Wayfarers
Canadian Achievers

Charles J. Humber

Editor-in-Chief

HEIRLOOM PUBLISHING INC.

CANADA HEIRLOOM SERIES
Volume I CANADA: From Sea Unto Sea (1986, revised 1988)
Volume II CANADA's Native Peoples (1988, revised 1989)
Volume III ALLEGIANCE: The Ontario Story (1991)
Volume IV PATHFINDERS: Canadian Tributes (1994)
Volume V WAYFARERS: Canadian Achievers (1996)

HEIRLOOM PUBLISHING INC.
6509B MISSISSAUGA ROAD NORTH
MISSISSAUGA ON L5N 1A6

Tel: (905) 821-1152
Fax: (905) 821-1158

Chairman William E. Melbourne
Secretary-Treasurer Phyllis L. Melbourne
Publisher Charles J. Humber
President Angela Dea Cappelli Clark
Editorial Coordinator Helen M. de Verteuil

Research, Editorial, and Sales Staff
Patricia Eden, Christine Hebscher, Paul Hultslander, Jennifer
Schultz, Claudia Willetts, Hughes Winfield. Also, Alexandrea
Clark, James Clark.

Production Consultant Arnold Diener
Cover Design Hart Broudy Designs
Book Design Amstier Communications: Peter Reitsma,
Kelly Closson, Craig Kirkham, Patricia Kruger,
Carl Messenger-Lehmann
Film DP&D Communications/Graphic Dimensions Inc.
Printing Arthurs-Jones Inc.
Binding Beck Bindery

WAYFARERS: Canadian Achievers
Printed and bound in Canada

Copyright 1996 by Heirloom Publishing Inc.
All Rights Reserved

Canadian Cataloguing in Publication Data
Main entry under title:
WAYFARERS: Canadian Achievers

(Canada heirloom series ; v. 5)
Includes bibliographical references and index.
ISBN 0-9694247-3-6
I. Canada — Biography.   I. Humber, Charles J.
II. Series
FC25.W38 1996   920.071   C95-930641-2
F1005.W38 1996

This book was typeset in Stone Informal

Printed on Luna Matte, 80lb text, manufactured in Canada
by Island Paper Mill

OPPOSITE: Photograph, *The Walk to Paradise Garden*, 1946, W. Eugene Smith
Courtesy, Jane Corkin Gallery, Toronto

*Dedicated to
the Wayfarers of
the 21st Century...*

CONTENTS

CONTRIBUTORS & ACKNOWLEDGEMENTS

J.M.S. Careless, O.C. (1981), Ph.D. (Harvard Univ.), F.R.S.C. Professor Emeritus, Univ. of Toronto; Author, *Canada: A Story of Challenge* (1953); *Brown of the Globe* (1959; revised, 1963); *The Union of the Canadas* (1967); *Colonists and Canadians* (1971); *Rise of Cities in Canada to 1914* (1978); *Pre-Confederation Premiers* (1980); *Frontier and Metropolis* (1989); Contributor, *CANADA From Sea Unto Sea* (1986; revised, 1988); *ALLEGIANCE : The Ontario Story* (1991); *PATHFINDERS: Canadian Tributes* (1994); Chief Historical Consultant, *Chronicle of Canada* (1990); Chairman, Board of Ontario Historical Studies Series.

Melbourne V. James
Freelance historical researcher and writer; President, Mel James & Associates, a PR consulting firm; Director of Information (ret'd) Bell Canada's Public Affairs Department (Ontario Division); Former Public Relations Writer with Bank of Montreal and CNR; For 18 years sat on Board of Couchiching Institute on Public Affairs (CIPA) and President, 1975-77; President, Canadian Public Relations Society (CPRS), 1974-75 and Chairman of its Foundation, 1988-91; Former PR Chairman, Toronto Board of Trade, United Way and Family Service Association; Recipient, the 25th Anniversary Medal of Her Majesty Queen Elizabeth's Coronation; Contributor, *PATHFINDERS: Canadian Tributes* (1994).

Larry Turner, B.Ed. (Univ. of Ottawa), M.A. (Queen's Univ.) Principal, Petherwin Heritage; Freelance historical researcher and writer; Associate, Commonwealth Historic Resource Mgmt. Ltd.; Author, *Merrickville: Jewel On The Rideau* (1995); *Ernestown: Rural Spaces, Urban Places* (1993); *Perth: Tradition and Style in Eastern Ontario* (1992); *Voyage of a Different Kind: The Associated Loyalists of Kingston and Adolphustown* (1984); Co-author, *Historic Mills of Ontario* (1987); Co-editor, *On a Sunday Afternoon: Classic Boats on the Rideau Canal* (1989); Contributor, *Canada From Sea Unto Sea* (1986; revised, 1988); *ALLEGIANCE: The Ontario Story* (1991); Past chairman, Friends of the Rideau. Co-authored *Rideau*, finalist for Ontario's Trillium Book Award, 1995.

Deborah Allan
Director of Public Affairs, Spar Aerospace Limited. Bachelor of Applied Arts in Journalism from Ryerson Polytechnic University.

Art Bailey
Retired after 35 years of service in the Federal Government of Canada. Served under C.D. Howe as staff economist, research analyst, and speech writer.

Murray Barkley
Doctoral candidate, Canadian History, University of Toronto. Proprietor, third generation, Barkley's General Store, Avonmore, Ontario.

A.J. Bauer
Retired Group Captain, RCAF. Spent career as pilot in Canada's Air Force. Founded Billy Bishop Heritage which purchased and turned the Billy Bishop home in Owen Sound, Ontario, into a museum honouring Canada's greatest flying ace.

Michael Beggs
Freelance journalist and former newspaper reporter. Graduated, University of Toronto, B.A. (Hons), 1983.

Wilfred Bigelow, M.D.
Retired Head, Cardiovascular Surgery, Toronto General Hospital and Professor Emeritus, Dept. of Surgery, University of Toronto. As a pioneering heart surgeon, Dr. Bigelow conceptualized the heart pacemaker.

Virginia Careless
Curator of History, Royal British Columbia Museum, specializing in domestic, social and cultural history. Graduated with M.A. from University of British Columbia (1974).

Derrick Crawley
President, Tri-Can Reinsurance, Toronto, and Tri-Can International, Bermuda. Graduate, University of London, England (B.Sc. Hons. Mathematics).

James Floyd
A graduate of the Manchester College of Technology, U.K. (1934). Chief design engineer for Avro Canada developing the Avro *C102 Jetliner*, chief engineer for the Avro *CF100* fighter aircraft, and vice president and director of engineering for the Avro *Arrow*, supersonic interceptor. Consultant to the British government for the development of the *Concorde*, 1965-1972. First non-American to be awarded Wright Brothers Gold Medal (1950).

Strome Galloway
Retired Colonel (1969), Canadian Army. Served overseas five years with The Royal Canadian Regiment in U.K., Tunisia, Sicily, Italy, and N.W. Europe. Honorary Editor Emeritus, Heraldry Canada. Columnist, Legion Magazine, 1974-1986. Military historian.

Patrick Hadley
Technical writer for Canadian Red Cross and author for a variety of writing projects. Obtained degrees in philosophy, psychology, and educational statistics.

Richard Levick
Freelance writer and public relations consultant. M.A., Journalism, University of Western Ontario.

John Parry
Freelance editor, editorial consultant and copy editor with a variety of publication houses and government ministries and agencies. Masters degrees from the University of London, U.K., University of Toronto, and McMaster University.

Charles Roland, M.D.
Jason A. Hannah Professor of the History of Medicine, McMaster University. Chairman, Dept. of Biomedical Communications, Mayo Clinic, Minnesota (1969-77). Curator, Osler Library, McGill University. Awarded Royal Society of Canada's Jason Hannah Medal for medical research (1995).

Ralph Sciullo, D.C.
A graduate of both McMaster University and the Canadian Memorial Chiropractic Institute. President, Hamilton, Ontario, Chiropractic Society. Member, Ontario, Canadian, American and International Chiropractic Associations.

D. McCormack Smyth, Ph.D.
Senior Scholar, York University. Founding Dean, Atkinson College, York University. Founding Chairman, the Churchill Society for the Advancement of Parliamentary Democracy.

Victoria Stewart
Well-known organizer, volunteer, lecturer, public speaker, historical researcher and lobbyist. Active in promoting North American Fur Trade Conferences and in generating heritage awareness about first nation peoples.

Patricia Stone
M.A. (Simon Fraser), M.A., (Concordia University). Teaching Master at Sir Sanford Fleming College.

Susan Tolusso
Senior Communications Manager with the National Film Board. Former reporter and editor with CBC Radio.

William Turner
Retired after 40 years in the space industry, including developing and marketing positions with de Havilland Aircraft and Spar Aerospace.

ACKNOWLEDGEMENTS Many wonderful people and considerate institutions have assisted in making *WAYFARERS: Canadian Achievers* a "cultural ambassador." Their sensitivity to our needs, general kindness and timely understanding in addition to their keen and overall interest have greatly helped to make this fifth volume of the ongoing *CANADA Heirloom Series* a visionary production spotlighting Canadian achievement on the world stage. Among others, they are:

Deborah Allan, Spar Aerospace; Army Headquarters Officers' Mess, Ottawa; Maral Bablanian, Annick Press; Joan Baillie; Belinda Bale, The National Ballet of Canada; Group Captain (ret'd) A.J. Bauer; Suzanne Bazzana, Firefly Books; Cynthia Bennell; Lyn Blenkorn, Canada Space Agency; Susan Bortot, United Parcel Services; Kathy Bridge, Provincial Archives of British Columbia; Anne Butler; James R. Campbell, Samuel E. Weir Collection & Library of Art; Stan Cappadocia; Greg Cappelli; Arthur Chamberlin; Communications DG4, Robert Levy, Ricki Normandin; Thora Cooke, The Western Canada Pictorial Index, Winnipeg; Sarah Cooper; Susan Corbeil, Unisource Canada Inc.; Amy Corner, Arthurs-Jones Inc.; Felicia Cukier, Art Gallery of Ontario; Lyn Delgaty, National Research Council Canada; Bev Dietrich, Guelph Museums; Irma Ditchburn, Gov't of Ontario Art Collection; Eric Doubt; Jane Edmonds, Stratford Festival Archives; H. Alan L. Emerson; Jim Etherington, London Life; Carol Ferguson; James C. Floyd; Wendy Frattolin, Kraft Canada; Dr. Alan Frosst; Charles E. Frosst Jr.; John Kenneth Galbraith; R.W. Ganong; Fred Gaskin; Wayne Getty; A.J. (Jim) Gibson; Isabel Gil, Bureau du Quebec; Stephen Gillis, Home Hardware; Paul Glover; David Gordon, Exec. Director, Mississauga Board of Trade; Lalage Hackett, Bureau du Quebec; Nora Hague, Notman Archives; Nasir Hasan; Conrad Heidenreich; Nick Henderson; Carl Hiebert; Doug Hull, Director General, Science Promotion & Academic Affairs, Industry Canada; Charles W. Humber; Scott N. Humber; Alan Jackson, Casavant Frères Limitée; Ian Jack; Robert F. James, Dofasco; Tony Jarvis, Industry Canada; Nick Javor; Birthe Joergensen, Canadian Opera Company; Margaret McCuaig-Johnston, Director General & Manager, Manufacturing and Processing Technologies Branch, Industry Canada; Judy Johnston, Royal Bank of Canada; Laurie Jones, National Film Board of Canada; Nena Jones, NASA; Richard and Pat Jones; Winnie Klotz, Photographer, Bronxville, New York; Michael Langlais; Judith LaRocque; Bradley Latham, DP&D Communications; Nathalie Lawson, Universal Press Syndicate; Bernard LeBlanc, Director, Musée Acadian, Universitée de Moncton; Marcel LeBlanc, DP&D Communications; Edwin Lewis; Lucie Linhart, The University of Lethbridge Art Gallery; Sandy Lizana, Great-West Life Assurance; J.C. (Cliff) Mackay, Spar Aerospace; Kathleen Mackenzie, St. Francis Xavier University; Hugh MacMillan; Patricia MacMillan; McMaster University, Sherri Cecil, Margaret Wilbey; Paul Maréchal, Power Corporation; Mary Willan Mason; Brian Masschaele, Simcoe County Archives; Terry McDermott; Tony McDermott; Duncan McGregor, Arthurs-Jones Inc.; Don McKibbon, Connaught Laboratories; William F. Mellberg, Flight Research, Park Ridge, Illinois; Susan Menzies, University of Ottawa Heart Institute; LaVera Miller, Ontario City Library, California; Dean Miller; Kirk Miner; Jeff Mitchell, *Port Perry Star*; Monarchist League of Canada; Betty Jo Moore, Museum of Mental Health Services (Toronto) Inc.; Rosemary Doyle-Morier; George Mowbray; Richard L. Muller; Rev'd. H.J. Nahabedian, Rector, The Church of St. Mary Magdalene; NASA; Sonja Noble, Librarian, *The Toronto Star*; Orchestré symphonique de Montréal, Sylvie Bouchard, Dominique Day, Christine St. Gelais; Ann Cameron Orr, CNIB; Charles Pachter; Louis Paquin; Stephen Pecar; Donald J.C. Phillipson; Paul Pivato; Corrie Pugh, *This Country Canada*; Angela Raljic, Ken Lister, Ethnology Dept., Royal Ontario Museum; Brian Reid; Lynn-Marie Richard, Maritime Museum of the Atlantic; Keith Richardson, Industry Canada; Sarah Robertson, Moore Corporation; Diane Roy, Kapuskasing; Lisa Russell, The Diocese of Ontario, Anglican Church of Canada; Rosemary Sadlier; Don Savaria, Crown Life; Dr. Ezra Schabas; Don J. Schalk, Jr., Spruce Falls Inc.; Stanley Scheer, Casavant Frères; Nugent Schneider; Kenneth Scott; Dr. Hugh E. Scully; Alek Shevchenko, Smith Falls Bookbinding; Harry (Buck) Sloat; D. McCormack Smyth; Maureen Stead, Harlequin Enterprises; Victoria Stewart, The Macdonald Stewart Foundation; Greg Sutton; Charles P. Taylor; Alexander Thain; Nathalie Thibault, Musée du Québec; Ken Thomson, Lord Thomson of Fleet; Harry Turner, National Research Council Canada; The Rt. Honourable John N. Turner, P.C.; William L. Turner; Linda Vachon, The Royal Society of Canada; Claire Versailles, Business Communication Management; David de Verteuil, The Laird Group; Vincent & Farrell Associates, New York; Peter J. Ward; Pat Wardrop; Leon Warmski, Archives of Ontario; Don Webster; Lorne Webster; Claudia Willetts; Gerald A. Willis, Absolute Color Slides; Nhanci Wright, Canadian Memorial Chiropractic College; Wyeth-Ayerst Canada Inc., Lori Poole, David Chown; Maureen Yacomine. We extend our deepest regrets to those we have unfortunately omitted from this august list of supporters.

A Message from the Governor General of Canada

For much of our history, we Canadians have faced great challenges. What we have accomplished in this country is remarkable. We have built prosperous communities, developed links of culture, transportation and communication and created a country that leads the world in many fields.

Yet, we rarely pause to proudly look back at what we have achieved. People say that we are modest by character and we are comfortable downplaying our successes. There may be truth in that but, perhaps, we have just been too busy building a country to truly appreciate our many accomplishments.

In Canada, tomorrow's challenge is just over today's horizon. We seem to have little time to congratulate ourselves on what we have done and to celebrate our achievements. That is why I am pleased to lend my support to the fifth volume of the *CANADA Heirloom Series, WAYFARERS: Canadian Achievers.*

The pages of this volume trace the lifeline of our country and its people. These 125 stories tell of creativity, determination and triumph. From the bark canoe that transported Native peoples and explorers to Marius Barbeau, who preserved French Canadian and Native folklore, to Margaret Atwood's ability to touch our hearts and souls, to the Acadians, whose resiliency is an example for the world, these vignettes describe an amazing diversity.

WAYFARERS is a reflection of Canada that is immense and vibrant. It portrays a country of energy, foresight and innovation. The Canadians who are chronicled are people who have dared to reach beyond the edge of their talents and who have succeeded.

These stories link us, as Canadians, to our past, to our heritage and to each other. They are stories that will inspire us as we ready ourselves to meet the challenges of tomorrow and of the new millennium.

*His Excellency The Right Honourable
Roméo LeBlanc,
P.C., C.C., C.M.M., C.D.
Governor General and
Commander-in-Chief of Canada*

Un Message du Gouverneur Général du Canada

Au cours d'une grande partie de leur histoire, les Canadiens ont eu à surmonter de grands défis. Nous avons réalisé des exploits remarquables dans ce pays. Nous avons bâti des communautés prospères, établi des liens culturels et des réseaux de transport et de communication, et créé un pays qui est à l'avant-garde dans de nombreux secteurs.

Pourtant, nous prenons rarement le temps de faire le bilan de nos réalisations. Les gens disent que nous sommes d'un naturel modeste et que nous aimons à minimiser l'importance de nos réussites. C'est peut-être vrai en partie, mais il se peut que nous ayons été simplement trop occupés à bâtir un pays pour apprécier pleinement tout ce que nous avons accompli.

Au Canada, le défi que nous réserve demain point déjà à l'horizon. Nous ne semblons guère avoir le temps de nous féliciter de nos succès. C'est pourquoi je salue avec plaisir la publication du cinquième volume de la série *CANADA Heirloom*, intitulé *WAYFARERS: Canadian Achievers.*

Ces pages nous font remonter le cours de la vie de notre pays et de ses habitants. Ces 125 histoires évoquent la créativité, la détermination et le triomphe. Du canot d'écorce qui a transporté les Autochtones et les explorateurs à Marius Barbeau, qui a préservé le folklore canadien français et autochtone, au talent de Margaret Atwood, qui sait nous émouvoir jusqu'à l'âme, et aux Acadiens, dont la ténacité sert d'exemple au monde entier, ces esquisses décrivent une diversité et un génie étonnants.

Le recueil *WAYFARERS* est une vaste fresque qui dépeint le Canada de manière saisissante – un Canada caractérisé par le dynamisme, la prévoyance et l'innovation. Les Canadiens qu'on y rencontre ont osé vaincre leurs limites.

Les histoires qui nous sont racontées dans ce livre nous rattachent à notre passé et à notre patrimoine commun comme Canadiens, tout en faisant ressortir les liens qui nous unissent. Ces récits nous serviront d'inspiration à l'heure où nous nous apprêtons à relever les défis de demain et d'un nouveau millénaire.

*Son Excellence le très honorable
Roméo LeBlanc,
P.C., C.C., C.M.M., C.D.
Gouverneur général et
Commandant en chef du Canada*

Photo: Peter Sibbald

INTRODUCTION

Spotlighting Wayfarers

WAYFARERS: *Canadian Achievers*, as the fifth volume of the *CANADA Heirloom Series*, spotlights 125 stories of Canadian achievement in a series of provident vignettes enhanced by a collection of rare and remarkable images and compelling graphics. The overall format, reinforced by refreshing research and scholarship, reflects the ongoing mandate of *Heirloom Publishing* to popularize Canada's rich culture, history and heritage by showcasing the dominion of the north on the world stage.

The publishers wish to thank His Excellency, the Right Honourable Roméo LeBlanc, Canada's 25th Governor General, for graciously accepting Heirloom's invitation to write the special message introducing this production. The Governor General's message, in addition to the cordial remarks by Diane Francis, Editor, *The Financial Post*, has greatly assisted in making *WAYFARERS* a distinguished "cultural ambassador."

Without the financial support, moreover, of Canada's business community, in general, and individual business establishments, in particular, *Heirloom* could never have succeeded in launching *WAYFARERS*, thus fulfilling its publication mandate to generate heritage awareness by celebrating global "wayfarers" identified inextricably with Canada.

Heirloom is also deeply grateful to History Professor J.M.S. Careless and historians Mel James and Larry Turner for undertaking the huge responsibility of writing the great majority of the vignettes published in this volume. Their participation plus the individual contributions of some 20 other personalities have greatly assisted Heirloom in completing an ambitious publication venture.

Gratitude is also extended to Amstier Communications, especially Peter Reitsma, for insisting on graphics and design commensurate with the subject material.

During the production of *WAYFARERS: Canadian Achievers*, *Heirloom Publishing* granted Industry Canada permission to supervise the overall digitization of the *CANADA Heirloom Series* for SchoolNet Digital Collections. Thanks to the guidance and advice of Doug Hull and other of his colleagues at Industry Canada, high school students from across Canada not only are being taught the digitization process but are making available for educational intentions the entire *CANADA Heirloom Series* on the Worldwide Web.

Finally, *Heirloom* would be very remiss in not acknowledging the immense contribution to this visionary project made by both William and Phyllis Melbourne, our colleagues. Their mentorship and business acumen steadfastly guided all of us to strive, to focus and to be of heart....

J. K. GALBRAITH

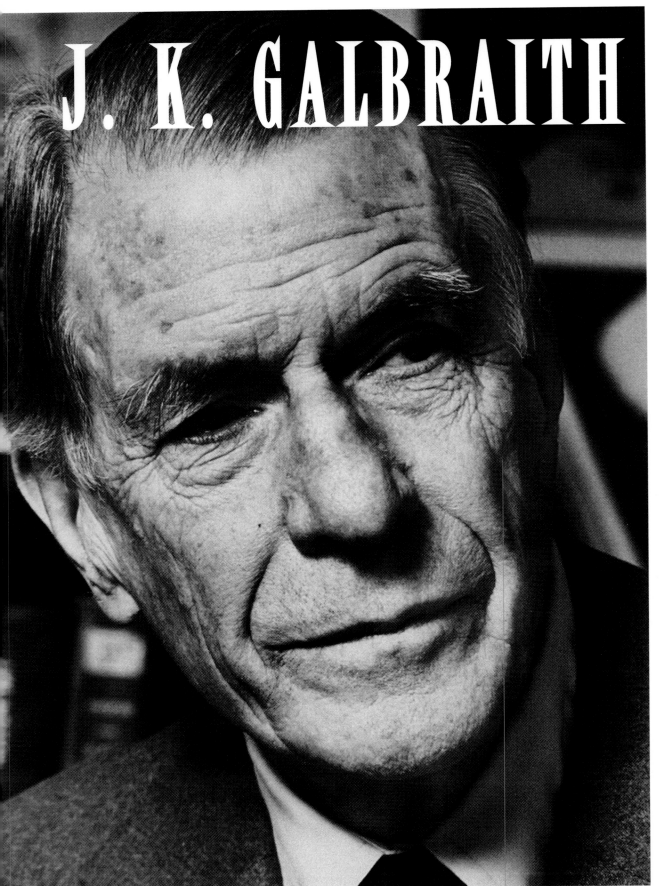

Canada's Gift to Harvard

During Canada's special year of centennial celebrations (1967), John Kenneth Galbraith proclaimed that "If I were still a practising as distinct from an advisory Canadian I would be ... concerned about maintaining the cultural integrity of the broadcasting system and with making sure Canada has an active, independent theatre, book-publishing industry, newspapers, magazines and schools of poets and painters." Arguably one of Canada's best-known personalities living outside his native homeland, Galbraith has been a major intellectual force in American liberalism for over half a century. [Photo, courtesy Harvard University/ Jim Kalett]

JOHN KENNETH GALBRAITH has been an economist, ambassador, professor, editor, activist, and novelist. He is known as the czar, in the early years of World War II, of price controls in the United States, author of a controversial report on the effectiveness of the bombing of Germany, a speech writer for J.F. Kennedy, President of the United States, and author of a book, entitled *The Scotch*, about his heritage and birthplace, Iona Station, Elgin County, in southwestern Ontario. It proved popular except to the people he affectionately described.

Its unpopularity in Elgin County was the direct result of his sardonic wit and sinewy frankness. He once wrote of his Highland heritage, "If a man didn't make sense, the Scotch felt it was misplaced politeness to try and keep him from knowing it." Some have tried to tell Ken Galbraith that he did not make sense as an economist, but books such as *The Affluent Society*, *The New Industrial State*, and *The Age of Uncertainty* (a 13-week BBC TV series and book) made him both a celebrity and the world's best-read and widely known economist.

Galbraith's interest in economics began when he was an undergraduate at the Ontario Agricultural College (now the University of Guelph) and he recognized that there was something wrong with a system that produced excellent livestock and excellent crops that could not be sold. In his final year, he investigated the reasons by interviewing tenant farmers: his thesis in 1931 led to a scholarship on agricultural economics offered at the University of California.

There his professors noted his writing skills (as an undergraduate at OAC he wrote a farmer's advice column for the *St. Thomas Times Journal*) and he became not only their student but also their scribe for various research projects.

On obtaining a Ph.D. in 1934, he joined Harvard University as an instructor. To further his knowledge on such subjects as economic principles, modern banking, and the economic beliefs of John Maynard Keynes whom he later met when he was granted a fellowship to Cambridge in 1937, he attended lectures given by leading professors. Before going to England, he married Catherine Atwater, a Smith College graduate, and became a U.S. citizen.

In 1939 he was made an assistant professor at Princeton. A year later he was asked to work as an economist in Washington and, in 1941, was named deputy administrator in charge of price controls for the office of Price Administration. "By 1943 we had virtually everything under control," Galbraith later recalled, to the chagrin of many. Before political pressure forced him to leave the Roosevelt administration in 1943, he admitted that "I reached the point that all price fixers reach – my enemies outnumbered my friends."

He joined *Fortune* magazine as a writer and later became an editor, returning to Harvard in 1948 because, as he wrote in his 1981 autobiography, *A Life In Our Times*, "I continued to believe that I should be at a university, teaching as necessary and writing on my own."

In 1952 he wrote two books: *The Theory of Price Control* and the first of a trilogy on economic theory, *American Capitalism: The Concept of Countervailing Power*, which examined the American free market economy and its control. The book was attacked and Galbraith admitted in his autobiography that "there was ... an erroneous implication in the title and a euphoric tendency in the text."

Galbraith produced the second volume of his trilogy in 1958. Influencing an entire generation, *The Affluent Society* was translated into a dozen languages and became an international best-seller. In it the 6' 8½" scholar examined, with biting candour and wit, the American obsession with overproduction of consumer goods and suggested more effort should be made to provide for such genuine needs as cleaner air, decent housing, and support for the arts.

Once again he was attacked for "an oversimplification of the issues," a charge also made about the third volume of the trilogy, *The New Industrial State*, written in 1967. One critic called it "classic Galbraithian heresy" ; another economist described Galbraith as "a very talented journalist but a bad economist." Galbraith admitted to errors in the third of the series but wryly observed in an interview, "It is not hard to admit errors that are cosmetically wrong. You can get a great deal of psychological pleasure out of saying 'God, what a broad-minded man you are, Galbraith.'"

Besides writing books, Galbraith became a noted speech writer and political activist when Adlai Stevenson ran for president in 1952. In 1955 he attended a Senate hearing to give evidence on the state of the stock market. A negative comment caused it to drop and a subsequent headline read, "Egghead Scrambles Market." In 1956 he went to India to take part in a study of its second five-year plan but got home in time to return to the political fray, writing not only on farm policy and economics for Stevenson again but condemning Nixon as vice president.

His political views and clout were further enhanced in 1960 when he not only wrote speeches for John F. Kennedy and, at the convention that nominated JFK for the presidency, was appointed floor manager for delegates west of the Mississippi. Shortly after winning office, Kennedy appointed Galbraith ambassador to India where he developed a close friendship with Prime Minister Jawaharlal Nehru and where his expertise in agriculture and economics was warmly welcomed. He was, however, critical of his own boss – Secretary of State Dean Rusk – and in July 1963 returned to resume his career at Harvard.

There he continued to lecture, write, make speeches and, in 1964, campaign for Lyndon Johnson's election. He had, however, serious reservations about America's growing involvement with Vietnam. He had visited the country at Kennedy's request while serving as ambassador to India and had reported that he was against the sending of troops to support the incumbent regime. When bombs were dropped on North Vietnam in 1965, Galbraith donned the mantle of an antiwar activist.

Galbraith supported Eugene McCarthy in 1968 and campaigned for George McGovern in

1972 while continuing to teach at Harvard and produce several more books including in 1968, a novel, *The Triumph*, "a sardonic comment on the fumblings and failures of American diplomacy." In the fall of 1972, he was invited with two other economists to visit China and, the following year, wrote a slim volume on his experiences. After he retired from Harvard in 1975, the BBC invited him to do a series of 13 TV shows entitled, *The Age of Uncertainty*, a series also shown in 1977 on CBC, PBS, and other educational stations. It reinforced the public's perception of him as an economist able to make "technical matters understandable with wit, brio and adroitness" and further added to his celebrity status.

Publishing books, speaking in public and receiving honorary degrees (he has more than 40 of them) have continued. As Peggy Lamson wrote in her 1992 biography, *Speaking of Galbraith*, he wrote 13 books by 1972 and 15 since, writing in longhand roughly four hours every morning at his home in Cambridge, Massachusetts, his farm in Vermont, or a chalet in Gstaad, Switzerland. He has written five more books since Lamson's biography, spoken a number of times in Canada where he still visits relatives and continues to comment on economic, social, and political issues of the day with an assurance that infuriates some, titillates others, but challenges all.

Mel James

Universities from around the world have recognized for over 50 years the achievements of the much respected Harvard University economics professor, John Kenneth Galbraith. In 1984, Galbraith, as viewed here, received an honorary Doctor of Letters degree from McMaster University (Hamilton, Ontario) in addition to addressing the graduating class.
[Photo, courtesy McMaster *Courier*]

WHEN, IN 1966, it was decided to name la Grande Salle of Montréal's Place des Arts, board members unanimously voted to name it Salle Wilfrid-Pelletier to honour the man known as the "grand man of music in Québec."

At the opening of that concert hall three years earlier, Pelletier, then 67, had been on hand to conduct the orchestra he had helped found – les Concerts symphoniques de Montréal (CSM). He called the event "the most moving time of my life," though, as conductor at the Metropolitan Opera of New York and as guest conductor of numerous other orchestras throughout North America, he had experienced many other occasions to compete with it.

The Montréal opening of the 2,982-seat hall was the culmination of a dream that had begun in 1934 when some prominent French-Canadian families had asked Pelletier to help his native city organize a new orchestra. Despite a heavy schedule with the Metropolitan,

Wilfrid Pelletier
Musique Maestro   **1896 - 1982**

La Grande Salle of Montreal's Place des Arts was renamed Salle Wilfrid-Pelletier in 1966. Seating nearly 3,000 subscribers, this home to symphony, opera, and ballet was inaugurated on September 13, 1963 with Pelletier as guest conductor. The hall's ambience and intimacy are equivalent to the great concert halls of Europe and America. [Photo, courtesy Orchestre symphonique de Montréal]

which he had joined in 1917, Pelletier jumped at the chance to take part and the following January, the CSM gave its first concert.

That, however, was only the beginning of his dedication to helping his native city establish a worldwide reputation in the field of music. In 1936, he founded the Matinées symphoniques pour la jeunesse which he directed for the next 25 years. He also established, in 1936, the Montréal Festival, an annual festival that, during the 1930s, featured such outstanding works as Bach's *St. Matthew Passion,* Beethoven's *Missa Solemnis* and *Ninth Symphony,* and Verdi's *Requiem.* In 1940, he introduced to Canadians the opera *Pelléas et Mélisande,* featuring tenor Raoul Jobin in a leading role, one of his numerous discoveries in his 50-plus-years as a musician and conductor.

Born in Montréal's east end in 1896, Pelletier was encouraged in his musical interests by his uncle, a local priest, who founded a band at the church and made Wilfrid, at age three, its mascot. An older brother introduced him to drums, and by age seven Wilfrid was not only performing with the band but knew most of the percussion instruments as well. His real interest, however, was piano, and a Mme. Françoise Héraly gave him free lessons since the family was poor (his father worked as a baker).

At 14, he was a pianist in the pit orchestra of Montréal's Théâtre National. There he heard his first symphony orchestra and, at His Majesty's Theatre, saw his first opera which was so thrilling that he decided he wanted to be a conductor. The following year he took his first step in that direction when the chorus master of the Montréal Opera Company hired him as a rehearsal pianist. In 1914

Before his appointment in 1935 as first artistic director of les Concerts symphoniques de Montréal, renamed l'Orchestre symphonique de Montréal in 1953, Wilfrid Pelletier had been identified with New York's Metropolitan Opera since 1917, rehearsing such operatic tenors as Enrico Caruso and Canada's own Edward Johnson and establishing a global reputation as conductor of the Met's Sunday Night Concerts. In a career spanning approximately sixty years, Pelletier conducted, among others, Chicago, Cincinnati, Detroit, San Francisco, Los Angeles, Montréal, Québec, and Mexico City symphony orchestras. [Photo, courtesy Orchestre symphonique de Montréal]

he won the Prix d'Europe contest sponsored by the Québec government, and later that year he went to France for the next two years to study piano, harmony, composition, and operatic coaching under, among others, Isidor Philipp, Marcel Samuel-Rousseau, and Camille Bellaigue.

On completing his scholarship, Pelletier decided to try his luck in New York where the Metropolitan Opera's newly hired French conductor, Pierre Monteux, gave him the job of coaching singers for the cast of *Samson and Dalila* starring Enrico Caruso. The manager of the Met, Giulio Gatti-Caszza, was so impressed that he hired Pelletier for the season. He stayed for another 32 years (1917-1949).

Working under such famous conductors as Bodansky, Moranzoni, Sarafin, and many others, Pelletier rehearsed the equally famous singers of the period – Caruso, Bori, Ponselle, Tibbet, and another Canadian, Edward Johnson. Liked and highly regarded by everyone, Pelletier became affectionately known as "Pelly" and, in 1919, was named assistant to the musical director of the touring company. While on tour, he was invited to conduct his first opera, Verdi's *Il Trovatore*. Other opportunities followed, and, in 1922, Pelly made his Met debut as conductor of *Carmen*. The same year he became conductor of the six-week summer opera season at Chicago's Ravina Park, an appointment that continued for a decade.

Numerous appearances as a conductor continued throughout the next four decades. In 1926 he started conducting the Sunday Night concerts at the Met and, in 1934, conducted radio programs such as the "Packard Hour" and the "Chase and Sanborn" concerts on Sunday afternoons. By 1937, he was placed in charge of and conducted the popular "Metropolitan Auditions of the Air," a program that led to the discovery of such outstanding vocalists as Leonard Warren, Robert Merrill, Eleanor Steber, Patrice Munsel, and Risë Stevens.

He was also discovering talent through his Matineés symphoniques pour la jeunesse in Montréal in 1935/36. When a youngster won a $25 prize for a little minuet composed for the piano, Pelletier made a point of obtaining the score, orchestrating it, having the symphony play it for the children at one of their concerts, and then introducing the young composer to the audience. "He had never heard a real symphony orchestra. He cried ... I cried ... everybody cried," Pelletier later recalled. The boy, incidentally, became the well-known composer, Clermont Pepin.

A 1982 article by Eric McLean, a Montréal music critic, recalls the Maestro's work with children. "He seemed happiest in the company of young people and the promising performance of a ten-year-old pianist could produce a sense of wonder in him," McLean wrote, later recalling one occasion when, although Pelletier was judging dozens of children playing the same obligatory Chopin waltz, he was moved to tears by one of the winning contestants.

In 1942, the Québec government asked Pelletier to organize a music conservatory in Montréal and appointed him director. Pelletier promptly hired world-famous teachers – a horn player from Toscanini's NBC Symphony, a percussion player from the New York Philharmonic, Grandjany for the harp – all to the chagrin of the government that wanted him to hire local people. "I had in mind to build good musicians," Pelletier told another

Montréal critic in 1965, pointing out that eventually these teachers would be replaced by the graduates of the Montréal and Québec City conservatories, the latter opening also under his direction in 1944.

In 1950, Pelletier retired from the Metropolitan but continued in demand as a conductor. He took charge of the l'Orchestre symphonique de Québec and brought it to full professional status by 1963. He was guest conductor for numerous operas performed throughout the United States and, in 1951, replaced Arturo Toscanini as conductor of a Beethoven Wagner program with Helen Traubel as soloist. Two years later, as conductor of the New York Philharmonic Children's Concerts, he became involved with children again for the next five years, turning that post over to Leonard Bernstein in 1958. In Montréal, his youth concerts appeared on Canadian television.

Appointed director of musical education in Québec and head of the musical department of the Ministry of Cultural Affairs in 1961, Pelletier continued to be a guest conductor into his 70s, appearing at the World Festival of Expo '67 as conductor of a gala concert marking the centennial of Confederation on July 1, 1967.

He received numerous honorary degrees in both Canada and the United States, was made a chevalier de la Légion d'Honneur by France, named a Companion of the Order of St. Michael and St. George by Great Britain, a knight of the Order of the King of Denmark, and, among other awards, made a Companion of the Order of Canada in 1968. His name has appeared on numerous record labels, including RCA and Columbia, with a selection of his 1930s recording of Verdi's *Otello* included in a special RCA album, "Opening Nights at the Met," released after the famous opera house moved to New York City's Lincoln Center.

In April 1981, Pelletier was one of the Canadians recognized by the Met when it dedicated its annual ball to Canada "in honour of the contribution of Canadians to classical music and to opera," and a month later he was in Montréal for an 85th birthday celebration. Married for a third time to American opera singer Rose Bampton in 1937, Pelletier continued to live in New York until his death in April 1982. Mayor Jean Drapeau of Montréal eulogized his life as one of "dedication, devotion, and generosity, a life of beauty." He was buried at the Bampton family plot in Wayne, Pennsylvania.

Mel James

Viewed conducting l'Orchestre symphonique de Montréal in the twilight of his career, Wilfrid Pelletier had a mission to instil a true love for symphonic music in a generation of young people who would carry his musical torch into the future. [Photo, courtesy Orchestre symphonique de Montréal]

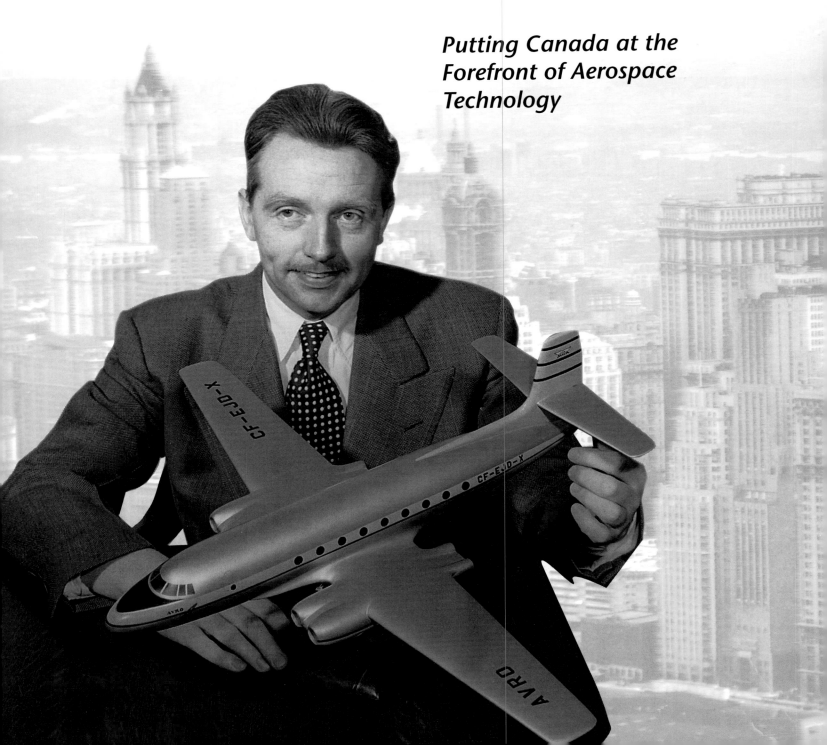

JAMES C. FLOYD

Putting Canada at the Forefront of Aerospace Technology

GREAT BRITAIN'S A.V. Roe Company (Avro) sent one of its bright young men in 1946 to join a new and small aircraft design team at its Malton, Ontario, plant. Little did Canada know at the time that it was getting an aircraft designer who not only would create the first commercial jet aircraft to fly in North America but would eventually assemble a team of brilliant aeronautical scientists, some of whom would later play a key role in America's *Apollo* project to put a man on the moon.

When James C. Floyd arrived in Canada at age 31, he already had an impressive record in aircraft design. Born near Manchester, England, by his mid-twenties Floyd was working on the first drawings of what was to become the *Lancaster* bomber of World War II fame. By age 29, he was chief project engineer, working on advanced projects including the application of jet engine technology.

Avro Canada was established as a result of the impressive workmanship on the *Lancaster* bombers at the Victory Aircraft plant at Malton during the war. Avro Canada took over this plant and sent Floyd to head a design team to develop a 30- to 36-seat jet-powered passenger plane for Trans Canada Airlines, the forerunner of Air Canada. When TCA backed out of the project (admitting later that they did not want to be the first to introduce jet service) Avro concentrated on making the plane suitable for airlines in the USA and Europe, eager, following the war, to update their passenger fleets.

In August 1949, just two weeks after Britain's de Havilland *Comet* had flown in Great Britain to win the honour of being the world's first jet transport to fly, Floyd's Avro *C102 Jetliner* took off from Malton airport and, by the end of October, was well into its flight testing program. The test pilot described the plane as "a perfect lady."

Promotional flights into the United States took that country by storm. One flight to New York took 59 minutes – almost half the time for regular flights – and another from Toronto to Chicago and New York prompted an American radio commentator to observe, "The record books of commercial aviation ... have been shot to pieces by the performance of the Canadian-built Avro *Jetliner*." The Rochester *Democrat and Chronicle* observed editorially about the same flight, "This should give our nation a good healthful kick in its placidity."

As a result, USA's National Airlines showed interest in signing a contract and the United States Air Force allotted funds to purchase 20 *Jetliners* for military operations. The Canadian government, however, reacting in part to the outbreak of the Korean War in June 1950, cancelled the project in 1951 in order to concentrate on the *CF100* – an all-weather, long-range fighter aircraft required by the RCAF.

Jim Floyd (left) with model of Jetliner in 1950 after being the first non-American to be awarded the prestigious and internationally renowned Wright Bros. Medal. [Photo, courtesy Avro Aircraft] Flown by chief test pilot Don Rogers, the Canadian Jetliner soars over New York City, April 18, 1950 – the first time that Americans had seen a jet passenger plane. [Photo, courtesy Bob Halford]

The all-Canadian Avro Canada CF100 Fighter. Close to 700 CF100s were built at Malton and ranged Canadian skies for well over a quarter of a century. It was also in NATO service with the Canadian squadrons in Europe and with the Belgian Air Force. [Photo, courtesy Brian Blatherwick]

In 1952, Avro attempted to revive international sales of the *Jetliner*. Howard Hughes of TWA became interested in purchasing a fleet of *Jetliners*, but negotiations were thwarted when C.D. Howe, cabinet minister responsible for aircraft production, hearing about this, bluntly wrote to Avro Canada that they were not to use the plant for the *Jetliner's* further development and ordered the *C102* "… to be moved out of any useful manufacturing space."

By1952, Floyd had become Avro's chief engineer in charge of all design, testing, research and experimental manufacture and had built up a growing team of experts to develop the *CF100* fighter aircraft which served the RCAF and NATO forces and which had been purchased by Belgium. The success of the *CF100* led to a 1953 RCAF specification for the development of a supersonic interceptor to destroy any enemy threat to the northern reaches of North America and this in turn gave birth to the *CF105* – the Avro *Arrow* project – one of the most advanced and ambitious military aircraft projects then being undertaken anywhere in the world.

While Jim Floyd plays down his part in the *Arrow* project by saying that it was produced "by a brilliant and highly sophisticated team of experts" and that his own role as vice-president of engineering was to "keep them all going in the same direction," historical records and honours suggest otherwise. In 1958, the Canadian Aeronautical Institute presented him with the J.D. McCurdy award, the citation reading in part, "The responsibility for the many decisions which had to be made in the design stages of such an aircraft rested to an unusually large degree on Mr. Floyd…. The quality of his technical judgment and of his infectious energy contributed to the speed with which the project has been carried through."

The first *Arrow* was produced by the end of 1957. When test flown in March 1958, it reached speeds in excess of 1,000mph. Over the next several months, five *Arrows* were completed. These flew at speeds around twice the speed of sound and caused great international interest. That October, Floyd was invited to give the prestigious British Commonwealth Lecture to the Royal Aeronautical Society in London, England, on the design and development of the *Arrow*.

But once again political considerations were to squelch Floyd's leadership role in Canadian aircraft development. In February 1959, Canadian Prime Minister John Diefenbaker announced the cancellation of the project, later ordering "all the aircraft, jigs and components, drawings, reports, films and everything associated with the *Arrow* program … to be destroyed." The 14,000 employees working on the project were laid off.

Floyd recalls that the cancellation of the project – and the break-up of the unique engineering team that had produced it – was devastating. Within weeks he was visiting many of the major aircraft companies in the USA to find work for his people. General Lauris Norstad, then head of NATO, described Floyd's group as "just about the best team that I have seen anywhere." Many from the team were placed with North American Aviation, Boeing, Douglas, Lockheed and other firms. Twenty-six of the Floyd group, led by Jim Chamberlin, described by Floyd as "a technical genius," joined the U.S. space agency as the result of an arrangement with NASA, to work on the *Mercury*, *Gemini* and later on the moon landings of *Apollo*.

The authors of *Apollo – the Race to the Moon* (1989) single out the work of these Canadians, writing, "As the Space Task Group's burden was threatening to overwhelm the entire project, the Canadian government unintentionally gave the American Space program its luckiest break since Wernher von Braun had surrendered to the Americans," adding that, while little public recognition was ever granted the Canadians, "their contribution was incalculable to the people within the programs." One of the group's top American engineers even claimed that the Canadians "had it all over us in many areas … just brilliant guys … bright as hell and talented and professional to a man."

"The same comments could have been said about many others that made their mark on the leading edge of technology in other countries, but were lost to Canada," Floyd laments. He turned down several lucrative job offers in the United States to accept an invitation from England to form a "think tank" to study advanced aviation technology and space vehicles, taking a number of ex-Avro Canada engineers with him. Their work also contributed to the development of the *Concorde*.

In 1961 he delivered a paper to the Royal Aeronautical Society on "Some Current Problems Facing The Aircraft Designer" that won him the Society's George Taylor Gold Medal for "its contribution to aeronautical science." The paper was so advanced that in 1988, 27 years later,

Jetliner *at Howard Hughes airfield in Culver City, 1952. Hughes was interested in purchasing a fleet of 30* **Jetliners** *for his TWA regional routes.* **[Photo, courtesy Don Rogers]**

The Avro Arrow *being rolled out on October 4, 1957,*
illustrating how big this all-Canadian aircraft was.
[Photo, courtesy Avro Aircraft]

The Arrow *in flight – beautiful but menacing to any potential intruder. On March 25, 1958, Jan Zurakowski became the first pilot to fly the famed* Arrow. *[Photo, courtesy Avro Aircraft]*

it was included in its entirety at the first World Conference on Hypersonic Flight in the 21st Century held at the University of North Dakota and sponsored by NASA and many other scientific organizations. One attendee, the honorary president of the Scientific Teachers Association of Ontario recalled, "My most vivid memory of the event was how revered Jim Floyd was in that company of experts. He was, in fact, the living symbol of the proud legacy this nation [Canada] has carved in aviation history." At the banquet given in Jim's honour at the conclusion of that conference, the chairman recalled that in 1950 Jim Floyd was the first non-American ever to receive the Wright Brothers Medal.

In 1962 Floyd established his own consulting firm and for 18 years worked with airlines and aviation companies worldwide (he was consultant to the British Ministry of Technology on the *Concorde* project from 1965 to 1973). He and his wife Irene, whom he had met when they were co-workers on the *Lancaster* bomber project in 1938, returned to Toronto after his retirement in 1980.

In 1986 Jim wrote a widely acclaimed book, *The Avro Canada C102 Jetliner.* In 1988 he was presented with a special award by the Aerospace Industries Association of Canada "in recognition of his service to the cause of aviation." He was named a Companion of the Order of Flight by the City of Edmonton in 1993, the same year that he was inducted into Canada's Aviation Hall of Fame. Now, in his eighties, he still passes on the stories of Canada's unique aviation heritage, particularly to young Canadians.

Mel James

-OUT OF FIRST AVRO ARROW, OCT. 4, 1957.

QUEBÉC CITY, the continent's only walled city, is North America's most fascinating urban area. Steeped in myth and romance, Québec city has experienced invasion, conquest, and political turmoil. Evoked as "the Gibraltar of America" by nineteenth century tourists seeking sublime and picturesque scenery, the old city is today celebrated by the United Nations (UNESCO) as a World Heritage Site. The historic district covers 135 hectares. With its harbour sector, religious institutions, and civil and military installations, it shares world status with only one other North American historic city centre, Mexico City, and with such other old cities as Florence, Istanbul, St. Petersburg, Damascus, Venice, Dubrovnik, Berne, Bath, Lima, Cracow, Quito, Toledo, Rome, and Warsaw.

Québec City

Medieval French City of North America

In 1985, UNESCO placed historic Québec City on the prestigious World Heritage List, the only North American urban site to earn this international recognition. Québec City's Lower Town, viewed here, was the site of Champlain's Abitation, 1608. Narrow streets, stone buildings dating back to the 1600s, public squares, museums, intimate cafés, and one-of-a-kind boutiques give this heritage quarter a medieval character unique in North America. [Photo, courtesy Carl E. Hiebert]

Jacques Cartier first explored the heights of Québec in 1535. In the general vicinity he found an Iroquoian village named Stadacona. In 1608, by the time Samuel de Champlain constructed the *Abitation* which indelibly marked the founding of New France in America, the village had disappeared. Located at a point alongside the St. Lawrence River where it narrows to 1 km, the town enjoyed the role of being an Atlantic seaport as well as an interior corridor to the Great Lakes watershed and beyond. The massive protruding Cap-aux-Diamants to this day dominates a riverscape and landscape that is compelling, strategic, and Christmas card picturesque.

Although it was captured by New England merchants in 1629 and the British on the Plains of Abraham in 1759, it was successfully defended against an invasion of American rebels in 1775. Throughout these years, Québec nevertheless sustained a central military, administrative, cultural, and religious role in New France. The population numbered only

Built in 1892 on the site of Château St.-Louis (1647) to resemble an European castle, Château Frontenac is one of Québec City's best-known and most visible landmarks. Dominating Place d'Armes, a large square in Upper Town used for military drills and parades during the French regime, this majestic sentinel overlooking the St. Lawrence River, 100 meters below, has hosted kings, queens, and heads of state. [Photo, courtesy Carl E. Hiebert]

Port Saint-Jean is one of several walled entrances into historic Québec City, the only fortified city north of Mexico. During Québec's Winter Carnival, each February, the popular mascot figure Bonhomme appears everywhere. [Photo, courtesy Québec Tourism/photographer, Luc-Antoine Courturier]

8,000 in 1760, but a century later it had risen to 60,000. The British invasion had infused the city with English-speaking traders and merchants who capitalized on the burgeoning lumber trade. However, the decline of preferential trade duties with Great Britain, the increasing role of interior trade with the United States, and the financial clout of upstream Montréal eclipsed Québec City's once dominant role on the St. Lawrence. A provincial capital since 1867, the city has amalgamated with many of its outlying municipalities, to form, today, a sprawling metropolitan area.

As the cradle of French civilization in North America, Québec, through four centuries of urban evolution, has sustained an authentic continuity. In its residences, churches, and institutions, the city cherishes some of Canada's most important landmarks; these include the Old Port, Artillery Park, the St. Louis Gate, the Ursuline Convent, Place Royale, the Plains of Abraham, the Citadel, Dufferin Terrace, Québec Bridge, the Colisée, and, on the skyline, the majestic Château Frontenac.

Québec has been the subject of many artistic interpretations and literary descriptions. Observing the exhilarating panorama from the citadel, Charles Dickens wrote:

> *The exquisite expanse of country, rich in field and forest, mountain height and water, which lies stretched out before the view, with miles of Canadian villages, glancing in long white streaks, like veins along the landscape; the motley crowd of gables, roofs and chimney tops, in the old hilly town immediately at hand; the beautiful St. Lawrence sparkling and flashing in the sunlight, and the tiny ships from below the Rock from which you gaze, whose distant rigging looks like spider's webs against the light...forms one of the brightest and most enchanting pictures the eye can rest upon.*

The cradle of French civilization in North America, Québec City historically consists of Upper and Lower Town quarters. Although much of Lower Town was destroyed by the great fire of 1682, by bombardment in the seige of 1759, and by neglect over the centuries, today its focal point is Place Royale where the humble Notre Dame des Victoires, viewed here, built in 1688, stands proudly refurbished on the site of Champlain's original Abitation. Some 60 buildings in the general area have recently been restored. In the centre of Québec City's oldest public square stands a bust of Louis XIV, a reminder of Québec's royal heritage. [Photo, courtesy Québec Tourism/photographer Jacques Boudreau]

Well before the modern heritage movement tried to restore and conserve the ambience and character of cities being transformed by urban growth and the automobile, Québec City was the subject of preservation concerns. Frederick Temple Blackwood, or Lord Dufferin, the Governor General of Canada between 1872 and 1878, utilizing the architectural skills of Thomas Seaton Scott in the Department of Public Works, initiated a project to save what became known as the Dufferin Terrace. He was aided by artist William Brymner whose drawings and paintings influenced J. W. Morrice and Maurice Cullen in their visual exploration of the city. To this day, Québec City continues to enjoy a rich artistic tradition.

Mazo de la Roche wrote in 1944:

> *Yet what traveller can name a city with a more romantic past or a more noble situation? It is a walled city. Even though some of the walls are gone, there still remain the massive gates to mark where they stood. The dignity, the character, the aloofness of the walled city remain. It stands on its mighty rock above the moving tides of the St. Lawrence, fortified, the dark Laurentians rising behind it, and, as though one great river were not enough to guard it, there flows on its northern side the St. Charles. Today it stands in its calm and its recollections, yet filled with active toil, a town of Medieval France in the New World.*

Historian David Thiery Ruddel has written: "Unique among cities, Québec has captured the hearts and minds of its inhabitants for centuries. Perhaps more than any other city in North America, Québec has stirred the imagination of artists, travellers, and historians."

Larry Turner

THE ART OF JAMES W. MORRICE, the Montreal-born painter who spent many years in Paris, was described by the heroine of W. Somerset Maugham's *The Magician* as "the most delightful interpreter of Paris I know, and when you have seen his sketches, and he has done hundreds, of unimaginable grace and feeling and distinction – you can never see Paris in the same way again."

Maugham's heroine was not alone in her praise of this artist, who, by the turn of the century, was Canada's most renowned international artist. Only a few years after he had made Paris his home, critics and artists were praising his work and inviting him to exhibit at various galleries in the city. Famed Canadian painter A.Y. Jackson recalled that Morrice, in his student days, had "opened our eyes to things no one ever thought of painting" and added that his "subtle colour harmonies and his seemingly careless technique appeared very radical to Canadians."

The son of a prominent Montreal merchant family of Scottish descent, Morrice showed an early talent for painting but complied with his father's wish by graduating from the University of Toronto Law School in 1889 before pursuing an art career. His father's friend, Sir William Van Horne, the first to buy one of his paintings, suggested James be sent to Europe for further art study.

After a brief stay in London in 1890, James went to Paris, enrolled at the Académie Julian, then worked with individual teachers including Henri Harpignies and America's James McNeill Whistler who became a friend and had a marked influence on his work.

Morrice opened a studio in Montmartre and became one of the crowd of expatriate and native-born painters to frequent the cafés on the Left Bank. There, while painting street scenes, barges on the Seine, the local circus, and the numerous cafés and garden parks of Paris, he met writers and fellow artists. Many of his original sketches and oils were made on small panels of blond wood.

After only a few years in Paris, Morrice became an established artist. His work was exhibited at several salons including the Salon d'Automne, which he described as "somewhat revolutionary at times" but with "the most original work." Critics were using words like "exquisite" to describe his work, often sold to prominent Parisians. In 1904, the French Government bought his "Le Quai des Grands Augustins" for its collection of Modern Foreign Art at the Jeu de Paume Galerie while the city of Lyons purchased one of his Canadian paintings. Museums in the USA, Russia, Luxembourg, even the Louvre, acquired other works. Only a few were bought in Canada – three of them by his father's Mount Royal Club in Montreal.

Although Morrice never again lived in Canada, he made annual winter visits to see family and friends in Montreal and, while there, painted the Quebec countryside. On one trip to Quebec's north shore he met and became friends with Newfoundland-born Maurice Cullen, a painter he considered "the man in Canada who gets at the guts of things." Later they worked

J.w D Morrice

1865 - 1924

"He has the most fascinating sense of colour in the world."

-Somerset Maugham

"Sainte-Anne de Beaupré, P.Q.," circa 1905, interprets the essence of a cold winter day in Quebec. The bleak, grey scene, dominated by cold snow and a colder sky, brilliantly contrasts with other Morrice canvases depicting lively summer café scenes in Paris or Venice, the shimmering beaches of St. Malo, and the sultry coast of Brittany. [Photo, courtesy Collection of Power Corporation of Canada]

together in Venice where Morrice gained further insight into the use of light on canvas.

Morrice made friends easily, among them artists such as Whistler, Matisse, Pendergast, and Lautrec and writers like Maugham and Arnold Bennett, the latter also thinly disguising Morrice in one of his novels. Bennett also wrote in his autobiography, "I found him a most distinguished person, full of right and beautiful ideas about everything." As young Eric Bell, later a noted British art critic, recalled, "Morrice found beauty everywhere, in streets, in cafés, in bars, in shop windows, circuses and penny steamers."

Even though able to afford a good life through both his family wealth and the sale of his work, Morrice lived simply. Kathleen Daly Pepper in her 1966 biography of Morrice wrote: "He practiced economy in all things – the detail of his work, in his spending and in the comforts of living. He liked to part neither with his money, nor his sketches."

In Bennett's autobiography, *Evening with Exiles*, Morrice's bedroom was described as "a monk's cell," and his studio as having two easels, one for unfinished pictures and the other for finished or near-finished paintings. On the wall were other paintings: one was of his young mistress (he never married) entitled "Lea in a Tall Hat" and others were colourful watercolours by the American artist Maurice Pendergast that he had received in exchange for some of his own work.

By 1914 his parents had died and, with the war in Europe disrupting the Paris he knew and loved, Morrice moved to London where, through the urging of art critic Roger Fry, the Tate Gallery bought his painting, "A House in Santiago."

Late in 1917 he returned to Paris and was asked by Lord Beaverbrook to become a war artist. During this assignment, which lasted only a few months, he made sketches and canvases portraying the aftermath of the great war. One seven-by-nine-foot mural of an endless line of troops marching through a muddy battlefield is now a part of the Canadian War Memorials Collection in Ottawa.

Connoisseur art dealer for over 50 years the late G. Blair Laing called James Wilson Morrice "one of the 20th century's most talented and lyrical painters." In the intensely creative atmosphere of France at the turn of the century Morrice ambitiously embraced the advanced art of his day. Influenced by peers such as Matisse, Marquet and Cézanne, the expatriote from Montreal is perhaps best known as a colourist. His composition virtuosity of integrating warm and cool colours, for many, was unexcelled in his day. [Photo, courtesy The Art Gallery of Ontario]

Always restless, Morrice made return trips to Morocco and Algiers to which he had travelled with Matisse in prewar times. He also revisited and painted in the West Indies, but his health was fast deteriorating – largely from excessive alcohol consumption – and in 1922 he painted one of his last major works, "The Port of Algiers." After that, finding he could no longer paint, he became frustrated and irritable. Ill for much of 1923, he spent that Christmas at Cagnes with Lea Cadoret, his mistress of many years.

Then, as Matisse later recalled, Morrice, "a little like a migrating bird but without any fixed landing place," went to Sicily and Tunis, dying there in a French military hospital on January 23, 1924. He was buried nearby with only the doctor, the clergyman, and the British consul in attendance.

Posthumously, before Canadians became aware that he was a significant painter of international stature, French galleries continued to recognize him as an outstanding artist. In 1926, the Paris Galeries Simonson held a comprehensive showing of his work. At home, the Art Association of Montreal was the first to honour him but, in 1927 and 1937, the National Gallery of Canada organized major exhibitions of his work. Canadians had at last acknowledged his greatness. "Today," writes Pepper, "Morrice's paintings hold their distinguished place in any modern gallery."

Mel James

*A **genius** in capturing the effect of sunlight on landscape, Morrice demonstrates his mastery of colour in "Palazzo Dario, Venice" (Venice at Sunset), oil on canvas, circa 1904. [Photo, courtesy Collection of Power Corporation of Canada]*

MARGARET ATWOOD was born in Ottawa in 1939 and spent her girl-hood summers in northern Ontario and Quebec where her entomologist father introduced her to the plea-sures of unspoiled wilder-ness, an influence which, to this day, reappears in her much admired writings.

MARGARET ATWOOD

Oracle for a National Culture

A brilliant scholar, she attended the University of Toronto, Radcliffe, and Harvard. She has served as the chairperson of The Writers' Union of Canada and has actively supported Amnesty International and P E N Canada. Margaret Atwood lives with writer Graeme Gibson and they have one daughter, Jess, who was born in the spring of 1976.

A decade after Margaret Atwood had won her first Governor General's Award, Tom Marshall commented, in an issue of the *Malahat Review* dedicated to her work, that "Atwood is young enough for us to suppose that her best work is in the future."

Thus far, Atwood, who is arguably Canada's best-known author both in her homeland and abroad, has written more than 30 literary works and has been translated into more than 25 languages. Although she has written non-fiction and children's literature, she is perhaps best known for her novels – *The Edible Woman* (1969), *Surfacing* (1972), *Lady Oracle* (1976), *Life Before Man* (1979), *Bodily Harm* (1981), *The Handmaid's Tale* (1985), *Cat's Eye* (1988), and *The Robber Bride* (1993), in addition to her numerous collections of poetry and short stories.

Atwood's first poetry emerged in the 1950s when she, a teenager, had no inkling of modern poetry. "In high school we did not study any Canadian poets; we studied dead English people. But there were a lot of people around my age who were coming into it, who had begun to write. There were people on the west coast and people here [Toronto] in the coffee-shop movement; there was that kind of public reading going on ... It was such a small community.... Something wiggled on one side of it and those on the other side felt the ripple."

In 1972 Atwood published her ground-breaking book, *Survival: A Thematic Guide to Canadian Literature*, in which her central thesis was that much Canadian literature is concerned with victimization by the natural environment.

When she won the Governor General's Award in 1966 for *The Circle Game* (she won the prize a second time in 1986 for *The Handmaid's Tale*), her prolific career was launched.

Several of Atwood's works have been turned into films including the poem "The Progressive Insanities of a Pioneer" and novels *Surfacing, The Edible Woman,* and *The Handmaid's Tale.*

Margaret Atwood has won wide international acclaim and numerous awards, highlighted by France's Le Chevalier dans L'Ordre des Arts et Lettres, England's *Sunday Times* Award for Literary Excellence, the Canadian Authors Association Award, the Ontario Trillium Award, the American Humanist of the Year Award (1987), the Ida Nudel Humanitarian Award, *Ms. Magazine's* Woman of the Year for 1986, the Welsh Arts Council International Writer's Prize (1982), and the *Los Angeles Times* Prize for Fiction in 1986. In 1987 and 1989, she was shortlisted for the Booker Prize and was made Companion of the Order of Canada in 1981.

Journalist Robert Fulford, longtime editor of *Saturday Night*, wrote in 1977 that Atwood, as "feminist, nationalist, literary witch, mythological poet, satirist, formulator of critical theories ... is beyond question the chief literary heroine of this era." He asked, "Who is Atwood? What is she up to? What is she up to now?" In 1995 she partly deflected a similar question in a *Poetry Canada Review*: "Biographically-minded people are constantly pushing interpretation towards the inner and personal and the subjective, but, in fact, a lot of what poets write about is there in the world. It's out there, not in here. Or it may be both, but it's certainly out there. So you're not writing about dire things because you happen to be oriented towards dire things; you're writing about dire things because they exist."

Patricia Stone

Opposite: "Margaret Atwood with Mug I," acrylic on canvas, 81x70cm, 1980 by Charles Pachter of Toronto and Miami Beach, Florida. [Painting, courtesy Charles Pachter]

Novelist, short story writer, poet, and critic, Margaret Atwood is viewed here with former teacher and mentor, Northrop Frye, left, and, right, George Ignatieff, Chancellor, University of Toronto, when she was honoured by her alma mater in 1983 with an honorary D.Litt. [Photo, courtesy Victoria College, University of Toronto]

Robert Service

1874 - 1958

Bard of the Midnight Sun

The strong life that never knows harness;
The wilds where the caribou call;
The freshness, the freedom, the fairness –
O God! How I'm stuck on it all.
　　　　"*The Spell of the Yukon*" (1907)

ROBERT W. SERVICE, "The Bard of the Yukon," "The Canadian Kipling," brought the magic of the Klondike Gold Rush to millions of readers worldwide. His writings captured the essence of Canada's Northern dimension, and his romantic imagination indelibly stamped the land of the midnight sun, northern lights, and arctic wilds upon the popular North American concept of Canada.

The claim is often made that Service has been the most widely read poet of the twentieth century. He certainly was the most successful in material terms, and while the self-deprecating Service would be the first to admit that quotability is no proof of literary merit, his works occupy more space in *Bartlett's Familiar Quotations* than those of all other Canadian poets combined. In the half century following the publication of *Songs of the Sourdough* in 1907, Service churned out more than a dozen other books of verse, numerous collected volumes, six novels, a two-volume autobiography, a song book, and a fitness guide. But his fame would have been assured had it rested solely upon that first slender volume (also released in the American market as *The Spell of the Yukon*), introducing as it did such immortal classics as "The Law of the Yukon," "The Shooting of Dan McGrew," and "The Cremation of Sam McGee." This modest tome for which Service is principally remembered began life as a "vanity" run of 100 copies as keepsakes to bestow "with apologetic wistfulness" upon kindly

Above: *Robert Service, viewed here, circa 1910, lived in this two-room cabin near Whitehorse on two different occasions: 1908-9 and 1911-12. It was here, before he ever went to the Klondike, that he wrote "The Shooting of Dan McGrew" and "The Cremation of Sam McGee." The cabin has been restored and during the summer tourists can see re-enactments of his poetry reading.* [Photo, courtesy Charles J. Humber Collection]

acquaintances. By 1940 it had sold over three million copies and "Dan McGrew" and "Sam McGee" had earned Service more than half a million dollars.

Service's interest in the Yukon came about almost by accident. Robert William Service was born in Preston, England, in 1874. The family moved to Scotland and Service was educated in Glasgow. He entered the Commercial Bank of Scotland and attended evening classes at the University of Glasgow, but soon gave up formal education in disgust. In 1896 he emigrated to Canada, arriving at Victoria, British Columbia, with five dollars in his pocket. For the next seven years he attended "the College of Hard Knocks, graduating without enthusiasm." Like Woody Guthrie or Steinbeck's migrant workers in a later era, he wandered up and down the west coast of North America "in vagabondage." Almost destitute, he found occasional work as a farm labourer, a potato digger, an orange picker, a tutor and handyman in a rural bordello, a dishwasher, a road worker, and a travelling balladeer. Riding the rails, frequenting soup kitchens, and begging for bread, he meandered towards Mexico in 1898, incredibly almost oblivious to the northward flow of the sea of humanity at the outbreak of the Klondike Gold Rush.

Tiring of the vagabond life and seeking security, in 1903 he accepted work as a bank clerk at the Canadian Bank of Commerce in Victoria. The following year he was transferred to Kamloops and almost immediately to the bank's branch in Whitehorse. There in the autumn of 1904, at the urging of Stroller White, the editor of the *Whitehorse Star*, he wrote his most celebrated verse, "The Shooting of Dan McGrew," as if "someone was whispering in [his] ear," and "The Cremation of Sam McGee" a month later while walking home from a party along a woodland trail "in a strange ecstasy." Thus it was that *Songs of a Sourdough*, containing Service's most renowned verse, was written before he ever set foot in the Klondike. Thanks in part to the wizardry of Robert Bond, William Brigg's best salesman, the collection "took off" in the spring of 1907 and went through 15 printings before the end of the year, each one larger than its predecessor, a feat unheard-of for Canadian verse.

Robert became Whitehorse's principal tourist attraction, so it was with a sense of relief that the shy and diffident bank clerk was transferred to Dawson in April 1908. Service had missed the heyday of the Gold Rush by a full decade and Dawson had now shrunk from 40,000 to just under 4,000 inhabitants. His new friend and neighbour, Laura Thompson (later Berton), mother of Pierre, had expected, based on his poetry, "a rip-roaring roisterer" but instead found a "shy and non-descript man in his mid thirties," prim and proper in his high starched collars, with a voice combining an "English inflection, an American drawl and Scottish overtones."

By November 1909, the royalty cheques had dwarfed his salary to such an extent that Robert retired from the Bank rather than accept a transfer. He devoted himself full time to his writing and turned out *Ballads of Cheechako* (1909), *Rhymes of a Rolling Stone* (1912), and his first novel, *The Trail of Ninety-Eight, a Northland Romance* (1910). Ironically for someone so mystically attached to the Canadian North, Service departed from the Yukon in the summer of 1912 and never returned. Laura Berton summarized his literary achievement in the

Yukon, noting that of the hundreds of writers who had spent their lives producing whole libraries on the North, many based on first-hand pioneering experiences, "only this quiet, colourless bank clerk succeeded in capturing the strange mixture of magic and tragedy, hope and heartbreak, of which the gold camps of the Yukon are compounded. It is a tribute to him that his books sell nowhere as well as they do in Dawson itself."

Service departed for Europe as *The Toronto Daily Star* war correspondent for the Second Balkan War. Settling in Paris in March 1913, he spent most of the remaining 46 years of his life in France, marrying Germaine Bourgoin in June 1913 and acquiring, that same summer, the other love of his life, "Dream Haven," his home in Lancieux, on the Emerald Coast of Brittany, just west of Dinard. Except for a five-year absence which he and his family spent in Vancouver and Hollywood during the Occupation, he would spend his summers in Brittany and his winters in Paris until 1929 and thereafter in Nice and later Monte Carlo. During World War I, he was briefly correspondent for *The Toronto Daily Star,* served with the Red Cross Ambulance Service Corps near Verdun, and finally was attached to the Canadian Expeditionary Force, receiving a commission to tour France and report on the activities of Canadian troops.

Following the War, Service continued to write verse and novels loosely based upon his experiences. He was never under any illusion as to the literary merits of his verse: he wrote it to sell. He also had a lifelong healthy loathing of academic, intellectual, and class pretensions. He felt that "stuffed shirtism" was "the camouflage of charlatans.... Dignified men are hypocrites and frauds. No man who has the honesty to see himself as he really is can be anything but humble. Only fools take themselves seriously...." As he explained in *Ballads of a Bohemian* (1921), "Imagination is the great gift of the gods. Given it, one does not need to look afar for subjects. There is romance in every face."

With Germaine and his young daughter Iris, Robert visited Hollywood in the early 1920s. He had received $5,000 for the film rights to *The Shooting of Dan McGrew* (1924), a remake of the 1915 version. In 1929, *The Trail of '98* was also made into a movie starring Dolores del Rio and Ralph Forbes. Service's own acting debut came in the 1942 remake of Rex Beach's *The Spoilers* starring Randolph Scott and John Wayne. In a scene with the film's dance hall heroine, played by Marlene Dietrich, Robert played himself, forty years younger, busily scribbling "The Shooting of Dan McGrew" in a corner of a saloon. Indeed, "Dan McGrew" had one more reincarnation of note in 1952 in the first-ever production of a ballet with a Canadian theme.

Robert Service died in September 1958, and that immortality he first sensed on opening the package containing his author's copies of *Songs of a Sourdough* in the Spring of 1907 has surpassed his wildest dreams. Memorials abound to his memory from the Yukon to Romania, where Queen Marie chose his verses in memory of their mutual friend, Colonel Joe Boyle (1867-1923), DSO, OBE. No poet save Robert Burns has enjoyed such a wide popularity with the common man, and high-profile fans include Ronald Reagan and the Queen Mother.

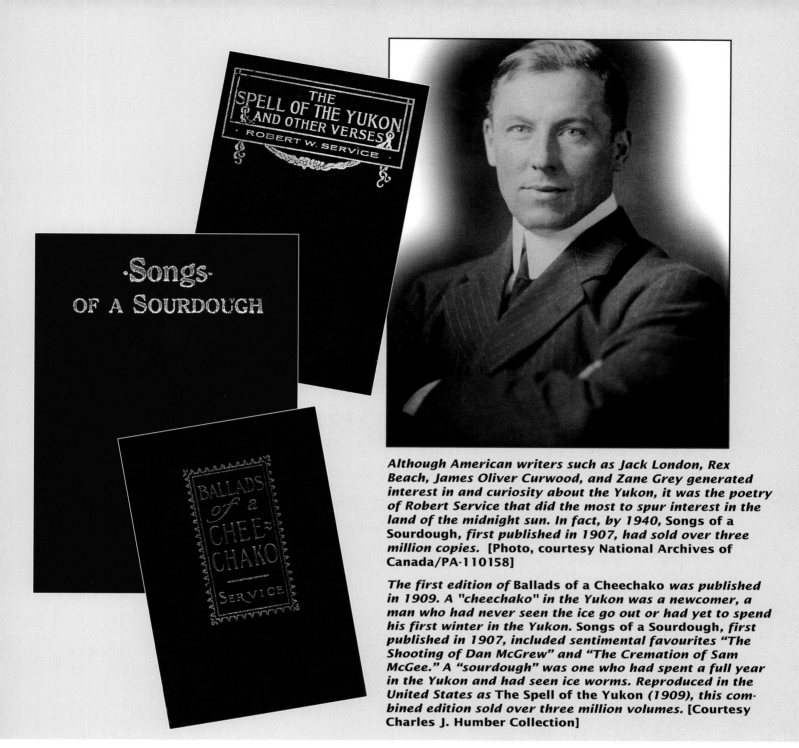

Although American writers such as Jack London, Rex Beach, James Oliver Curwood, and Zane Grey generated interest in and curiosity about the Yukon, it was the poetry of Robert Service that did the most to spur interest in the land of the midnight sun. In fact, by 1940, Songs of a Sourdough, *first published in 1907, had sold over three million copies.* [Photo, courtesy National Archives of Canada/PA-110158]

The first edition of Ballads of a Cheechako *was published in 1909. A "cheechako" in the Yukon was a newcomer, a man who had never seen the ice go out or had yet to spend his first winter in the Yukon.* Songs of a Sourdough, *first published in 1907, included sentimental favourites "The Shooting of Dan McGrew" and "The Cremation of Sam McGee." A "sourdough" was one who had spent a full year in the Yukon and had seen ice worms. Reproduced in the United States as* The Spell of the Yukon *(1909), this combined edition sold over three million volumes.* [Courtesy Charles J. Humber Collection]

Of those he made famous through his writing, "The Ragtime Kid," Hartley Claude Myrick, passed away in Seattle in July 1950. "The Lady known as Lou," cabaret singer Lulu Johnson, was drowned when the Canadian Pacific Steamer, *Princess Sofia,* sank in the Lynn Canal on October 25, 1918. And Sam McGee, a Dawson prospector whose name Robert had lifted from the Bank ledger and who actually came from Lindsay, Ontario, left the Yukon in 1909, settled in Great Falls, Montana, and was eventually decently interred in Beiseker, Alberta, having spent much of his life responding to queries about whether he was "warm" enough yet. But Robert Service lives on in the Canadian national imagination which his writings did much to stir and inspire.

Murray Barkley

Feeding the World

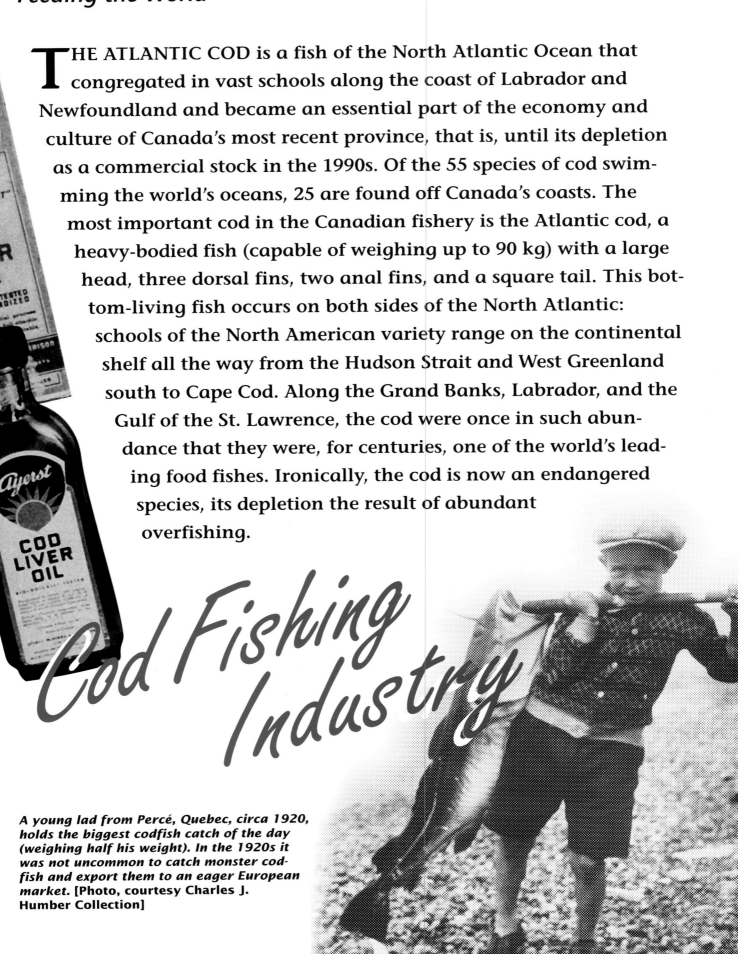

THE ATLANTIC COD is a fish of the North Atlantic Ocean that congregated in vast schools along the coast of Labrador and Newfoundland and became an essential part of the economy and culture of Canada's most recent province, that is, until its depletion as a commercial stock in the 1990s. Of the 55 species of cod swimming the world's oceans, 25 are found off Canada's coasts. The most important cod in the Canadian fishery is the Atlantic cod, a heavy-bodied fish (capable of weighing up to 90 kg) with a large head, three dorsal fins, two anal fins, and a square tail. This bottom-living fish occurs on both sides of the North Atlantic: schools of the North American variety range on the continental shelf all the way from the Hudson Strait and West Greenland south to Cape Cod. Along the Grand Banks, Labrador, and the Gulf of the St. Lawrence, the cod were once in such abundance that they were, for centuries, one of the world's leading food fishes. Ironically, the cod is now an endangered species, its depletion the result of abundant overfishing.

Cod Fishing Industry

A young lad from Percé, Quebec, circa 1920, holds the biggest codfish catch of the day (weighing half his weight). In the 1920s it was not uncommon to catch monster codfish and export them to an eager European market. [Photo, courtesy Charles J. Humber Collection]

The shallow waters of the continental shelf, in particular the Grand Banks off Newfoundland, were an ideal habitat for Atlantic cod. Swirling currents that mixed warm waters from the Gulf Stream with the icy waters from the Labrador current and the fresh waters from the St. Lawrence encouraged a rich growth of plankton, smaller fish, and their predators. The great advantage of cod as a food fish was that it could be easily caught, dried, or salted, transported long distances, and preserved for several months.

The European exploitation of the cod fishery centuries ago set in motion the acquisition of North America, the development of mercantile networks and possessive imperial regimes that had affected areas far beyond the Grand Banks. British, French, and Dutch seafaring traditions were built in part on the "nursery for seamen" that the fishing industry created. Canadian historian, Harold Adam Innis, in his famous *Cod Fisheries: The History of an International Economy (1940)*, maintained that maritime fishing had a complex impact on the rest of North America, the West Indies, Western Europe, South America, and the Mediterranean. Fishing was a core activity that reinforced shipping, shipbuilding, and trade.

In 1497 John Cabot described the Grand Banks as so "swarming with fish [that they] could be taken not only with a net but in baskets let down with a stone." In describing Newfoundland in 1497, Cabot used the Portuguese name *baccalaos*, which meant "Land of Cod." Normans, Bretons, Basques, and Portuguese pioneered the trans-Atlantic fishery early in the sixteenth century, with the English from the west country dominating the Avalon peninsula after 1570. By 1575, the more than 300 French, Portuguese, and English vessels fishing on the banks created local competition among 100 European ports. By the time the Pilgrims landed at Plymouth, Massachusetts, in 1620, the cod fleet exceeded 1,000 vessels and the fishery slowly shifted from one that was migratory in nature to one that involved planters and overwinterers. As Spanish and Portuguese fleets declined, the English, French, and, later, New Englanders, competed along the continental shelf. By the Treaty of Utrecht in 1713 which acknowledged England's claim to Hudson Bay and ceded Acadia and Newfoundland to England, the cod fishery was one of the great industries of the western Europe economy. At the end of the American Revolution in 1783, as many as 1,500 vessels were fishing for cod, not to mention other vessels seeking various other fish species as well as whales. So abundant was the yearly catch that no talk of stock depletion or species extinction would take place for another 200 years!

Patterns of eighteenth century fishery included the dominance of crews and vessels from Waterford, Ireland; from Poole, Exeter, and Dartmouth in England; and from Norman communities in France, especially St. Malo. In France, codfish was the "beef of the sea" and the French continued to fish from bases around the Gulf of St. Lawrence and St. Pierre and Miquelon in spite of growing English dominance. In Europe, northern regions preferred wet or salted cod; Mediterranean countries acquired the more thoroughly processed and preserved dry cod. In 1772 the largest distributor of cod in Europe was the port city of Marseille which then redistributed it throughout the region to Spain, Italy, and other Mediterranean locations.

As late as 1900, three-quarters of the fish caught by Newfoundlanders was cod. One of the offshoots that sustained the cod fishery was the popularity of cod liver oil as a primary source of vitamin A. Before the 1920s, most cod liver oil was supplied by Norwegian sources until research in Newfoundland by Ayerst, McKenna, and Harrison Ltd. proved the potency and value of oil extracted from cod off the Grand Banks. Cod liver oil thereafter became a worldwide phenomenon, especially in the provision of vitamins to children.

The cod fishery, now nearly gone the way of the dodo, also contributed to a major economic theory developed by Canadian economists and historians relating to empire,

Curing and drying codfish at the turn of the century was a common sight in Canada's maritime provinces. Here codfish are being dried, circa 1920, on a two-tier wharf in Yarmouth, Nova Scotia. [Photo, courtesy Charles J. Humber Collection]

Fish Curing, Yarmouth, N.S.

Gaspé fishermen prepare the day's cod catch. In the background is Percé Rock, one of the most spectacular landmarks in all of Canada. Until recent times, beach scenes such as this 1920s view, depicted seagulls hovering above fishing workbenches while boats, drawn ashore by teams of horses, waited for early morning fishermen to ply the ocean another day. [Photo, courtesy Charles J. Humber Collection]

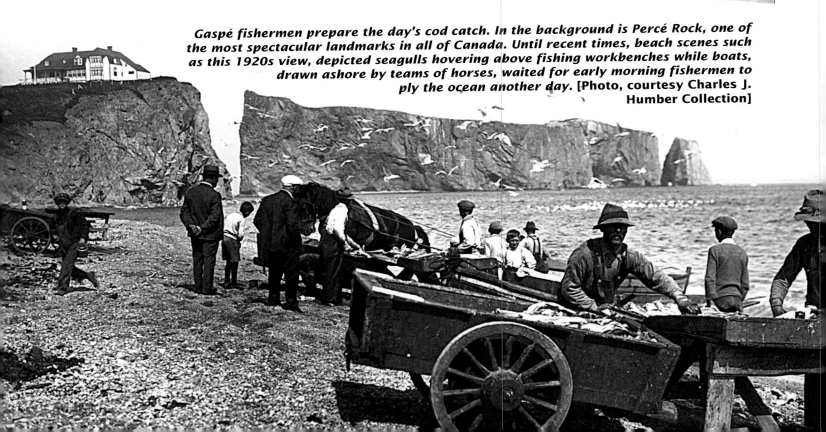

communications, staples, and metropolitanism. The study of the cod fishery, in addition to other Canadian staple products such as fur, lumber, and wheat, has provided economic models applied to other parts of the world where resources, transport, mercantilism, and power controlled the system and pace of development. In the words of Graeme Patterson, both Harold Adam Innis and Marshall McLuhan "believed the world was and continues to be shaped by communications systems ... the causes and effects of changes such as these are worldwide and not merely national or continental in extent." Innis revealed that the study of the exploitation of cod and beaver within the framework of an intellectual concept was merely elementary to McLuhan's understanding of the global village.

Larry Turner

Canada's codfish industry extended into Labrador where curing and drying of cod on raised platforms covered all the open spaces of little fishing villages. This view, circa 1910, captures a satisfying moment for Labrador fishermen having just completed the task of preparing cod for market. [Photo, courtesy Charles J. Humber Collection]

Finding space for the drying and curing of codfish in Annapolis, Nova Scotia, at the early part of the 20th century proved difficult. Catches were so plentiful, that the platforms of railway stations – even the tracks – became surfaces for codfish curing. [Photo, courtesy Charles J. Humber Collection]

Margaret Newton

Defeating Wheat Rust Disease

1887 - 1971

MARGARET NEWTON was in her final year for a B.S.A. degree at McGill University in 1917 when one of her professors was summoned to Ottawa to help solve the problem of rust that was ruining the wheat crops of prairie farmers. He asked if she would look after his experiments on grasses while he was away and sent her additional cultures. In carrying out an experiment on the new cultures, she discovered the key to the wheat rust problem and spent the rest of her professional life seeking solutions that made her a world-famous plant pathologist.

Her discovery was, at first, merely an observation. After having applied ten spores of rust to ten identical specimens of wheat – all from the same plant – she noticed that one of the resulting patches of disease was different. It was smaller and less damaging. This led her to wonder whether there was more than one kind of rust or whether this particular specimen of wheat was more resistant.

When Margaret showed her results to the professor on his return to McGill, he realized she was on the right track. In other words, the key to solving wheat rust was to develop grains resistant to many different "races" of rust. "Scientists from all over the world will flock to see this," he declared, for wheat rust in North America and Europe alone was annually destroying countless millions in both bushels and dollars.

The daughter of a wealthy English-born father who settled in Montreal when he was 21, Margaret was one of five children, four of whom became agricultural scientists with Ph.D. degrees. Her doctorate was obtained at the University of Minnesota in 1922. By then, she was already recognized for her research and spent the next decade, first as an associate professor of biology at the University of Saskatchewan and later as senior plant pathologist at the newly created Dominion Rust Research Centre in Winnipeg. There she supervised a number of scientists while carrying out her own research, sometimes to the point of exhaustion, to identify different "races" of rust.

In 1933 the Russian government offered her $10,000 and a staff of 50 scientists with all travel expenses paid. It even included a fleet of camels for her travels through desert country, but, when her brother Robert pointed out that her absence would put "Canada's work in the field back many years," she turned down this offer.

Margaret's life-long research included isolating some 150 different races of rust that occurred in Western Canada. She did this by exposing them to the wheat to be grown in a given area and developing a host index that recorded the "races" and relative frequency of each invading Canada. She also gave lectures in the U.S.A., at such European cities as Moscow, Leningrad, Amsterdam, and at Cambridge University in England. In addition, she wrote 42 papers focusing on the subject before ill health forced her to retire in 1945.

Her illness was lung trouble – a kind of silicosis brought about as a result of her long years working with rust spores. When the Canadian government hesitated about paying her a full pension, Western farmers showed their appreciation for her work by petitioning Ottawa with the observation that "This woman has saved the country millions of dollars." She got a full pension.

Scientific societies and numerous associations and institutions recognized her accomplishments. Awarded an FRCS in 1942, she also became the first woman to receive the Flavelle Gold Medal from the Royal Society of Canada in 1948. She also won the Outstanding Achievement Award from the University of Minnesota in 1956. By then she had retired to Victoria, British Columbia, where the University of Victoria named a women's residence in her honour. In 1992 – 21 years after her death in Victoria – her work was again recognized when she was inducted into the newly created Science Hall of Fame in Ottawa.

Mel James

While still a student at McGill, Margaret Newton worked on the first scientific survey of wheat rust in Canada and was possibly the first Canadian woman to undertake a life-long research career. In 1948 she received the Royal Society of Canada's prestigious Flavelle Medal for her outstanding contribution to biological science. [Photo, courtesy National Research Council]

PERCY WILLIAMS

The World's Fastest Human – in 1928   **1908 - 1982**

WHEN PERCY WILLIAMS of Vancouver won the 100- and 200-metre sprints at the Amsterdam Olympics in 1928, his triumphs set off one of the greatest celebrations for an individual in Canada's history. He was, according to David Wallerchinsky, author of *The Complete Book of the Olympics*, "greeted with an enthusiasm reminiscent of the ancient Greek Olympics."

There were a number of reasons for this. Percy was the obvious underdog. Only one Canadian had ever won a short distance race at the Olympics and that was 20 years earlier when Bobby Kerr won the 220-yard sprint. Percy was a skinny 20-year-old just out of high school who had never before competed in the 100-metre distance against such international stars as Frank Wykoff and Bob McAllister, both of the U.S., or Charles Borah of the U.S. and Hermit Koernig of Germany, famous for their internationally acclaimed 200-metre victories. He was also self-effacing. Writing in his diary after winning the Canadian Olympic trials in Hamilton, he mused, "I can't quite understand yet, but they say winning the 100 metres puts me on the boat to Amsterdam."

He arrived in Amsterdam without his coach, Bob Granger, who first saw him run as an 18-year-old at a high school track meet in Vancouver and virtually decided then and there that he could make him a winner at the 1928 Games. Granger had been left behind for lack of money, but funds were quickly raised by Williams' mother and others in Vancouver to

Percy Williams of Vancouver won gold medals in both the 100- and 200-metre events at the 1928 Amsterdam Olympics, the only time a Canadian has accomplished this extraordinary feat. This view, often attributed to his 100-metre victory at Amsterdam, actually records his stunning 100-yard victory two years later at the British Empire Games in Hamilton. [Photo, courtesy Ontario Track and Field Association]

enable him to take a freighter a few days later to be on hand to coach Percy through the gruelling preliminary and the final races of the sprint competition.

Because there were 87 competitors for the 100-metre sprint, Percy was required to run three heats before the final. After winning the first and second heats, he made a modest observation in his diary: "I always imagined it (the Olympics) was a game of heroes. Well, I'm in the semi-finals myself so it can't be so hot." In the semi-final he came second to McAllister and then had two hours to kill before the final. Granger had him read a book and, just before the race, gave him a rubdown with coconut butter.

As he lined up between McAllister and Jack London, a 200-pound Guyanese running for Great Britain, he looked even skinnier than his 126 pounds. Others in the final were Wykoff, George Lammers of Germany, and Wilfred Legg of South Africa. After two false starts, the third was perfect for Williams as he shot into the lead and held onto it to win one yard ahead of London with Lammers third. Granger later described his own reaction to it as "ten seconds of breathless living," but Williams recorded, "Well, well, well. So I'm supposed to be the World's 100-metre champion (Crushed Apples). No more fun in running now."

The next day the trials began for the 200-metre event. He won the first and then discovered that both Borah and Koernig would be competing in the next trial. Since only the winner and runner-up would move on, he had to beat one of them and Granger wisely counselled, "Don't try to win. Run to beat whoever is running second." Koernig won and Williams edged Borah. The next day in the semi-finals he eliminated Charlie Paddock, another favourite from the U.S., so the final pitted him against an American, Jackson Sholtz, another Canadian, John Fitzpatrick of Hamilton, Jacob Schuller and Koernig of Germany, and Walter Rangeley of Great Britain. The field was the fastest ever assembled up to that time.

Granger had new words of advice, telling his charge that Koernig was the man to beat. "He's a front runner and if you come out of the curve even with him or just ahead of him, you will kill his inspiration and win." Williams did just that. They came out of the curve, neck and neck, and 50 yards from the finish line, Percy shifted gears and shot passed Koernig to win by a yard over Rangeley. Koernig ended up in a dead heat with Sholtz for third place.

Bobby Kerr, captain of the 1928 Olympic team and the only other Canadian to ever win the event, hugged Williams at the finish line. "Won't Granger be pleased?" Percy gasped as the crowd went wild. General Douglas McArthur, then president of the U.S. Olympic Committee, declared, "The Canadian Percy Williams is the greatest sprinter the world has ever seen and he will be even greater before his career is ended," while Percy told reporters, "My lucky coin in the race was getting off to a good start." His diary noted "Telegrams galore. The girls' team sent flowers to me. Hot Dog!"

On arriving in Canada on September 14, he received more than just congratulatory messages. His mother was on hand to meet him as the ship docked at Quebec City and the mayor gave him a gold watch. Boarding a train, Percy and his mother received numerous other gifts and greetings. In Montreal Mayor Camillien Houde urged him "to stay

Canadian." In Toronto, thousands cheered him at the Canadian National Exhibition. Hamilton gave him a gold key and Winnipeg declared a "Percy Williams Day" at the Polo Park racetrack. Thousands even showed up in Calgary where the stopover lasted only 15 minutes.

But all of the ceremonies paled in comparison to his welcome home in Vancouver where people jammed not only the train station but several downtown blocks as a school band played "Hail the Conquering Hero." Schools were let out and 2,000 school children led a parade, with Percy, Granger, the Mayor, and the Premier seated in a touring car, to Stanley Park where 20,000 people were on hand to see "Peerless Percy," as the papers dubbed him, presented with a brand-new Graham-Page coupe as well as a trust fund for his education that amounted to $14,500. Granger too was recognized, receiving $500 in gold. "Oh what a homecoming," declared Premier S.F. Tolmie. "Never has there been such joy and pride."

Williams' double victory caused some American sportswriters to suggest he won because

BOBBY KERR

1882-1963

THE first person to congratulate Williams after he won the 200-metre event at the 1928 Olympics was Canada's only other winner of it, Bobby Kerr of Hamilton. Kerr had won the same event at the 1908 Olympics in London, England, and was in Amsterdam 20 years later as captain of the Canadian Olympic team.

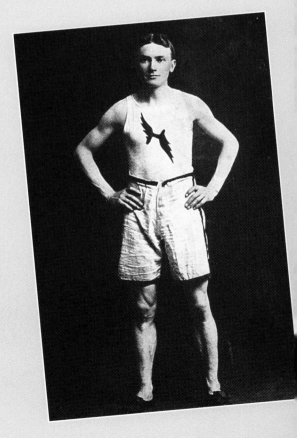

Born in Enniskillen, Ireland, in 1882, Kerr moved with his family to Kemptville, Ontario, when he was five, but they settled in Hamilton 18 months later. Bobby loved to run, but, because he began working in his teens he had to squeeze in training after his 12-hour day. As a result, he was 20 before he first gained prominence as a premier runner, winning, in 1902, the 100-, 440-, and 800-yard races at the Hamilton Coronation Games. The following year, the man destined to become the fastest human won the 100- and 200-yard events at the YMCA championships. He then spent his own savings from his company fire brigade job to go to St. Louis for the 1904 Olympics.

Kerr lost in a qualifying round but, once back in Hamilton, entered meets wherever he could in Canada and

of the soft track conditions existing in Amsterdam, a claim Percy put to rest the following winter when he took part in several U.S. indoor track meets, setting one world record for the 45-yard distance and equalling three others. In August 1930, he set a new world record of 10.3 seconds for 100 metres in Toronto. Previously, he had tied the world mark for the 100-yards at 9.6 seconds. He also won the 100-metre race at the British Empire Games in Hamilton two weeks later but pulled a muscle in his thigh. Percy never reached the same form afterwards, being eliminated in the second qualifying run for the 100 metres at the 1932 Olympic Games in Los Angeles. Percy retired to become a successful insurance agent and take up golf. In 1950 he was voted by Canadian Press as the country's top track and field performer of the half century but later admitted he never really enjoyed running. "Oh I was so glad to get out of it all," he said in a 1954 interview. He never married but lived with his mother until her death and then alone until he was found dead at his home from a heart attack at age 74 in 1982.

Mel James

in U.S. border cities. Over the next three years he set new Canadian records for the 40, 50, 60, 75, 100, 150, 220 yards and the 100 and 200 metres. In 1907 he won both the 100- and 200-yard Canadian titles and had 39 other first-place finishes. He continued his string of victories in 1908 by sweeping the sprint events at the Ontario and Canadian Games before going to London to compete in the Olympics.

Being entered in two events, Bobby, like Percy, had to compete six times over a period of four days in order to qualify and reach the finals. On the morning of July 22, for instance, he won the semifinal in the 200-metre semifinals and, that afternoon, placed third for the bronze medal in the 100-metre final. The next day he captured the Gold in the 200-metre final.

It was a popular win in London as British fans looked upon Bobby as representing the Empire. In Hamilton, the news of his victory set off a celebration of bell ringing, whistle blowing, and a flag-raising ceremony at City Hall. When he arrived home in August, a gala parade was held in his honour and gifts were showered on the world-champion hero in much the same way as Williams would be fêted some 20 years later in Vancouver.

There was, however, a big difference between the only two Canadian men who have ever won Olympic gold medals at those distances. Kerr remained active in track and field activities for years. He attended four Olympiads in various capacities, served as honorary secretary of the Canadian Olympic Association, and was everything from an official starter to meet director and chairman of numerous other track and field meets for years. When Kerr died in 1963 at age 81, Ivan Miller, sports director of the *Hamilton Spectator*, wrote, "Oldtimers will remember with deep nostalgia the torchlight parades that welcomed Bobby back from conquest after conquest, and they'll miss the modesty that set apart a man who just did his best."

Mel James

Bobby Kerr, first to cross the finish line in the 200-yard final at the 1908 London Olympics, was the first Canadian sprinter to win an Olympic gold medal. [Photo, courtesy Charles J. Humber Collection]

In 1960, Lt. Col. Edwin A. Baker received from Helen Keller, in New York, the first international award of the American Foundation for Overseas Blind. [Photo, courtesy Canadian National Institute for the Blind]

Sightless Seer   **1893 - 1968**

EDWIN ALBERT BAKER

AMONG THE THOUSANDS of young men who marched off to the First World War and never again saw their home country was Colonel Edwin Albert Baker. Col. Baker lost his eyesight at Flanders Fields on October 10, 1915, while serving in the 6th Field Company of the Canadian Engineers. Despite his disability, he became a world leader in the provision of services for the visually handicapped, a founder of the Canadian National Institute for the Blind (CNIB) and its managing director for forty-two years.

Born on the waterfront of Lake Ontario in Ernestown Township west of Kingston in 1893, Edwin had just graduated from Queen's University with a degree in electrical engineering in 1914 when he enlisted for the war. After his tragedy, he found inspiration at St. Dunstan's Blinded Soldiers' and Sailors' Hostel, in London, England, operated by Sir Arthur Pearson who promoted a philosophy of independence and self-reliance.

Back in Canada, Baker met and married a daughter of "Black Jack" Robinson, the editor of the Toronto *Telegram* who helped Edwin get a job at the Ontario Hydro Electric Commission.

In 1916 Baker joined the board of a library renamed, in 1917, the Canadian National Library for the Blind. Baker and six others then organized the CNIB in 1918 and Baker became its managing director in 1920. Baker realized the limitations facing the disabled and the lack of training facilities for them. His goal was to establish the kinds of institutions he had "witnessed" in Britain and give "a new outlook" to rehabilitation centres. His philosophy stated, "You can't judge anyone by what he's lost – only by what he does with what's left."

His role at the CNIB soon made the institution world renowned. He promoted special provision for disabled veterans, workmen's compensation, medical research into disabilities,

Lt. Col. Edwin A. Baker, O.B.E., C.C., M.C., Croix de Guerre, B.Sc., LL.D., U.E. [Photo, courtesy Canadian National Institute for the Blind]

eye-saving classes, special transportation arrangements, education, library services in Braille, and an eye bank. Always taking note of irony in his position, Baker once said, "Part of my job is to open society's eyes. By a twist of fate, I've turned from electrical to human engineering."

In the international sphere, Baker headed the Sir Arthur Pearson Club of Blinded Associations, was a trustee of the American Foundation for the Blind, and a founder and, in 1951, the first president of the World Council for the Welfare of the Blind. When he retired in 1962, the E. A Baker Foundation was established to set up further research into the causes of blindness and the means of prevention.

Three sons and a daughter were born to Edwin and Jessie and they were raised like any other children on the block. Their father taught them to swim, fish, camp, and play baseball.

He was an inspiration to many when services were scant and when a social stigma was attached to those with disabilities. He peeled away ignorance, taught by example, lobbied on behalf of others, and was a leader extraordinaire. His elevation to the position of Lieutenant Colonel in his old regiment is a measure of the esteem in which he was held by his peers.

Edwin Baker's honorary awards were many. Some were of international distinction. Among others, he was awarded the Military Cross, the Croix de Guerre, made an Officer in the Order of the British Empire, was the first recipient of the Helen Keller Award presented by the American Foundation of Overseas Blind, and Helen Keller personally presented him with the American Migel Medal in 1951. Among the first to be awarded a Companion of the Order of Canada in 1967, Baker, at the time, was honoured by Governor General Roland Michener who observed, "... there are no limits to what anyone of us can accomplish in the service of mankind."

Baker is remembered today as a very special individual who taught that the disabled and handicapped can perform serious and demanding work. One tribute stated that, without him, "all sightless and amputee Canadians would have faced a longer and more difficult struggle against tradition and prejudice." After his death in 1968, the *Toronto Star* saluted him in an obituary: "Both those that see and those that do not should be grateful that Edwin Baker saw things as he did."

Larry Turner

Joseph B. MacInnis

DR. JOE MACINNIS was born in Barrie, Ontario, in 1937. His father's career as a pilot with the RCAF might have foretold his son's future distinction in high-risk endeavours. Certainly his Isle of Mull Scottish heritage helps to explain both a general penchant for adventure and a particular affinity for the sea.

Unfortunately, because MacInnis Sr. died in an air crash over Trenton when his son was just one year old, his father's influence essentially had to be nature rather than nurture. Soon after this tragedy, the MacInnises left Barrie for Toronto, which has been Joe's headquarters ever since. He spent his high school years at Upper Canada College.

His love of swimming increased as the skill developed at summer camp. By 1956 he was a candidate for Canada's Olympic swimming team. Like many bright young men, he concealed his brains behind the "jock" smokescreen. But the brains were there and came into heavy use when he began medical school at the University of Toronto.

After he graduated in 1962, MacInnis found a way to tie all his interests together. A critical event was his involvement as an intern in caring for a man who almost died of decompression sickness. MacInnis's love of swimming had led him to SCUBA diving. There is much physical risk involved in diving; medical consultation often is needed. Being a physician who was also a trained SCUBA diver, MacInnis was a natural to join the fledgling Ocean Systems Inc. founded by Edmund Link. This involvement took him to deep waters all over the world and to his involvement as medical director of dives that set many world records.

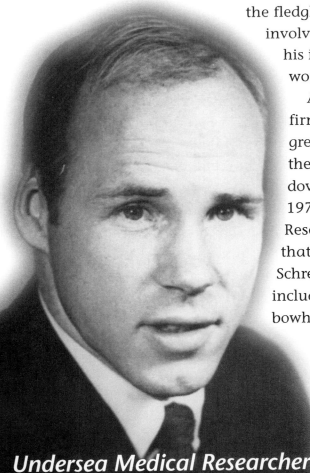

Although his early career was centered with American firms, MacInnis has kept a permanent home base in the greater Toronto area. By 1970, his endeavours were shifting to the Arctic where he filmed harp seals, searched for shipwrecks, dove under the North Pole (the first person to do so), and, in 1975, escorted Prince Charles on a dive under Arctic ice at Resolute Bay. He led a dive under the North Pole in 1979 that included the then Governor General of Canada, Edward Schreyer. His ongoing involvement with the undersea world has included research into six-gill sharks, harp seals, narwhals, and bowhead and beluga whales.

As creator and president of Undersea Research Ltd., he has worked under contract on numerous governmental

His hobbies have become his profession. Dr. Joe MacInnis, one of the world's leading authorities in underwater medicine and exploration technology, is a celebrated high-risk explorer.

Undersea Medical Researcher

and corporate projects in cooperation with firms such as IBM Canada, Petro-Canada, Canadian Airlines, and the Donner Foundation.

In 1969 and 1970 he was responsible for the Sublimnos Project, which established an underwater station for research and education 12 metres below the surface of Lake Huron. Two years later he established and directed "Subigloo," the world's first polar diving station that allowed men to explore beneath the polar ice cap.

His commitment saw spectacular results in 1980 with the discovery of *HMS Breadalbane*. This, MacInnis's second attempt, was crowned with success when the wreck finally was located on the sonar screen. *Breadalbane*, the northernmost known shipwreck, had been lost during the search for the Franklin Expedition and had been lying on the bottom of the Northwest Passage since 1853. In 1981 the team returned, aided by support from the National Geographic Society. Using a remotely controlled submersible, the researchers were able to take still and video photographs of the ship 100 metres down. The thirty-metre-long, three-masted ship is remarkably well preserved in the icy arctic waters. In 1983 MacInnis led manned dives to the wreck. Research into this rich and invaluable discovery continues.

MacInnis has also dived to a much more famous wreck, perhaps the world's most famous – the *Titanic*. Not only did he serve as consultant to the discovery team in 1985, but he was also co-leader, in 1991, of the deep-diving expedition to film *Titanic* in the IMAX format. The product was *Titanica*. MacInnis made the last of the seventeen dives to the wreck, this one being to the ship's bridge.

In the summer of 1994, he probed the wreck of the legendary *Edmund Fitzgerald*, sunk during a fierce storm in November 1975 with the loss of all 29 crewmen, a catastrophe made known through the mournful song written and performed by Gordon Lightfoot.

Other diving expeditions have taken MacInnis to Lake Baikal, the Bahamas, the Gulf of Mexico, the North Sea, Lake Huron, the Caribbean, the Gulf of St. Lawrence, and 10,000 feet into the Pacific Ocean. One assignment was a Pan-American jet recovery off Caracas, Venezuela. Another was the recovery from the bottom of Lake Mead, Nevada, of a light plane that contained secret nuclear power data. From these many adventures have come numerous articles, both popular and scientific, and several books, movies, and television programs. One of MacInnis's books, *Underwater Images*, indicates the breadth of the man, for it contains his poetry.

MacInnis sees the lakes and oceans in far broader terms than as environments to be conquered and used. Rather, he espouses the concept of mutual existence and of a balance between man and technology. His current interests are focused particularly on attempts to educate the public on the need to save the Great Lakes. There is a great urgency to accelerate this process, especially to eliminate the contamination of the food chain by toxins.

MacInnis has been honoured often for his accomplishments which encompass fields as disparate as archeology, deep-water medicine, diving technology, exploration, and literature. He has received the Queen's Anniversary Medal and, notably, in 1976 he was awarded the Order of Canada.

Charles Roland

HOMER & CO. ROSSEAU.

OCOLATES • GANONGS • GB • CHOCOLATES • GANONGS • GB

Chocolatiers to the World

THE GANONG FAMILY

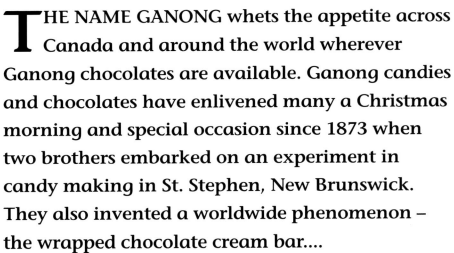

THE NAME GANONG whets the appetite across Canada and around the world wherever Ganong chocolates are available. Ganong candies and chocolates have enlivened many a Christmas morning and special occasion since 1873 when two brothers embarked on an experiment in candy making in St. Stephen, New Brunswick. They also invented a worldwide phenomenon – the wrapped chocolate cream bar....

Contemporary with the discovery of ice cream, refrigeration, and a craving for sweets was the establishment of the Ganong name. The company chose the literary Acadian heroine "Evangeline" as its symbol in 1904, even though the Ganong family name was French Huguenot in origin and the Ganong ancestors had arrived in New Brunswick as United Empire Loyalists in 1783. "Evangeline" manifested the virtues of "purity, excellence, and constancy, romance, sentiment, and sweetness," a wonderful

Above:
Ganong confectioners were being established across Canada by 1900. This early photograph taken in Rosseau, Ontario, in front of Homer Wade's country store suggests that people in remote areas of near northern Ontario were gratifying sweet tooth cravings by 1900. [Photo, courtesy Hugh MacMillan]

Left:
Ganong's Evangeline Chocolate Cream was the original chocolate cream bar and sold for 54 years. There were earlier "bars" without wrapping which were sold elsewhere by the pound. But it was the 5 cent Evangeline bar, wrapped in foil so as to keep better in pockets, that initiated chocolate bar sales all over North America. [Photo, courtesy R. Whidden Ganong]

packaging concept for a chocolate factory and a suitable symbol of their maritime identity.

Founders James Harvey (1841-1888) and Gilbert White Ganong (1851-1917) decided to pool resources into a general store in St. Stephen in 1873 where they found a market for confectioneries. In 1884 the partnership was dissolved: James expanded into successful soap production, and Gilbert maintained the candy company known as Ganong Brothers.

The expansive Maritime shipping tradition demanded supplies for trade as well as for the shipping fleet. The Caribbean trade brought sugar to the shores of New Brunswick and Nova Scotia where, by the 1880s, refineries were in operation at Moncton and Halifax. In 1889 the Ganongs flourished behind a protective trade barrier. As a result of hiring several candy-makers it developed new products such as penny candies and lozenges. It introduced the wrapped chocolate bar in 1906 and invented the milk chocolate bar by 1910. With growing tastes and markets, there was a veritable explosion on the confectionery business at the turn of the century. Ironically, several fires at the Ganong plant in St. Stephen served to encourage new methods of processing and production. This, in turn, kept the company ahead of other American and Canadian competitors.

Under the management of Arthur D. Ganong (1877-1960), a son of James, the company reached new heights of production between 1917 and 1930 when, during the latter year, there were 700 employees at St. Stephen, many of whom were women. The difficulties of the Depression, war rationing, and excise taxes on confectioneries almost strangled the company. One bestseller from 1925 (except during the war) was a combination chocolate and peppermint bar known as "Pepts." Postwar innovations in marketing and packaging revived the company, especially with television advertising. Because of a growing Asian market, a plant was opened in Bangkok, Thailand, in 1989.

Several members of the Ganong family made their name in managing, directing, or marketing the company products. Gilbert W. Ganong, a founder, served as a member of parliament and was appointed Lieutenant Governor of New Brunswick; William F. Ganong, a son of the other founder, James, was a passionate student of his beloved province as an historian, cartographer, botanist, and linguist. He canoed and mapped its waterways, translated and preserved the oral traditions of the Micmac and Maliseet, and promoted the New Brunswick museum in Saint John. He is best known for translating and editing works by early explorers Champlain, Denys, and Le Clerq. In 1931 he won the Tyrrell Medal of the Royal Society of Canada.

Prestigious Ganong products still come from its original family base in St. Stephen where president David Ganong caters to a world culture demanding sweet tooth gratification.

Larry Turner

A selection of chocolatier sundries from the candy factory of the Ganong Bros. Limited, established in 1873 in St. Stephen, New Brunswick. [Photo, courtesy R. Whidden Ganong]

The Queen's Plate

Since 1860....

IN JULY 1859, directors of the Toronto Turf Club received word that Her Majesty Queen Victoria "had been graciously pleased" to grant a Plate of 50 Guineas "to be run for in Toronto or such other place as Her Majesty might appoint." It was in answer to a petition they had made in April and it launched what is today the oldest consecutive thorough-bred horse race in North America, the Queen's Plate.

The first winner the following June was not a three-year-old and had to win two out of three one-mile heats before the owners could claim the guineas. All three heats were required: the top four horses of the first race took part in the second and third contests after a 20-minute rest ordered by the Turf Club's President, Casimir Gzowski. The horses had to have been bred in Upper Canada and not previously have won a race. This rule was criticized later.

Above: *The running of the Queen's Plate is North America's oldest, continuously run stakes race. Known as one of the year's premier thoroughbred horse racing events worldwide, when the first Plate was run at the New Woodbine racetrack, viewed here, near Malton, Ontario, in 1956, 20,000 race fans turned out to witness Canadian Champ stride to royal victory.* [Photo, courtesy The Toronto Star/Jeff Goode]

While the Carleton course located in what was then the city's outskirts at Keele south of Dundas Street was suggested in the original petition, the royal proposal "or such other place as Her Majesty might appoint" came into being early. The 1864 running, for instance, was held at Guelph where for the first time a filly won over 11 other entries. Two years later the scene was Hamilton where some of the 5,000 spectators tried to enter the area reserved for the "well-to-do." "Hamiltonians, it seems," explained the reporter for the *Spectator*, "always observe Her Majesty's birthday with unbridled enthusiasm," adding, "liquor and beer on empty stomachs may have triggered the loutish behaviour." A horse named Beacon won in two heats.

The tenth running took place at London and the favourite, Bay Jack, a four-year-old colt and half brother to Beacon won. Later the colt toured the continent and in 1872 made further headlines when he was given too much laudanum by a jockey at Strathroy and died of poisoning. A jockey went to jail but, to this day, historians are not sure if this was the jockey who had administered the drug.

Trouble of a different kind erupted at the 15th running in Hamilton when Charles Boyle, a well-known trainer, failed to let go of Emily, the horse he had trained and was holding, when the starter dropped the flag. She lost and her owner, Thomas Charles Patteson, complained about the defeat until his death in 1907.

Patteson was an Eaton and Oxford graduate who emigrated to Canada in 1858. He became a politician, manager, and editor of *The Toronto Mail*, establishing friendships with both the Governor General and the Prime Minister. He owned a stable and cattle farm and was critical not just of Boyle's blunder but of horseracing activities generally. In 1881 he won the support of Toronto's leading citizens as well as the local newspapers to create the Ontario Jockey Club with Gzowski as first president. That year the Queen's Plate, after travelling to such cities as Prescott (1877) and Ottawa (1880), returned to the new Woodbine track in Toronto.

Still problems remained. Many of the horses and the jockeys were ill-trained. In 1885, for instance, the winning horse, Willie W., broke away two or three times and caused "tedious delay." A jockey who broke a leg at the half-mile post in 1890 recalled that two steeplechase races were run before a carriage ambulance reached him.

In 1894 the battle for the 50 guineas was mild compared to the battle in the OJC boardroom when Patteson and two other directors tried to oust William Hendrie as president. They failed and were themselves removed from the board, but only after Patteson and Hendrie nearly came to blows. Among those stepping in to stop the fracas was Joseph Emm Seagram of Waterloo whose champion horses would dominate the Queen's/King's Plate for years and whose distilling would become world famous.

In 1902 the 50 guineas were awarded to the winner of the King's Plate for the first time following the death of Queen Victoria. The race continued to be called the King's Plate when George V became King in 1911. By 1915, anti-German feeling had caused the directors to ask one trainer of German background to withdraw from the race and to persuade another owner of German parentage to sell his best possible entry. Despite this, Charles Millar, a noted lawyer of German parentage, entered two horses that came in first and second. He got a law partner to pick up the guineas on his behalf. *The Toronto World* reported that "he was Canadian all over ... and has been so devoted to his old mother that he never married." According to Louis E. Cauz in his history entitled, *The Plate – A Royal Tradition* (1984), the war also prompted directors to allow horses to be trained outside the country and George Hendrie of Hamilton sent Springside to Kentucky before the colt returned to capture the guineas in 1918.

Crowds and excitement for the event continued through the 1920s. The biggest upset occurred in 1924 when Maternal Pride, with only one last-place finish as a two-year-old, won, and paid $193.35 on a $2 bet. The first radio broadcast of the event took place in 1925.

The Depression saw the demise of some stables, forced others to reduce their holdings, and caused the Jockey Club to see smaller crowds and offer smaller purses. Only 12,000 were on hand for the 1931 running; the purse of $7,850 plus the 50 guineas was $5,000 less than a year previous. R.S. McLaughlin's

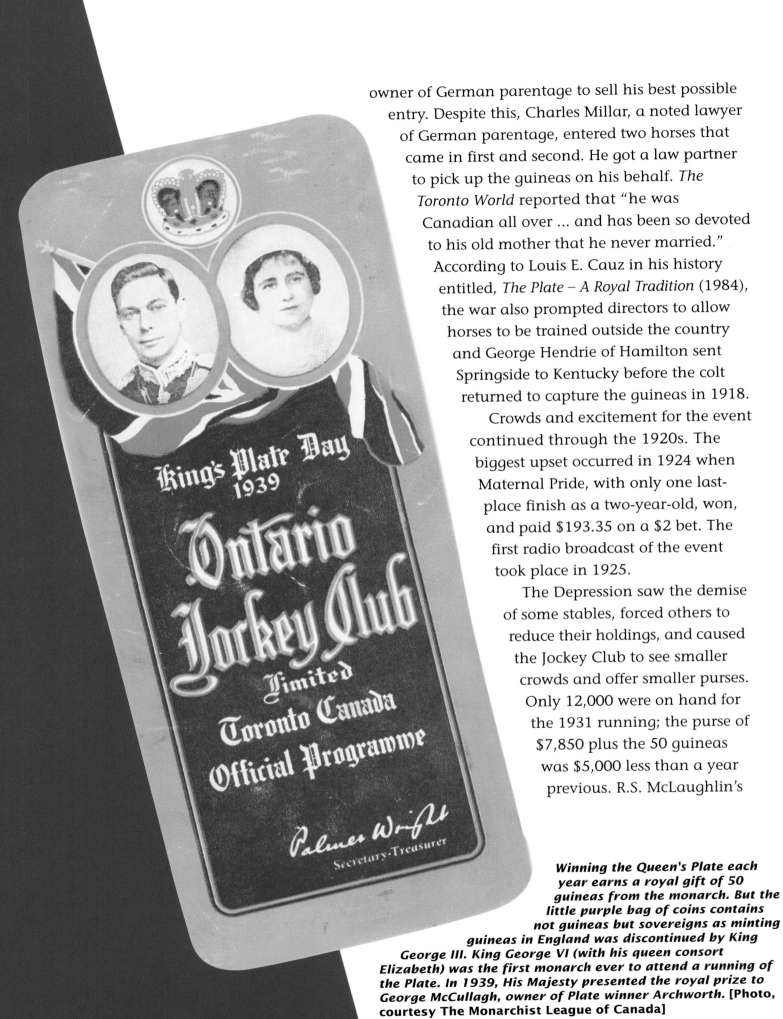

Winning the Queen's Plate each year earns a royal gift of 50 guineas from the monarch. But the little purple bag of coins contains not guineas but sovereigns as minting guineas in England was discontinued by King George III. King George VI (with his queen consort Elizabeth) was the first monarch ever to attend a running of the Plate. In 1939, His Majesty presented the royal prize to George McCullagh, owner of Plate winner Archworth. [Photo, courtesy The Monarchist League of Canada]

Horometer was such a sure bet for the 75th running in 1934 that it paid only $2.10 on a $2 bet. Excitement ran high in 1939 as King George VI and Queen Elizabeth presented the guineas to George McCullagh, owner of Toronto's *Globe and Mail*.

In 1944 the race was opened to any Canadian-bred horse and in 1948 the prize went to Jim Fair, a dirt farmer from the Brantford area, whose horse, Last Mark, was believed to be four rather than a three-year-old. Whatever the age, the colt swept to victory over Lord Fairmond ridden by one of the world's most successful jockeys, Canada's Johnny Longden, who would eventually win 6032 races including America's Triple Crown (1943) but never, despite four attempts, the Plate.

The next year Edward Plunkett Taylor won the guineas for the first time. Horses from his stable, Windfields Farm, dominated the Plate over the next 15 years, his greatest victory occurring in 1964 when Northern Dancer, winner of the Kentucky Derby and the Preakness earlier that year stood in the winner's enclosure at Woodbine. The next year saw the first winner foaled from outside Ontario (Alberta). In 1968 Max Bell's horse, Merger, became the second Alberta horse to win. A year later the popular Cuban-born jockey Alvelino Gomez had his fourth plate victory, a feat later accomplished by Canada's Sandy Hawley who won his first and second Plate races in 1970 and '71. The 1980 race, won by another Alberta horse, was dedicated to Gomez, who had been killed in a tragic accident at the Woodbine track a week earlier.

Mel James

The first running of the Queen's Plate in 1860 was celebrated at the Carleton Racecourse situated on a farm in an area later to be called West Toronto Junction. Between 1864 and 1880, the race for Queen Victoria's royal donation of 50 guineas was run on eleven different tracks outside Toronto including turfs at Kingston, Prescott, Ottawa, Picton, Whitby, Barrie, Guelph, St. Catharines, London, and Woodstock. During this time rural breeders dominated thoroughbred racing. When the neoteric racetrack at the New Woodbine, near Malton, opened in 1956, the annual running of the Queen's Plate in northwest Toronto now had a racetrack palace to showcase the oldest, North American continuous thoroughbred racing event. [Photo, courtesy Charles J. Humber]

HAROLD INNIS was a trailblazer in analyzing and interpreting Canada's distinctive economic history. His masterly studies of the historic Canadian fur trade as well as of Canada's cod fishing industry brought him international recognition as an eminent scholar. But he also researched and wrote brilliantly about railways, the forestry and mining industries, and many other themes in Canada's economic growth. In later years, foreshadowing media gurus such as Marshall McLuhan, a university colleague, he crowned a brilliant academic career with innovative inquiries of world scope into communications media and communications theory. Thus, this outstanding economist who taught for over thirty years at the University of Toronto made signal contributions to world learning.

Born near Otterville in southwestern Ontario in 1894 and educated at McMaster and the University of Toronto, Innis served overseas in World War I. Wounded and invalided home in 1917, he pursued his economic studies at the University of Chicago until, in 1920, he became a lecturer in Toronto's political economy department. His doctoral thesis, published in 1923 as *A History of the Canadian Pacific Railway*, demonstrates that Innis recognized the relationship between the forces that engineered this transcontinental rail line and Canada's own natural and historic lines of water communications.

At the same time, he was looking for an all-Canadian formula, not those of American or British-trained colleagues, to apply to his country's economic development. Accordingly, his first classic work, *The Fur Trade in Canada* (1930) – aptly subtitled *An Introduction to Canadian*

Blazing the Communications Trail   **1894 - 1952**

HAROLD ADAMS INNIS

To research his first major work, **The Fur Trade in Canada,** *Harold Innis extensively travelled Canada's fur trading routes. His investigations led him to Churchill, Manitoba, in 1929, the year before his important tome was published. At this time he explored by canoe the Churchill River watershed of northern Manitoba. [Photo, courtesy University of Toronto Library]*

Economic History – opposed the "continentalist" American approach to Canada's past experience by asserting that the country's political borders were really those marked out by its primary staple fur trade (rooted as it was on the St. Lawrence-Great Lakes system) that had expanded to continental limits long before the Americans spanned the continent themselves.

Taking much of a decade to produce, this major study first introduced his "staple thesis" of economic development. Ten years later, his next large study, just as impressive, was called *The Cod Fisheries: The History of an International Economy*. Here Innis reinforced his "staples approach" to Canada's even earlier basic staple trade. Yet he dealt not only with the fisheries' Canadian context but also with their European links and communications that certainly reached far beyond continental bounds. And *that* study led even more widely to his last pioneering studies. Published in the early fifties, *Empire and Communications* (1950), *The Bias of Communications* (1951), and *Changing Concepts of Time* (1952) opened wide the way to global examinations of mass media and their effects on human history, economy, and society. Though Innis died in 1952, at just 59, his impact by then – and since – could well be termed monumental. In fact, one could argue that this trilogy created the essential foundations for exploring how the media generates and controls public opinion.

Innis, of Loyalist descent, produced many other valuable works whether teaching, researching, or sitting on Royal Commissions of inquiry. These works, for instance, included *Peter Pond, Fur Trader and Adventurer* (1930), *Problems of Staple Production in Canada* (1933), *Settlement and the Mining Frontier* (1936), and *Political Economy in the Modern State* (1946). His writing style, often involved or difficult, was packed with solid information. In person he could at times seem distant, yet he was eager to talk with those who cared seriously, and, at times, was warm and witty. His close students and friends could testify to that – that it was a privilege to know and admire this influential Canadian scholar.

J.M.S. Careless

A brilliant economic historian respected internationally, Harold Adams Innis, who spent nearly 32 years as a University of Toronto faculty member, later turned his attention to understanding the important role emerging communications technology would have in the development of a post-war economy. Considered today a trailblazer for the likes of Marshall McLuhan, Innis pioneered studies in both Canada's Fur Trade and Cod Fishery. [Photo, courtesy Thomas Fisher Rare Book Library, University of Toronto]

THE NATIONAL FILM BOARD OF CANADA

Eyes of Canada

THE DEPRESSION approached a grim 10th birthday, the menace of world war intensified, and the power of the Hollywood film production industry stole momentum from both. In Canada, the government wanted to put film to good use at home.

Such were the times in 1938 when the politicians invited Scottish born John Grierson, a visionary with a proven track record in making exceptional documentaries, to immigrate to Canada to study the Canadian government's use of film. His report led directly to the establishment, in 1939, of the National Film Board (NFB) with Grierson as its first commissioner. He envisioned the NFB becoming "the eyes of Canada." Sixty years later, the Board is globally acclaimed as an icon among documentary producers.

Hired in peacetime, Grierson went to work in support of the war effort and began building the NFB's reputation with persuasive dramatizations such as *Canada Carries On* and *The World in Action*. But he envisioned a broader public service role for the NFB beyond the war years, of interpreting Canada

In 1995, Canada's National Film Board won its 10th Oscar for Bob's Birthday, *co-directed by Alison Snowden and David Fine.* [Photo, courtesy National Film Board of Canada]

to Canadians and Canadians to each other and the world. Grierson also required that all major NFB films of this era be translated into French, years before the Board established a separate French Program branch.

In 1950, the "official" mandate of the NFB was set down in The National Film Act. It required the NFB to "produce and distribute and to promote the production and distribution of films designed to interpret Canada to Canadians and to other nations."

But the seeds of spectacular projects in which animators interpreted the world to Canadians had been planted years earlier. One of the people most identified with the history of the NFB, Norman McLaren, became director of the Board's Animation Department in 1943. The public marvelled at McLaren's artistic brilliance as an animator. He produced a series of masterpieces, such as *Neighbours* – the Oscar-winning 1952 film inspired by the Korean War – where the battle of two men over a flower that borders each man's property leads to a devastating "war" and ultimately to the death of both, and *A Chairy Tale* (1957), and *Pas de deux* (1965).

The Film Board grew quickly and, thanks to its "travelling theatres," could boast that millions of Canadians saw its productions each year – to say nothing of the thousands of prints circulating internationally. Still, the filmmakers longed to apply the precepts of photojournalism to their craft, to capture insights, catalytic and intimate moments on film.

Film Board experts systematically worked with emerging technologies to devise portable equipment which eventually allowed synchronized recording of picture and sound by the late 1950s. This liberating leap forward led later to the filmmaking style known originally as Candid Eye and later as direct cinema/cinéma direct.

An important example of the roots and rationale of cinéma direct was *Les Raquetteurs*, a 1958 film examining a snowshoe congress in Sherbrooke, Québec. The filmmakers called it a sociological documentary and, as writer Gary Evans explains, it was an exciting new film form since "it showed the common people in tribal ritual."

The cinéma direct style gave rise to many classic productions, including Donald Brittain's *Memorandum*, a study of a Holocaust survivor, Claude Jutra and Michel Brault's *Québec-U.S.A. ou l'invasion pacifique*, Hubert Aquin and 28 filmmakers' *À St.-Henri, le 5 septembre*, Colin Low and Wolf Koenig's *City of Gold*, Koenig and Roman Kroitor's *Lonely Boy* and *Glenn Gould: On the Record*.

The pattern of NFB research advancing the artistry of filmmaking has been repeated over and over. Once image and sound capture had become relatively portable, NFB tech experts turned their attention to the engineering of a wireless microphone prototype, a marvel first tested by crews filming *Stravinsky* in 1963. At the moment the composer assumed the mic, Evans writes, its chief designer, Marcel Carrière, "achieved the transcendence of which documentary film-

Logo of the National Film Board, recognized internationally as a symbol for excellence in filmmaking.

makers had long dreamed – the subject was freed completely from the hardware. Carrière finished perfecting the prototype while shooting the Film Board's second English feature, *Nobody Waved Goodbye,* in 1964.

During Canada's Centennial year the Board initiated two watermark programs: Challenge for Change and Société nouvelle.

Challenge for Change encouraged filmmakers to explore social problems such as poverty, racism, and sexism, simultaneously affording the productions an opportunity to help the disadvantaged improve their situations. Notable titles – which tended to create controversy and reflect the social unrest of the decade – included *The Things I Cannot Change, Pow Wow at Duck Lake, You Are on Indian Land,* and *Working Mothers.*

Société nouvelle offered Québecois filmmakers opportunities to address what they saw as social ills. During the '60s, the artists' thrust was to discuss the need for recognition of Québec's distinct society within Confederation. Many controversial films emerged as part of

John Grierson, left, NFB's founding commissioner, and Ralph Foster, Chief of Graphics Division for NFB, examine one of the many posters circulated and popularized by the NFB during Canada's war effort in 1944. [Photo, courtesy National Film Board of Canada]

Société nouvelle, several of which preceded the larger national unity debates led by the Parti Québecois. Some titles are: *Cap d'espoir, On est au coton, Un pays sans bons sens,* and *Québec, Duplessis et après.*

During the following decade, the Film Board saw considerable decentralization. The credo of "democratization" was being promoted throughout the federal government. The Film Board responded by establishing production and distribution offices for both English and French programs outside Montreal. Board staff could then establish production relationships with local filmmakers and could meet their library and educational clients – and, increasingly, television programmers and other distribution partners – face-to-face.

Canada's NFB has achieved an international reputation for excellence in the production of films although the Board's artistic creations cover an astonishingly wide variety of issues and topics, the NFB consistently maintains a Canadian sensibility and focus of concerns. It releases films produced by both English and French program branches, its production achievements not just limited to fine documentaries and animation. Much celebrated fiction and docudrama is associated with the NFB and with Board co-productions. Notable examples include John N. Smith's *The Boys of St. Vincent* (co-produced by Les Productions Télé-Action), Denys Arcand's *Jésus de Montréal* (co-produced by Max Films and Gérard Mital Productions), Cynthia Scott's *The Company of Strangers*, Jean Beaudin's *Mario*, Paul Cowan's *Justice Denied*, and *The Kid Who Couldn't Miss*.

One of the Board's most recognizable symbols is its logo. Designed in 1968 by Georges Beaupré, the drawing represents a human figure in which the head resembles the eye's iris. The upraised arms and joined hands suggest celebration. The bold lines of the logo suggest the art of the Inuit and First Nation peoples.

At about this time, Roman Kroitor and Colin Low assisted in the development of the IMAX screens, an innovative technology that is now seen in theatres around the world – a direct result of the NFB's willingness to support experimental filmmaking.

Also known and loved around the globe are such celebrated films as Claude Jutra's *Mon oncle Antoine*, Grant Munro and Gerald Potterton's *My Financial Career*, "Co" Hoedeman's *The Sand Castle*, Richard Condie's *The Big Snit*, Cordell Barker's *The Cat Came Back*, Bernard Longpré's and André Leduc's *Monsieur Pointu*, Jean Beaudin's *J.A. Martin, photographe* and Tahani Rached's *Au Chic Resto Pop*.

The NFB has won more than 3,000 awards, and by 1996 had been nominated for 60 Oscars and had won 10. In 1994 alone, films produced by the NFB won close to 100 awards across Canada, throughout Europe and in United States. Oscar awards won by NFB films as *Neighbours* (1952), *Every Child* (1979), *If You Love This Planet* (1982), *Flamenco at 5:15* (1983), and, in 1995, *Bob's Birthday*. In 1989, the NFB received an Honorary Oscar "in recognition of its fiftieth anniversary and its dedicated commitment to originate artistic, creative and technological activity and excellence in every area of film-making."

The NFB received almost $66 million in 1996/97 to make and distribute films and audiovisual products that convey Canada's social and cultural realities. An additional $10 million is generated by a variety of sales and videos both in Canada and around the world.

A major techological innovator in the world of filmmaking, the NFB has been responsible for dozens of important breakthroughs, including the development of a digital sound library management system; digital footage, frame and time counter; an electronic film subtitling system; and the first large-scale audiovisual server in Canada, the CinéRobothèque. It continues to produce state-of-the-art films every year. Current research projects include a computer animation workstation and the establishment of a digital imaging service for film ensure a pre-eminent role for Canada's National Film Board in the 21st century.

Patricia Stone/Susan Tolusso

Mary (Molly) Brant

1736 - 1796

MOLLY BRANT KOŇWATSI'TSIAIÉŇNI
CANADA
POSTAGE POSTES
34

Woman of Two Worlds

MARY ("MOLLY") BRANT was one of the most influential people in the American Revolution because of, not in spite of, her being a woman. Bridging two cultures as distinct as the European and the Mohawk of the Six Nations Iroquois, Koňwatsi'tsiaiéňni forged between her people of upper New York and the British a consensus that altered the destinies of both peoples. While her younger brother, Joseph Brant (Thayendanegea), was admired and mythologized for his urbane acculturation and zealous support for the British during the Revolution, Molly Brant enjoyed a higher status as the relict of a powerful British land baron and Indian agent, and as a diplomat and stateswoman at the head of a society of Six Nations matrons who wielded immense power and authority in traditional Iroquoian government.

Mary Brant was probably born in 1736 of mixed Onondaga and Wyandot parentage in the Upper Mohawk castle of Canajoharie in New York where the Mohawks controlled the river of the same name. The Mohawks, the easternmost nation of the Six Nations Iroquoian Confederacy, had strong connections with former Dutch and English trading partners. Molly married, in "the custom of the country," Sir William Johnson, a greatly admired landowner and the first superintendent of the northern Indians of British North America. From their

Above: *Six years older than her famous brother Joseph (1742/43-1807), Molly Brant was married by Mohawk rites to Sir William Johnson, colonial baron, whose leadership in upper New York state made him an influential voice throughout the Mohawk Valley. Following Sir William's death in 1774, Molly wielded considerable influence over the Iroquois Confederacy. Whenever their loyalty wavered, Koňwatsi'tsiaiéňni, as she preferred to be called, was able to convince the Confederacy to continue their support for Britain throughout the American Revolution. Because of their loyalty,* *the Six Nations Confederacy was dispossessed of its extensive lands following the Treaty of Paris (1783). The Iroquois, including Molly Brant and her seven children, were consequently forced to flee as refugees with some 7,000 other U.E. Loyalists to Quebec, (divided into Upper and Lower Canada in 1791), a British colony that rejected rebellion during the American Revolution. This Canada Post stamp, issued in 1986, commemorates the 250th anniversary of the birth of Koňwatsi'tsiaiéňni.*
[Photo, courtesy Canada Post Corporation]

alliance at least seven children were born at Johnson Hall. Although his will when he died in 1774 recognized her only as a "prudent faithful housekeeper," she was left a legacy of land, money, and a black female slave.

The American Revolution forced the Iroquois to take sides and the Brants argued persuasively that the Six Nations would best be served by the British. Molly was highly esteemed in the Six Nations Confederacy as the head of a society of matrons who influenced councils of war and young warriors. While living in the Mohawk Valley she aided other Loyalists taking refuge, and in August of 1777 successfully warned the British of an advancing American army later defeated at the Battle of Oriskany. Members of the Six Nations who sided with the Americans, especially the Oneida people, enacted revenge on Molly by sending her fleeing with her family to other Six Nations communities and finally to Canada — first to the Niagara area and later to Fort Haldimand on Carleton Island in the St. Lawrence River.

The home of Sir William Johnson (1715-1774) is an historical landmark in upper New York state. Molly Brant, Sir William's wife, was responsible for the management of Johnson Hall which entertained, as illustrated in this E.L. Henry painting, large numbers of Iroquois and other guests who lodged there for extensive intervals until 1777 at which time she fled the baronial estate, and her ancestral lands, for Canada. [Photo, courtesy Albany Institute of History and Art]

Indian agent Daniel Claus commented in 1779, "One word from her goes farther with them (the Iroquois) than a thousand from any white man without exception who in general must purchase their interest at a high rate." Alexander Fraser, commanding Carleton Island in 1779-1780, declared that the Indians' "uncommon good behaviour is in a great measure ascribed to Miss Molly Brant's influence over them, which is far superior to that of all their Chiefs put together."

The war had inconvenient consequences for the Loyalists who became refugees in a new land, and tragic consequences for the Loyalists Iroquois who were forced to give up ancestral lands because of their loyalty to the British. Following hostilities, Sir Frederick Haldimand as governor of Quebec made arrangements for Molly that included a house built at Cataraqui (Kingston) in 1783 as well as an annual pension. She also received compensation for her great losses. These material gains never came close to making amends for the sense of dispersion and displacement experienced by her people. When she returned to her beloved Mohawk Valley in 1785, she could not be enticed to stay. Eventually she was buried in 1796 in St. Paul's Anglican churchyard, Kingston.

Historian Barbara Graymont wrote that Molly Brant was "a woman of high intelligence and remarkable ability who was at ease in two cultures. Mary Brant personified the dignity and influence accorded to respected mothers among the Iroquois people."

Larry Turner

As wife of Upper Canada's first Lieutenant Governor, Elizabeth Simcoe sketched scenes between 1792-96 of Upper Canada which today are invaluable historical documents. This sketch of Kingston, U.C., in 1792, is where Molly Brant lived out the last days of her life and where she was buried in 1796. [Photo, courtesy Macdonald Stewart Foundation, Montreal]

Surgeon with a Global Mission

ACHARLOTTETOWN PATRIOT review of the play *McClure* put it succinctly: "This is a show every Canadian should see, written about a man every Canadian should know."

This was referring to Robert Baird McClure and his work as a missionary doctor in China and Taiwan between 1923 and 1948. What author Munro Scott did not describe in the 1986 production – but did in a two-volume biography written earlier – was McClure's other 30 years as a medical missionary in the Gaza Strip, India, Borneo, Peru, and Zaire, before he retired in his 78th year.

Bob McClure's colourful life began in Portland, Oregon, where he was born in 1900 because his father, also a missionary doctor, had sent his wife and two young daughters out of China during the Boxer Rebellion. The following year the family were reunited at Weihwei, Honan province, China, where Bob learned Mandarin before English and spent most of his first 15 years attending the mission school there.

He completed high school in Toronto and graduated from the University of Toronto Medical School in 1922 before returning to China in 1924 to replace a United Church missionary doctor who had been murdered by bandits at a hospital in Hwaiking. There Bob not only performed surgery but also made numerous mechanical improvements that included enhancing the lighting in the operating room by using skills learned earlier when he had worked summers at a Toronto factory.

In 1926, Amy, a student nurse he had met at university, arrived in China to marry him but within one year they had the first of many separations when nationalist fervor forced

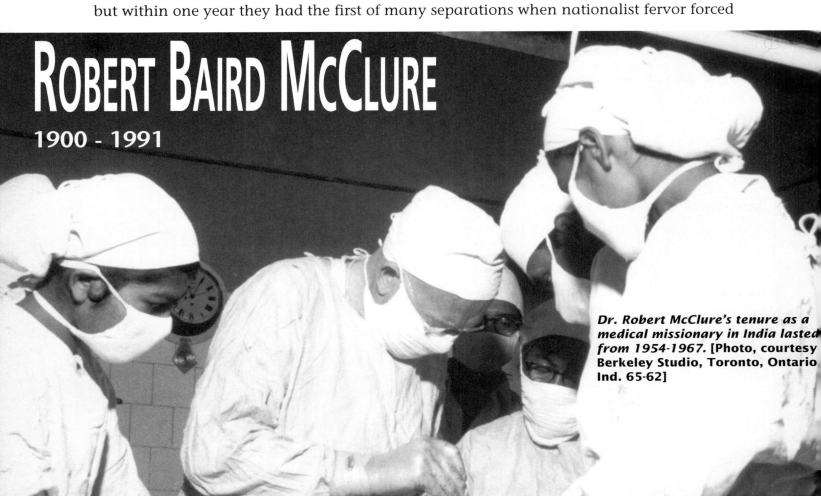

ROBERT BAIRD McCLURE
1900 - 1991

Dr. Robert McClure's tenure as a medical missionary in India lasted from 1954-1967. [Photo, courtesy Berkeley Studio, Toronto, Ontario. Ind. 65-62]

foreigners to leave. They later settled in Taiwan where two of their four children were born.

A study leave in 1930 enabled Bob to become a Fellow of the Royal College of Surgeons at Edinburgh University before returning to Hwaiking as Chief of Surgery. There, by teaching a number of Chinese enough about medicine to be able to do x-rays, lab tests, and minor surgery, he also developed a rural medical system that extended over an area of 5,000 square miles. He affectionately referred to these assistants as his "quacks."

A radiology course in Sweden in 1934 and a donation of radium by Vincent Massey, later Canada's Governor General, enabled Bob to become the first missionary doctor to provide radium treatment to cancer patients in inland China.

Soon after the outbreak of the Sino-Japanese war in 1937, McClure was seconded to the International Red Cross (IRC) as Field Director for North and Central China. This entailed attending civilians injured from massive air raids, feeding and housing refugees, seeing that wounded soldiers were treated in field and missionary hospitals, and establishing orphanages. Because of bombed trains and rail lines, Bob often travelled by bicycle so that as Scott wrote in *McClure: The China Years of Bob McClure* (1977), it became "an almost routine day for McClure to cycle a hundred miles, hold some meetings, inspect some stores and end up doing some surgery in a mission operating room."

Despite his Red Cross connection, McClure was captured by the Nationalists, and since he was not a communist, was questioned personally by Mao Tse-tung as to why he helped the Chinese. He also had a price put on his head by the Japanese as a suspected spy. He also met Madame Chiang Kai-shek and the Generalissimo who, in 1938, asked him to attend an IRC meeting in England. This was followed by a fund-raising tour that eventually took him to Toronto where he arrived a week ahead of his family who had been detained in Japanese territory for a year before being allowed to leave China.

When Bob returned to China via India in February 1939, he was only the second person to drive a vehicle over the Burma Road. In charge of moving medical and other supplies into China over the newly created road, Bob wrote to Amy, "It seems funny for a surgeon to be doing this work in wartime." Soon, however, as there was no other medical person present, he became involved in medical work.

That December he was severely injured when pinned between two trucks and was invalided home to Toronto in March. In another speaking tour that followed, he

A medical missionary for more than half a century, Dr. Robert McClure was one of the world's great humanitarians of the 20th century. [Photo, courtesy Berkeley Studio, Toronto, Ontario, Ind. 65-57]

criticized Canada for selling nickel to Japan. Although the charge was not denied, McClure was summoned to Ottawa where Prime Minister Mackenzie King ordered him to apologize publicly or go to jail. An angry McClure wrote the apology.

Before returning to the Burma Road in command of a Quaker-sponsored Friends Ambulance Unit (FAU), he also applied for and became one of two civilians to take pilot training with young Norwegian volunteers being trained in Canada by the Toronto Flying Club. When Burma fell to the Japanese and supplies were airlifted over the Himalayas to China, McClure organized local villagers as stretcher-bearers for downed air crews; he himself parachuted from rescue planes a number of times to treat the injured before they were carried to field hospitals.

In December 1943, McClure collapsed from fever and overwork. His rehabilitation in Toronto soon turned into another tour that raised funds from numerous sources including $500,000 from the Canadian Red Cross. By May he was back with the FAU whose activities later included taking over some of the missionary hospitals as the Japanese retreated. China, however, continued to be torn by civil war between the Nationalist and Communists forces and, in December 1948, after seeing his Hwaiking hospital reduced to rubble and on learning that his eldest daughter was ill, he left China.

Back in Toronto he joined a clinic but within eighteen months he was reapplying for mission work. India seemed likely, but when a former colleague of the FAU wired that a hospital treating Arab refugees in the Gaza Strip needed a surgeon, McClure arranged with the United Church for him to serve there for a year. He stayed three, and, when he left to take over a hospital at Ratlam, India, in 1954, the new hospital superintendent wrote of his departure: "I have certainly never seen any group of people who loved their chief more than did the hospital staff, the patients, and the people of the city of Gaza."

His start at the hospital at Ratlam did not provoke the same affection when he fired some incompetent staff members and was critical of others who did not measure up to his demands. McClure's enthusiasm and outlook, however, soon affected the staff positively. He introduced programs to train lab and x-ray technicians, conducted public health seminars, and held screenings to identify and treat TB patients. On one occasion he amazed the operating room staff while performing major surgery on a woman whose husband, standing by to give a blood transfusion, disappeared. McClure promptly climbed onto the donor's gurney, gave his own blood, and then

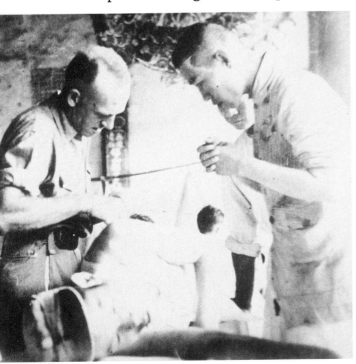

Dr. Robert McClure's missionary service as medical surgeon in China began in 1923 and lasted for nearly one-quarter of a century. [Photo, courtesy The United Church/Victoria University Archives, Toronto/Accession No: 76.001 P 4383]

completed the operation. Later McClure wrote to a colleague that he loved his medical work in India and "if I am spared for ten years to do this work it will be the height of my ambition."

In 1956 Amy joined him at Ratlam and during the next 11 years McClure added a dental clinic, inoculated thousands of children with polio vaccine that he had Connaught Laboratories donate, battled both Indian and Canadian bureaucracies, personally acknowledged all gifts and donations sent to the mission hospital, and continued to perform annually hundreds of operations that included numerous reconstructive surgeries on people deformed by leprosy.

When McClure retired in November 1967, there was once again an outpouring of affection as hundreds swamped the train station, weighing both Bob and Amy down with traditional garlands and flowers.

In 1968 he was elected Moderator of the United Church of Canada – the first layman to hold that office – and for the next two and a half years his outspoken views on everything from the lack of parishioner generosity to his belief in removing life-support systems in cases of irreparable damage or agonizing terminal illness made headlines across Canada.

He refused the $16,000 annual salary and, when he travelled throughout Canada and made trips to Britain, the Middle East, and Africa, his expenses were such that one senior member of the clergy commented, "The church may have had better Moderators, but it never had a cheaper one."

On stepping down as Moderator in 1971, McClure went to Southeast Asia to do a family-planning survey for Oxfam and, by year end, he and Amy were at a Methodist mission hospital in Borneo. McClure had volunteered to be an assistant surgeon but, when the chief surgeon decided not to return he felt compelled to continue performing all manner of emergency and scheduled operations for eight months before being relieved. He then concentrated on his family-planning programs and developed a kit to reduce the number of baby deaths caused by tetanus.

In 1975 he spent six months in Peru as an assistant surgeon, and a year later held a similar post for a few months on the island of St. Vincent. On returning to Toronto, McClure read that a hospital in Zaire required an assistant surgeon for a short term and promptly volunteered. He paid his own air fare to Kimpese to work in a modern hospital with a well-trained and efficient multiracial staff. He was amazed and amused one day when, during an operation, the three attending nurses began to sing a hymn and the female patient, under a local anesthetic, joined them. Bob later recalled humorously that the hymn was "Nearer My God To Thee."

Home from that experience, McClure gave up the scalpel but the following summer relieved a doctor for two months at Port Simpson, B.C., and then continued speaking and raising funds for hospitals and missionaries in third world countries until he died of cancer in 1991, two weeks before his 91st birthday.

Mel James

RICHARD MAURICE BUCKE

Medical and Spiritual Revolutionist

1837 - 1902

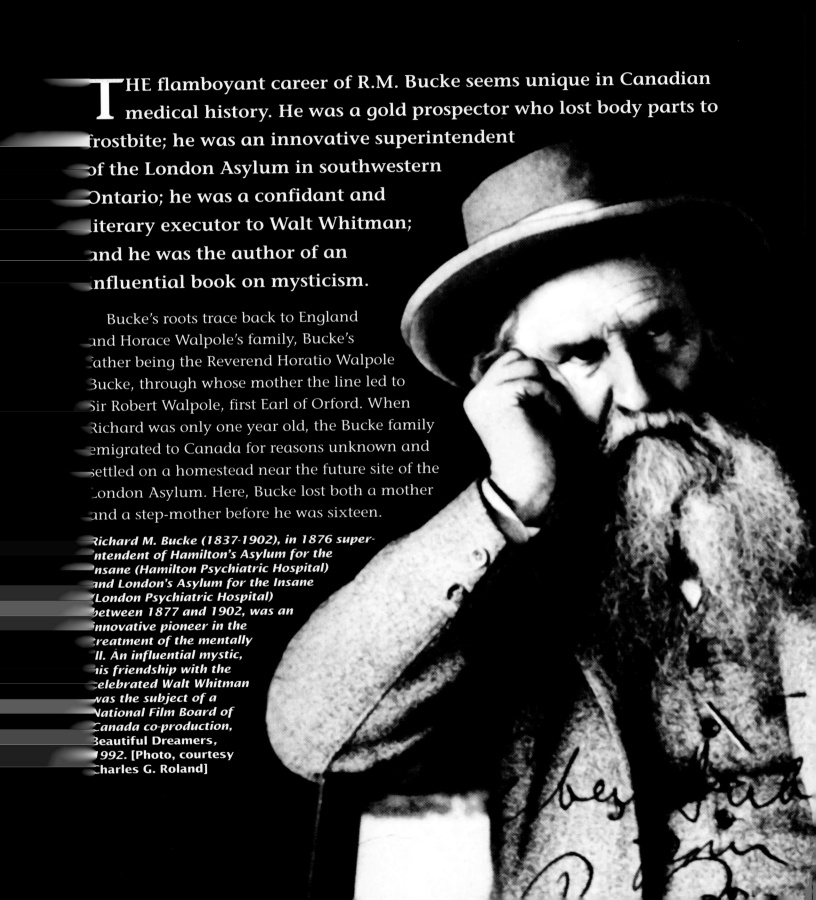

THE flamboyant career of R.M. Bucke seems unique in Canadian medical history. He was a gold prospector who lost body parts to frostbite; he was an innovative superintendent of the London Asylum in southwestern Ontario; he was a confidant and literary executor to Walt Whitman; and he was the author of an influential book on mysticism.

Bucke's roots trace back to England and Horace Walpole's family, Bucke's father being the Reverend Horatio Walpole Bucke, through whose mother the line led to Sir Robert Walpole, first Earl of Orford. When Richard was only one year old, the Bucke family emigrated to Canada for reasons unknown and settled on a homestead near the future site of the London Asylum. Here, Bucke lost both a mother and a step-mother before he was sixteen.

Richard M. Bucke (1837-1902), in 1876 superintendent of Hamilton's Asylum for the Insane (Hamilton Psychiatric Hospital) and London's Asylum for the Insane (London Psychiatric Hospital) between 1877 and 1902, was an innovative pioneer in the treatment of the mentally ill. An influential mystic, his friendship with the celebrated Walt Whitman was the subject of a National Film Board of Canada co-production, Beautiful Dreamers, 1992. [Photo, courtesy Charles G. Roland]

His mother may have been worn out from delivering and caring for ten children in not much more than a decade.

His father had brought a voluminous library to Canada, and this became Bucke's university. He had no formal schooling before attending McGill University, but he arrived there remarkably well educated. The home library is said to have contained several thousand volumes in seven languages.

There was, however, a substantial hiatus between his losing his stepmother in 1853 and his attending university. At age sixteen, Bucke decided to pursue the great American adventure by trekking west looking for gold. He approached this experience gradually, spending three or four years working at a wide variety of jobs in Ohio, Louisiana, and on steamboats on the Mississippi and Ohio rivers. When he decided to cross the continent to the Pacific, he was hired on to help escort a wagon train from Fort Leavenworth to Salt Lake City.

From there the men set up groups of five or ten, bought a wagon for each group, and headed west through hostile Indian territory. They fought through to the mountains and became gold miners in the most westerly areas of Utah. Then, in 1857, Bucke set out for California to find silver.

Soon he was in serious trouble. Food ran out. He was badly frostbitten and irredeemably lost. Near death, he stumbled upon a mining camp where he recovered, but one foot and part of the other had to be amputated. The stumps would take forty years to heal completely.

He returned home at age 21 having experienced remarkable adventures paid for with part of his body. But his spirit was vigorously alive. Enabled to study medicine by means of a small legacy from his mother, he went to McGill in 1858.

After graduation and a period of study in England and Paris, Bucke returned to western Ontario in 1863 to practise general medicine throughout much of the 1860s and early 1870s. But he also made several trips to Great Britain, and on one of these he had a transcendental experience that profoundly affected his life.

In 1876 he obtained the position of superintendent at the Asylum for the Insane in Hamilton, Ontario. After a year there, he competed successfully for the similar post at the London Asylum for the Insane, recently vacated by the death of his predecessor.

Bucke first read the poetry of Walt Whitman while he was a general practitioner and became exaggeratedly enthusiastic about Whitman's qualities as a mystical poet, philosopher, and man. They met in 1877. Their names were to be connected throughout Whitman's lifetime, and indeed still are in many ways. Bucke found his hero godlike and from this time on they corresponded frequently, with Bucke often visiting the poet in New Jersey and Whitman spending four months with the Buckes in London. Bucke grew a beard like Whitman's and, in many photographs, can scarcely be distinguished from Whitman. Ultimately Bucke had his friend William Osler undertake the medical care of his friend.

At the London Asylum, Bucke increasingly sought to minimize the use of physical restraint that was so much a part of asylum "care" until well into the nineteenth century in

Brought in 1838 to Upper Canada (Ontario) at age one, Richard Bucke grew up in this pioneer family farm near London, Ontario. The drawing was rendered by his father in the 1840s. [Photo, courtesy Charles G. Roland]

both Europe and North America. At the London institute there were 900 patients, roughly half of them women; on average, about half of the patients, once admitted, stayed in the

asylum longer than a decade. By 1882 Bucke had ceased to prescribe alcohol, considered by most a sheet anchor of therapy. Bucke also became a pioneer in his treatment of the mentally ill, in Canada at least, by greatly increasing the freedom of movement for most of his patients, a policy in direct opposition to tradition and convention which kept patients in physical restraint.

Several of Bucke's books made his name widely known even though superficially they might seem directed to specific audiences. First, he published, in 1879, his psychiatric speculations in a book entitled *Man's Moral Nature*. Briefly, his thesis was that moral sense in humans was mediated via the sympathetic nervous system and that this innate moral sense was becoming more common. Though it sold poorly, the book was the first Canadian monograph on psychiatry. In 1883 he followed this work with his authorized biography of Whitman, someone who, he believed, showed to a marked degree the moral sense he referred to in *Man's Moral Nature*.

But most important in attempting to understand Bucke's continued worldwide influence nearly a century after his death is his last and major opus, *Cosmic Consciousness*. Published in 1901 and still in print today, this has become a classic of mysticism. This volume was the logical sequel to his earlier books. In it Bucke posited a third type of consciousness among humans. There is, first, the simple consciousness of existence and, second, a higher level of self-consciousness. Bucke added a third and profoundly higher level, "cosmic consciousness," which he believed to have been attained by only a few dozen individuals by 1901. These include Jesus, Buddha, Mohammed, Dante, Whitman, Francis Bacon, Blake, as well as Bucke himself. He believed that the occurrence of this special form of consciousness was increasing and attainable, eventually, by all. Whether this may turn out to be the case, only the future can tell.

Just a few months after *Cosmic Consciousness* appeared, Bucke fell on an icy porch, fractured his skull, and died. He had been well appreciated by his professional colleagues, who saw him elected a charter member of the Royal Society of Canada, president of national and international societies, as well as a distinguished professor at Western University in London, now the University of Western Ontario.

Charles Roland

Magical Master of Myth and Marvel

ROBERTSON DAVIES, was one of modern Canada's most venerated authors whose constituency extended far beyond his country. Exuding eminence, Davies continued a brilliantly productive literary career right up to his death in 1995. He had been, in his time, a novelist, essayist, playwright, journalist, critic, scholar and, as well, an actor – an early interest that influenced him, both in his writings and in his own dramatic presence as the magical "Man of Myth."

Born at Thamesville, Ontario, in 1913, the third son in the well-to-do family of Senator Rupert Davies, newspaper publisher, he moved as the family's business concerns required, first to Renfrew, thence to Kingston where his father owned the local *Whig-Standard*. As a child, young Rob Davies acted in amateur plays in Kingston and thus acquired an early passion for theatre. When he was sent to Toronto's prestigious Upper Canada College – shy and sensitive as he was, neither an athlete nor a classroom leader – he adopted the shielding, dramatic

1913 - 1995

Sometime journalist, publisher, editor, novelist, playwright, actor, and professor, Robertson Davies, once considered a potential recipient of the 1993 Nobel Prize for Literature, was born "in the cusp of Leo and Virgo with Mercury in the ascendant." This probably explains why this Canadian literary figure had a resplendent aura of magic, myth, and marvel. [Photo, courtesy Peter Paterson]

persona of an urbane British-accented gentleman of taste. Afterwards, at Queen's University from 1932 to 1935, despite all his native intelligence, he did not proceed to a degree. But then he moved on to Oxford and flourished in its stately (and dramatic) surroundings, taking a B.Litt degree in 1938 while also zestfully acting in Oxford's notable Dramatic Society. In 1940, in fact, Davies joined the-still-more-noted Old Vic Theatre Company in London where he also married its stage manager – known since Oxford days – his lifelong wife, Brenda.

Davies returned to Canada in 1940 as literary editor of *Saturday Night*. In 1942 he became the editor of the Peterborough *Examiner*, another of his father's papers, and also its increasingly popular columnist, "Samuel Marchbanks," whose witty comments and humorous accounts would later be published in three volumes between 1947 and 1967. In 1955, Davies advanced to publisher of the *Examiner*, a post he held till 1965 although by that date he had entered the scholarly world and, more than that, had already produced a whole stream of other writings: articles, plays, and high-quality novels.

His first play, *Eros at Breakfast*, won a Dominion Drama Award in 1948 and was followed by *Fortune, My Foe*, published in 1949; *My Heart's Core* appeared in 1950. Then came a series of novels: *Tempest-Tost* (1951), *Leaven of Malice* (1954) (which won the Stephen Leacock Medal for humorous writing), and *A Mixture of Frailties* (1958). This trio was succeeded in 1961 by something completely different – his perceptive collection of scholarly essays, *A Voice from the Attic*, which garnered another literary prize, the Lorne Pierce Medal in 1961. By now Davies was settling into academic life, having in 1960 begun teaching literature and drama at Trinity College in the University of Toronto as he would do over the next 20 years. Furthermore, in 1963 he was also made Master of Massey College, the University's new college for chosen graduate students and associated senior staff; and in that position he presided elegantly but warmly till his retirement in 1981: a courtly guide and mentor, a kindly counsellor, and a sparkling raconteur. His writing activities went on apace. He produced a new trilogy of novels: *Fifth Business* in 1970 (which, according to the *New York Times*, earned "major acclaim"), *The Manticore* (1972), and *World of Wonders* (1975). References to the stage, along with others reflecting on image arts and Jungian psychology, marked these outstanding, fascinating novels. An unstoppable Robertson Davies continued to flow steadily on, issuing *The Rebel Angels* (1981), *What's Bred in the Bone* (1985), and still other works, including *The Lyre of Orpheus* (1988) and *Murther & Walking Spirits* (1991) to arrive in 1994 at his last novel, *The Cunning Man* (1994).

The charm, insight, and excellence of Davies' complex and prolific outpourings brought unprecedented reflected glory to Canada. And "Dr. Davies," superb in his flowing white locks and beard, his protuberant brow, and his swirling cloak and broad-brimmed hat, will remain among many other distinguished but more utilitarian-seeming Canadian wayfarers, a theatrical figure in the best sense.

J.M.S. Careless

Canada's "Ancient Mariner"

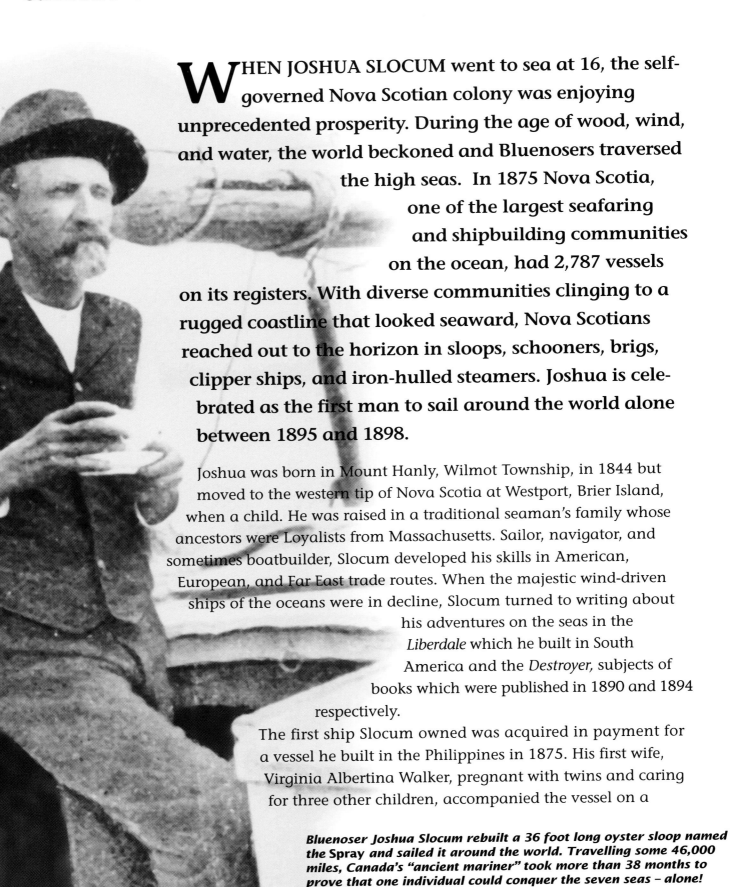

WHEN JOSHUA SLOCUM went to sea at 16, the self-governed Nova Scotian colony was enjoying unprecedented prosperity. During the age of wood, wind, and water, the world beckoned and Bluenosers traversed the high seas. In 1875 Nova Scotia, one of the largest seafaring and shipbuilding communities on the ocean, had 2,787 vessels on its registers. With diverse communities clinging to a rugged coastline that looked seaward, Nova Scotians reached out to the horizon in sloops, schooners, brigs, clipper ships, and iron-hulled steamers. Joshua is celebrated as the first man to sail around the world alone between 1895 and 1898.

Joshua was born in Mount Hanly, Wilmot Township, in 1844 but moved to the western tip of Nova Scotia at Westport, Brier Island, when a child. He was raised in a traditional seaman's family whose ancestors were Loyalists from Massachusetts. Sailor, navigator, and sometimes boatbuilder, Slocum developed his skills in American, European, and Far East trade routes. When the majestic wind-driven ships of the oceans were in decline, Slocum turned to writing about his adventures on the seas in the *Liberdale* which he built in South America and the *Destroyer,* subjects of books which were published in 1890 and 1894 respectively.

The first ship Slocum owned was acquired in payment for a vessel he built in the Philippines in 1875. His first wife, Virginia Albertina Walker, pregnant with twins and caring for three other children, accompanied the vessel on a

Bluenoser Joshua Slocum rebuilt a 36 foot long oyster sloop named the Spray *and sailed it around the world. Travelling some 46,000 miles, Canada's "ancient mariner" took more than 38 months to prove that one individual could conquer the seven seas – alone!* [Photo, courtesy Public Archives of Nova Scotia, 1981-478, Walter Teller Collection #19]

Siberian fishing expedition. Her story as a mariner's wife can only be imagined: she loved the sea as much as he did and bore all seven children on board ship. She died in Sydney, Australia, in 1884.

Opportunities declined for sailors with the scope and experience of Slocum. Labouring in a Boston shipyard, he rebuilt in 1893 a derelict oyster sloop which would become his personal window on the high seas. In the words of biographer Brian D. Murphy, Slocum "withdrew from the human world and made the ocean his country." On April 24, 1895 he set out in the *Spray* for a personal trip around the world, one of the last maritime feats not yet accomplished by people in search of adventure. In his 36' 9" long, 14'2" wide, 4'2" deep vessel, only 13 tons gross, he left Boston for a visit to his Yarmouth area home in Nova Scotia before crossing the Atlantic to Gibraltar. Concerned about pirates in the Mediterranean and Red seas, he changed course for the Straits of Magellan and the Pacific Ocean, his reputation preceding him. Religious and romantic, he visited the island where Alexander Selkirk, the inspiration for Robinson Crusoe, was left stranded and also visited the widow of author Robert Louis Stevenson at Upolu in Western Samoa. He spent Australia's summer giving tours of his boat so that by the time he reached South Africa he had received sufficient notoriety to be received by Boer leader Paul Kruger and explorer Henry Morton Stanley. After 46,000 miles he arrived a celebrity at Newport, Rhode Island, on June 27, 1898.

JOSHUA SLOCUM 1844 - 1909

Slocum's reputation grew with the publication in 1899 and 1900 of his serialized "Sailing alone around the world" in *Century Illustrated Monthly Magazine* and with the release of it in book form in 1900. At the turn of the century, Joshua Slocum represented the progressive explorer setting new standards of seamanship while yearning nostalgically for a declining world of wind and sail. The shift of sailing from commercial to recreational spheres provided a platform to celebrate Slocum's contribution as an individual who challenged the world and to offer new goals in feats of accomplishment. The Slocum Society in the United States perpetuates his memory as one man against the elements, an early breed of navigators sailing for the winds' sake alone.

Joshua Slocum became an American citizen, suffered personal tragedies that landed him in jail, and retreated from world attention. Nevertheless, he is remembered as a symbol of a Nova Scotian seafaring tradition that reached around the world and as an individualist who challenged one of the last frontiers of unique adventure. On November 14, 1909 he sailed from Massachusetts for the South Seas, but the oceans he had earlier conquered single-handedly reclaimed him. He was never seen again.

Larry Turner

Clarence M. Hincks

Mental Health Crusader

1885 - 1964

CLARENCE HINCKS, while director of the Canadian Mental Health Association, announced on CBC cross-Canada radio that he was manic depressive. In mid-twentieth century Canada, the mentally ill were still seen as creatures to be hidden away. It took real courage for Hincks to proclaim his illness. But he did so for humanitarian purposes.

Clare, as he was generally known, was born in the town of St. Marys, Ontario. The son of a clergyman, he studied at the University of Toronto, graduating in medicine in 1908. He left his first practice in Campbellford, Ontario, after refusing to carry out an abortion of convenience for a prominent citizen.

As a young practitioner in Toronto, Hincks became involved with examining schoolchildren, particularly those who were having trouble keeping up in the school system. It was in Toronto's school system that his life's calling began. Many of the children he was called upon to see were classified, in the unfortunate jargon of the day, "feeble-minded." Others were labelled "idiots." In general, they were thought of as unteachable and the question often was whether they should be isolated in one of the establishments devoted exclusively to such persons. But there were still other children who had no discernable reason for having the troubles they exhibited in school.

Hincks was convinced that there was no reason to be pessimistic about many of these children. He identified their unrecognised condition with his own life experiences. Although he had had a healthy, vigorous childhood and youth, when still a university student Clare had his first episode of mental illness. At the time, he had lost all interest in his surroundings and his studies. Many long days he had lain abed, convinced that nothing would ever interest him again. He was wrong, of course, and it was the recovery that so impressed him. He knew from personal experience that mental illness was not necessarily permanent. This first insight led to his lifetime involvement with the mentally ill. His dramatic revelation on CBC radio in 1962 describing his recurring illness was intentional: he wished to destroy the fear felt by much of the public about mental illness.

In August 1913, Hincks attended a medical meeting in Buffalo, New York. He paid his expenses by writing an account of the meetings for the *Toronto Daily Star*. At Buffalo he first learned about the Stanford-Binet tests that measure intelligence quotient, or one's IQ. But perhaps the most significant discovery was a publication by the American, Clifford Beers, called *A Mind That Found Itself*. Beers had been institutionalized in the eastern United States because of a severe depressive illness that sounded much like Hincks' own problem.

Beers had been institutionalized in the eastern United States because of a severe depressive illness that sounded much like Hincks' own problem. Beers had recovered after a two-year illness and had written his book during convalescence. It, and its author, played a major role in establishing the mental hygiene movement in North America. It was from the nascent American organization that Hincks took inspiration to establish something similar in Canada.

The initial organization in Canada, the Canadian National Committee for Mental Hygiene (CNCMH), owed much to Clare Hincks, to Dr. Colin Russell of Montreal, and to Dr. C.K. Clarke in Toronto as well as to the generosity of wealthy Canadians, in particular Lady Eaton. Hincks not only demonstrated superb organizational skills but proved over and over again that he was one of Canada's adroit fundraisers.

Clare devoted his considerable energy to pushing for the establishment of the CNCMH patterned on Beers' young group in the USA. From the initial formative meeting in February 1918 to its incorporation by federal charter on April 26, 1918, Hincks travelled the cities of Ontario and Quebec, seeking both professional and fiscal cooperation. It is a great tribute to so many individuals that the organization became a functioning entity so quickly.

The work of the CNCMH was much advanced by provincial surveys made early in the Committee's existence. For example, in 1918 Hincks and C.K. Clarke were invited to Manitoba to survey the mental institutions of that province, their first major activity after incorporation. At the outset they wisely established a policy of reporting directly to the government and thereby avoided the confrontational stance of later organizations that chose to release findings to the press first.

What Clare found during the three-week survey in Manitoba was sensational. The various institutions and/or hospitals were seriously overcrowded. Patients who should, ideally, have been separated were lumped together. Some should not have been patients at all. Moreover, some of the custodial care was appalling as exemplified by the naked woman who had been locked in a dark closet without furniture for two years.

The government of Manitoba reacted positively to the confidential report tendered by the CNCMH. So did other governments over the years. Surveys were made in other provinces. Governments became more and more comfortable in their dealings with the medical staff of the CNCMH.

As efforts increasingly focused on direct contact with the Canadian public, the Committee, in 1950, changed its name to the Canadian Mental Health Association. Made Medical Director of the CNCMH in 1924, Hincks continued in this office with the CMHA until his retirement in 1952. By then, at least partly because of the accomplishments of this organization, public perception of mental illness had changed significantly. Many other countries had studied and copied the approach of the CMHA. Institutions had become more humane, and patients often did better while confined in them. As a result of the work of the CMHA, today mental illness is much better understood.

Hincks was not a traditional medical researcher. His contributions to medical literature were few and basic. But his influence, support, and assistance helped to create and push forward a multitude of necessary projects. Clarence Hincks was greatly responsible for changing the bogeyman attitude to mental illness that had prevailed for thousands of years. This was his greatest achievement.

Charles Roland

TIMOTHY EATON

1834 - 1907

TIMOTHY EATON, founder of the huge all-Canadian department store chain bearing his name, began with a small dry goods business in Toronto in 1869. By his death in 1907, he had built up a giant retail store in Ontario's capital city along with a country-wide mail-order business and a big new branch store in Winnipeg, the first of many such "T. Eaton Company" business establishments that, in time, would spread all across Canada when Timothy's family successors extended the Eaton empire. Yet it was master merchant, Timothy, who led in the crucial period of development that spanned nearly forty years, a period of time in which he instituted the very concept of "Department Store," an idea that flourished not only in Canada but also in London, Paris, New York and, in fact, worldwide.

Timothy was born in 1834 on a tenant farm near Ballymena in Northern Ireland to an Irish Presbyterian family that took its faith very seriously, as did he. As a boy he worked in a local general store, but, at 20, in 1854, he followed two older brothers to Canada where they established a general store at St. Marys, in what became southwest Ontario. But Timothy looked to greater things and thus moved on to Toronto in a time of fast-rising city markets where, in 1869, he opened his own store on Yonge Street near Queen – an unfashionable

Master Merchant, Department Store Monarch, Prodigious Prince of Retail, Timothy Eaton not only revolutionized shopping but masterminded the moving of merchandise by mail-order. [Photo, courtesy T. Eaton Collection/Archives of Ontario]

area that he would totally change partly because of two striking innovations he made in retailing: sales for cash only and satisfaction guaranteed or money refunded. The first precept did away with age-old haggling and barter that always left the merchant uneasy about meeting costs and his customer about getting the best price, while the second assured the buyer of a secure choice – now and later. And so, with policies that would spread across department store business, Timothy Eaton excelled in a growing enterprise that enlarged from dry goods to clothing, housewares to furniture, and, in due course, to stationery, hardware, electrical goods, and still more.

In 1883 he opened a new, far larger store on Yonge Street. With four shopping floors, two elevators, electric lighting, concerts, and ladies' restrooms, the flagship Toronto store was aggressively modernized, no doubt because of the new rival store of Scottish immigrant, Robert Simpson, just across the street. In truth, the proximity of the two big shopping enterprises facilitated astute shopping since buyers could readily compare price tags at both stores. In 1884 Timothy Eaton expanded his customer base beyond city limits (in time followed by Simpson), for he sought to gain prosperous rural markets by establishing a mail-order catalogue and service. Eaton's mail order spread fast: a whole new building was erected in Toronto for its operations that ultimately reached "from sea unto sea." Meanwhile, business increased in the Toronto store which introduced more elevators, installed escalators, and was serviced by a host of delivery wagons, neatly painted in red and black, with polite, uniformed drivers and well-groomed, patient horses.

Timothy Eaton stressed not only quality goods, prices, and customer service but also fair labour practices. Early in his business endeavours, he began closing his store at eight in the evening, two hours earlier than any of his competitors, thus affording his staff time for rest and relaxation. He also closed on Saturday afternoons during July and August, another innovation for that time. A thoroughly earnest Protestant of his era, he condemned smoking, drinking, dancing, and card playing – and would not, did not, sell liquors or tobacco. Nor had he changed by the time of his death in 1907.

When he left his thriving 9,000-employee company to his sons, he had, with his successful policy of "Satisfaction Guaranteed, or Money Refunded" done his helpful best to entrench a commercial ethic.

J.M.S. Careless

Timothy Eaton's commercial career as a merchandising genius had its roots in both Kirkton and St. Marys in southwest Ontario. The first T. Eaton & Co. store (inset) was established at 178 Yonge St., Toronto, two years after Canada's Confederation in 1867. [Photo, courtesy T. Eaton Collection/Archives of Ontario]

ON AUGUST 20, 1884, a telegram from Britain's Colonial Secretary to Canada's Governor General, Lord Lansdowne, made an unusual request. It asked that 300 "voyageurs" be recruited as steersmen for boats on a military expedition up the Nile River for the relief of Khartoum where Sir Charles ("Chinese") Gordon, Governor General of the Sudan, was being besieged by a fanatical leader known as "The Mahdi" and his followers.

Initially, Britain's Prime Minister Gladstone and his cabinet had debated whether to send relief, but worldwide press and public pressure resolved the issue, and General Garnet Wolseley was appointed to rescue Gordon. Wolseley, a British Army officer who had taken part in quelling the 1870 Manitoba uprising, recalled the skills of the voyageurs handling the boats on that difficult expedition and believed they could be an essential factor in moving troops and supplies up the treacherous rapids and cataracts of the Nile River. The telegram, probably written by Wolseley, offered the volunteers $40 a month for six months, a suit of work clothes, free travel and rations.

Nile River Expedition

1884 - 1885

Canadian Boatmen Challenge the Nile

It also suggested that they be under the command of three Canadian officers and accompanied by a priest. Lansdowne forwarded the wire to Prime Minister Sir John A. Macdonald who, to avoid political reaction, suggested that Britain carry out and pay for the recruiting. As a result, Lansdowne's military secretary, Lord Melgund (later Fourth Earl of Minto and a future Canadian Governor General), was put in charge of recruiting. In less than a month, 386 Canadian voyageurs boarded a British steamer at Quebec City bound for Alexandria.

While called voyageurs, they were not veteran canoeists of the fur trade but mostly raftsmen of the lumber trade, skilled at riding timber rafts and logs down turbulent rivers to the sawmills each spring. There were French, English, first nation peoples, and Métis recruits in the group that came mainly from the Ottawa and Peterborough areas of Ontario, the Caughnawagna reserve, and Trois Rivières in Quebec. The 92 from Winnipeg included not only Indians and expert canoeists but lawyers, teachers, and other men merely seeking adventure.

Accompanying them were four officers, a regular Canadian army doctor, and a priest. The priest, Father Arthur Bouchard, who had earlier served as a missionary in the Sudan, spoke Arabic and was thus a great help to both the men and officers under the command of Major Frederick Denison. Denison, a Toronto lawyer, alderman, and militia officer, won, with his tact and understanding, the respect of the tough and boisterous voyageur recruits.

At Quebec City, the Governor General saw them off and skilfully reminded them, in both French and English, that, even though they were not going to serve as soldiers, they nevertheless should display "many of the best qualities of a soldier" in their work on the Nile.

The greatest imperial drama of Queen Victoria's later years involved Canadians whose unique water skills were needed to transport British forces through the many cataracts of the upper Nile River in an attempt to rescue Sir Charles Gordon, besieged at Khartoum in the mid-1880s. [Originally appeared in Illustrated London News]

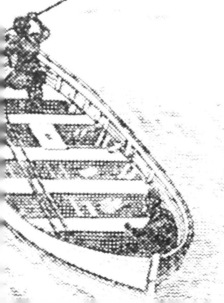

After stops in Sydney, Nova Scotia – where three decided to quit and one Nova Scotian was recruited – and Gibraltar to fuel the ship, they arrived at Alexandria and boarded 40 whalers towed behind the Khedive's yacht for a pleasant voyage up the Nile River to Wadi Halfa. There they were welcomed by General Wolseley who noted privately that they "were a rough looking lot."

This was an opinion shared by many British officers and journalists, one writing that they were mutinous, another reporting that many carried bowie knives and were drunk upon arrival at Wadi Halfa. The criticisms prompted Denison to write: "I hear some lying accounts of my men have been telegraphed out from Assuan, saying they were mutinous etc. It is all manufactured." About their arrival at Wadi Halfa he wrote, "I rather fancy the man must be a fool," pointing out that the story was written the day before they even arrived there.

At Wadi Halfa the Canadians soon won respect rather than scorn. Working from dawn to dusk – a 13- to 14-hour day – they skilfully guided the 30-foot whalers carrying three to four tons of supplies and as many as 12 fully equipped soldiers through rapids and cataracts. Their British commandant wrote, "It is extraordinary to see the rapidity with which the expedition travels since the Canadians have arrived."

Progress, however, remained frustratingly slow despite the skills of the Canadians. Some of the cataracts became so swift and dangerous that the soldiers, normally equipped with oars to row the boats, went ashore to tow them with only the voyageurs remaining on board to manoeuvre the loaded vessels around treacherous rocks often hidden in muddy water. Six voyageurs were drowned, two were killed in an accident, and eight died of smallpox or typhoid fever.

The slow progress also created another problem: the six-month contract was running out and, despite an increase in pay to $60 a month and new clothing to those whom Denison wished to retain, fewer than 100 agreed to stay.

The need for boatmen, however, lessened considerably when Wolseley sent half his forces across the desert. Late in January 1885, those electing to return to Canada left Wadi Halfa for Cairo where they were given a grand tour of the city and the pyramids. A British General inspected them and praised their work.

This was one of several commendations they received. Lord Wolseley wrote to Lord

Prior to their departure for the Nile River, Canadian voyageurs assembled on Ottawa's Parliament Hill on September 13, 1884. In all, some 386 Canadians would cross the Atlantic in an historic attempt to rescue Sir Charles Gordon under seige at Khartoum. [Photo, courtesy National Archives of Canada]

Lansdowne at Ottawa, exclaiming that "the services of these voyageurs has been of the greatest possible value." Another senior officer "doubted whether the boats would have got up at all ... and if they had ... the loss of life would have been much greater than has been the case." One soldier wrote, "These imported voyageurs, greatly discredited by some of the commentators on this campaign, were absolutely indispensable."

The returning voyageurs sailed on a troopship bound for Ireland where some stopped over, leaving 260 for the trip to Halifax. There they made a colourful scene on March 4, sporting turbans and pith helmets, and carrying spears, shields, and other African souvenirs that included cockatoos and monkeys. Two days later they were cheered by Ottawa crowds as they paraded to an armoury for a welcome home banquet. A local paper headlined its story: "Hurrah stout hearts, well and bravely have you done your duty."

The voyageurs remaining in Egypt pushed further up the Nile until February when it was learned that Khartoum had fallen and that General Gordon had been among those massacred. By early April it became clear there was no further need for the boatmen. They then sailed from Wadi Halfa on a steamer to Cairo, where another tour of the city was arranged before they boarded a ship for England. Denison, promoted to Lieutenant Colonel, was not with them as he had been hospitalized on arriving in Cairo with typhoid fever. Two others died of smallpox in London: a Peterborough boatman and William N. Kennedy, an officer who had enlisted and accompanied the Winnipeg volunteers.

The smallpox outbreak prevented a planned inspection by Queen Victoria at Windsor Castle but she sent a message expressing how pleased she was "by the reports of the energy and devotion they had shown in the arduous duties performed by them on the Nile."

The British war office also showed its appreciation by assigning a guide to show them "some places of interest and amusement" in London before the majority embarked on a Montreal-bound ship on May 15. Late in June, Denison arrived home in Toronto where he resumed his law practice and learned he was awarded the C.M.G. for his service in Egypt. Abbé Bouchard became a parish priest in Quebec and Trinidad, dying on the Caribbean island in 1896 at age 51 – the same year Denison also died of cancer at age 49, after serving as Federal Member of Parliament for a Toronto riding.

Mel James

William C. Macdonald

Tobacconist with a Heart
1831 - 1917

ONE of the most important benefactors of Canadian education was Sir William Christopher Macdonald. His statesman-like manner of giving unconditionally earned him the deepest respect of all who knew him. Shunning publicity, he basked privately in the achievements of others whom he helped – with or without their knowledge.

William was a direct descendant of Ian Og, guardian of Clanranald and first Chief of Glenaladale and Glenfinnan, Invernesshire, Scotland. The duties of the clan protector were passed down from one generation to another. William, however, significantly broadened the definition of the word "clan" to encompass one's country.

The sixth of seven children, William was born on February 10, 1831, to the Honourable Donald Macdonald, Member (later President) of the Legislative Council of Prince Edward Island, and Matilda Brecken. By the age of 16, after heated disagreements with his father, he ran away to Boston, Massachusetts, to become "a minor in a counting room." Within two years, the business acumen and single-minded determination to succeed that would take him to the heights of Canadian finance began to bud.

Following a brief and near ruinous 1851 venture in shipping consigned goods from Boston to Charlottetown, William and his brother Augustine left Massachusetts for safer home ground. Early the next year, they resurfaced as "Montreal oil and commission merchants." While profits were reasonable, William was still unsatisfied.

When Queen Victoria knighted Sir William Macdonald in 1898, Her Majesty declared the Montrealer as "the greatest philanthropist in the British Empire." [Photo, courtesy Macdonald Stewart Foundation]

As with most nineteenth century young men, his dream was to become wealthy, and, by using common sense mixed with frugality and unrelenting resolve, he was determined to "turn his signature into gold."

On the eve of the American Civil War in 1858, "McDonald Brothers and Co., Tobacco Manufacturers" was established. By 1866 the name was changed to "W.C. McDonald," with William as sole proprietor. Because the corporate logo was a heart-shaped tin label, the product became known as "the tobacco with a heart," an appropriate slogan considering that most of the company's profits were later spent on Canadian youth.

Business grew steadily. Paper work was William's number one enemy, but the simplicity by which he ran his company assured economic stability and success. Purchases by "unknown" merchants were paid for in cash; those few granted accounts settled before another order was filled. Buyers were responsible for delivery of their goods – William was "in the business of manufacturing tobacco, not transporting it." As his tobacco products fast became the favourites across the country, there was no choice but to accept his demands.

Citing smoking as a "wasteful habit" and the chewing of tobacco as "disgusting," he sought a way in which his profits could benefit society at large. With this new purpose, consciously or not, William assumed the hereditary duty of guardian, thus becoming one of Canada's preeminent humanitarians.

His general interest focused on the country's youth and the quality of their education. If they were to succeed, education would have to be the key. Much of his knowledge was acquired by reading reports and magazines well into each night while standing at his own library lectern. Getting children to school was not as difficult as keeping them there. It would take meaningful and inspiring training to achieve that, and he was determined to provide it.

Interestingly, given that he himself was a school dropout, his initial patronage in this field, in 1870, was ten annual matriculation scholarships to McGill University that continue to this day to provide funds for scholarships in the Arts Faculty.

In 1883 he was nominated to the Board of McGill Governors and, until his death, 35 years later, neither the university nor its students ever had a more knowledgeable or generous benefactor. Deficits were discreetly covered; endowments of Chairs and gifts of land and equipment were anonymously given in addition to tuition fees and scholarships for hundreds of youth he never met.

William's passionate regard for agriculture began to soar, ironically, as a direct result of his election in 1887 as a Bank of Montreal director. On reviewing the Bank's progress, he noted increased economic growth in rural areas where dairy and livestock farming dominated. This awakened his interest in English-speaking farmers in Quebec, his home province, and led to "The Macdonald Movement for Rural Education."

McGill meanwhile continued to prosper from his generosity: the Macdonald Physics and Chemistry buildings, and, jointly with Thomas Workman of Montreal, the Macdonald Engineering building, all with fully funded faculties, were opened. As well, William had the Engineering building reconstructed after it was destroyed by fire. Before classes were recommenced, however, William tested the contractor's guarantee that it was now fireproof by igniting, inside the structure, wood shavings that indeed caused only slight damage. The building and contractor were then deemed trustworthy.

An example of the expertise with which he staffed his faculties was the appointment of Ernest Rutherford, who had been working on radioactive transformation of the elements at Cambridge University. Appointed as Macdonald Professor of Physics, Rutherford went on to win the Nobel Prize for chemistry in 1908 for his work at McGill and later was knighted for his efforts that precipitated the splitting of the atom.

Having already refused that honour once, William consented, in 1898, to being knighted by Queen Victoria, who, unaware that his efforts had just begun, described him as the greatest philanthropist in education in the British Empire.

It was said of Macdonald that "to be of service to others on lines of his own choosing was with him a passion." That passion was ignited in 1899 when he began to work with Dr. James W. Robertson, then Dominion Commissioner of Agriculture and Dairying. Together, with the aim of keeping the children on the farms, they launched an experiment of introducing nature study and gardening into country schools. Sir William astutely knew the importance of spirituality and believed that, if children learned to feel a closeness to the earth, then perhaps they would not be lured to the big cities.

This endeavour was so successful that it caused the formation of Macdonald Consolidated Schools which offered not only gardening and nature study but manual (practical) training and household sciences as well. Schools were established in Prince Edward Island, Nova Scotia, New Brunswick, Quebec, and Ontario.

Sir William also provided transportation – horse-drawn wagons to facilitate the children's attendance. As well, he awarded scholarships that enabled teachers to attend courses at Chicago, Cornell, Columbia, and Clark universities in the United States and at the Ontario Agricultural College in Guelph. Instructors were paid out of the Macdonald Training Fund and, by 1907, more than 20,000 young people were benefiting from his efforts.

When Lord Strathcona donated Strathcona Hall to Montreal's Young Men's Christian Association, Sir William, who, although spiritual, did not incline to any one religious denomination, stated, "Lord Strathcona has given a building for the Christians; I will give a building for all students of the University." The Students' Union Building was the fulfillment of his promise.

No one threatened the integrity of McGill without experiencing Macdonald's wrath first-hand. A syndicate of Montreal businessmen, some rumoured to be McGill governors, bought

Sir William provided transportation to facilitate children attending the Macdonald School in Middleton, Nova Scotia. [Photo, courtesy Macdonald Stewart Foundation]

land on the southwest corner of the University grounds on which they planned to build a hotel. When this news reached Sir William, he threatened the men with exposure and financial ruin and demanded the land, gladly paying $500 more, while firmly stating that he would "not have McGill made the backyard of any hotel." Two years later, he added 25 acres of prime Montreal property thereby extending the main campus to the north on which its gymnasium, stadium, and Douglas Hall were built.

Ontario experienced his openhandedness by way of the Macdonald Institute at Guelph. Established to improve rural education, it also helped Adelaide Hunter Hoodless of Hamilton, Ontario, founder of the first Women's Institute, to provide better training of women in household sciences. Sir William, a confirmed bachelor albeit one who ardently believed in the ability of women, gave the school and residence, along with his encouragement. The Ontario government maintained the buildings and teaching staff.

Of all the gifts Sir William bestowed upon his countrymen, the greatest, given in 1907, was Macdonald College of McGill University at Ste. Anne de Bellevue, Quebec. Primarily an agricultural college, it would also provide for household sciences and teachers' training. The college reflected the broadminded characteristic of its founder, and benefited not only Canadians, but people worldwide. Like McGill, it continues to this day to maintain a solid international reputation.

Sir William did not confine to eastern Canada his efforts to establish a level of excellence in education. He also provided funding for the consolidation of Vancouver and Victoria colleges into the McGill University College of British Columbia, which evolved into the University of British Columbia. As well, he financially assisted the University of Alberta on the appointment of its first president.

When nominated President and Chancellor of McGill early in 1914, Sir William expressed his "earnest hope that no harm should ever come to the university in consequence of this election." None ever did save for the vast void left upon his death in Montreal on June 9, 1917. His will included munificent bequests to the faculties of medicine and music, and travelling fellowships in the Faculty of Law that allowed English-speaking Quebec lawyers to study the French language in France.

The compassion of this shy, unpretentious, self-made tobacconist was measured by the willingness of others to help themselves. This was the spirit of his philanthropy that even today, through his enduring munificence, continues to serve his "clan" well.   *Victoria Stewart*

Sir William Macdonald culminated his educational philanthropy with the founding of the Macdonald Institute on the Ontario Agricultural College campus at Guelph, Ontario, in 1903. In 1964 the OAC was renamed the University of Guelph. [Photo, courtesy Macdonald Stewart Foundation]

John G. FitzGerald

1882 - 1940

Canada's Public Health Visionary

VIRTUALLY every Canadian child today is protected from a host of deadly infectious diseases thanks to the bold vision of Dr. John G. FitzGerald, founder of Connaught Laboratories and a leading proponent of Canada's modern public health system.

Above: Dr. John FitzGerald founded Connaught Laboratories in 1914. [Photo, courtesy Connaught Laboratories]

Right: The humble birthplace of Connaught Laboratories: the Barton Ave. stable where Dr. John FitzGerald and his first employee, William Fenton (at doorway), began producing diphtheria antitoxin for the first time in Canada. The stable now stands at Connaught's research and manufacturing complex in North York. [Photo, courtesy Connaught Laboratories]

When John FitzGerald began practising medicine in Toronto at the beginning of this century, impoverished parents of children stricken with diphtheria often made a tragic mistake. Unable to afford enough of the costly, imported diphtheria antitoxin to treat each child effectively, they would share the medicine among the children, thereby leaving all at risk to the deadly disease. In those days, one out of every six children infected with diphtheria died.

This tragedy inspired the young, University of Toronto-trained physician to search for a way of bringing these new disease-fighting medicines – vaccines and antitoxins – to the public at the lowest possible cost.

Graduating in 1903 as the youngest member of his medical class, FitzGerald began his career in psychiatry. A growing interest in the possibilities of preventive medicine drew FitzGerald to the emerging field of bacteriology pioneered by Dr. Louis Pasteur of France. In 1909, he began lecturing on the subject at the University of Toronto and travelling the world to learn more.

FitzGerald spent the summers of 1910 and 1911 studying at the renowned Pasteur Institute in Paris and Brussels. While there, he learned not only of the latest advances in "microbics," as microbiology was then known, but also of Pasteur's strong belief that scientific knowledge should be applied to public health to benefit all people, regardless of economics and geography.

In Pasteur's philosophy, FitzGerald found a focus for his own frustrations about the state of preventative medicine in his native country. At the time, only smallpox and typhoid vaccines were being produced in small quantities in Canada. And while products such as diphtheria antitoxin could be imported from the United States, their cost was often beyond the reach of poor families and there was little guarantee of supply.

Through his studies at the Pasteur Institute, the Lister Institute in London, England, and with New York City's Department of Health, FitzGerald also recognized that knowledge was as vital as medicine in the fight against disease. Learning about a disease and how it was spread was important not only to the finding of a cure, but also in teaching others how it could be prevented. In this combination of research, production, and teaching, FitzGerald believed he had found a formula for reforming public health services in Canada.

His opportunity came in 1913 when he was appointed associate professor in the University of Toronto's new Department of Hygiene. That summer, FitzGerald took the first step in his plan by producing Pasteur's rabies treatment for the Ontario Board of Health in a small University laboratory above a jewellery store in downtown Toronto. Until then, rabies treatments had to be imported from New York at an exorbitant price.

Later that year, he approached the University with a proposal to set up laboratories as part of its Department of Hygiene where high-quality antitoxins and vaccines could be manufactured at costs low enough for them to be widely available. Yet FitzGerald's ideas met with skepticism since they represented a somewhat radical departure from the University's strictly academic traditions. Without the University's approval, the impatient FitzGerald decided to plunge ahead anyway.

Using money from his wife's inheritance, he built a small stable on Barton Avenue west of the University where he began to inoculate four horses with diphtheria bacteria, the first step in preparing the life-saving antitoxin. Within months, he was producing it at one-fifth of the cost of the imported product. This led to a contract with the Ontario Board of Health, which then undertook one of the first free distributions of medicine by any government in Canada.

These successes finally convinced the University to back FitzGerald's plan and he was given laboratory space in the basement of the medical building. Issuing his first progress report on June 30, 1914, FitzGerald outlined the new laboratory's role:

> *The fundamental idea underlying the project was the production of all sera and vaccines of value in public health work and their distribution at cost. It was expected that the active cooperation of public health authorities in Canada would be obtained, and this has, in large measure, been realized.*

In one bold, impetuous stroke, FitzGerald had given Canada the ability to develop and produce life-saving vaccines and antitoxins and helped set the stage for the nation's modern, publicly funded public health care system.

The outbreak of the war in August 1914 threatened to undermine the support for FitzGerald's project as the University began focusing on helping the war effort. Ironically, the war was to give a "shot in the arm" to the fledging laboratories. In 1915, FitzGerald was asked by Col. Albert Gooderham of the Canadian Red Cross to begin producing large quantities of tetanus antitoxin for the Canadian Army.

Also known as "lockjaw," tetanus was infecting troops wounded in France, adding the threat of death by disease to the perils of the battlefield. FitzGerald, who had already enlisted in the Canadian Army Medical Corps, agreed to begin providing the much-needed antitoxin at cost, significantly less than $1.35 per dose cost of imported product from the United States. Suddenly, FitzGerald's back street stable and basement laboratory were propelled to the front line of the war effort.

To help increase the laboratory's production capacity, Gooderham donated a 57- acre farm 15 miles north of Toronto where stables and a modern laboratory building were constructed. Officially opened in October 1917, the new facility was named the "Connaught Antitoxin Laboratories and University Farm" after the Duke of Connaught, third son of Queen Victoria and a recent Governor General of Canada.

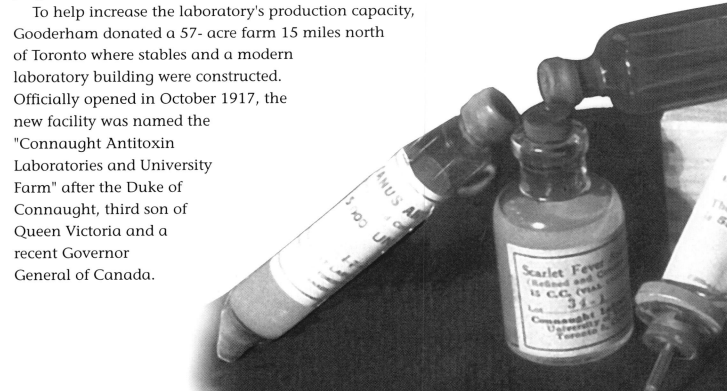

By the war's end in 1918, the expanded laboratories had supplied more than 250,000 doses of tetanus antitoxin to the army at 34 cents a dose and produced more than one million doses of smallpox vaccine and several other much-needed vaccines and sera.

Soon after the new laboratory opened, the ever-restless FitzGerald was on his way to the Western Front after obtaining a transfer to the British Army's Medical Corps. During the last six months of the war, he commanded a mobile laboratory and served as assistant advisor of pathology to the Fifth British Army. In the meantime, FitzGerald's close friend, Dr. Robert Defries, managed Connaught's activities – a role he would often fill while FitzGerald pursued new projects.

Returning from overseas, FitzGerald resumed his teaching post at the University and his position as the Director of Connaught Laboratories. In 1920, he was appointed to the Dominion Council of Health, a new agency responsible for coordinating federal and provincial health programs. The Council was patterned on an earlier scientific advisory body that FitzGerald had created at Connaught. Following a sabbatical year at the University of California in 1922, FitzGerald was made a member of the Rockefeller Foundation's International Board of Health.

With the Foundation's backing, FitzGerald was soon able to complete the third stage of his public health vision for Canada – research, production, and education. In 1925, the Foundation provided funding to the University of Toronto to establish a School of Hygiene. Opened in 1927 with FitzGerald serving as its first director, it was the first learning institution in Canada dedicated to public health and preventative medicine.

In the meantime, Connaught Laboratories had achieved worldwide recognition in 1922 as the first

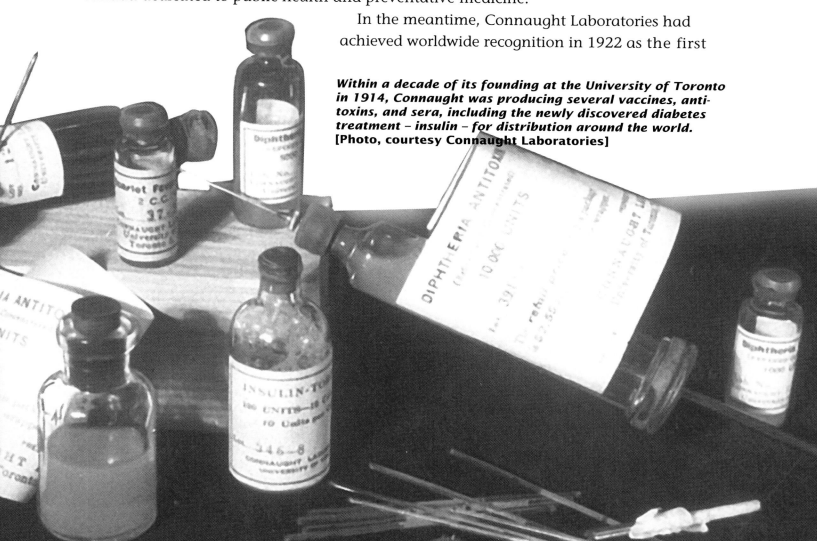

Within a decade of its founding at the University of Toronto in 1914, Connaught was producing several vaccines, antitoxins, and sera, including the newly discovered diabetes treatment – insulin – for distribution around the world. **[Photo, courtesy Connaught Laboratories]**

In the summer of 1910, Dr. John FitzGerald (in white coat} began his lifelong association with the Pasteur Institute of France where he learned how Louis Pasteur's life-saving vaccines and antitoxins could be produced for public distribution in Canada.
[Photo, courtesy FitzGerald Family]

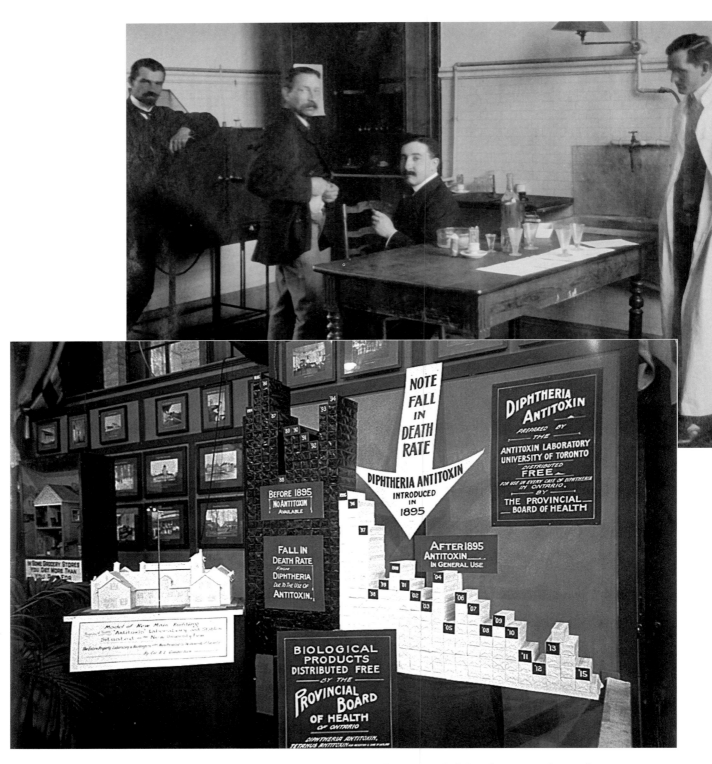

A display at the Canadian National Exhibition in 1920 shows how diphtheria antitoxin had reduced the death rate from the disease. The antitoxin was the first of many biological products prepared by Connaught at costs low enough to be distributed free by the Ontario Board of Health.
[Photo, courtesy Connaught Laboratories]

organization to produce insulin in large quantities. This breakthrough treatment for diabetes had recently been discovered by Dr. Frederick Banting and Charles Best at the University of Toronto. Soon afterward, thanks to FitzGerald's connection with the Pasteur Institute which had developed the new vaccine, Connaught became the first North American laboratory to field-test and produce an immunizing diphtheria toxoid.

Throughout the 1930s, FitzGerald assumed even greater responsibilities both at home and abroad. In 1932, he was appointed Dean of Medicine at the University of Toronto, a position he would hold for three terms. With Defries' steadfast support, he continued as Connaught's Director as the laboratories expanded their research and production of vaccines and sera against other infectious diseases. FitzGerald also served as member or Director of several medical and research organizations both in Canada and the United States. On the international scene, he was a member of the League of Nations Health Committee and travelled extensively as a scientific director of the Rockefeller Foundation's International Division.

Sadly, by the late 1930s the restless energy and infectious enthusiasm that had enabled FitzGerald to accomplish so much and attract others to his cause began to wane. Throughout his life, he had suffered from severe headaches brought on by restless work habits and a worsening manic-depressive condition. Worn out physically and mentally, in 1938 FitzGerald suffered a severe mental breakdown that brought an end to his brilliant career. Tragically, he ended his own life in June 1940.

A year after his death, FitzGerald was honoured by Donald T. Fraser in the *Proceedings of the Royal Society of Canada* with the following eulogy:

> *To few are given the qualities of executive ability, singleness of purpose, imagination and vision, combined with gentleness, modesty, and charm of character in such large measure as Dr. FitzGerald possessed.*

The small Barton Avenue stable where FitzGerald produced his first batches of diphtheria antitoxin stands today among several modern research and manufacturing buildings at Connaught Laboratories' facilities on the northern edge of Metropolitan Toronto. Surrounded by suburban sprawl, the former Gooderham farm is now headquarters of the largest vaccine manufacturer in North America.

At Connaught, research scientists carry on FitzGerald's fight against such modern-day infectious diseases as AIDS, influenza, and whooping cough. His former stable has been replaced by high technology biofermentation plants that produce millions of doses of vaccines annually for distribution around the world.

And in a final irony, the story of John FitzGerald and Connaught Laboratories has come full circle. In 1989, the company became a member of the Pasteur Merieux group of companies of France. Nearly 80 years had passed since an idealistic young doctor from Canada spent a summer in Paris learning how to bring Louis Pasteur's new life-saving vaccines and sera "within reach of everyone."

Richard Levick

Jack Miner

1865 - 1944

Wildlife Conservationist

J ACK MINER grew up near the shores of Lake Erie in proximity to both the industrial complex of Detroit-Windsor and one of North America's great bird migration fly-ways. He was an avid hunter, but the relentless development of the region, the declining quality of the Great Lakes, and the threat of wildlife extermination converted Jack Miner, trapper and market hunter, into Jack Miner, conservationist and world wildlife spokesperson. Not unlike converted big-game hunters in Africa, Miner awakened to the crisis slowly but then threw himself with religious zeal into the protection of wildlife.

Born John Thomas Miner at Dover Centre (Westlake), Ohio, on April 10, 1865, he moved with his family to Kingsville, Essex County, in southwestern Ontario in 1878 and soon bonded with the land as a consummate hunter. He hunted for fun and profit, his friends and relations marvelling at his natural instinct and energy in the bush. His affinity with the wild and his sense of sight, smell, and direction led to his being credited in his lifetime with the finding of thirteen people who had been lost in the forest.

In 1888 he married Laona Wigle and subsequently fathered four sons and a daughter. Then, at the turn of the century, a series of tragedies occurred: his daughter died suddenly in 1897 and, on an autumn moose-hunting trip to Quebec in 1898, his brother Ted died in a tragic accident. By 1900 Jack had learned to read, had discovered the Bible, and had experienced a religious conversion; in these life crises he began to interpret the

Jack Miner first began tagging waterfowl in 1909. Here, in 1915, he releases the first goose with a biblical verse inscribed on the band. [Photo, courtesy The Jack Miner Foundation]

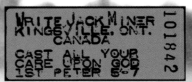

WRITE JACK MINER
KINGSVILLE. ONT.
CANADA
CAST ALL YOUR
CARE UPON GOD
1ST PETER 5-7

101842

biblical pronouncement, "Let man have dominion over all," as being a call for responsibility and stewardship, not exploitation and subjugation of nature. In 1904, his faith was put to a test when his oldest son Carl died suddenly at age thirteen. He tried to overcome tremendous grief through his conservation efforts.

Both the Atlantic and Mississippi flyways converged near the family brickyard in Kingsville, ten miles from the now famous Point Pelée which Miner helped designate a National Park in 1918. The plight of birds became a focus for his attention, especially as a result of the extinction of the passenger pigeon (last recorded in Canada in 1902). After Miner purchased seven pinioned geese from a local trapper and in 1904 flooded one of the brickyard pits, he attracted Canada geese to his property. Soon he was feeding migrating flocks of geese, ducks, doves, and songbirds in a series of artificial ponds and was on his way to becoming "Wild Goose Jack," a worldwide symbol of conservation efforts.

In 1904 the Kingsville site was one of the first bird sanctuaries in North America. In August 1909, Miner tagged his first wild duck with a hand stamped aluminum band. The band was recovered five months later by Dr. W. Bray of Anderson, South Carolina (the first complete banding record). Data from thousands of subsequent taggings over the next six years was instrumental in the Migratory Bird Treaty of 1916 between Canada and the U.S. In 1915, with a flash of inspiration, he added a short verse of biblical scripture to his duck and goose bands. This was his unique way of passing on God's promises to those who recovered the bands.

Jack Miner's reputation grew and he became a much sought out lecturer on conservation and on his methods of banding, research, and habitat preservation. He spoke across the North American continent, wrote two books on the subject, in 1929 was awarded the outdoor gold medal in the U.S. and in 1943, a year before his death, an O.B.E. for "the greatest achievement in conservation in the British Empire." In 1931 he organized the Jack Miner Migratory Bird Foundation which was incorporated as a philanthropic body in both the U.S. and Canada. The Jack Miner League, similar to the Izaak Walton League, spread across Canada in the 1920s and 1930s. He took to the radio waves in support of junior bird clubs, encouraging children to build bird boxes for a wide variety of songbirds. His prophetic concerns over the condition of the Great Lakes, voiced as early as 1927, warned of future battles for the environment well before this became an international and political concern. When National Wildlife Week was created in his honour, it was to a deserving pioneer of conservation who offered practical advice in a relative vacuum of scientific information on the relationship of birds and animals to their environment. Jack Miner had the instinct for preservation.

Larry Turner

During their annual migration, geese by the thousands stop to feed at the Jack Miner Bird Sanctuary in Kingsville, Ontario. Many are banded, contributing to the research of the migratory birds of North America. [Photo, courtesy The Jack Miner Foundation]

Creating the World's Largest Business Form Company

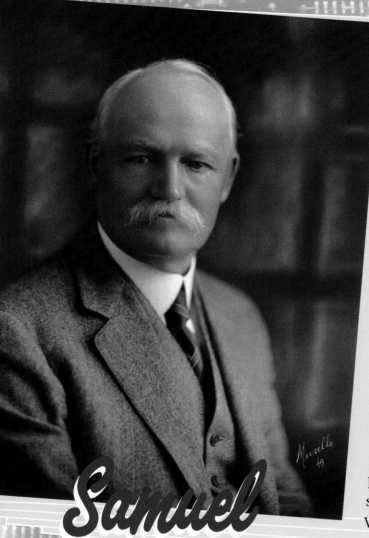

Samuel John Moore

1859 - 1948

INVENTIONS often seem remarkably simple in hindsight and, not only are they often taken for granted, but the systems they have replaced may now seem incomprehensible.

Samuel Moore did not invent the concept of the business form, but when he saw it, he knew what to do with it. He quickly recognized the revolution it would have on administrative procedures, the enormous effect on the commercial flow of sales transactions, and the strong impact on modern business management. Samuel Moore latched onto a concept that not only became one of the foundations of the "Gospel of Efficiency" but also helped define the Progressive era of late nineteenth century North America. He introduced a mass-produced stationery form that slashed time and money from the cost of doing business, and, in doing so, built an international empire based in Toronto.

Samuel John Moore was born in England on August 3, 1859 and was only a youngster when his parents, Isaac and Louisa (Chapman), settled in Barrie, Ontario. Samuel's introduction as a "printer's devil" at the tender age of 12 took place at the Barrie *Examiner* newspaper, where he eventually became a local editor before setting out to find his fortune in Texas at the age of 20. When Samuel returned to Canada, he soon formed a partnership with J.W. Bengough to publish *Grip*, the satirical paper that lampooned Canadian politics through Moore's pen and Bengough's cartoons. In 1882, John R. Carter, a drygoods store clerk, wandered into Bengough, Moore & Co., Printers and Publishers, and showed Samuel a simple sales book in which a sheet of carbon paper inserted between two pages could give both customer and store proprietor a record of a transaction. Business would never be the same.

In a rapidly expanding urban economy, the means by which accounts were kept and invoices made required a legion of bookkeepers, copyists, and clerks for mundane and repetitive paperwork. The invention of carbon copy and mass-produced sales slips and business forms had an impact similar to that of the typewriter and the copy machine on later evolutions in the business world.

Samuel Moore pioneered a consortium of companies in Canada, the U.S., and around the world (Britain and Australia) which designed, printed, and bound a wide range of business forms to serve diverse purposes. By 1929 a major network of Moore companies had emerged as Moore Corporation Limited, the largest producer of business forms in the world.

In 1934, at the 50th anniversary of the salesbook industry, the scope of Moore's initiative was reflected in the statement by the Sales Book Manufacturers Association president that the industry "is the reflection of the vision and energy of Samuel J. Moore." He went on to laud the career of the industry's most enthusiastic advocate: "Mr. Moore proved himself a master salesman, as well as a capable organiser and an efficient manufacturer. He was both a correct interpreter of events and the apostle of an idea."

The abundantly successful enterprise spawned interests in other endeavours, including directorships of numerous companies. Of one of these, the Metropolitan Bank of Canada, he was a founder in 1902. The bank was later merged into The Bank of Nova Scotia where Moore served as President, Chairman of the Board, and eventually Honorary Chairman.

Samuel Moore's business life was intertwined with his devout volunteerism both as a layman in the Baptist Church and an organizer in the Young Men's Christian Association (YMCA). In the heady days of building the YMCA into one of North America's foremost institutions, Moore chaired the international convention in Toronto in 1894 and was elected a life member. In 1911 Moore underwrote a world tour by John R. Mott to organize the World Student Christian Federation. Mott later went on to found the World Missionary Conference, to help found the World Council of Churches, and to win a Nobel Peace Prize. In 1963 the S.J. Moore Educational Scholarship was endowed in Moore's memory by the YMCA.

For more than 35 years, Moore found time in his busy schedule to assist the Baptist Church. He superintended Toronto's Dovercourt Baptist Church Sunday School, chaired the Layman's Missionary Conference in 1909, sat on the executive board of the Baptist World Alliance in 1911, and presided over the Baptist Convention of Ontario and Quebec in 1920.

Samuel Moore always kept a motto clipped and pasted in the front of his constant companion, the Bible. It read *"Consult Wisely, Resolve Firmly and Execute with Inflexible Perseverance."*

At the establishment of the YMCA S.J. Moore Educational Award in 1963, Arthur G. Walwyn acclaimed Moore as "a great Canadian Christian, an eminently successful business man and one whose life was a great example and inspiration to all who knew him." *Larry Turner*

OPPOSITE:
When Samuel Moore was fêted at Toronto's Royal York Hotel on his 75th birthday, **The Financial Post** *described him as one whose career had "outshone that of Horatio Alger's most ambitious boy wonder."*
[Photo, courtesy Moore Corporation]

Mr. Samuel Moore, relaxing with his wife and two of their three daughters, Violet and Tillie, circa 1910.
[Photo, courtesy Moore Corporation]

Hugh Allan

1810 - 1882

Formidable Financier and Shipping Sultan

Former president of the Montreal Board of Trade (1851-1854), Sir Hugh Allan was knighted by Queen Victoria in 1871. [Photo, courtesy National Archives of Canada/C-26668]

MONTREAL SHIPOWNER, would-be builder of the Canadian Pacific Railway, Hugh Allan was an enterprising nineteenth century financier who was born in 1810 at Saltcoats beside the entry to the Firth of Clyde where much of Scotland's Atlantic shipping and shipbuilding had concentrated. In 1822 his father, a Clydeside sea captain, began his own regular transatlantic service between Glasgow and the St. Lawrence with one sailing vessel. The next year his son went to work, at 13, as an office boy at Greenock on the Clyde. At 16, young Hugh then moved overseas to a Montreal merchandising house that was also shipping agent for his father's growing service. There he flourished in Canada's top commercial city, becoming junior partner in a Montreal ship brokerage and shipbuilding firm. In 1839, under Hugh's influence as a senior partner, the same firm expanded into shipping. In fact, under his direction the firm went on to produce Canada's celebrated "Allan Line" of transatlantic transport.

With financial help from his father and brothers in Scotland, Allan's partnership bought both sailing craft and the new ocean vessels, enlarging their business over the 1840s until in 1852 they incorporated as the Montreal Ocean Steamship Company. Moreover, as President of the Montreal Board of Trade (1851-1854), Allan by 1853 had induced the Canadian government of the day to subsidize mail carriage between Montreal and Britain, and in 1856, helped by friends in the Conservative party, had taken away the valuable sea-mail contracts from competitors. The Allan line also bought or built non-propeller steamers (faster and safer than the old paddlewheelers) and continued to improve ship technology, even introducing in 1879 the first all-steel steamship launched on the Atlantic. Meanwhile, Allan Lines had supplied transport for British and French troops in the Crimean War of the 1850s, later carrying British forces to Africa. Hence, Allan was knighted in 1871 in recognition of his services both to Canada and the British Empire.

In other fields of enterprise, he was president of the Montreal Telegraph Company that pioneered telegraphic links in Canada. He was also a founder of the powerful Merchants Bank of Canada, established in Montreal in 1861. Additionally, he owned Nova Scotia coal mines, Quebec and/or Ontario tobacco, paper, textile, and steel plants. In particular, he headed the Canadian Pacific Railway Company – a line promised to British Columbia on its entering Confederation in 1871 – that would knit up the young Canadian transcontinental union. After winning the federal election of 1872, Sir John A. Macdonald's government had passed a C.P.R. bill offering $30 million and 50 million acres of western lands to the company that would accept the challenge. Despite hot competition from a Toronto-centred group, the Montreal-based consortium led by Sir Hugh Allan was finally awarded the multi-million dollar contract.

In the spring of 1873 the Allan CPR success changed to disaster when news leaked out that he had provided $360,000 to fund their 1872 elections to such leading Conservatives as Sir George-Étienne Cartier, the Quebec leader, and Sir John A. Macdonald in Kingston, Ontario. These election "bribes" mocked the Canadian public and were certainly exploited by the Liberal opposition. At any rate, the Macdonald government fell in what was termed the Pacific Scandal and Allan's railway undertaking totally collapsed, delaying the CPR until the 1880s. Nevertheless, the big shipping magnate with his many other interests went onward until his death at Edinburgh in 1882. And his life of enterprising achievement was not all that significantly lessened by the grand "Scandal" for which he is all too readily remembered. *J.M.S. Careless*

Better known as the "Allan Line," the Montreal Ocean Steamship Co. was headquartered for many years in downtown Montreal at the corner of Craig and Bleury Streets.

Depicted on a toleware cigarette case (c. 1905), the S.S. Victorian *was the first ocean liner driven by turbine engines.* [Photos, courtesy Charles J. Humber collection]

EDSON LOY PEASE

1856 - 1930

Coin of the Realm

William Notman photograph of Edson Pease in 1908.
[Photo, courtesy McCord Museum of Canadian History, Notman Photographic Archives]

AMONG THE most stable enterprises at home and abroad are Canada's national banks. Supportive legislation, economic growth, and international expansion provided a solid foundation for these institutions. Bankers, however, as the administrators and investors of economic growth, seldom receive the same recognition as that accorded the builders: the architects, developers, planners, and engineers. Edson Pease is no exception. However, in the first two decades of the twentieth century, he mapped out a strategy that turned a provincial bank into a national and international force known today as Royal Bank of Canada.

Edson Loy Pease was born at Coteau Landing on the St. Lawrence River near Montreal, Quebec, in 1856, the twelfth of 14 children born to a dry goods merchant. Pease left school at age 14 to work as a telegraph operator, and at that job he learned the importance of fast, timely information. Historian Duncan McDowall has noted that Pease's birth in proximity to the commercial empire that was the St. Lawrence River and his experience with the telegraph gave him a transcontinental vision when in 1883 he was hired as an accountant by the Merchants' Bank of Halifax.

In turning a provincial bank into a proud national business establishment, Edson Pease urged that a branch be established in Montreal in 1887. By absorbing existing banks in

Ontario and Quebec and, bypassing the Prairies, setting up new branches in British Columbia, the Merchants' Bank of Halifax had achieved national scope even before January 2, 1901 when it became the Royal Bank of Canada. Pease used a policy of balancing those areas that saved at low interest rates with those that borrowed at high rates. The western boom, accompanied by immigration, the rise of the wheat staple, and the Laurier era in national politics, gave the bank ample opportunity to build a national infrastructure. In 1899 Pease was appointed a joint general manager of the Bank with David Duncan. Pease was responsible for Montreal westward and was the dominant force in decision making. In 1908 Pease was appointed vice-president of the Royal Bank and, in 1916, assumed a new role as chief executive and managing director. Between 1899 and 1922 when he retired, Pease, by turning to amalgamations within Canada and expansion beyond, set a national scope and international foundation for the Royal Bank.

Mergers made the Royal Bank Canada's leading institution. Between 1910 and 1918, the height of Pease's power, the Royal Bank opened or acquired 526 new bank branches in Canada, including The Traders Bank of Canada in 1912 and the Quebec Bank in 1917. Previous to Pease's arrival, or before he became the dominant force in the Bank, the Merchants' Bank of Halifax had set up connections with Bermuda and with St. Pierre and Miquelon in 1882 and 1884 respectively. In 1899 the Bank opened international branches in New York City and Washington state, and made a major intrusion into sugar-rich Cuba. Between 1907 and 1920, the Royal Bank set up branches in 17 Caribbean islands, 6 South American and 3 Central American countries. It also had export branches in London, Paris, and Barcelona. Under the management of Pease, the Royal not only became a great international bank but set a style that defined a Canadian banking tradition distinct from those of other countries, most noticeably England, France, and the United States. Canadian banks such as the Royal were, in some cases, the only or, certainly, the most significant Canadian presence in several countries in the western hemisphere before the emergence of Canadian diplomatic or consular ties.

Edson Pease, one of the visionary founders of the Bank of Canada as a central institution with controls on national bank note circulation and the regulation of internal credit, foreign exchange, and monetary policy, rigorously campaigned for a central bank as early as 1918, but it was not until after his death in 1930 and after the Great Depression had savaged the social, political, and economic underpinnings of the world that the Bank of Canada was born in 1935.

Canadian banks have long been known for their prestige and stability in international affairs, and Edson Pease played a considerable role in fashioning the Canadian style abroad. Through his creation and direction of Canada's largest bank and his setting in motion the idea of a government-controlled central bank for the regulation of monetary policy, he was a most significant player in Canada's financial coming of age. Edson Pease had an enormous impact, both at home and abroad, on the character and growth of Canadian banking.   *Larry Turner*

The 101 branches of the Toronto-based Traders Bank, Toronto headquarters viewed here, joined the Royal Bank system in 1912. Edson Pease also supervised the merger of the Quebec Bank in 1917 and the Northern Crown Bank in 1918, assuring that his policy of expansion would create a banking conglomerate from sea to sea. [Photo, courtesy Charles J. Humber Collection]

La Famille Casavant

The largest Casavant organ in the world is installed at the Broadway Baptist Church, Fort Worth, Texas. With 10,615 pipes it is one of the world's largest organs. It was installed at a cost of almost four million dollars in 1996. [Photo, courtesy Casavant Frères Ltée]

Piping Music Around the World

THE PIPE ORGAN is universally recognized for its ability to fill vast halls, naves, and theatres with immense, amplified, vibrating sound. The pipe organ is most recognized in religious music where organs grace most of the great cathedrals and thousands of smaller Christian churches around the world. Indeed, the pipe organ became as crucial an addition to church interiors as stained-glass windows. The organ represents a continuing tradition of sacred music in the church and symphonic music elsewhere. Casavant Frères Limitée of St. Hyacinthe, Quebec, is a world leader in organ making: more than 3,700 of its organs constructed since 1880 can be found in churches, opera houses, and music halls in Europe, Africa, Asia, Australia, and the Americas.

While attending a college to study Latin in 1834, Joseph Casavant (1807-1874), a blacksmith by trade, by completing a half-built organ to widespread satisfaction, became the first Canadian-born organ builder of note. By his retirement in 1866, he had built 17 organs including major ones at the Roman Catholic cathedrals of Ottawa and Kingston in 1850 and 1854 respectively. Some of his original pipes still survive at the church of Mont-Ste.-Hilaire, Quebec. Joseph passed on his passion for organ making to sons Samuel-Marie (1850-1929) and Joseph-Claver (1855-1933) who were the founders of the great tradition of Casavant Frères Limitée.

The first Canadian organ maker of note, Joseph Casavant (1807-1874), created the foundations for Casavant Frères Ltée, one of the world's largest organ-making firms, founded in 1879 by sons Claver and Samuel. [Photo, courtesy Casavant Frères Ltée]

The Casavant brothers learned their art from Eusèbe Brodeur, who took over their father's establishment, and from John Abbey in Versailles, France, as well as from experiences gained from visits to organ builders in Europe in 1878-79. They established themselves on the site of their father's original workshop at St. Hyacinthe in 1880 and the business continues to date.

The reputation of Casavant organs was based on ingenuity and craftsmanship. The brothers experimented in the 1890s with adjustable-combination pedals, electro-pneumatic traction, all-electric systems and installed the first of these kinds of organs. Claver became known for his voicing and Samuel for his mechanics. Like string instruments, pipe organs could not be mass-produced in factories but required a level of craftsmanship that involved workshops, master builders, and the voicing of instruments before shipping and after installation.

Late-Victorian and Edwardian Canada witnessed an explosion in the number of churches erected in expanding rural and urban areas. Several manufacturers of pianos attempted to keep up with the demand by also building organs. However, the Casavant tradition grew and Casavant Frères built their first organ in Ontario in 1887, exported their first organ to the U.S. in 1895, and built an organ in the Yukon during the 1898 Gold Rush. They had built 100 organs by 1899, 200 by 1904, and 500 by 1912. The company experimented with manufacturing organs at South Haven, Michigan, from 1912 to 1918, even diversifying into furniture and cabinet making in Quebec.

In 1930 the Casavant brothers were awarded the Grand Prix in Antwerp, Belgium, at an international exhibition where European firms traditionally dominated the competition. After the deaths of the brothers in 1929 and 1933, the company continued operations, but its quality was revived only in the late

In this view, Claver Casavant is seated at the five-manual console of the Casavant organ installed at Toronto's Royal York Hotel in 1929. [Photo, courtesy Casavant Frères Ltée]

From the small town of St. Hyacinthe, Quebec, Casavant Frères Ltée was customizing organs and shipping them worldwide by the 1920s.

This 1927 photograph demonstrates an organ shipment being prepared for Salisbury, Rhodesia. **[Photo, courtesy Casavant Frères Ltée]**

fifties when a team of managers and technicians re-introduced tracker-action organs and built some of the finest and largest organ works around the world.

The Casavant name continues to define excellence in the building and maintenance of organs. The largest organ in the firm's illustrious career was completed in 1996 at Broadway Baptist Church in Fort Worth, Texas; the construction utilized a pioneering method of combining different mechanisms into a replication of a French romantic organ. Called the Rildia Bee O'Bryan Cliburn organ, its 10,615 pipes, 129 independent stops, and 191 ranks make it larger than the great Casavant organs at the Victorian Arts Centre in Melbourne, Australia; the Calvary Episcopal Church in Pittsburgh; and the Basilica de Santa Maria de Guadalupe in Mexico City.

In the 1930s, Casavant Societies were formed in Montreal and Toronto to celebrate and promote "the organ as an instrument in its own right, not necessarily associated with religious services; to make known its rich repertoire from all periods by means of performances of the highest calibre; and to grant bursaries to young organists." The Casavant name literally defines the organ-building tradition in Canada, a continuing art form that pipes music in all ten provinces, all 50 states in the United States, and in many countries around the world.

Larry Turner

Master Military Engineer in Africa

BEFORE THE FIRST World War, a Montreal newspaper poll rated him one of the ten greatest Canadians. Both Winston Churchill and Lord Kitchener considered him one

Percy Girouard
1867-1932

of the most brilliant men of his time. Both summoned him at critical moments to take on work of the greatest importance. His name was Edouard Percy Cranwell Girouard, and he was the son of a French-Canadian Montreal lawyer and an American mother of Irish parentage. Today, it is doubtful if one Canadian in a thousand has heard of him.

Born in 1867, Percy Girouard graduated from the Royal Military College in Kingston, Ontario, at age 19 and accepted employment as a surveyor for the recently completed Canadian Pacific Railway. His two years with the railway gave him the basic experience that would forge his brilliant military career.

By 1888 he had obtained a commission in the British Army Royal Engineers. His first eight years of military service were uneventful. However, being traffic manager of the railways within the Royal Arsenal got him thinking about the ways the twin rails of steel could move armies and their supplies in the event of a major war. His great opportunity came in 1896 when the British government decided to begin the reconquest of the Sudan. Lord Kitchener, the British commander of the Egyptian Army, was ordered to advance up the Nile to Dongola. He had heard of the young French-Canadian's love affair with railways and their potential use in military campaigns. Although the British had earlier failed to realize the military potential of railways, Girouard had studied in every detail their use and management by both the French and Germans during the Franco-Prussian War of 1870.

Lieutenant Girouard's services were requisitioned. When he arrived in Egypt, he was appointed Director of Railways and told to build a railway across the great Sudan desert at the rate of a mile a day. A railway battalion was formed and work began on the mammoth task. Construction averaged 1-1/6 miles of track laid per day, the best day seeing three miles laid. When the 588 miles of track were laid, delivery of supplies began. Kitchener was able to bring to his forming-up place the troops, ammunition, and supplies required to effect the defeat of the Sudanese and the annexation of the Sudan. The Battle of Omdurman achieved these goals. Meanwhile, Girouard, now lieutenant-colonel, was awarded the Distinguished Service Order and also became the president of both the Egyptian state railways and Alexandria harbour. For a young man of 32, he had achieved a great deal.

In October 1899, the Boer War began in South Africa. Girouard was reinstated in the British Army and sent to South Africa as Director of Railways for the British campaign. His reward was a knighthood. After the war, Sir Percy had the task of reorganizing the South African railways so that they could better serve the new nation – the Union of South Africa. When his job was completed, Sir Percy returned to the United Kingdom.

Three years later, he was contacted by Winston Churchill who had met him in South Africa and knew of his work there as well as of his previous success in pushing steel across the Sudanese desert. Churchill, as under-secretary of state for the British colonies, wanted to set up a railway system in Nigeria. He recalled Girouard's accomplishments. "Where is Girouard?" he asked. "Get him."

In order to facilitate the railway, Churchill appointed Sir Percy High Commissioner of Northern Nigeria and promised him a free hand.

In February 1907, Sir Percy Girouard embarked to Nigeria as High Commissioner and Commander-in-Chief. Two years later, he was made Governor and Commander-in-Chief of the whole of British East Africa, a post he held for the next three years. His regime was outstanding: when he resigned in 1912 and decided to re-enter the industrial world, the press expressed dismay.

After the outbreak of World War I, Lord Kitchener, now the secretary of state for war, summoned Girouard into the army with the rank of major-general. A year later, the government formed a directorate of munitions with Lloyd George as the Minister of Munitions. Girouard, Director of the War Office Munitions Department, was made his right-hand man. Unfortunately, Lloyd George and General Girouard did not see eye to eye. Consequently, Girouard left the army, again entering the industrial sphere. He died in 1932 at age 65 and is buried in Brookwood Cemetery, south of Woking in Surrey.

Canada has great reason to be proud of Sir Percy Girouard who, as a young Canadian army engineer, supervised the construction of the railway across the arid African desert at a rate of more than a mile a day.

Strome Galloway

A Royal Engineer Officer sketched the building of Girouard's Sudan railway for Graphics, 1897. [Private collection]

Bruce Chown 1893 - 1986

Battling Pediatric Blood Disease

ERYTHROBLASTOSIS FETALIS, or hemolytic disease of the newborn, can still kill babies. Fortunately, thanks to the work of medical investiga-tors, preeminent among whom was Dr. Bruce Chown, the disease can be prevented.

Bruce Chown was born in 1893 in Winnipeg, a city that would be the site of his medical and scientific career. The name Chown was well-known in his native city as his father, H.H. Chown, was dean of the Manitoba Medical College while Bruce was a youngster.

Bruce enrolled at McGill but, before he completed his studies, World War I began and Chown enlisted in the Canadian Field Artillery. For his bravery under fire in France, he earned the Military Cross.

Upon returning to Canada he completed his BA and then returned to Winnipeg to pursue a medical degree. After graduation in 1922, he completed postgraduate work in pediatrics at Columbia, Cornell, and Johns Hopkins universities. By 1925 he was one of only a few thoroughly trained pediatricians in Canada and the only one in Manitoba.

Initially, Dr. Chown had a private practice but at the same time he was establishing himself as a respected pathologist at Winnipeg Children's Hospital. But by the 1930s he had become a full-time pathologist, and a few years later he was led into the research area in which he made such major contributions.

Hemolytic disease of the newborn occurs because human beings have blood that is either Rh-positive or Rh-negative (this is only one of many complexities in the structure of blood; each of us has a basic blood type of O, A, B, or AB, but each of these types exists as either Rh-positive or Rh-negative). If an Rh-negative mother has an Rh-positive baby (which may well occur if the father is Rh-positive), she may develop antibodies in her blood against Rh-positive blood. If she then has a baby who is Rh-negative, as she is, there will be no difficulties, but if her second (or later) baby is Rh-positive, the antibodies in her blood can damage or destroy the red blood cells of that baby. A child diagnosed as having erythroblastosis fetalis can be affected in many ways, from mild anemia to jaundice and prematurity. In the past, many newborn deaths occurred because of this problem.

The corollary is that nowadays this once devastating disease has become a rarity. The methods of Bruce Chown and the other Winnipeg investigators have been disseminated around the world. Potentially harmful antibodies can be tested for, and, usually, blocked. When erythroblastosis does occur, whole-body transfusions of the affected baby can effectively flush out the offending and sometimes lethal antibodies.

Charles G. Roland

Bruce Chown conducted important research with several co-workers in Winnipeg to elucidate the cause and find a way to control the blood disease caused by the Rhesus factor. [Photo, courtesy Charles G. Roland]

JOHN KORDA P. ENG.

Satellite Pioneer

IT IS 1996. In the sweltering heat of the Mission Director Centre in Kourou, French Guiana, Canada's John Korda is watching the clock count down the final minutes before the launch of yet another telecommunication satellite. As the satellite's Launch Director, on his shoulders rests the final authority to proceed with the launch – and the final responsibility for any failure. But Korda himself is unperturbed – after all, he is wearing his "lucky" polyester suit and it has never before let him down. As the clock nears zero, he takes a final puff on his cigar and then makes his decision....

The space age has brought with it many technological innovations, but perhaps none can match in sheer impact the world-spanning influence of the telecommunication satellite. The commercial satellite industry is now very big business indeed, with total costs per satellite launch sometimes exceeding three hundred million dollars. Perhaps the most important individual in any satellite launch is the Launch Director, the overall manager of the entire process of actually getting a satellite off the ground and into space.

The Launch Director must have a thorough knowledge of the satellite, its rocket vehicle, the weather, the Worldwide Tracking System that enables launchers to keep track of their 'bird," and a myriad other factors. It is the Launch Director who makes the final "go/no go" decision, and it is the Launch Director who is held ultimately responsible for the success or failure of the launch. The Launch Director must have both the strength of will to maintain iron control of the activities of hundreds of people and the intuition to make launch decisions based on little more than a "gut feeling" that the moment is right.

Of all the Launch Directors in the history of the telecommunication industry, only one, Telesat Canada's John Korda, has maintained a career-long record of no satellites lost in launch. For Korda, this achievement is even more spectacular, considering that his career spans virtually the entire history of the commercial telecommunication satellite. In a very real sense, Korda was present at the creation of an industry that today is changing the lives of individuals in every country on the globe.

John Korda was born in Budapest, Hungary, on March 14, 1929. He studied mechanical engineering at university but left Hungary without his degree in December 1956, shortly after Soviet tanks crushed the Hungarian Revolution. Despite the dangers of crossing the border to escape Hungary, Korda felt he had to leave his homeland because he sensed that his opportunities had become limited. Korda can recall to this day the vivid emotions he felt as he left everything behind him and ventured forth into an unknown world.

Accompanied by his wife Hedy (Hedwig), Korda spent several months in Vienna before obtaining his Canadian visa. He and Hedy took a thirty-four hour flight to Montreal, then

Opposite: *An Ariane 4 launcher blasts off from its launch pad in Kourou, French Guiana. John Korda's remarkable record has included working with European, American and Chinese launch vehicles.*
[Photo, courtesy Telesat Canada and Arianespace]

crossed Canada by train. It was this experience that enabled Korda to understand the vastness of Canada, as well as to improve his command of the English language.

At Hedy's urging, Korda returned to university, receiving his engineering degree from the University of British Columbia. In 1963, he began work in Ottawa with Computing Devices Canada, and in 1965 he joined the aerospace engineering department of RCA Montreal (now Spar Aerospace). It was, Korda recalled later, a special era in the history of the telecommunication industry. "Space was a cottage industry back then," he said. "In the sixties, we got to dabble in everything. There were no ready-made experts around." In those years, Korda worked on the experimental Canadian satellites *Alouette* and *ISIS*, and gained a reputation as an individual always willing to learn, to expand his professional horizons.

It was this desire to grow that led Korda to leave Canada in 1969, sensing that greater opportunity lay in the United States. But in 1970, newly formed Telesat Canada hired Korda, who has remained with them ever since. It was a critical time, not only for the Canadian satellite industry, but for the commercialization of space as a whole.

In 1970 most involvement in space was still strictly governmental, fueled by the demands of the Cold War. Space remained ripe for commercial development, but it was Canada and not the great powers that stepped most boldly into the void. The challenge for Canada, as Korda saw it, was that "any fool can build with unlimited funds. The goal was to make space operate as a *business*."

Despite its small population, Canada was the third nation on Earth to have a satellite in space and the first to have a *commercial* domestic operator of geostationary satellites – Telesat Canada. And it was John Korda whom Telesat Canada chose to be Launch Director on every one of its satellite launches. Since his hiring by Telesat, Korda has launched sixteen satellites with no losses, including two satellites for Brazil and two for the United Kingdom, one of which was Britain's first Direct Broadcast Satellite. In addition, Korda became the first western Launch Director to work with the People's Republic of China when a satellite he helped launch for Hong Kong-based Asiasat rose into space atop a Chinese *Long March* rocket.

Now Korda's career is approaching its climax. He was Launch Director for TMI's first mobile satellite, launched early in 1996 on the French *Ariane* rocket. Ever since he was Launch Director for the first *Anik* satellite in 1972, Korda has worn what he calls his "lucky suit," a decidedly unfashionable wide-lapelled polyester two-piece complete with bell-bottomed pants. Korda wore the same suit for the 1996 launch and smoked his trademark cigar. According to plan, the *Ariane* rose from its launchpad in French Guiana to begin yet another perfect satellite launch, the latest in John Korda's career of successes.

Looking back on his life with satellites, Korda believes that over the years he has accumulated a storehouse of experience and not just knowledge. The most important advice he gives to young engineers and scientists interested in careers in space industry is this: "Don't just look for a job. Look for an avocation – a calling. And above all, don't lose your spark, your capacity to *dream*."

Korda is a recognized authority by the satellite insurance industry, a tribute both to his success and to that of Telesat Canada. In a world in which satellite communication has helped to revolutionize politics, economics, and culture, John Korda must be considered one of the most influential figures – a pioneer in an industry whose effects even now are sweeping the globe.

Patrick Hadley

John Korda with an Anik E satellite. The satellite is folded up and is being packed into the fairing of an Ariane 4 launcher. This photo was taken in Kourou, French Guiana, at the European Space Centre. At this point the satellite is fueled. The highly poisonous nature of the propellants explains the need for the safety mask. [Photo, courtesy Telesat Canada and Arianespace]

WHEN JOHN WILLIAM DAWSON arrived as the fifth principal of Montreal's McGill University in 1855, there was clearly a bright future ahead. The 35-year-old native of Pictou, Nova Scotia, had previously served as Superintendent of Education for his home province and was building a reputation as one of North American's leading authorities on fossil plants, but few could have predicted the breadth of influence that Dawson would exert during his 38-year tenure as head of McGill.

JOHN WILLIAM DAWSON

Trailblazer of Modern Science

As an administrator, teacher, proponent of educational progress, and leader in civic affairs, he oversaw its growth from fledgling facility to world-class university. A groundbreaking geologist and paleobotanist as well as the author of more than 400 scientific papers and books, Dawson was destined to become the first Canadian-born scientist of international stature, laying down much of the foundation within his country for twentieth century science.

Dawson's fascination with natural history dated back to his boyhood when he began collecting fossil plants from the Nova Scotia coalfields as well as shells, insects, and rare birds. His discovery of fossil leaves in a shale which he and his schoolmates had excavated and shaved to make slate pencils earned favourable notice from a local authority. "And from that time on," Dawson would later observe, "I became a geological collector."

In the summer of 1841, when Great Britain's foremost geologist, Sir Charles Lyell, paid a trip to Pictou's famed coalfields, the 21-year-old Dawson was selected as his principle guide. Lyell would become a lifelong mentor, inspiring Dawson's studies in Natural Science at Edinburgh University. Dawson returned to Canada in 1847 with a Scottish wife (Margaret Mercer) and qualifications as North America's first trained exploration geologist.

With a growing reputation as a scholar and lecturer, he was appointed Superintendent of Education for Nova Scotia in 1850. Over the next three years he worked tirelessly to raise school standards and founded a normal school and, in his off hours, he accumulated geological data on his travels around the province. In the same year that he assumed the principalship at McGill (1855), Dawson published one of his most acclaimed books, the comprehensive *Acadian Geology*, and was narrowly passed over for the position of chair of natural history at Edinburgh University.

He found a significant challenge waiting for him at McGill, an institution with low enrollment, minimal resources, and inadequate buildings. Dawson managed to gain the support of Montreal's business community and thereby transformed it, over the next 38 years, into one of Canada's leading universities.

A brilliant professor of natural history and agriculture, he dedicated himself to building a strong faculty in the physical and biological sciences and engineering, presided over the opening of the McGill University Library and the acclaimed Peter Redpath Museum of Science, and waged a successful 20-year fight to have a woman admitted into McGill's bachelor of arts program. He became the first president of the Royal Society of Canada (1882) and was long-time president of the Botanical Society of Montreal. Well-known Canadian humorist and McGill economics professor Stephen Butler Leacock once observed, "More than that of any man or group of men, McGill is his work."

Frustrated that his administrative commitments at McGill left him with little spare time for geological field trips, Dawson nevertheless published about 10 scientific papers per year at McGill while establishing himself among the top world scientists of his day.

A devout Christian, teetotaller, and anti-Darwinist, Dawson dedicated more than 100 articles to the relationship between religion and science, writing in 1860 that "a godless view of nature would lead to the degradation of man."

His refusal to accept the emerging theories on evolution and the presence of earlier continental glaciers across Canada led to Dawson's disrepute among a new generation of scientists. However, these failings should in no way discount his contribution as a leading nineteenth century expert on fossil plants and trailblazer of modern science in Canada (pushing for the institution of higher degrees, lifelong research, and the publication of research results).

Known in international circles as "Principal Dawson," he was the only person to ever serve as president of both the British and American Associations For the Advancement of Science, was awarded the Lyell Medal by the Geographical Society of London in 1881 for outstanding achievements, and was knighted by Queen Victoria in 1884 for his public services.

Along the way, he inspired many young Canadians to choose a career path in science, including sons George Mercer Dawson, geologist, who served as director of the Geographical Survey of Canada from 1895 to 1901, and William Bell Dawson, surveyor, who is best known as engineer and superintendent of the Tidal Survey, Canadian Department of Marine and Fisheries, 1893-1924.   *Michael Beggs*

1820 - 1899

Canada's 20th century scientific community owes much to the foundation created by John William Dawson (1820-1899), the first Canadian-born scientist of worldwide reputation. [Photo, courtesy National Archives of Canada/C-49822]

Roloff Beny

Artist of Canvas and Camera

1924 - 1984

ROLOFF BENY was 13 years old when he sold his first painting and 15 when he won a four-week scholarship to the Banff Summer School of Fine Arts. He wasn't known as Roloff then but as "Wilfred," the second son of Charles Beny, a car dealer in Medicine Hat, Alberta. At Banff he met other art students and discovered, "I was not necessarily an oddity for wanting to devote my life to painting."

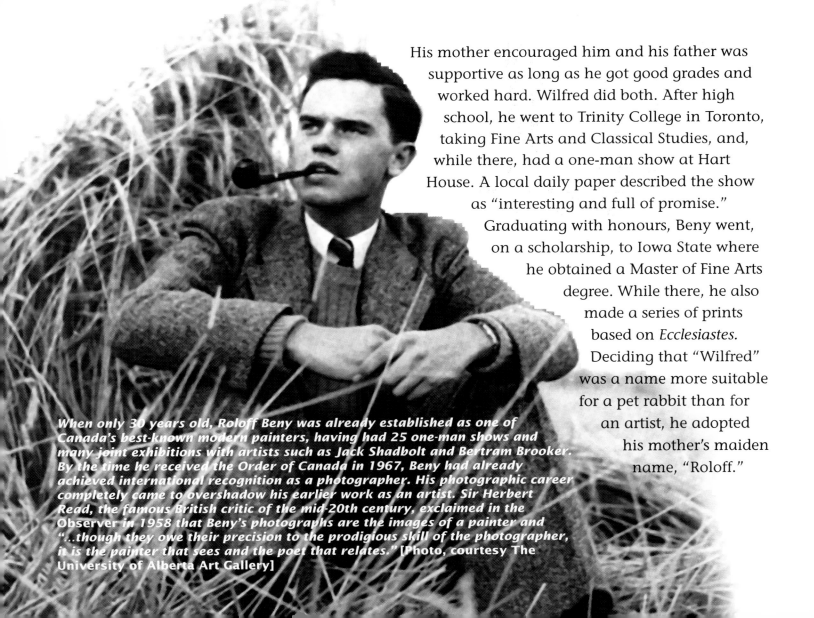

His mother encouraged him and his father was supportive as long as he got good grades and worked hard. Wilfred did both. After high school, he went to Trinity College in Toronto, taking Fine Arts and Classical Studies, and, while there, had a one-man show at Hart House. A local daily paper described the show as "interesting and full of promise." Graduating with honours, Beny went, on a scholarship, to Iowa State where he obtained a Master of Fine Arts degree. While there, he also made a series of prints based on *Ecclesiastes*. Deciding that "Wilfred" was a name more suitable for a pet rabbit than for an artist, he adopted his mother's maiden name, "Roloff."

When only 30 years old, Roloff Beny was already established as one of Canada's best-known modern painters, having had 25 one-man shows and many joint exhibitions with artists such as Jack Shadbolt and Bertram Brooker. By the time he received the Order of Canada in 1967, Beny had already achieved international recognition as a photographer. His photographic career completely came to overshadow his earlier work as an artist. Sir Herbert Read, the famous British critic of the mid-20th century, exclaimed in the Observer in 1958 that Beny's photographs are the images of a painter and "...though they owe their precision to the prodigious skill of the photographer, it is the painter that sees and the poet that relates." [Photo, courtesy The University of Alberta Art Gallery]

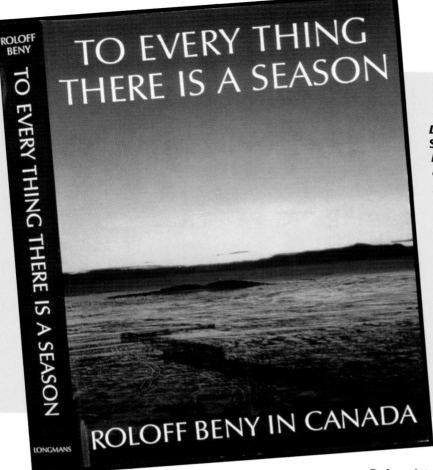

ROLOFF BENY

TO EVERY THING THERE IS A SEASON

TO EVERY THING THERE IS A SEASON

LONGMANS · ROLOFF BENY IN CANADA

Dust jacket for **To Everything There is a Season: Roloff Beny in Canada.** *Published to commemorate Canada's centennial, this lavish publication was produced by Thames and Hudson Limited for Longmans Canada in 1967. The 56 colour plates, 144 photogravure plates and 10 maps and line drawings are interwoven by commentary from famous historical figures and contemporary Canadians. Other countries such as Japan, India, Italy, Iran, and Iceland were lavishly photographed by Beny and celebrated in coffee table books making Beny famous as a globetrotting photographer with a painter's eye.*

Fellowships took him next to Columbia University and the Institute of Fine Arts at New York University where, at one group exhibit, critics, New York papers, and the *Art News* singled out his work. He also sold some prints of his *Ecclesiastes* to Harvard, Yale, the Library of Congress, and a complete set of his lithographs won first prize at the Brooklyn Museum.

In 1948 he was invited to Greece by his Trinity College mentor, Dr. Homer Thompson, head of the American school of Classical Studies in Athens, who appreciated Roloff's background in classical studies and talent as an artist. Roloff loved Greece but, before the year ended, he was in Venice where he sought out Peggy Guggenheim, a famous American collector of contemporary art.

Beny was particularly adept at meeting and charming rich and famous people, and Peggy became a supporter and friend. She arranged a one-man show for him that attracted many well-known people. Roloff admitted in his diary, "People of power, position and accomplishment intrigue me because I admire them and because they inspire me to do better."

A bout with rheumatic fever in 1950 brought Roloff home to Lethbridge where his parents had resettled, and he began work on *Aegean Notebook*, the first of his 16 books. *Mayfair* magazine wrote about the book and it sold out.

His health restored, Beny moved to Toronto where John and Signy Eaton arranged a one-man show of his work. He soon moved on to Paris and held a one-man show at the Palais Royale. Other shows were scheduled for Milan and London, prompting Reuter's News agency to report, "The Alberta boy is a minor rage in European art circles."

Another fellowship took him back to New York where, to bolster his income, Roloff also did fashion photography. He had first become serious about photography in 1951 when he and an ex-roommate at Trinity had travelled through Europe, and Roloff had taken photographs if he couldn't stay to sketch a scene or building. Gradually Roloff had found he was taking more than "mere snapshots for future reference. I still saw them as an adjunct to my painting but began to . . . compose my photographs as I did my drawings."

In January 1956, he held his first photographic exhibition in London. He also met the founder of Thames and London Publishing Company and suggested a photographic volume "... on the art and architecture of the Mediterranean world with essays by famous authors on their favourite parts of that world." He suggested such people as Jean Cocteau, Sir Herbert Read, and Bernard Berenson whom he had met earlier and photographed, recording in his diary, "After all, I had no reputation as a photographer and if the book was to sell, I needed those names because my ambitions for the book were enormous, megalomaniac and sumptuous."

Two years later *The Thrones of Earth and Heaven* was lavishly launched at London, New York, and Rome. Beny planned the launchings with an eye to publicity and promotion, suggesting, in London for example, that guests dress in red, black, and white to reflect the colour scheme of the book jacket. He even served colour-coordinated refreshments. The crowds came and *Thrones* became an artistic success, winning the International Prize for Design at the Leipzig Book Fair and numerous other commendations.

From then on, Beny concentrated on photography, seldom mentioning his former artistic career. By the time *Thrones* was published, he had settled in Rome where he made friends with the famous and near famous, dressed eccentrically, threw extravagant parties, and worked hard photographing for a number of leading journals and magazines. Growing bored, he proposed a book based on the ancient civilization of Greece, *A Time of Gods*.

Next, he was sponsored for a round-the-world trip to make a photographic interpretation of the travel book, *Pleasure of Ruins*, the first book to introduce his colour work. This was followed by his book on Canada, *To Everything There Is a Season*, which appeared in time for the nation's centennial in 1967. At its launch in Toronto, he met Jack McClelland, who later became his publisher for several volumes and his friend. *Japan in Colour* was also published in 1967 and he donated some of his early art works to the University of Lethbridge.

McClelland published *India* in 1969 and a book on Ceylon in 1971. On its completion he was asked by the president of Italy, "When are you going to do my country?" In 1974, *In Italy* appeared, the launch being spread over eight days.

Beny then got the Shah and Shahbanou of Iran to commission him for two books on their country. He became a close friend of theirs over the next four years, but as biographer Mitchell Crites, who travelled with him throughout Iran, recalled in his 1994 book, *Visual Journeys*, the friendship made him enemies everywhere because "imperial patronage made him arrogant and demanding."

After completion of the second volume in 1978, further books on Iran were being considered by Beny and McClelland but only months later, the Shah was forced into exile. Beny met Egyptian President Anwar Sadat to seek support for a book on that country but the project was stymied by government officials. The Alberta government also backed away from a proposal to secure his archives when opposition was voiced by the press, public, and even the art community who "resented Roloff's flamboyant expatriate status." Alberta bought only his Canadian work.

In 1980, an exhibition featuring photographs from his Canadian book was shown in Rome and in 1981, the two books, *Churches of Rome* and *Odyssey, Mirror of the Mediterranean*, were published. In 1982, a solution was found to have his archives sent to the University of Lethbridge while he drove himself that year and the next to complete five separate projects: revisiting Greece for *The Gods of Greece*, doing photography for *Rajasthan: Land of Kings*, photographing Iceland, and working on the architectural and people volumes of his own *Visual Journeys* project. "I'm a workaholic," he noted in his diary. "Until they cart me away, I'll still turn out books." Another entry reflected his attitude towards work. "My books are my lifelines – the ladder from the well of my loneliness."

When he made these entries he had no reason to believe that he soon would be "carted away." Shortly before any of these projects were published, Roloff died of a cerebral hemorrhage in the bath of his Rome apartment on March 16, 1984. His ashes were buried, along with copies of his published books, beside his mother in the family plot at Medicine Hat.

Mel James

Roloff Beny, left, at the National Gallery of Canada, Ottawa, with Charles Comfort, Gallery Director, October 4, 1964. The National Gallery purchased, in 1948/49 Beny's Ecclesiastes *series of prints.* [Photo, The University of Lethbridge Art Gallery]

Bluenose & Angus Walters

International Sailing Champions

IN 1937 the schooner *Bluenose* was reproduced on the Canadian ten cent piece in tribute to a sailing vessel that had brought international fame to Canada as the greatest "salt bank" racer ever to ply the waters of the Grand Banks. Nearly sixty years later, the Canadian Mint is still producing this coin.

The *Bluenose's* claim to fame began in 1921.

In 1920, Senator W.H. Dennis, owner of the Halifax *Herald*, had initiated and sponsored a trophy to be awarded to the sailing champion of the North American fishing fleet, thereby formalizing the race rivalry that had been going on unofficially for years between the fishermen of Lunenburg, Nova Scotia, and Gloucester, Massachusetts. A $4,000 prize accompanied the trophy.

The Lunenburgers were stung when the first race, held in October 1920, went to the Americans. Consequently, in 1921, according to historian C.J. Snider, "Some good Halifax sports joined with thrifty Lunenburgers and a few central Canada 'angels'" to build a vessel that would regain the International Fisherman's Trophy and asked William J. Roué, a local sailing enthusiast with a reputation for designing yachts, to produce a sure winner. In March 1921, the *Bluenose* was launched at the town's Smith and Rhuland Shipyards where a doubtful senior partner of the yard commented, "I don't think nothing of her. We built her as close to the Roué lines as we knew how. If she's a success, he gets the praise. If she's a failure, he gets the blame."

One not sharing that view was Angus Walters, the part owner and future captain of the *Bluenose* who had gone to sea on his father's schooner in 1895 at the age of 13 and now, 26 years later, had become a respected, salty-tongued skipper known for hoisting plenty of sail and for his uncanny ability to find fish.

Walters, a part owner and captain of three schooners before the *Bluenose*, had some design changes made before taking her to fish off the Grand Banks (only proven fishing vessels could compete) and, in October, sailed to Halifax for the trials against other Canadian vessels. *Bluenose* won, proving to be exceptionally strong on windward tacks, and then met America's finest, the *Elsie*, in a best two-out-of-three series over a 40-mile course near Halifax. Interest ran high as newsmen from major papers across the continent and thousands of Nova Scotians watched the *Bluenose* easily win two in a row.

Above: *The American schooner,* **Gertrude L. Thebaud,** *challenged the* **Bluenose** *on several occasions between 1930 and 1938, the* **Bluenose** *winning four out of seven races. The last race was off Gloucester, Massachusetts, in 1938, when the* **Bluenose** *was 17 years old and its skipper a young 56 years.* [Photo, courtesy Charles J. Humber Collection]

Right: *Painter, Nicholas John Henderson, born in Jones Falls, Ontario, was able to reproduce the* **Bluenose** *in meticulous detail because, as friend of ship captain, Angus Walters, he was able to sail aboard the* **Bluenose** *before he painted her in 1930. Subsequently reproduced on a calendar, this pulchritudinous rendition of the* **Bluenose** *became the inspiration for immortalizing Canada's best-known sailing vessel on the Canadian dime.* [Painting, courtesy Nick Henderson/Photo, courtesy Geoff Webster]

Angus Walters (1882-1968) was a fisherman born in Lunenberg, Nova Scotia. Made skipper of the Bluenose in 1920 because of his ability to find fish and get the most speed out of his vessels, he and the Bluenose achieved much international fame in a decade of sailing races and were inseparable until he was forced to sell the Bluenose in 1942. [Photo, courtesy Maritime Museum of the Atlantic, Halifax, Nova Scotia]

This victory over Gloucester's best now prompted the Americans to build two vessels, the *Henry Ford* eventually winning out to compete in Gloucester in October 1922. Light winds prompted officials to call off the first race as the two schooners approached the starting line, but both skippers, who knew each other well, decided to race anyway. The *Ford* won but exceeded the six-hour time limit, the same thing happening in a second race. A few days later, in a stiff breeze, the *Bluenose* proved to be an easy champion, the *Ford* breaking her topmast in the second encounter.

For the 1923 contest, Gloucester built the *Columbia* to be captained by Newfoundland-born Ben Pine, a much respected skipper of the Gloucester fleet. In the first race off Halifax, the *Bluenose* was edged into shallow water and, to avoid being run aground, Walters, as permitted by the law of the sea, manoeuvred his vessel so that the *Columbia* had to swing away or collide. In the partial collision that ensued, the *Bluenose* dragged the *Columbia* for a short distance before breaking free and winning the race.

That controversial finish was nothing compared to the statement that followed the next race. On the night before, officials had decided that all navigation buoys be passed on the seaward side and sent copies of their decision in sealed envelopes to the schooners. Walters saw the letter on his bunk but did not open it and failed to pass one of the buoys as ordered. He won the race but, during the banquet that followed, he and Pine were summoned and told that as a result of a complaint by a U.S. committee member, the *Columbia* was being declared the winner, thus making a third race necessary. Walters' refusal made front-page instead of sports-page headlines across the continent. His suggestion that the *Bluenose* be credited with the first race and that two more be held if necessary to determine the winner was, in turn, refused. When officials warned him he would lose the prize money, Walters' reply, according to biographer G.J. Gillespie, "didn't mince any words." "You can go to hell with it," he said. "I'm sailing back to Lunenburg."

For the next eight years there was no further contest for the trophy which remained in Lunenburg. The *Bluenose* plied her trade as a "salt banker" until 1930 when Gloucester, celebrating its 300th anniversary, changed the rules so that the *Bluenose* could take part in races for the Lipton Cup established earlier by Sir Thomas Lipton, the tea magnate and sailing enthusiast, for competition among Gloucester vessels.

The Gloucester group entered a new schooner, the *Gertrude L. Thebaud*, and, in a light wind, the *Bluenose* lost the first race. In the second, Walters was ahead when a shift in the wind caught the *Bluenose* skipper off guard and the *Thebaud* won. "I didn't use my head," Walters declared afterwards. "I should have kept the *Thebaud* covered but I split tacks and lost the race."

The *Bluenose* still held the International Fisherman's Trophy, however, and the *Thebaud* victory made the Gloucester people eager to recapture it. A competition was held off Halifax in 1931. This time the *Bluenose* won the first race by almost three miles and the second by two.

The Depression scuppered further races, the *Bluenose* plying her trade off the Grand Banks until the summer of 1933 when she sailed up the St. Lawrence and into Lake Michigan to represent Canada at the Chicago Century of Progress Exposition. On her return, she docked in Toronto for another welcome and stayed there over the winter months. In 1934, it was suggested that the *Bluenose* represent Canada at the 1935 Silver Jubilee celebrations of the reign of King George V and Queen Mary, and, while at Spithead, Walters was invited to the Royal Yacht where the King presented him with that vessel's mainsail.

On her homeward trip, the *Bluenose* encountered such violent storms that she almost sank. Major repairs were required after she finally limped into Lunenburg. The following year she was fitted with diesel engines to enable her to compete with the powered vessels being introduced to the fishing fleets. Walters also faced another challenge for, as the Depression continued, prices dropped so low that there was no money to be made in fishing. When dealers refused to pay a quarter of a cent more per pound, Walters, as president of the skipper organization, tied up the Lunenburg fleet in 1937 – a move that won the support of the fish handlers in Halifax and the public in general and made the dealers quickly offer concessions for a settlement.

In 1938 Boston wanted a race between the *Bluenose* and *Thebaud* held off its coast, promising an additional $8,000 besides the prize money – a handsome sum in Depression times. It was agreed that, in a best three out of five series, two of the races would take place at Boston and any subsequent races at Gloucester. All five were required before the 17-year-old *Bluenose* won the final race at Gloucester three minutes ahead of its rival. The prize money, however, was not forthcoming. Eventually only $5,000 of the additional funds was received. "I think that put a crimp in the fisherman's races for good," Walters later observed.

The outbreak of World War II most assuredly did. Still owing $7,200 for the diesel engines and gear installed in 1936, the owners showed little interest in saving the *Bluenose* from the auction block. A suggestion that the Canadian government take over the *Bluenose* was ignored and a plan to save her by selling shares to Canadians for one dollar each with no dividends paid also came to nothing. Walters scraped together the $7,200 to pay the bill and become the major shareholder. By 1942, however, with the vessel moored idly at dockside, Walters agreed to sell her to the West Indies Trading Company to carry freight between the islands.

Walters later recalled that, when he cast her lines off in May 1942, "There was a lump in my throat. Somehow I knew it was goodbye. We'd seen a lot together in fair weather and foul, and the *Bluenose* was like part of me."

He was right. It was goodbye. On January 30, 1946, a wire flashed the news that the *Bluenose* had struck a reef on the Haitian coast and sunk, leaving Captain Walters with only memories of the *Bluenose* until his own death at his native Lunenburg in 1969.   *Mel James*

EMMA ALBANI

1850 - 1930

*Queen of Europe's
Opera Houses*

ALTHOUGH BORN and christened Marie-Louise-Cécile-Emma Lajeunesse at Chambly, Québec, it was as Emma Albani that she became Canada's first internationally acclaimed diva. A favourite of Queen Victoria, she visited Buckingham Palace and Balmoral Castle, sang at the White House and before the Tsar of Russia at St. Petersburg, won the hearts of Berliners for her Wagnerian performances, and was a principal star at London's Covent Garden for more than two decades. Today, however, Canada's premiere nineteenth century diva is virtually unknown.

Emma, the daughter of a music teacher, studied music four hours a day from the age of five. At eight, she was "... able to read at sight almost all of the works of the old masters as well as modern composers." After her mother's death when Emma was seven, she attended the Couvent du Sacré Coeur in Montréal where her father was a music teacher. There she became so proficient as a composer, pianist, organist, harpist, and singer that she was not allowed to compete for the music prizes.

She considered being a nun, but the Mother Superior, Madame Trincano, persuaded her to pursue a musical career. "God has given you a beautiful voice," she told Emma, "and I think it is clearly your duty to use it."

By then she had already performed a number of times, one of the most auspicious being a concert for the oldest son of Queen Victoria when, as the Prince of Wales in 1860, he officially opened Victoria Bridge in Montréal. Over the next 40 years he heard her sing many times and, in 1901, as King Edward VII, invited her to sing at a private family funeral for Queen Victoria.

In 1865, at age 18, Emma graduated from the convent. Her father then moved the family to Albany, New York, to further develop her skills. There she became the soprano soloist, organist, and choir director of St. Joseph's Church until 1868 when the bishop personally helped organize two concerts to raise funds so that she could study in Paris. Later, in Milan, she studied with Maestro Francesco Lamperti, who taught her for several months before agreeing that she could make her grand debut as Amina in Vincenzo Bellini's *La Sonnambula*

Above: *Emma Albani's autograph, 1896, the year of her nationally acclaimed transcontinental tour from Halifax to Vancouver.* [Photo, courtesy Charles J. Humber collection]

The beautiful voice of Emma Albani was heard round the world in a career spanning more than four decades. The diva performed at Paris' Elysée Palace, Milan's La Scala, London's Covent Garden and Crystal Palace, and Scotland's Balmoral Castle. Well known throughout all of Europe as well as Russia, India, Ceylon, Australia, New Zealand, South Africa, and Mexico, she sang coast to coast in Canada and the U.S.A. The Prince of Wales while visiting Canada in 1860 heard her sing and, never forgetting her voice, persuaded her to perform at Windsor Castle for the private family funeral, in 1901, of his mother, and Emma's friend, Queen Victoria. This oil on canvas, Marie-Emma Lajeunesse, Madame Albani *was rendered in 1877 by William Hicock Low.* [Photo, courtesy Musée du Québec 49.83]

Emma Albani wearing the cross given her by Queen Victoria after a command performance at Windsor Castle in 1874. [Photo, courtesy National Library of Canada]

at Messina in Sicily. After she had rehearsed her first aria, the conductor told Emma, "My child, your success is assured and it will be very great." Her elocution master suggested she use the name of a famous old Italian family whose members had all died except for an aging Cardinal, and it was as Emma Albani that Sicilian audiences cheered her. When she sang the same opera at Aci Reale, a reviewer wrote, "Fancy the *Sonnambula,* that superhuman and inimitable idyll, with this young creature in it from beyond the Atlantic, and yet with such a vast perception of Italian art."

After a triumphant season in Malta in 1870-71, where she starred in Rossini's *The Barber of Seville*, she returned to Aci Reale for a benefit performance which became two performances when the crowds broke down the doors to hear the rehearsal. Following the benefit, shops were shut, and the Mayor and Council, along with some 5,000 people, saw her off at the station, bound for England to meet Frederick Gye, manager of Covent Garden, who decided she should make her debut at the start of the 1872 season.

Success followed success in London. It began with *La Sonnambula,* which she later sang in Moscow and again, in 1874, in her operatic debut at New York's Academy of Music. In 1875 she played Elsa in Wagner's *Lohengrin.* Always the perfectionist, before appearing in that role she went to Germany for two weeks of intense study with a German conductor.

When she visited Berlin in 1882 to play Elsa, Kaiser Wilhelm I summoned her to his box and named her a Royal Court Singer. A reviewer wrote that Madame Albani, in the German tongue, conjured up, "The most poetical, but likewise most difficult character of Elsa with such consummate mastery that the audience is aroused by her to enthusiasm."

By then, Emma was Madame Gye in private life, having married Frederick's son Ernest in 1878. Later that year, Ernest became manager of Covent Garden after his father's death. Emma continued using her professional name and was in much demand not just for operas but also for oratorio festivals at which she was the star soloist. These festivals, held in many

English cities, were even more popular than operas.

In 1883 a second American tour included an invitation to sing at the White House and a visit to Montréal where she shook hands with up to 2,000 people at a city hall reception. "The afternoon was like a holiday, shops were closed, crowds were in the streets and we were cheered all the way back as we returned from the Hôtel de Ville to our hotel," she recalled in her autobiography, *Forty Years of Song*.

After a performance in Montréal, one reviewer wrote, "A voice of exquisite sweetness and wonderful power, compass and freedom, aided by an art so great that it concealed every evidence of itself filled the room and enthralled those who heard it." In 1889, however, George Bernard Shaw, reviewing her performance in Handel's *Messiah* found her "... too bent on finishing 'effectively' to finish well."

Despite Shaw, more tours followed in various European countries and in North America where, at the New York's Metropolitan Opera in 1890, she became the first Desdemona in Verdi's *Otello*. She remained as the Met's leading soprano for the 1891-92 season and played Senta in *The Flying Dutchman* before concluding her appearances in opera in the United States. She continued singing operas in England and Europe for another four years, winning praise especially for her performance as Isolde in *Tristan and Isolde* at Covent Garden in 1896 – the last year she sang opera. One reviewer wrote, "To hear the music sung perfectly in tune was alone a treat that was well nigh a revelation."

Concert tours continued for more than another decade before she retired: Austria, Australia, and South Africa in 1898, tours of Canada in 1903 and '06 and of Ceylon and India in 1907 as well as South Africa and New Zealand. Retirement, however, was not kind to Emma and her husband. Even though she had earned considerable sums during her years as a performer, some bad investments forced them into near poverty following her retirement.

In order to live comfortably, Emma sold some of the many gifts she had received from royalty and others. She also sang in music halls and taught voice, but as these steps failed to enable Emma and Ernest to maintain their home in London's Kensington district, they rented it out and leased a smaller one. In 1920 the British government granted them an annual pension of 100 pounds. When Prime Minister Mackenzie King visited her in 1924, he was shocked to find Emma "old and feeble and dependent ... married to a man named Gye who is quite as helpless as herself." He tried to get a pension approved in Canada but lacked a majority government and the motion was defeated. He appealed to the Québec government, pointing out, "her name has been too splendidly associated with the name of our country to let it suffer this kind of eclipse" but the appeal was ignored.

Following the death of Ernest in 1925, her financial situation prompted two major concerts: one in London that featured some of her protégées and the other staged at the fort in the town of her birth, Chambly. The latter, sponsored by the Montréal newspaper, *La Presse*, raised $4095.55 and that, along with the proceeds of the London event, enabled her to move back to her Kensington home and live in comfort until her death in 1930.

Mel James

Daniel David Palmer

THE PRACTICES and traditions of the healing arts known today as chiropractic have been exercised for centuries. "Adjusting" the osseous (bony) structures of the body, particularly the spine, skull, and pelvis, has long been in regular use to treat various ailments of the human body. The specific modern healing art called chiropractic began in 1895 in the small Mississippi River town of Davenport, Iowa. Here Daniel David Palmer, a 50-year-old Canadian immigrant, began the profession as practised today and devoted his entire life to establishing it as a rational science, art, and philosophy.

D.D. Palmer's father, Thomas, was born in 1823 in Prince Edward Island. A shoemaker, then grocer, Thomas eventually became a Port Perry, Ontario, school director and local postmaster. He and his wife, Catherine McVay, had three sons and three daughters. Daniel David, the eldest, was born March 7, 1845.

By the time he was eleven, D.D. had acquired the equivalent of an eighth grade education and was well into the study of high school subjects when his education was cut short. His father's business failed in 1856, and the family moved to the United States, leaving D.D. and his younger brother, nine-year-old Thomas, in Canada.

In 1865, D.D. and Thomas, now aged 20 and 18 respectively, left Port Perry because of lack of opportunity and walked south to Whitby, Ontario, on the shores of Lake Ontario. There they bought boat passage to Buffalo, New York. Three months later they rejoined their parents and siblings in Iowa.

Shortly after his arrival, 21-year-old D.D. became master in a one-room schoolhouse on the prairies. Over the ensuing years, three children were born to D.D. and his second wife, Louvenia. Despite successes with farming, beekeeping, and horticulture, D.D moved the family and married for a third time when Louvenia died.

It was during his stay in Illinois that D.D. became interested in spiritualism in addition to the art of "magnetic healing" which held that a magnetic field emanated from the body and that magnetic healers, by passing their hands over their patients' bodies, could influence this field and thereby the health of their patients. D.D. studied this and set up practice in Iowa as

Founder of Chiropractic

1845 - 1913

In 1946, the town of Port Perry, Ontario, celebrated an "old boy" by unveiling a monument to honour Dr. Daniel David Palmer, born there in 1845 and the founder of chiropractic. Canada Post Corporation, to celebrate 100 years of chiropractic, in 1995, honoured D.D. Palmer with a commemorative stamp. Today, the Scugog Shores Museum Village in Port Perry is currently negotiating with the American Chiropractic Association, owners of the Palmer homestead, to purchase this historic home and move it to the site of the Port Perry Heritage Village. This photo of the bearded D.D. Palmer, who died in 1913 at age 68, was taken in the early 1900s. [Photo, courtesy the Canadian Memorial Chiropractic College, Toronto]

D.D. Palmer, Vital Healer.

In his book *The Palmers*, Dr. Daniel Palmer, D.D.'s grandson, outlined his grandfather's personal working style:

> *D.D. described his method of practising magnetic healing. He would develop a sense of being positive within his own body, sickness being negative. He would draw his hands over the area of pain and with a sweeping motion stand aside, shaking his hand and fingers vigorously taking away the pain as if it were drops of water.*

A lapel pin of the Palmer School of Chiropractic dated 1923. [Photo, courtesy Lucille Elliot Longfield]

D.D. was apparently financially successful as a magnetic healer, averaging $3,000 to $4,000 per year income at a time when a suit cost $6.00 and a hotel room $2.00 a day.

Just as D.D.'s natural intellectual affinity attracted him to the concepts of magnetic healing, the creation of the healing art now called chiropractic came about from the melding of the scientific and the metaphysical.

On September 18, 1895, the profession of chiropractic was born when D.D. performed his first adjustment on a janitor in the building where D.D. had his office. As he reported in *The Chiropractor's Adjuster*:

> *Harvey Lillard...had been so deaf for 17 years that he could not hear the racket of a wagon on the street or the ticking of a watch. I made inquiry as to the cause of his deafness and was informed that when he was exerting himself in a cramped, stooping position, he felt something give in his back and immediately became deaf. An examination showed a vertebra racked from its normal position. I reasoned that if the vertebra was replaced, the man's hearing should be restored. With this object in view, a half hour talk persuaded Mr. Lillard to allow me to replace it. I racked it into position by using the spinous process as a lever and soon the man could hear as before. There was nothing "accidental" about this as it was accomplished with an object in view, and the expected result was obtained. There was nothing "crude" about this adjustment; it was specific so much so that no chiropractor has equalled it.*

Following the proceeding, D.D. Palmer began exploring and developing his radical theory that suggested decreased nerve flow may be the cause of disease and that misplaced spinal vertebrae may cause pressure on various nerves thereby impeding impulses. If the spinal column were correctly positioned, he reasoned, the body would be healthy. The name he coined for the art was chiropractic from the Greek *cheir* meaning "hand" and *praktos* meaning "done."

Individuals with all kinds of health problems were responding to Palmer's new "hand treatments" – those with sciatica, asthma, skin conditions, digestive problems, migraine headaches, epilepsy ... the list went on and on.

In 1897 D.D. decided to teach his "big idea" to others and opened a chiropractic school. By 1902 fifteen people had graduated from the Palmer Infirmary and Chiropractic Institute. One of the earliest graduates was D.D.'s son, Bartlett Joshua (B.J.) Palmer, who would later become as memorable a figure in chiropractic history as his father, becoming known as the Developer of Chiropractic.

The turn of the century was a time of rapid change in health care as alternatives to allopathic medicine gained ground. Chiropractors, unlike medical doctors, were not officially licensed by government. It was not surprising, therefore, that Palmer, in 1906, was the first of hundreds of chiropractors convicted of practising medicine without a licence. He was sentenced to 105 days in jail. After serving 23 days, he paid the $350 fine to be released. But while in his cell he wrote prophetically:

> The advancement of all sciences, especially where there has been such a radical change, have been attended with persecution. In fact, it seems necessary in order to bring it to public attention. Thousands are now talking about chiropractic and its discoverer who never heard of it before. The jailing of D.D. Palmer, a man who is ahead of the times, a man who dares to think, even in a cell, where the walls are iron and the floor the best cement, will not check the onward march of the science he has discovered.

After his release from prison, Palmer opened new schools along the West coast, although most of them were short-lived. In spring 1911, D.D. took up residence in Los Angeles where he continued to lecture and write. His two most prominent works were *The Science of Chiropractic* and *The Chiropractor's Adjuster*.

D.D. Palmer died on October 20, 1913, at home in Los Angeles. The cause of death was typhoid fever; he had been ill for 28 days.

The singleness of purpose toward which he dedicated his life, his quest for the cause of disease and the restoration of health, was an all-consuming mistress. At his memorial service his long-time patient and confidant, Rev. Samuel H. Weed, eulogised:

> I firmly believe that God raises up men for special purposes, and that he raised up D.D. Palmer for the purpose of giving to the world this science in the beginnings....

Ralph Sciullo

1995 marked the 150th anniversary of the birth of Daniel David Palmer. It was also the 100th anniversary of the founding of chiropractic and the 50th anniversary of the opening of the Canadian Chiropractic College in Toronto. The 1,000 lb memorial bust was rededicated in Palmer Memorial Park at the corner of Water and Queen Streets in Port Perry, Ontario, in 1995. [Photo, courtesy Port Perry Star/Jeff Mitchell]

DANIEL·DAVID
PALMER

FOUNDER·OF
CHIROPRACTIC
SEPTEMBER·18
·1895·
BORN·PORT·PERRY
MARCH·7·1845
·DIED·
OCTOBER·20·1913

"I·HAVE·NEVER·CONSIDERED
IT·BENEATH·MY·DIGNITY·TO
DO·ANYTHING·TO·RELIEVE
HUMAN·SUFFERING"

NOBEL LAUREATES

Eight Scientific Researchers Who Discovered...

GUESSING THE NUMBER OF CANADIANS who have won the Nobel Prize for scientific discoveries might well be a question for the TV game show *Jeopardy*, but the answer would be open to debate, for at least three of the eight recipients were born in other countries and four of the five native-born winners were recognized for research accomplished in the United States.

Six scientists have won outright or jointly won, a Nobel Prize for chemistry and two have won for physics. Three of the chemistry winners were born elsewhere: Gerhard Herzberg, born in Germany, left in 1935 because his wife was Jewish; John Polanyi, a University of Toronto professor, was also born in Germany; and Michael Smith, now at the University of British Columbia, is a native of Blackpool, England.

The first Canadian-born chemist to win the Nobel Prize was Henry Taube, from the mixed-farming community of Neudorf, Saskatchewan, for studies accomplished at three American universities. The other two, natives of Montreal, were Rudolph Marcus and Sidney Altman.

Two Alberta-born scientists have won the Nobel Prize for physics: Bertram Brockhouse in 1994 for discoveries made 40 years earlier at Chalk River, Ontario, and Richard Taylor for researching subatomic particles called "quarks." He was jointly awarded the Nobel Prize with two Americans in 1990.

Gerhard Herzberg

After Dr. Herzberg came to Canada as a 31-year-old accomplished scientist, he remained at the University of Saskatchewan for a decade, becoming a Canadian citizen in 1945. Following a three-year stint at the University of Chicago's Yerkes Observatory, he was hired as principal research officer for the Division of Physics at the National Research Council (NRC) in Ottawa. He became director a year later and, in 1955, director of the Division of Pure Physics.

By then his interest had shifted to the more difficult spectroscopic analysis of free radicals (atoms or molecules with at least one unpaired electron). This research led to his Nobel Prize for chemistry in 1971.

Herzberg was president of the International Union of Pure

Gerhard Herzberg left Germany for Canada in 1935. A highlight of his near 50-year career at Ottawa's National Research Council was winning the 1971 Nobel Prize for chemistry for research work in the spectroscopic analysis of free molecules. [Photo, courtesy National Research Council/Harry Turner]

and Applied Physics from 1957 to 1963. He has won numerous worldwide honours from universities and scientific societies, including honorary doctoral degrees from both Oxford and Cambridge Universities. When the Nobel Laureate reached retirement age in 1969, the NRC made him a Distinguished Research Scientist so that he could continue his research at the lab (renamed the Herzberg Institute of Astrophysics in 1975 as a further honour to him). At the age of 92 he is still working there....

Professor John Charles Polanyi, of the University of Toronto, whose scientific career began at Ottawa's National Research Council, celebrates with colleagues and friends the rewarding news that he had just co-won the 1986 Nobel Prize for chemistry for his research work on infrared chemiluminescence. [Photo, courtesy The Toronto Star/ B. Weil]

John Polanyi

The study of molecular reaction also led to John Polanyi's winning the 1986 Nobel Prize for chemistry, awarded jointly with two Americans. John was born in Berlin in 1929. His parents were Hungarian, and his father, a distinguished theologian and philosopher, moved to England as a world-famous science professor in 1933 to teach chemistry at the University of Manchester. John entered that university as a student in 1946, and after receiving his Ph.D. there in 1952, spent two years at the NRC in Ottawa as a postdoctoral fellow before taking further studies at Princeton University in 1954.

Joining the faculty of the University of Toronto in 1954, the future Nobel Laureate began his 30-year investigation into chemical reactions. The research that eventually involved the analysis of infrared emissions from a newly formed molecule became instrumental in the development of the laser and led ultimately to his shared Nobel Prize.

When the John Polanyi Chair in Chemistry was established in 1994 at the University of Toronto, ten other Nobel Prize winners attended the ceremonies including Gerhard Herzberg and Michael Smith, the 1993 winner of the Nobel Prize for chemistry.

Michael Smith

Professor Smith, head of the Biotechnology Laboratory at the University of British Columbia, attributes much of his success to "luck" though others who have worked with him talk of his organizational skill and aver that he is a workaholic and perfectionist.

When he was a youth in Blackpool, England, a top-notch chemistry teacher "turned him on" to science. After attending the University of Manchester, he came to Canada in 1956 to do postdoctoral studies at UBC.

Selected to head the chemistry lab at the Vancouver-based

Professor Michael Smith came to Canada in 1956 to pursue postdoctoral studies at the University of British Columbia. He jointly won the Nobel Prize for chemistry in 1993 for developing ways to create mutations in DNA. [Photo, courtesy The University of British Columbia]

Fisheries Research Board of Canada, Smith combined his new job with teaching graduate students, a sideline frowned upon by his superior at the Board. In 1966 that problem was solved with "another bit of luck" when the Medical Research Council of Canada made him a "career investigator" with an annual grant of $100,000.

Smith's Nobel Prize was jointly awarded for developing a way to create mutations in DNA (deoxyribonucleic acid). His findings have empowered research scientists today to change DNA chemically, and thereby create a mutation, affording researchers, moreover, an opportunity to discover precisely how cancer and virus genes work.

Shortly after receiving his $500,000 award, Smith announced that half of it was being donated for schizophrenia research at the University of Toronto.

After graduating with a Ph.D. from McGill University in 1946, Montreal-born Rudolph Marcus commenced a research career at Ottawa's National Research Council. Postdoctoral research led to studies in the United States. His theories on "electronic transfer" at the California Institute of Technology won him a Nobel Prize for chemistry in 1992. [Photo, courtesy The Toronto Star/Tony Bock]

Rudolf Marcus

In 1992, Montreal-born Rudolph Marcus was attending a scientific conference in Toronto when notified that he had won the Nobel Prize. Marcus later recalled his mother's promise years earlier that he "would go to McGill someday." He did graduate from McGill with a Ph.D. in 1946 and began working on "front line research" at Ottawa's National Research Council. There he developed a keen interest in theoretical chemistry. With no postdoctorate studies available in Canada, he left Canada for the University of North Carolina.

While later teaching at Brooklyn's Polytechnical Institute in 1951, he began reading "everything that was available in electrostatics." This led to his theories on electronic transfer cited in his Nobel award. At the California Institute of Technology, his research intensified and although a number of administrative posts were offered, he declined them all because "I've not wanted anything to interfere with my love of problems and research."

In order to maintain professional status in California, Marcus became an American citizen in 1958. When this legal requirement was changed in the 1970s he applied for dual citizenship, but Canadian law ironically required he had to live in Canada for five years before he could apply. Because he was unable to attain dual citizenship, the 1992 prize for chemistry is shown as won by a U.S. citizen.

Henry Taube

Much the same occurred to Henry Taube whose education started in a Saskatchewan one-room school. After obtaining a B.Sc. in 1935 and an M.Sc. two years later at the University of Saskatchewan, he moved to the University of California for additional graduate work and became involved in inorganic chemistry studies. Unable to find employment at home, he joined the faculty at Cornell University in 1941, moving, in 1946, to the University of Chicago. On becoming professor at Stanford University in 1961, he "saw the field of inorganic chemistry wide open to him for studies in depth."

His research there which led to his 1983 Nobel Prize in chemistry concentrated on the transfer of electrons in metals which, according to a biographical sketch in *Nobel Laureates*, "paved the way not only for our present understanding of the structure and reactivity of classical coordination complexes but has also been the basis for discussion for the behaviour of metal ions in biological systems."

Today, the Nobel Laureate is the author of more than 300 papers. Moreover, mainly because of the infectious enthusiasm and creative approach to chemistry that Taube has passed on to his colleagues, nearly half of some 200 graduates and associates of Taube's "school" have become professors and scientists at leading U.S. and foreign universities.

Sidney Altman

Sidney Altman jointly won the Nobel Prize in 1989 for a fundamental biochemical discovery that some RNA molecules could themselves act as catalysts of biochemical reactions or enzymes. It is described as a major breakthrough in understanding the roll in cells of RNA, which had previously been thought to act only as a carrier of genetic information.

Born in 1939, the son of Russian and Polish immigrants who ran a small grocery store in Montreal, Altman was a bookish child fascinated by atoms and modern nuclear physics. He

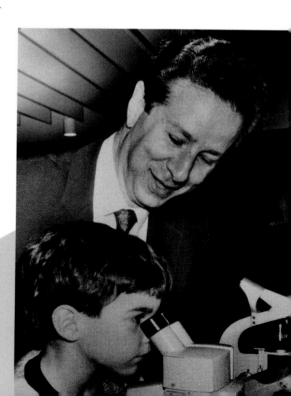

enrolled as a physics major at the Massachusetts Institute of Technology (MIT) but, while he showed an interest in laboratory research and was a keen student, his overall grades were not particularly outstanding until his senior year.

Obtaining a B.Sc. from MIT in 1960, Altman went to Columbia University. While attending Columbia, he worked as a science and poetry editor for Collier Publishing. He left Columbia early, however, and obtained a job screen writing at Canada's National Film Board but never showed up for work when assigned to write a script for a military training film. After a brief fling at translating a French novel into English, he went to Boulder, Colorado, as a science writer and student at a summer institute in physics.

Eventually, after joining the biophysics department of the University of Colorado Medical School in Denver, he continued his studies and obtained a Ph.D. in biophysics. Postdoctoral studies followed at Harvard and Cambridge University where the former hockey player at MIT began his research on the RNA enzyme. In 1971, the future Nobel Laureate returned to the U.S. as an assistant professor at Yale University, becoming professor in 1980, chairman of biology in 1983, and dean of Yale College in 1985.

Richard Taylor

Richard Taylor became the first Canadian Nobel Laureate in physics for proving that protons and neurons are not fundamental particles but are made up of smaller components called "quarks," named so by Murray Gell-Mann, an American scientist who, in the early 1960s, theorized the existence of subatomic particles and adopted the word "quarks" from James Joyce's novel, *Finnigan's Wake*.

A native of Medicine Hat, Alberta, Taylor obtained both a B.Sc. and M.Sc. in physics at the University of Alberta before moving to Stanford University in 1952 for doctoral studies. By 1954 he was working at Stanford's High Energy Physics Laboratory, with its newly installed linear accelerator.

Later, after a three-year stint in France, Taylor returned to the U.S., receiving his doctorate from Stanford in 1962. He participated in the design of a new, much larger linear accelator being built at Stanford. Over the next decade he helped build associated equipment for experiments using the accelerator. He became a faculty member at Stanford in 1968. Taylor, who has never taken out American citizenship, was awarded the 1990 Nobel Prize in physics along with two MIT scientists for confirming Gell-Mann's theories. They also saw some effects of the "gluons" – electrically neutral particles that bind the quarks together.

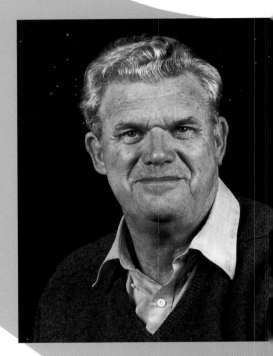

Richard Taylor became the first Canadian to win a Nobel Prize for physics, jointly awarded to him in 1990. He was born in Medicine Hat, Alberta, completing both his B.Sc. and M.Sc. degrees at the University of Alberta. The future Nobel Laureate then went to California's Stanford University, completing his doctorate in 1962. With colleagues elsewhere, his research proved that protons and neutrons are not fundamental particles but are made up of smaller components called "quarks." [Photo, courtesy Stanford University Library via Richard Taylor]

Bertram Brockhouse

The high-speed accelerator used by Taylor and his colleagues was a far cry from the equipment used by Bertram Brockhouse while working at Chalk River, Ontario, in the 1950s, but his work there at proving "what atoms do" made him the 1994 recipient of the Nobel Prize for physics, shared with Clifford Shull of MIT who was also doing atomic research in the 1950s.

Born in Lethbridge, Alberta, in 1918, Brockhouse attended high school in British Columbia, worked as a radio repairman and served in the navy before returning to college as a veteran and graduating in mathematics and physics from the University of British Columbia in 1947. He took his M.A. and Ph.D. degrees at the University of Toronto and was invited to do "neutron scattering experiments" at the NRC's Atomic Energy of Canada.

There, Dr. Brockhouse invented an instrument that enabled him to bombard solid materials with slow-moving neutrons produced in the reactor and that, in time, "allowed him to calculate the strength of the forces that bind atoms together." At about the same time, Shull, the co-winner, was carrying out experiments in which neutrons were deflected to provide a picture of the position of atoms, but their discoveries, though known in the scientific community, went virtually unnoticed elsewhere.

Ten years after he retired as professor of physics at McMaster University, at Hamilton, Ontario, and some 42 years after his groundbreaking research at the Chalk River nuclear laboratories in northern Ontario, Bertram Brockhouse shared the Nobel Prize for physics in 1994. [Photo, courtesy McMaster University Times]

In 1962, Dr. Brockhouse joined the physics department at McMaster University and by 1967, as former chairman Dr. Martin Johns recalled when the Nobel Prize was announced in 1994, Brockhouse, the chairman of the department, had "a cadre of young scientists second to none in Canada." Dr. Brockhouse had been retired for ten years and "was surprised when he heard the news on his telephone answering machine at home." Dr. Johns, however, said the award "comes as no surprise since they [the scientific community] had been waiting for decades for this to happen."

~ ~

While scientists have won most of the Nobel prizes awarded to Canadians, four other Canadians have been recipients and have won international acclaim. Lester B. Pearson won the prize for peace in 1957, while serving as Canada's Secretary of State, and three men won for discoveries in medicine. Dr. Frederick Banting was Canada's first winner, in 1923, for co-discovering insulin, followed by Dr. Charles Huggins of Halifax, who won it in 1966, for research at the University of Chicago on the hormonal treatment of prostate cancer, and Dr. David H. Hubel, born in Windsor, Ontario, and a graduate of McGill, who worked at the Montreal Neurological Institute before moving to the United States. He shared the 1981 Nobel prize for research in neurobiology conducted at Harvard University.

Mel James

WHEN Edward Plunket Taylor was named the first recipient of the Man of the Year Sovereign Award in 1976, Milt Dunnell, sports columnist of the *Toronto Daily Star*, headlined his column, "Taylor's Always Man of the Year," and added, "It's a good thing they didn't make the award retroactive. Taylor's trophies and trinkets would have to be delivered by truck. The last time he wasn't Man of the Year in Canadian Thoroughbred Racing was the year before he came in."

Taylor "came in" as far as horseracing was concerned as early as 1936 when he hired his first trainer, Bert Alexandra, bought the one horse Alexandra owned, and commissioned him to buy more with the $6,000 he allotted for this. Alexandra went to Pimlico and came home in time for the week-long races at Woodbine that May with eight horses picked up through claiming races. By the end of the Woodbine week, three of the horses had won twice. This not only gave Taylor his money back but also ownership of all eight horses.

To promote one of the many brands of beer he had bought up in the early 1930s and later consolidated into Canadian Breweries Limited, Taylor had his horses run under the stable name Cosgrave. The name "Cosgrave" was retained for several more years, its horses eventually winning more than 350 races.

In World War II, "E.P." served as a dollar-a-year man. That arrangement almost ended in December 1940 when the ship he was on, along with Canada's then Minister of Munitions and Supply, C.D. Howe, and other government officials, was torpedoed crossing the Atlantic. They were rescued by a captain who broke regulations to pick them up. Taylor was later assigned key jobs in the USA and Britain before returning to his own corporate and thoroughbred interests, the latter leading to a directorship of the Ontario Jockey Club (OJC) in 1947. "E.P." soon became OJC's largest single shareholder and successfully lobbied the provincial government to reduce the tax on betting. He also developed plans – as he had done in the brewing industry – to consolidate the numerous but poorly equipped tracks around the province into fewer but more profitable operations. By then he had won the King's Plate for

Opposite: *E.P. Taylor built up one of Canada's largest and most successful industrial empires after World War II. He turned a hobby of owning, breeding, and racing thoroughbreds into an empire of champions. In so doing, his Windfields Farms created an unsurpassed equine gene pool.* [Photo, courtesy Canadian Press]

the first time with Epic in 1949 and, following another King's Plate victory with Major Factor in 1951, helped promote the first "Horse of the Year" award at Toronto in 1952.

As the principal speaker at that event, Taylor went public about the need for "improvement in racing itself, better conditions for horsemen, and more facilities for the public." He also improved his own stable facilities by buying out Colonel R.S. McLaughlin's Parkwood Stud in Oshawa and hiring several experts to oversee Windfields Farm that would make him Canada's leading thoroughbred breeder and owner.

In 1954, Taylor made another innovative and sportsmanlike move when he announced that all his yearlings would be offered for sale each spring and that he would retain those not bought, a move that gave other owners an opportunity to buy quality thoroughbreds to compete with him. As a result, Taylor-bred horses won a dozen Queen's Plate races over the next 15 years, with his own stable entries in the winner's circle nine times.

On becoming chairman of the Jockey Club's executive committee in 1953, Taylor began, with the club's backing, to put his 1952 call for improvements into action, buying and rebuilding the Fort Erie track, renovating Woodbine (renamed Greenwood) and buying and shutting down other money-losing tracks around the province. He also quietly bought up land for a new track near Toronto's international airport, turning it over to the Jockey Club at cost. The OJC also won the right to extend the racing season from 84 to 196 days.

Called New Woodbine, the track was opened with fanfare in 1956 with a Taylor horse winning the first event over 14 others. In 1957 Lyford Cay, a horse he had sold at the yearling sale two years earlier that had been returned to him because of a suspected knee problem, won the Queen's Plate.

A walk he took many times in a hobby/career lasting almost 50 years, E.P. Taylor leads Lord Durham, in 1973, with Sandy Hawley aboard as winning jockey, to the champion's circle of the Coronation Futurity, the premier Canadian racing event held annually for two-year-old thoroughbreds. [Photo, courtesy The Toronto Star/ Ron Bull]

Taylor was president of the Jockey Club for the 100th running of the Queen's Plate and invited Queen Elizabeth II to be present. She and Prince Philip came and, although Taylor's own horse was not the favourite, it won, making a Taylor-owned horse the winner for the fifth time in a decade.

In 1960, Taylor's finest thoroughbred to date, Victoria Park, was third in the Kentucky Derby and second in the Preakness before winning the Queen's Plate. Victoria Park also set a track record at Delaware but a bowed tendon ended his racing career later that summer. The Queen Mother was present to hand the "50 guineas" to Taylor in 1962 and a year later Taylor was again in the Queen's Plate winner's circle. Several things occurred that year, however, to make that victory anything but popular. One of the favoured horses from Texas was prevented from running on a technicality and some blamed Taylor's power for the decision. Canada's high unemployment and other economic woes were also attributed, in part, to capitalists such as Taylor, so the crowd booed when Taylor held up the cup over his grey topper.

The next year, however, all was forgiven as Taylor's Canadian thoroughbred, Northern Dancer, winner of both the Kentucky Derby and the Preakness, romped to victory at the Queen's Plate in what proved to be his last race, also because of a bowed tendon.

By then, Taylor, with two farms in Ontario and still another Windfields Farm in Maryland, was one of the most honoured and successful thoroughbred breeders in the world. As early as 1953, he had been made an honorary member of the Jockey Club of New York. In 1965 he was the first Canadian to be elected president of the Thoroughbred Racing Association and in 1970, he became the world's leading breeder of thoroughbreds when his stock earned more than $1.7 million. Three years later he stepped down as chairman of the Ontario Jockey Club and was honoree at a dinner that raised $50,000 to establish the E.P. Taylor Equine Research Foundation to provide for the advancement and improvement of equine medicine, surgery, and husbandry.

In 1974 he was named Man of the Year by the Thoroughbred Racing Association and was elected to Canada's Sports Hall of Fame. By then, since he was offering every horse he bred at major North American yearling auctions – and selling most of them – Taylor's winning entries under his own colours of turquoise and yellow polka dots were less frequent. In 1975, Taylor-bred horses won $2,366,571 breaking the world record; again in 1976, of his 252 starters, 151 were winners with total earnings of $3,022,181.

These achievements were cited at the Man of the Year Sovereign Award sponsored by the Jockey Club of Canada, the *Daily Racing Form*, the Canadian Thoroughbred Horse Society and the National Association of Canadian Race Tracks. A year later the Thoroughbred Racing Association also honoured him with its prestigious Eclipse Award as the leading breeder of thoroughbreds in North America, the first Canadian so honoured.

On May 1, 1996, exactly 60 years to the day after Annemessic became Taylor's first winner, plaintively, the Taylor family announced that it was selling off its breeding stock, ending a fabulous racing empire which won more than 10,000 races and enters the record books as the world's leading breeder of stakes winners at 349 wins.

Mel James

WHEN A CUSTOMER at a small Greek restaurant in Toronto could not pay his bill, the owners were given two tickets to a Metropolitan Opera performance at Maple Leaf Gardens. They gave the tickets to their son to take his sister for her sixteenth birthday. She was initially not pleased with the idea but was so awed by the performance that she decided she too would sing opera. Today she is the world-renowned diva, Teresa Stratas.

Teresa Stratas

Strat128pheric Voice

At the time of seeing *La Traviata* Teresa had hoped to become a nightclub singer. She had already played at some clubs and had sung on radio but, on seeing the Verdi masterpiece, she discovered that there was, to opera, not only a wonderful story, sets, costumes, and fabulous music but, as she told Harry Rasky, author and producer of a film and book about her titled *StrataSphere,* "the most incredible, extraordinary part of it all, was the people opening their mouths, making incredible sounds come out of the human body." She promptly approached the Royal Conservatory of Music in Toronto and when she refused to be put off by a secretary before she sang for someone, Dr. Arnold Walter, founder and head of the opera faculty, agreed to hear her. Teresa, not knowing anything classical, sang "Smoke Gets in Your Eyes." Walter listened and was so impressed with her voice that he arranged for her to see Irene Jessner, a former Metropolitan Opera soprano turned teacher who was equally impressed with her voice and she became her only singing instructor.

Teresa's first professional appearance was as Mimi in *La Bohème* at the Canadian Opera Festival in 1958. A year later, as a co-winner of the Metropolitan Opera auditions, she sang bit parts with them and performed in other operas in Vancouver, Athens, and London, England, before being selected by Rudolph Bing, general manager of the Metropolitan Opera, to replace an indisposed singer as the slave girl Liu in *Turandot.* That happened in 1961 and caused one reviewer to suggest, "It is to be hoped she will be given further significant roles before the season's end."

Her career took flight. In 1962, Alan Rich of the *New York Times* praised her "Mimi" in *La Bohème* at the Met as "full of grace, charm and insinuation." That year she also sang at Milan's famed La Scala, toured Russia with l'Orchestre symphonique de Montréal, and a year later received 16 curtain calls in Leningrad when she sang, in Russian, the role of

Pagliacci *(1892)*, *Leoncavallo's popular opera, has afforded sopranos such as Teresa Stratas, viewed here as Nedda, the opportunity to sing with passion one of the great dramatic arias in all opera.*
[Photo, courtesy Winnie Klotz via the Metropolitan Opera, New York]

Tatiana in Tchaikovsky's *Eugene Onegin*. Her success in Moscow was marred, however, when she walked off the stage after the second act because she felt the Bolshoi Theatre audience did not appreciate her, not realizing that Russian audiences applauded only at the end of a performance.

The misunderstanding got worldwide attention, and subsequently failures to appear have contributed to her status as the temperamental Stratas. But throughout the 1960s, '70s and early '80s, her performances at the Metropolitan and virtually all the major opera houses in the U.S. and Europe won her a faithful following and critical acclaim. She had over 30 roles in her active repertoire, roles that covered a great vocal and dramatic range. These included *La Traviata* in Munich which set off a record 43-minute ovation; Desdemona in *Otello* at Expo 67; Despina in Mozart's *Così Fan Tutte* and Susanna in *The Marriage of Figaro* at the Salzburg Festival; Nedda in *Pagliacci* and Queen Isabella in *Atlantida* at La Scala. Elsewhere, and especially at the Metropolitan, there were Mozart's Cherubino and Zerlina, Puccini's Cio-Cio-'San, Mimi, Liu, and Magda in *La Rondine*, Richard Strauss' Composer, Offenbach's Périchole and Antonia, Menotti's Sardulla in *The Last Savage*, Marie in *The Bartered Bride*, Debussy's Mélisande, Humperdink's Hansel, Tchaikovsky's Lisa in *Pique Dame*, Massenet's *Manon*. In 1979, in Paris, she created the title role of Alban Berg's complete *Lulu* (the first time the "forbidden" third act was performed), described as the greatest musical event in Europe since World War II.

Not all of the 300 international music critics attending sang her praises, but enough did to identify her as the one and only Lulu and the role as a highlight of her then 20-year career. *New York Times* critic Harold C. Schonberg called the role "murderous ... vocally and dramatically," and of her performance wrote, "Her marvellous blend of singing and acting abilities far outweighed her lack of ease with some of the unconventional high-flying notes of the jarring score."

Numerous articles appeared in North America and Europe following *Lulu* which she also performed at the Met later, before singing Kurt Weill's *The Rise and Fall of the City of Mahagonny*. By the beginning of the early '80s, her desire for privacy made her more selective in her public appearances. As she told Rasky, "I am basically a very introverted person leading a very public life," thereby giving a partial explanation for her series of departures from stage appearances in the latter part of the '80s.

In 1981, for instance, she backpacked through India, visiting Mother Teresa's Mission of Charity in Calcutta and volunteering to work there. Between 1983 and 1989 she did not sing at all at the Met, but made films of such operas as *La Traviata* and Monetti's *Amahl and the Night Visitors* and recorded songs written by Weill that had been kept by his wife, Lotte Lenya, who became Teresa's friend during the rehearsals for *Mahagonny*.

In 1987, Teresa starred in the Broadway musical, *Rags,* and, although it closed after four performances, she won a Tony as the best actress in a musical. That year her singing the role of Julie in a recording of Jerome Kern's *Showboat* prompted *New York Times* critic Alan Rich to write, "The Stratas Julie, like the Stratas Lulu, or the Stratas Kurt Weill, is the incomparable dramatic creation of an artist with an uncanny ability to get under your skin at every turn of phrase ... a phenomenal artist."

Following her appearance as Lulu in Brussels, 1988, she returned to the Metropolitan and triumphed in all three operas of Puccini's *Il Trittico*, created Marie Antoinette in the world premiere of Corigliano's *Ghosts of Versailles*, and scored major successes as Marie in Poulenc's *Dialogues of the Carmelites* and with repeats of Liu, the Composer, and Jenny. Among her many filmed performances (in addition to *La Traviata* and *Amahl)* are *Salome*, *La Rondine*, *Lulu*, *Pagliacci*, *The Bartered Bride*, *Mahagonny*, *La Bohème*, *Eugene Onegin*, *Così Fan Tutte*, *Tabarro*, and *Ghosts of Versailles*.

While Teresa indicated as early as 1966 in a *Maclean's* magazine story that she would give up singing before people asked, "Stratas – is she still singing?" and that she might return to Canada to form her own opera company, there is no sign that either will happen. Still petite and trim (five feet tall and just over 100 pounds), she continues to captivate and enthrall audiences and critics alike with her acting and magnificent voice. Still one to shun publicity and relish privacy, she admitted in a rare interview with the *New Yorker* magazine in 1994, "Opera is not life. It's part of life, of course, but it isn't life itself," adding after a pause, "I couldn't live without singing. At least I wouldn't want to."

Mel James

When Teresa Stratas sang at the Canadian National Exhibition, as viewed here, in 1962, her operatic career was in full flight. Already a star with New York's Metropolitan Opera, her stratospheric rise as an international diva included triumphant performances at Milan's La Scala and a victorious tour of Russia. At the time she was 24 years old. [Photo, courtesy *The Toronto Star*]

Canadian Astronauts

On Top of the World

MARC GARNEAU AND ROBERTA BONDAR are two Canadian wayfarers who, as crew members aboard United States space-shuttle missions, were literally the first two Canadians to journey right out of this world. Captain Garneau flew in the shuttle craft *Challenger* in 1984; Dr. Roberta Bondar, in the *Discovery* in 1992. That these two Canadian astronauts shared in American space adventures was not surprising, given important links between research endeavours in both countries. Above all, Canadian aeronautical research designed and produced the "Canadarm," a complex, computerized device "... mounted on shuttles, which would set out or retrieve telecommunications satellites in space – or, in time, repair them in their orbits far above the Earth."

Canada's role in space has stayed both valuable and continuing. Garneau and Bondar, as the first two of a group of Canadian astronauts carefully selected and trained for space missions, were followed by "back-up" comrades including Ottawa-born Steve MacLean, whose mission STS-52 took place October 22 - November 1, 1992 and Chris Hadfield of Milton, Ontario, whose November 1995 voyage into space was aboard the *Atlantis*. The same, indeed, was true of American astronauts themselves, where a number of equally ready and able candidates for shuttle flights were left on standby, perhaps never to take that breathtaking skyward leap. But Garneau and Bondar were the very first Canadians to join that special group of human beings who actually left this planet, wayfared into the immensities beyond, and successfully returned.

Marc Garneau, born at Quebec City in 1949 and fluently bilingual, graduated from Collège militaire royal de Saint-Jean in 1968, then from Royal Military College in 1970. In 1973, he earned a Ph.D. in electrical engineering at the University of London, England. Joining the Canadian naval forces, he first served as a combat systems officer. In Halifax where he was a weapons instructor, he designed a simulator for training officers in missile systems. Chosen as a member of the first Canadian astronaut team in late 1983, he took on duties with the space program at the National Research Council (NRC) in Ottawa, and then, in October 1984, was selected to fly aboard the Challenger out of Cape

Canada's original space team, December 1983, included top row from left: Ken Money, Roberta Bondar, Bjarni Tryggvason, and bottom row: Steve MacLean, Robert Thirsk, and Marc Garneau. Thirsk, a medical doctor and engineer, embarked on the longest space shuttle flight in history aboard the Columbia on June 20, 1996. While in space he studied the effects of low-level gravity on living organisms. [Photo, courtesy National Research Council]

Chris Hadfield, addressing Spar Aerospace employees in Brampton, Ontario, following the STS-74 mission aboard Atlantis. He was the first Canadian to fly as Mission Specialist, the first Canadian to board the Russian Space Station Mir, and the first Canadian to operate the Canadarm in space. [Photo, courtesy Spar Aerospace Limited]

Kennedy in Florida. On his eight-day voyage beyond the Earth, Garneau carried out experiments in space science that dealt both with a "space vision system" developed by the NRC and also with problems of living in space – notably with nausea more troublesome than "sea" sickness! Continuing in the astronaut program on his return, Marc Garneau retired from the navy in 1989 and as Canada's pioneer astronaut, returned to space aboard *Endeavour* in May 1996, becoming the first Canadian to fly aboard the space shuttle twice.

Roberta Bondar, first Canadian woman in space, was born in Sault Ste. Marie, Ontario, in 1945, took a bachelor's degree in science at the University of Guelph in 1968, a master's degree at the University of Western Ontario in 1971, and a Ph.D. at the University of Toronto in 1974. She branched from Zoology into neurobiology and medicine, joining the medical faculty of McMaster University. She also taught at the University of Ottawa from 1985-89. On becoming Chairman of the Life Science Committee for Space Stations at the NRC, she took flight surgeon's training, then went to the Sunnybrook Medical Centre in Toronto. Also chosen as an astronaut, after repeated delays that included the tragic loss of the *Challenger* and all on board in 1986, she took off, at last, in January 1992 aboard the *Discovery*. Roberta Bondar did crucial work on weightlessness in space. No less enthusiastic since her return to earth, she has taught at universities from Hamilton to New Mexico where she has demonstrated her pride in Canada's space program.

J.M.S. Careless

ONE OF CANADA'S most enduring cultural symbols is the canoe. It forms a link in our collective stream of memory from first nation peoples who originally designed the bark craft to voyageurs who today paddle Canada's waterway highways recreationally in modern canvas, fiberglass and aluminum canoes. A product of the forest, used to explore the waterways and vault landscapes, the canoe is unquestionably the quintessential vehicle that ushered people to the interiors of a grand new country. Its very essence evokes spirituality, solitude, and patriotism, deep personal feelings reverentially recorded by adventurous Canadians:

Following one canoe pilgrimage into the sanctuaries of Canada's vast wilderness, the Rt. Hon. **John Turner**, former Canadian Prime Minister, observed devotionally: "Before us had been a big unspoiled, majestic country of treeless land and water, game, and birds in their undisturbed habitat. Wildlife bloomed everywhere. I wondered how long this river would remain untouched and unspoiled. How much longer would this solitude last? What a privilege to have run these waters.... We had travelled one of the last frontiers of the world. Because we love the country, we are careful to leave it as we found it, with no signs of our passing. I have never felt more Canadian than when alone with my thoughts in the remote northern vastness."

One of Canada's great promoters of wilderness travel by canoe, the late **Eric Morse**, the first and only Canadian ever made an Honorary Director of the Explorers Club International, theorized that "... as much history could be learned from a canoe as from a history book."

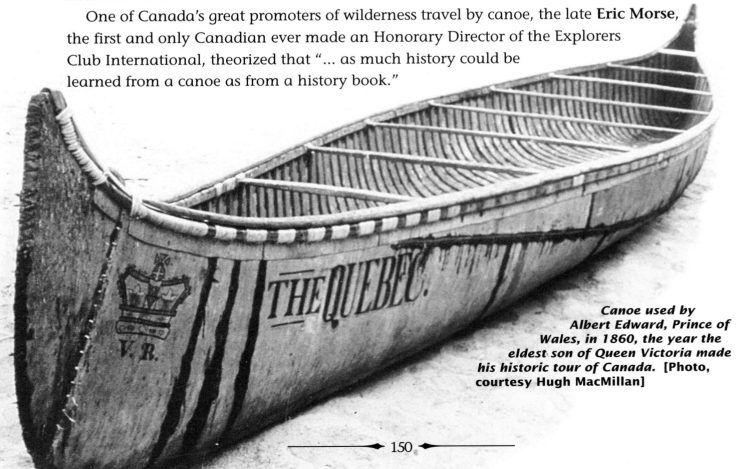

Canoe used by Albert Edward, Prince of Wales, in 1860, the year the eldest son of Queen Victoria made his historic tour of Canada. [Photo, courtesy Hugh MacMillan]

Pierre Berton has proposed that Canadians "... are a nation of canoeists, and have been since the earliest days, paddling ... up the St. Lawrence, across the lakes, over the portages of the Shield, west along the North Saskatchewan through the Yellowhead gap and thence southwest by the Columbia and Fraser rivers to the sea. When somebody asks ... how Canada could exist as a horizontal country with its plains and mountains running vertically, tell him about the paddlers."

According to C.E.S. Franks, "Canada is a northern nation. A strong element of nordicity in the Canadian landscape of the imagination is essential for it to be our homeland. Canoeing, properly placed in its historical and cultural context, is contributing to this important component of nation building."

Each time he paddled down one of Canada's fur-trading routes, Blair Fraser, Ottawa editor of *Maclean's* who tragically drowned in a canoeing accident on the Petawawa River in 1968, felt that canoe trips were akin to passing through "an empty area of forest and plain in which a man could still enjoy the illusion of solitude. This is the quality that makes Canada unique and gives root to Canadian patriotism."

Another former Canadian Prime Minister, the Rt. Hon. Pierre Elliot Trudeau, conjectured that canoeing generated the virtue of patriotism: "Canoeing forces you to make a distinction between your needs: survival, food, sleep, protection from the weather. These are all things

Canonized Cultural Symbol

that you tend to take for granted when you are living in so-called civilization, with its constant pressures on you to do this or that for social reasons created by others, or to satisfy artificial wants created by advertising. Canoeing gets you back close to nature, using a method of travel that does not even call for roads or paths."

Contending that the "... canoeist should know the ironic role of the canoe in the evolving Canadian culture...," Bruce Hodgins believes in "the canoe's mythological purity as a symbol" and understands all too well that the canoe, per se, has unfortunately "led to the continuing destruction of wilderness and the degradation of environment."

Queen's University professor **James Raffan** in *Wild Waters* (1986) fondly reminisced after one wilderness venture: "Around quiet campfires on the Coppermine, smoke from gnarled wood tweaked our imaginations as we talked of native people and read from the journals of Samuel Hearne and Sir John Franklin. Like never before I felt a part of our Canadian past. I realized that the river routes that reticulate this land from sea to arctic sea bear the very essence of who we are. By paddling the Coppermine, stripped of school and its interpreters, I was experiencing the land much as Hearne, Franklin, and its native custodians had left it centuries earlier."

Larry Turner

The subject of this Arthur Heming (1870-1940) painting on canvas is the rapids-running incident on the French river during Alexander Mackenzie's 74-day journey of discovery to the Pacific Ocean.
[Photo, courtesy Government of Ontario Art Collection, Toronto]

Most of Cornelius Krieghoff's 2,000 paintings read like a gripping narrative, especially those canvases depicting wilderness canoeing and camping expeditions. This Krieghoff canvas, "Shooting the Rapids," 1860, demonstrates Krieghoff's fascination for this subject as well as his passion for Canada's brilliant autumn colours. [Photos, courtesy National Archives of Canada/C-4668]

Temple
of Science

NATIONAL RESEARCH COUNCIL

Originally called the National Research Laboratories when it opened in 1932, the main building of the National Research Council is often cited as "the temple of science." Located in Ottawa, the granite and sandstone ediface is enhanced by 16 Doric columns and huge entrance doors of sculptured bronze. [Photo, courtesy National Research Council]

"**A**THE BEGINNING of the long dash, following ten seconds of silence" thousands of Canadians each day at 1:00 p.m. EST, check the time on their watches and clocks against the official time signal broadcast by the National Research Council of Canada. Few of them realize that the time signal is generated by the world's first atomic clock – just one of many discoveries, inventions, and innovations that NRC scientists have brought to Canadians' daily lives.

In its 80-year history, the National Research Council (NRC) has provided guidance and support to Canadian research scientists in practically every field of human endeavour from agriculture and health care to oceanography and space exploration. Such common items as cooking oil, home furnaces, and most of Canada's buildings have been improved thanks to the inquiring minds at the NRC. At the same time, its scientific research has helped keep Canada at the forefront of such specialized fields as lasers, aerospace, ultrasonics, and chemical engineering.

That is precisely the role envisioned for the NRC when its forerunner the Honorary

Advisory Council for Scientific and Industrial Research, was established by the federal government in 1916, in the middle of World War I. The war's huge demands on Canada's industrial research and production capacities had underlined the need for directing and coordinating scientific and technical research on a national basis. The Council's mandate, by stressing that its research "is absolutely necessary in order to enable us to compete with progressive countries in the great race for national expansion," also envisioned a role beyond wartime.

The Council's initial activities were limited to providing scholarships to promising graduate students and research grants to universities. It had no laboratory facilities of its own. Yet within a year, with the development by researchers at McGill University of an effective system of fog signals, the Council's efforts had resulted in success. After the war, the Council supported projects geared to peacetime needs. In 1920, for example, it sponsored research on preventing the discoloration of canned lobster meat that led to improved revenues for the Atlantic fishery.

By 1924, the Council had established its own library of research and technical journals which today has become the largest collection of its kind in North America. During the next year, it set up its first model laboratory on the top two floors of an office building in downtown Ottawa. One of its first research projects on processing magnesite helped in the development of Canada's magnesium mining industry.

The Council did not have a home of its own until 1932 when its large central laboratory was officially opened on Sussex Drive in Ottawa. Later referred to as "the temple of science," this massive granite and sandstone structure was adorned with 16 Doric columns and huge entrance doors of sculptured bronze. A biblical quotation selected by Prime Minister Mackenzie King is carved in stone above the main entrance. It reads:

Great is truth, and mighty above all things;
it endureth and is always strong;
it liveth and conquereth for ever more;
the more thou searchest,
the more thou shalt marvel.

Housed in this magnificent facility, the newly named National Research Council established four professional divisions – chemistry, physics and engineering, biology and agriculture, and research information – and began a period of steady growth. In 1938, the laboratories began producing its own electricity from a hydro generating station on the nearby Rideau River Falls.

NATIONAL RESEARCH COUNCIL

THE INSCRIPTION OVER THE MAIN ENTRANCE WAS CHOSEN FROM THE APOCRYPHAL BOOKS OF ESDRAS BY THE RIGHT HONOURABLE W. L. MacKENZIE KING.

NATIONAL RESEARCH LABORATORIES

"GREAT IS TRUTH AND MIGHTY ABOVE ALL THINGS. IT ENDURETH AND IS ALWAYS STRONG. IT LIVETH AND CONQUERETH FOR EVER MORE. THE MORE THOU SEARCHEST. THE MORE THOU SHALT MARVEL."

The outbreak of war in 1939 caused the NRC to switch its entire efforts to wartime research. During the war years, the NRC staff expanded from 300 in 1939 to more than 3,000 by 1945. Several new research laboratories were also built along Montreal Road, east of Ottawa. NRC scientists contributed some of the war's most significant scientific advances

Canada has an array of astronomical instruments for observing the heavens, most of which are available to scientists as national facilities under the aegis of the National Research Council. One of the world's largest optical telescopes, located at the summit of Hawaii's Mauna Kea, is jointly owned by Canada, France, and the State of Hawaii. It took eight years to build and its mirror measures nearly 3.7 metres in diameter. As viewed here, the concave surface, accurate to a few millionths of a centimetre, was ground, polished and prepared by personnel at the Dominion Astro-physical Observatory. [Photo, courtesy National Research Council]

including the development of ultrasonics for antisubmarine warfare, major improvements to aircraft detection by radar, the production of RDX (a new explosive more powerful than TNT), and the nuclear research that led to the development of atomic power. A major breakthrough credited to NRC scientists was the development of the anti-gravity suit that prevented pilots from "blacking out" during violent flight manoeuvres.

One of the more bizarre projects undertaken by NRC scientists was research on creating giant floating airfields of ice that could be used as waypoints for aircraft crossing the Atlantic Ocean. Code-named Habakkuk, the project had been enthusiastically endorsed by British Prime Minister Winston Churchill. Even though the Habakkuk research resulted in greater knowledge of refrigeration and the properties of ice, the project was abandoned because the cost of building such an airfield would likely cost more than a traditional aircraft carrier!

Not all of NRC's war efforts were as dramatic as its role in developing Canada's first atomic reactor at its Chalk River facility or as fanciful as its Habakkuk research. Yet much of the NRC's wartime research in food processing and packaging, aircraft de-icing, the treatment of burns and shock, mineral processing and production placed Canadian scientists in the forefront of many of these fields.

The NRC's successes in wartime assured its future by 1945 when peace came. Instead, the postwar years saw rapid expansion of the NRC's scientific divisions and facilities as the Council turned its attention to the needs of Canada's new-found industrial capabilities. The scientific discoveries and innovations supported by NRC research during this period range from the exotic to the everyday.

For instance, its expertise in radar helped Trans-Canada Air Lines (TCA) set up the world's first civilian radar installation for air traffic control. Its nuclear research also led to the first-ever use of Cobalt-60 radiation in the treatment of cancer. On the home front, the NRC played a key role in the development of canola (rapeseed), which is used to produce cholesterol-free cooking oil and margarine. Its scientists also discovered a natural substance that keeps cocoa suspended in chocolate milk, milkshakes, and puddings – to the delight of children everywhere!

In the field of aeronautics and space science, NRC's research has resulted in significant improvements in aircraft and rocket design and in the development of highly specialized instruments such as the crash position indicator (CPI) used to locate lost aircraft. Its astronomers have also played key roles in the measurement of quasars (gigantic star clusters), the discovery of the second "black hole" in space and in identifying the billion-year age differences between star clusters in the universe.

Capable of measuring correct time within an accuracy of three parts in one hundred billion, the atomic clock is Canada's basic time standard. Designed by the National Research Council in 1958, it is the most precise clock known to man. [Photo, courtesy National Research Council]

Through its health care research, the NRC's research and technologies have led to several new procedures and instruments for diagnosing and treating diseases and injuries. It has also been responsible for the development of vaccines against meningitis and for the use of genetic engineering to have bacteria produce human insulin. The Council's new technologies created to help disabled persons include one of the first wheelchairs for quadriplegics, an ultrasound object detector for the blind, and a portable speech synthesizer for severely disabled children.

In the field of transportation, NRC's research has solved a wide variety of problems that include the siltation of harbours, the freezing over of railway switches in winter and the need for increased energy efficiency of transit buses. It even developed, for the repair of potholes, a much more durable substance comprised of asphalt, liquid sulphur, mica flakes, and polyester fibre.

Agricultural research has, since its inception, been one of the NRC's mainstays. This work has involved creating new disease- and cold-resistant strains of various crops, the cloning of

Below: *In 1942, Britain's High Commissioner approached Dr. C.J. Mackenzie, then acting president of the National Research Council, with a top secret proposal: if Canada would provide a laboratory, the team of physicists working on the nuclear research project at Cambridge, England, would be transferred to Canada and a joint British-Canadian research effort established. Mackenzie immediately recognized that Canada could be on the ground floor of a great new technological advance. He took the proposal to C.D. Howe, the powerhouse behind Canada's wartime industrial effort. When "The Minister of Everything" approved the idea to build a pilot plant on the Chalk River for the production of plutonium from uranium using heavy water as a moderator, he launched Canada into the nuclear age. The Chalk River complex, viewed here, circa 1949, became the site of the first reactor built outside the United States. The cooling tanks are seen in the foreground.* [Photo, courtesy National Research Council]

Above: *Dr. W.R Franks (1901-1986), viewed centre explaining the working of his anti-gravity suit invention to a pilot, took charge of a wartime research effort investigating anti G-suit possibilities. His invention of the pressure suit allowed pilots to carry out high speed manoeuvres without losing consciousness. To continue studying the complex effect of G-forces on aircrew, the National Research Council was persuaded to build a human centrifuge which later became the basic research instrument for determining reactions of the human body to flight and which also led to perfecting space suits now playing such an important role in the conquest of outer space.* [Photo, courtesy National Research Council]

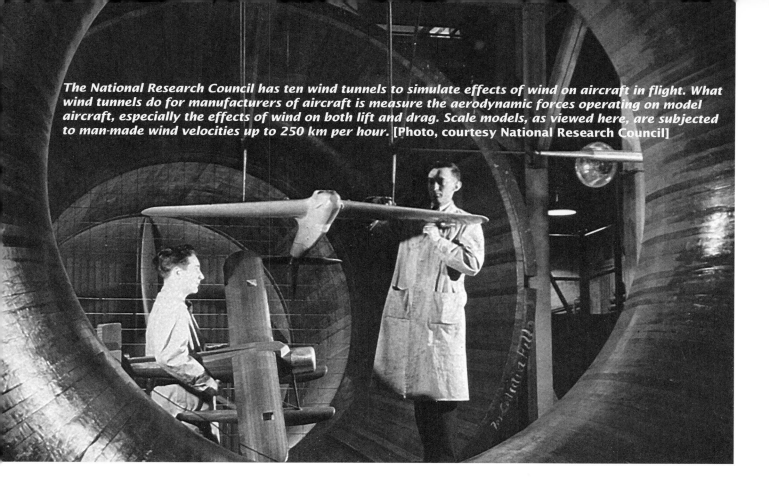

The National Research Council has ten wind tunnels to simulate effects of wind on aircraft in flight. What wind tunnels do for manufacturers of aircraft is measure the aerodynamic forces operating on model aircraft, especially the effects of wind on both lift and drag. Scale models, as viewed here, are subjected to man-made wind velocities up to 250 km per hour. [Photo, courtesy National Research Council]

plant tissues through deep freezing, and the development of better packaging and transportation for such perishable foods as meat and fish.

Society's growing concerns about the environment have also led the NRC to focus its research on pollution control and abatement in such areas as PCB incineration and the treatment of toxic waste from pulp mills.

Not all NRC's research is dedicated to solving humanity's most difficult problems; some projects are simply interesting or fun. For example, NRC had a hand in developing the first, all-fiberglass hockey stick, in building a bobsled for the Canadian Olympic Team, and in designing the massive torch for the 1988 Winter Olympics in Calgary.

Developing methods of extremely precise measurement has always been one of the NRC's strengths. In 1967, it developed the world's best potentiometer, a device for measuring electrical current that is so accurate and stable that it could not be calibrated against any similar device at that time. About the same time, the NRC began developing gauges that would be used by the Apollo astronauts to measure gases in the moon's atmosphere.

But it is the so-called atomic clock, developed by the NRC in 1974, that exemplifies the high scientific standards and down-to-earth practicality of the Council's researchers over the past 80 years. Capable of measuring time to within an accuracy of three parts within one hundred billion, this super clock is not used just for esoteric scientific experiments: it also enables Canadians to answer the question "What time is it?" as accurately as anyone in the world.

Richard Levick

JOHN D. MACNAUGHTON

Ensuring Canada's Place in Space

WHEN A FASCINATION FROM CHILDHOOD with machines and engines of all kinds converged with a wonderment over the marvellous possibilities of space, the result was a visionary Canadian professional engineer and executive responsible for that acme of Canadian technology: Canadarm.

John D. MacNaughton retired in 1996. During his 42-year engineering career that coincided with the dramatic growth of Canada's space industry, he successfully guided Spar Aerospace Limited to the forefront of Canada's entire space program. [Photo, courtesy Spar Aerospace Limited]

John MacNaughton's reflective demeanour belies a persistent nature that does not accept 'no' for an answer. It is this quiet determination, coupled with a talent to envision finished products and programs, that has directed his 42-year career in Canada's space industry. In fact, these traits that have allowed MacNaughton to build a great and successful career for himself are the very foundation of Canada's current space program.

Born in Moose Jaw, Saskatchewan, and raised in Victoria, British Columbia, MacNaughton studied aeronautical engineering at de Havilland's Aeronautical Technical School and attended London University's Hatfield College in the U.K. There, away from his parents' watchful eyes, he took up a long-time passion: motorcycle racing. Aboard his 350cc Velocette, he careened around corners, face as close to the ground as his feet. This sensation of man and machine working together as parts of the same whole sealed his decision to spend a lifetime with designs and mechanisms that would hurl Canada onto the world stage as a source of the world's leading space engineers – the smallest country of its kind to enjoy such a reputation.

John MacNaughton is one of Spar's original employees. Spar began as the Special Products and Applied Research Division of de Havilland Aircraft. It had developed a unique product, the STEM antenna, which was used in the early 1960s on *Alouette I*, Canada's first scientific satellite. By the time Spar became a separate public company in 1967, STEM represented 40 per cent of the new company's sales.

From *Alouette,* STEM ushered Spar – and MacNaughton – into a whole series of space projects and programs: the Manned Space Program that included *Mercury, Gemini, Apollo,* and *Skylab;* additional space science projects in the U.K., the U.S., Japan, France, and Germany that included *ISIS, Skylark* and *Dragon.* It also introduced MacNaughton to space scientists at universities around the world.

Through such broad exposure to the business, he developed the team concept of addressing Canadian space projects in a regionally effective manner, bringing together companies and academia. As the founding Chairman of the Aerospace Industry Association of Canada's (AIAC) Space Committee having to deal with key people in many federal and provincial government departments, he gained considerable insight into the mechanics of government. He went on to develop the AIAC's policy paper on space which was instrumental in the formulation of the Science and Technology Minister's space policy of the early 1970s. Among this policy's recommendations was that Canada consider joining the robotics area of the space shuttle program. And Canadarm was conceived. But a conception is not a birth, and as he began work on the Canadarm program in earnest, MacNaughton realized there was much to be done. He had a vision of space shuttle robotics that could be spun off to operate commercially in other hostile environments: undersea, and in nuclear reactors. No such research was under way in Canada. All of his work on the subject was from ground zero. But through sheer determination, and with the cooperation of key players in the National Research Council and the Department of Supply and Services, he worked with the many levels and organizations within the Canadian, U.S., and European governments to bring the vision to

John MacNaughton's passion for the motorcycle took root while he was attending school in the United Kingdom. There he became fascinated with the sensation of working with a machine that could careen around corners with his face as close to the ground as his feet. Viewed here as a student in the early '50s, John sits on his 350cc Velocette. [Photo, courtesy Spar Aerospace Limited]

reality. The result was a memorandum of understanding between Canada's National Research Council and NASA – the original draft of which was penned by MacNaughton himself.

MacNaughton expanded the original rationale for collaborating with the European Space Agency. His plans to gain access to the European market and to its research and development contracts and to forge new industrial links were a prescient view of the global market we live in today.

As the prime architect of Canada's industrial strategy for extending our domestic space industry, he was a key player in the development of Canada's various long-term space plans. The first phase of these programs resulted in such world-leading technological breakthroughs as *Radarsat,* a satellite that can see through clouds and darkness to return accurate images of earth from space, and Canadarm and its offspring: the robotics for the International Space Station. Phase II, now under way, moves these into the next technology generation.

MacNaughton has spent his life furthering Canada's technological and business progress, first in the international space industry and later into such other high technology areas as telecommunications. Spellbound by the power that the microprocessor has unleashed on industry and society and aware that not seizing the opportunities it offered was tantamount to corporate suicide, he led Spar through one of the most successful – and dramatic – reinventions in Canadian business. He maintained Spar's position as Canada's premier space company, while expanding its commercial business and moving into international communications and software markets. Communications and software now represent 45 per cent of the company's revenues compared to 5 per cent in 1991. Spar Aerospace has entered new international markets previously untried by members of the Canadian industry; 60 per cent

John D. MacNaughton breaks ground in 1976 for Spar Aerospace's new Simulation Facility for the Remote Manipulator Systems Space Division in Mississauga, Ontario. [Photo, courtesy Spar Aerospace Limited]

of the company's revenues are derived outside of North America compared to 25 per cent in 1991. Commercial sales accounted for 56 per cent of 1995 total revenues compared to only 19 per cent in 1991.

His profession, his industry, and his country have recognized MacNaughton for his many contributions and accomplishments. Among the honours bestowed upon him are the Casey Baldwin Award (the Canadian Aeronautics and Space Institute, 1963), Engineering Medal (Professional Engineers of Ontario, 1965), Public Service Medal (the National Aeronautics and Space Administration [NASA], 1982), McGregor Award (the Royal Canadian Air Force Association, 1983), the McCurdy Award (Canadian Aeronautics and Space Institute, 1983), System Professional of the Year (Association of Systems Management, 1983), Thomas W. Eadie Medal (Royal Society of Canada, 1984), Canada's 125th Anniversary Commemorative Medal, 1993.

As Chairman of the National Quality Institute, John MacNaughton expresses his strong convictions about Canada's need for international excellence and competitiveness. His position as a Director at Large for Junior Achievement of Canada reflects his commitment to encourage youth and thereby ensuring Canada of high-quality future recruits. He has a strong sense of nationalism and is a member of the Canadian Council for Canadian Unity. He is also a fellow and Past President of the Canadian Aeronautic and Space Institute, a former director and member of the Executive Committee of the Canadian Advanced Technology Association, and past Vice Chairman of the Aerospace Industries Association of Canada.

John MacNaughton: a thinker and a doer; a dreamer and a builder.

William Turner/Deborah Allan

David Allanson Jones

Bee King of the Nineteenth Century

1836-1910

THERE MIGHT STILL have been a Clarksville, Ontario, today if David Allanson Jones hadn't decided to keep bees. Instead, the community in Simcoe County originally called Clarksville is known as Beeton in honour of the man who became widely known as the "Bee King of Canada" and internationally regarded as an expert apiarist.

Jones was 31 when, in 1867, the same year Canada was confederated, he and a brother moved to the growing community of Clarksville in Whitchurch Township, Ontario, to establish a general store. Three years later Jones purchased two swarms of bees from a neighbouring hive and within months offered the world his first patented hive, somewhat immodestly called "The Jones Perfection Bee Hive." He described it as double-walled – the internal wall being all tin and glass.

The following year Jones wrote to the *American Bee Journal* that he had experimented by placing six stocks in movable comb hives and one in a box – and reported, "The box stock never yielded any surplus until transferred, and then only 31 lbs in comb and five by extractor – 36 lbs in all. From my other six stocks I have taken nine swarms and 1,707 pounds of beautiful honey."

In 1872, when his brother (later Senator L.M. Jones) moved to Brantford, Ontario, D.A. Jones gave up the store and opened a planing mill. He also established a factory to produce window sashes and doors and to invent and produce beekeeping equipment.

As bees were not native to North America but brought here by early settlers, new breeding stock had to be imported. When Jones could not get the government interested, in 1879 he made a trip at his own expense to Cyprus and Palestine with a fellow beekeeper from the United States. Returning in June

David Allanson Jones (1836-1910), world-renowned breeder of bees, was a 19th century pioneer of the North American beekeeping industry. The town he immigrated to in 1867 was named Clarksville, near Barrie, Ontario. In 1874 it was renamed Beetown (now Beeton) to honour this apiarist entrepreneur. [Photo, courtesy Simcoe County Archives]

The Canadian Bee Journal *was founded in 1885 by David Allanson Jones. When fire destroyed his business establishment in 1893, the D.A. Jones, Limited operations in Beeton conducted by Jones ceased.* [Photo, courtesy Simcoe County Archives]

1880 with several hives from those two countries, Jones was ready to expand his beekeeping.

Three colonies for mating were established on three Georgian Bay islands named Palestine, Cyprus, and Carniola, the queens being returned to Beeton after they began laying their eggs. An article in the American publication, *Bee Culture*, reported in 1881, "The bees gather very little and must be fed continually through the summer season. They are taken to these islands in the Spring and returned to Beeton in the Fall – a rather costly and tedious process."

This was so unprofitable in fact that *Bee Culture* reported three years later that, although the queens sold for as high as $15 and were distributed throughout Canada and the U.S., repeat orders were not numerous "as the bees were found too cross in temperament."

In 1885 Jones founded *The Canadian Bee Journal*. He promised to print articles from leading beekeepers throughout the world and to present, periodically, questions raised by students at weekly conventions. Young men from both the U.S. and Britain learned beekeeping from him at Beeton while being paid 12 cents an hour.

Jones' beekeeping enterprise lasted until June 1893 when a fire destroyed his factory and printing plant, and a bacteria called foulbrood, which attacked honeybee larvae, swept the province and destroyed much of the industry.

He then turned to building up the community, an interest he had shown since his arrival. Land that he had purchased over the years was turned into lots and he had the streets lined with pollen- and nectar-producing trees such as soft maple, basswood, and elm, some of which still enhance the community where he died in 1910.

In 1957, the Ontario government erected a cairn citing him as a "world renowned breeder of bees and pioneer of the North American beekeeping industry." The Ontario and Georgian Bay Beekeepers Associations and local governments also unveiled a cairn in the Presbyterian Cemetery to recall his work as an apiarist, editor, and generous community leader.

Mel James

Hume Cronyn

Celebrating Sixty-five Years on Stage and Screen

HUME CRONYN was 19 and a first-year dropout from McGill University in 1930 when he told his mother and two older brothers that he wanted to be an actor. A brother, 18 years his senior, bluntly asked, "How many years do you think you can afford to waste?" Angry and hurt, Hume stormed out of the family estate at London, Ontario, but on his return his mother had a proposal: go to McGill for another year, and "if at the end of that time you still wish to go into the theatre, I will see to it that you go to the Royal Academy of Dramatic Arts in London, England, or the American Academy in New York as you choose."

Even before entering the American Academy in 1932, Cronyn made his professional stage debut in Washington after appearing in plays at McGill and the Montreal Repertory Theatre in 1930 and '31 respectively. More than 65 years later, the list of stage plays, films, and TV appearances that he has performed in or directed and the honours received takes up seven pages in his 1991 memoir, *A Terrible Liar*, titled so because, as he wrote, "... memory can be a judicious editor, omitting trial and tribulation. It can also be a terrible liar...."

Other writers and critics, however, have confirmed his outstanding contribution as actor, director, producer, writer, and teacher. One wrote, "Although he is frequently cast in the role of an old man, Hume Cronyn is not a 'type' character; his talents are too protean to be limited to any one kind of role." Walcott Gibbs described his performance in *The Honeys* as "astonishingly resourceful," and Brooks Atkinson wrote that he was brilliant in the role of Julian in *A Day by the Sea.*

Cronyn, however, is best-known for his appearances with his British-born wife, Jessica Tandy, who died in 1995. Married 53 years, they appeared together so often on stage, screen, radio, and television that one book on outstanding actors wrote their biographies as a single article. It cited their performances in such hits as *The Fourposter* and *The Gin Game.*

Most of the time they received rave reviews but ran afoul of Brooks Atkinson for *The Man in the Dog Suit.* When Cronyn wrote his one and only letter to a critic to complain, Atkinson responded, "Let me say that I am sorry to have given you a bad time. But since I know the quality of the work that you and Jessica do, I could not help brooding in the theatre over the problem presented by a play I think is below your standards of artistic taste."

After graduating from the New York Academy in 1934, Cronyn spent nearly ten years on stage before Alfred Hitchcock cast him in *Shadow of a Doubt* for his first movie role. Cronyn's performance was described in the *New York Times* as "a modest comic masterpiece" and other movies quickly followed. These included *Phantom of the Opera, The Cross of Lorraine,* and *The Seventh Cross* which won him an Academy Award nomination in 1944 as best supporting actor. "I didn't win," Cronyn recalls in his memoir. "Barry Fitzgerald did for a beautiful job

Hume Cronyn's career on stage, screen, radio, and television has spanned more than 65 years. A brilliant character actor, he often teamed with his wife, Jessica Tandy, to the delight of audiences across North America and Europe. [Photo, courtesy *The Toronto Star*/Jeff Goode]

in *Going My Way.*"

While life in Hollywood "was full of unexpected joys," Cronyn returned to stage work in 1948. His first play lasted eight performances. In 1949, he jumped at the opportunity to play Hamlet with a touring company and humorously commented on one media headline that read, "Hamlet on the Half Shell." "While somewhat obscure I don't think it can be described as congratulatory." In 1964, however, playing the role of Polonius with Richard Burton as Hamlet, Cronyn won a Tony Award.

By then he had also starred in the 1963 opening season of the Tyrone Guthrie Theater in Minneapolis playing in such roles as Harpagon in Moliére's *The Miser*, which *Life Magazine* called "easily the most entertaining U.S. production of Moliére ever given" and Willie Loman in *Death of a Salesman* with Jessica playing his wife, Linda.

Early in 1965, they were summoned to the White House to entertain President and Lady Bird Johnson along with members of the Cabinet, the Supreme Court, and a number of editors, business leaders, and university presidents. Later that year they returned to the Guthrie Theater to perform in *Richard III* and *The Cherry Orchard*. In 1969 Ontario's Stratford Festival audiences saw Cronyn in *Hadrian VII*, and he returned with Jessica in 1976 for roles in *The Merchant of Venice* and *A Midsummer Night's Dream*. They also went to Cronyn's native city of London to perform in *The Many Faces of Love*.

In 1978, Cronyn coproduced *The Gin Game* which won a Pulitzer Prize and went on tour in the United States. It played in Toronto before going to London, England, and the USSR until December 1979. He then played Hector Nations in *Foxfire*, a play he co-authored with Susan Cooper and performed with his wife Jessica at the Stratford Festival, 1981, and at the Ethel Barrymore Theater in New York from November to May 1982.

Sandwiched between long-running stage plays and tours were movies and television productions. In 1963, he spent months in Italy playing Sosignes in *Cleopatra* starring Richard Burton and Elizabeth Taylor but most of his performance ended on the cutting-room floor. Canadian Norman Jewison directed Cronyn in *Gaily, Gaily* in 1968. Films made in the 1970s and '80s included *The Parallax View, Garp, Impulse, Cocoon,* and *Cocoon: The Return*. His first appearance in television was on NBC in 1939; he produced and directed *Portrait of a Madonna* starring Jessica in 1948 and both a radio and television series of *The Marriage* with Jessica in 1953-54. On seven occasions he performed live in *Omnibus*, the acclaimed TV series. He continued making TV productions mainly with Jessica until shortly before her death.

Cronyn, a recipient of the Order of Canada, has won numerous awards in his 65-year career. He was nominated six times for a Tony and won it in 1964 for his role as Polonius. He received the New York Drama League's Delia Austria medal for his performance as Jimmie Luton in *Big Fish, Little Fish*, The Los Angeles Drama Critics Circle Award for best actor as Captain Queeg in *Caine Mutiny Court Martial,* the Straw Hat award for best director in the 1972 production of *Promenade All*, and an Obie Award for his Off-Broadway performance in *Krapp's Last Tape*.

He and his wife Jessica won awards for *The Gin Game*, and among the many other tributes paid to them was one by the Academy of Television Arts and Sciences, in 1989, for 50 years of television performances.

In 1979, Hume Cronyn was elected to the Theater Hall of Fame, won honours from the National Press Club, and the Commonwealth Award for Dramatic Arts in 1983, and was a co-winner, with Susan Cooper, of the 1985 Christopher Award and Writers Guild Award for the screenplay, *Dollmaker*, an ABC teleplay. In 1990, he won an Emmy for the TV miniseries called *Age-Old Friends* and returned to the White House to receive the National Medal of Arts award from President George Bush for "special recognition of outstanding contribution to the excellence, growth, support and availability of the arts in the United States."

Mel James

A scene from the 1976 Stratford Festival production of A Midsummer Night's Dream *featuring, left to right, Larry Lamb as Snout, Bernard Hopkins as Snug, Rod Beattie as Quince, Hume Cronyn as Bottom, and Richard Whelan as Flute. [Photo, courtesy Stratford Festival Archives/Photographer, Robert C. Ragsdale]*

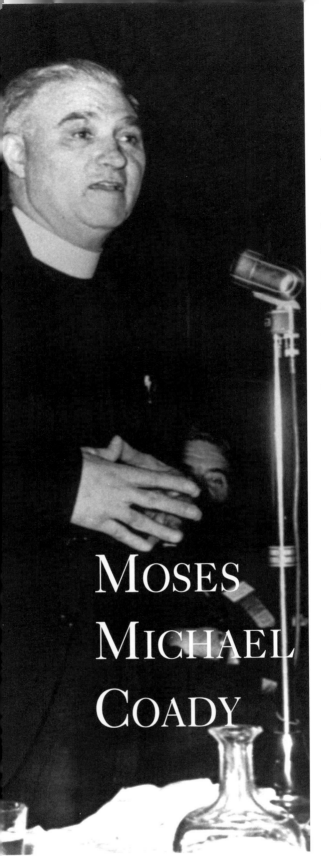

MOSES
MICHAEL
COADY

1882 - 1959

Making Men and Women "Masters of Their Own Destiny"

NOT ALL PARTS of Canada have enjoyed continuous economic rewards from the land or the sea. From eastern Nova Scotia came a response to regional poverty and the Great Depression that grew to define a method of community visioning in many Third World countries. Father Moses Michael Coady, co-founded, with Father J.J. ("Jimmy") Tompkins, the Antigonish Movement as an outgrowth of an extension department of St. Francis Xavier University. It articulated a social and economic message that had profound implications. In a dominantly Scottish Catholic community in Antigonish County and parts of Cape Breton Island, Coady challenged Catholicism to respond to a liberal call for action, responsibility, and social self-understanding.

Father Moses M. Coady was born at North East Margaree, Nova Scotia, on January 3, 1882. Before undertaking studies in philosophy and theology in Rome, he studied at the Provincial Normal College, Truro, Nova Scotia, and received his B.A. at St. Francis Xavier University (1905). In 1939 he wrote *Masters of Their Own Destiny*, a book which is still in print in seven languages. In this Canadian classic, Coady outlined his perception of cooperative action and consciousness raising among the traditionally powerless and poorly educated.

As founding director of the extension department in 1928, Coady and others organized study groups among farmers, fishermen, and industrial workers to give them a

First Director of the Extension Department at St. Francis Xavier University, Antigonish, Nova Scotia, Father Moses Michael Coady (1882 - 1959), viewed at microphone addressing a convention in the 1940s, conducted a remarkable program of adult education for the fishermen of Canada's maritime provinces. While pioneering the organization and expansion of cooperatives and credit unions, his work contributed greatly to the well-being of outreach communities and hundreds of isolated families. "Self-help" could easily have been the motto of this giving, caring priest. The "Antigonish Movement" which he co-founded is carried on today in the Third World by the Coady International Institute. [Photo, courtesy St. Francis Xavier University/Angus L. Macdonald Library]

sense of practical empowerment to set up cooperative stores, factories, and credit unions. He articulated a new vision of social organization and a radical analysis of a malfunctioning economy. As a grass roots movement, it was both a call to action that had an unprecedented impact on local communities and a means of effectual organization both at home and abroad. Coady helped to organize the Nova Scotia's Teachers' Union, the United Maritime Fishermen, and what loosely became known as the Antigonish Movement. From the 1930s this movement combined social and economic approaches that, by the 1940s, were readily adapted to situations in Europe, Latin America, and Asia.

Father Coady was careful to present his ideas within the context of Catholic social teaching and he kept the Antigonish Movement politically neutral. Although he distanced himself from socialist movements then active in North America, he did oppose "the bourgeoisie" who, at the expense of primary producers and workers, lived by dividends, rent, and interest. Some of his followers contributed to the electoral success in Cape Breton of the Co-operative Commonwealth Federation.

By stressing the idea of beginning small and of amalgamating to become more powerful, Coady eschewed head-on challenges with larger economic, religious, and political institutions. His movement dovetailed with other national and regional cooperative movements, but, disputatiously, its impetus had as great an influence beyond Canada's borders, especially in areas of underdevelopment where the vision had practical and immediate application.

The Antigonish Movement developed into multimillion dollar enterprises that revived a region and influenced the entire cooperative movement both in Canada and portions of the United States. As a liberal Catholic movement focusing on adult education, it was an exciting and innovative concept. The Antigonish Movement, a pioneer of distance learning and cooperative management, was a significant national and international force for responsibility, awareness, and change. In 1959, the year of his death, the Coady International Institute in Nova Scotia's St. Francis Xavier University was opened to continue his goal of self-awareness, social action, and cooperative management in the Third World. This institute, in educating community organizers around the world and advising Canadian foreign aid programs, has made a significant contribution.

Moses M. Coady will be remembered as a practical visionary who, through the Antigonish Movement, offered individuals and communities, frustrated by social and economic despair, an applied and successful alternative.

Larry Turner

Premier Joey Smallwood was active in Newfoundland's cooperative movement in the 1920s. This view captures him, left, with M.M. Coady, centre, and Angus Bernard MacDonald, right, at the Congress of Nova Scotia cooperatives held at St. Francis Xavier University, July 1951. MacDonald joined St. Francis Xavier's Extension Department in 1930 as associate director. At the time of this picture, he was national secretary of the Co-operative Union of Canada. His devoted work made Canada a sponsor of CARE, the international aid program. [Photo, courtesy St. Francis Xavier University/Angus L. Macdonald Library]

Father of Irrigation

George Chaffey

1848 -1932

Ontario, California, was a planned community. Euclid Ave., 200 feet wide, was the show-place main street of the entire West. Viewed here, circa 1890, Ontario, California was a brilliant experiment in rural planning. As a model colony, it was featured at the St. Louis World Fair in 1902. [Photo, courtesy Ontario City Library, California/Model Colony Room Collection]

Born one year before the 1849 California Gold Rush, George Chaffey, from Brockville, Ontario, found gold of a different kind in the desert regions of Southern California – untapped fresh water for the irrigation of model colonies he planned to build! By the early 1880s, he and brother William formed a partnership with plans to irrigate the San Bernardino Valley. Communities such as Ontario and Etiwanda, irrigated by fresh water canals, sprung up. The rush to populate this valley would eventually create one of the great fruit bearing regions in the world. Viewed here, circa 1893, George Chaffey reflected in later years that his greatest achievement was diverting the waters of the Colorado River to irrigate a vast desert he named the Imperial Valley, a place name reflecting more his monarchial roots in Canada than his adopted republic roots in California. [Photo, courtesy Ontario City Library, California/Model Colony Room Collection]

C ANADA IS FAMOUS for the fresh water contained in the lakes and rivers that define great expanses of its landscape. Some of Canada's most famous scientists, biologists, geologists, and engineers have received global fame and recognition for their attempts to control and utilize these water resources. One of these was George Chaffey, who made his mark, first in Canada, then internationally in both the United States and Australia.

Born in 1848, George was the eldest child of George Chaffey and Ann Marie Leggo of Brockville, Canada West (Ontario). George Chaffey Sr. had established a shipbuilding operation in Brockville before venturing to Kingston in 1859. The precocious George Jr. attended the esteemed Kingston Grammar School for only a short time. His first love, engineering, could not be satisfied in school, therefore, by the age of 14 he was apprenticed as a marine engineer on Lake Ontario steamships. George then learned administrative skills in Toronto at the bank of his Uncle Benjamin Chaffey. There in 1869 he married Annette, the only daughter of Thomas McCord, the city chamberlain. In the decade of the 1870s, he formed, with his father, a partnership that specialized in building shallow-draught steamers for the Great Lakes and Ohio River trade.

In 1878, George Sr. was enticed to join a Canadian settlement in Riverside, California, where the Santa Ana River irrigation scheme had earlier been established. George Jr. followed a younger brother, William Benjamin (1856-1926) to the settlement in 1880, and they formed a partnership based on the success they had witnessed within the irrigation scheme. They purchased land and water rights on the Cucamonga Plain (presently in San Bernardino County), designed extensive irrigation colonies, and planned towns at Etiwanda and Ontario based on the sale of blocks of land serviced by a mutual non-profit irrigation company. Their vigorous plans included innovative techniques in irrigation management: their model colonies were featured at the World's Fair in St. Louis in 1902. George also invested in electric lighting and telephones in California, and as president and joint engineer of the Los Angeles Electric Company, he made the southern California city the first in the United

William Chaffey, viewed here in 1886, although identified with his older brother in developing the San Bernardino Valley in Southern California, is perhaps better known in South Australia, where today he is looked upon as the father of irrigation in Australia's Murray River Valley. [Photo courtesy Ontario City Library, California/Model Colony Room Collection]

States to be lighted by electricity.

In 1885, a future Prime Minister of Australia, Alfred Deakin, chairman of a royal commission on water supply in Victoria, Australia, visited Ontario, California, and met with the Chaffeys. Excited by the challenge of droughts and deserts on the other side of the Pacific, George visited Melbourne in 1886, hastily told William to sell their California interests, and made plans for huge irrigation colonies in the Murray River valley at Mildura in Victoria and at Renmark in South Australia. The Chaffeys ran into serious problems trying to plant an individualist Californian model in the deserts of Australia, but these colonies eventually were successful and the brothers today are considered largely responsible for the development of Australia's fruit industry.

Encumbered by debts and royal commissions (Chaffey Brothers Limited went into liquidation in 1895), George Chaffey left Australia in 1897, returning to California to invest in subdivision ventures near Los Angeles, irrigation projects, and banking partnerships, the latter with his son Andrew. One of George Chaffey's greatest accomplishments was diverting the waters of the Colorado River to irrigate a portion of the desert he named Imperial Valley, today one of the richest agricultural areas of the western United States.

In an article, "Brockville Boys at Home and Abroad," published in 1914 in the Brockville *Recorder*, the reporter editorialized: "Thirty years ago, a stretch of desert, covered by cactus and sagebrush, inhabited only by quail, jackrabbits and their kind: today the beautiful, smiling town of Ontario, hundreds of freight cars bearing away the golden harvests of the orchards and the product of the town's factories. Ontario is the 'model colony' – the pride not alone of San Bernardino County, but all of Southern California. How was it done? Irrigation and enterprise. And who did it – the Chaffey brothers, Brockville boys."

George Chaffey was a pioneer in agricultural technology, designing irrigation systems that altered the landscapes and prospects of Pacific rim settlements in both California and Australia. He and his younger brother were innovators whose far-reaching efforts made possible the agricultural revolution that opened vast arid areas for agriculture and allowed food to be grown throughout the year and transported to areas that could not sustain year-round growth. He grew up fascinated with the study of engineering on the lush north shore of Lake Ontario and is credited, along with his brother William, with founding several communities in some of the driest regions of the world, the most important of which are Ontario, Mildura, and Renmark. William, who remained in Australia until his death in 1926, is remembered as an Australian pioneer. Statues of him stand today in both Renmark and Mildura. George died in Ontario, California, in 1932, one of the most significant planners and developers in American west coast history. It is fitting that the Chaffey name survives in Ontario, Canada, at a lockstation located on one of the greatest engineering achievements in its day, the Rideau Canal. Chaffey's Locks was named for Samuel, a great-uncle of George and William.

Larry Turner

Chaffey College, Ontario, California, as it appeared in 1887. Originally a satellite campus of the University of Southern California and founded by George Chaffey in 1882, it first opened for classes in 1885. [Photo, courtesy Ontario City Library, California/Model Colony Room Collection]

WHEN, IN 1916, EMILY MURPHY was appointed the first female magis- trate in the British Empire, she had written four books, pushed for the passage of the Dower Act which awarded a wife one-third of a husband's estate, inaugurated a movement to found the Victorian Order of Nurses in Edmonton, Alberta, paved the way for the election of women as school trustees, was the first woman member of the hospital board of Edmonton, and was President of the Canadian Women's Press Club.

Emily Murphy

Clarion Crusader
1868 - 1933

These achievements led the legal committee of the Council of Women of Edmonton to ask her advice when they [the Council] were refused admission to witness the trial of a group of prostitutes because "they might hear what was not fit for their ears." She suggested to the provincial Attorney General that there should be a special court for cases dealing with women and children. He promptly agreed and urged her to become its magistrate. While not trained in law she had some knowledge of the profession as three of her brothers were lawyers. They urged her to take the job. A week later, June 19, 1916, she was appointed.

The third child and first daughter of the promi- nent Ferguson family of Cookstown, Ontario, Emily was also well-educated, having graduated from the Bishop Strachan School for girls in Toronto before marrying,

Granddaughter of Ogle R. Gowan, founder of the Orange Association of British North America, Emily Murphy was the champion leader of five Alberta women who campaigned to have women declared "persons" in 1929 and whose names appear today on a plaque near the main door of the Senate Chamber in Ottawa. [Photo, courtesy National Archives of Canada/PA-138847]

at 19, Arthur Murphy, an Anglican minister, in 1887. For the next decade they lived in Forrest, Chatham, and Ingersoll, Ontario, before they went in 1898 to England where Arthur took a missionary post. This prompted her to write her first book, entitled *Impressions of Janey Canuck Abroad* (1901).

On their return from Great Britain, they settled in Swan River, Manitoba, where Emily began writing for the Winnipeg *Telegram*, until moving to Edmonton in 1907. Her second book was a collection of sketches of life at Swan River entitled *Janey Canuck in the West* and two more followed: *Open Trails* in 1910 and *Seeds of Pine* in 1914. That year Emily met and became a close friend of still another staunch supporter of women's rights, Nellie McClung.

Never at a loss for words whether in her writing or on the bench, Emily described her first day in court as "as pleasant an experience as running a rapids without a guide." Her second case involved lawyer Eardley Jackson who objected to Emily as a judge since a woman, by law, was not considered a person. She noted the objection but continued the hearing and clearly won her point when the Alberta Supreme Court later ruled that "women could not be disqualified from holding public office on account of their sex."

Jackson was later heard to declare in court, "To hell with women magistrates. This country is going to the dogs because of them." He promptly received a letter from Emily: "Unless I receive from you an unqualified apology in writing, I shall regretfully be obliged to henceforth refuse you admittance to this Court in the capacity of Counsel."

As a magistrate for 15 years, she made an exhaustive study of the drug problem and wrote a series of articles for *Maclean's* magazine that became her most important book when published as *The Black Candle* in 1922. According to Christine Mander's 1985 biography of Emily, it caused "a profound stir nationwide among law enforcement and social welfare agencies, the medical profession, and the general public." It also caused passage of new laws that remained in effect more than 40 years.

Emily's biggest victory for women in general began in 1927 when a brother discovered "that any five persons had the right to petition the government for ruling on a constitutional point." Since women were not considered "persons" under the terms of the British North American Act and could not, therefore, be appointed to the Senate, Emily asked McClung and three other Alberta women to sign a petition that went to the Privy Council in England before a judgment, rendered in 1929, overturned a ruling of the Supreme Court of Canada to declare that "women are eligible to be summoned and become members of the Senate of Canada."

Ill health caused Emily to step down as an active magistrate in 1931, by which time she was "liked and respected by the police, clerks, bailiffs, librarians, and even lawyers." It remained, however, for her old nemesis, Eardley Jackson, to pay the final tribute when, in 1933, Emily attended a court hearing she was interested in and Jackson, now a judge, introduced and welcomed her, observing, "A feminine note missing from this building is brought back by the kindly smiling countenance of this beloved lady." She thanked him and that night died in her sleep.

Mel James

Roy Herbert Thomson

1894 - 1976

Paper Chaser

THE CREATION, development, and success of the international Thomson organization is one of the most remarkable commercial achievements in the twentieth century and perhaps in the entire history of business in the Western World. By the mid 1990s this corporation – an enterprise involved with newspapers, specialized information, publishing, and leisure travel – had annual revenues of over eight billion dollars. It was engaged in a variety of business activities, particularly the publishing of newspapers in North America and a wide range of information and publishing products throughout the world. This vast commercial group grew initially from the hard work, experience, and business abilities of one man – Roy Thomson.

Success did not come early or easily to Thomson, a genial, hardworking extrovert. Born in Toronto, the son of a barber, he dropped out of high school at 13 and then studied bookkeeping for a year at a privately owned business school. He paid his fees by working as a janitor. At 14, having learned the basic elements of financial accounting, young Thomson went to work as a bookkeeper for a cordage company.

During his first twenty-five years in the business world, Thomson worked vigorously and accumulated much valuable experience but had little financial success. He went from the cordage business into farming and lost money. Then, with his brother, he sold auto parts and tires. Again he had financial troubles. In 1930 he secured a franchise to sell radio sets in North Bay, about 200 miles north of Toronto, but since radio reception was poor, he concluded that the most effective way to sell his radio sets was to establish a local radio station. By good fortune, he secured a local broadcasting licence, acquired a transmitter, and began to operate his own radio station – CFCH – in North Bay. As he lacked the money necessary to pay employees, he did most of the station's work himself until it was generating sufficient revenue to pay the wages of the necessary staff. At the same time he continued to sell radio sets.

During the economic depression of the 1930s, only determined, optimistic and intuitive people like Thomson, who knew how to test hunches and act on them, had the courage to launch into businesses in which they had no previous experience. Thus it is not surprising that he ventured into both radio broadcasting and newspaper publishing.

The rise in the price of gold in 1934 increased business activity in such Northern Ontario mining communities as Timmins and Kirkland Lake. He established a second radio station (CKGB) and shortly thereafter made a deal to acquire from a local proprietor in Timmins a small weekly newspaper – the *Timmins Weekly Press*. In less than two years, against all apparent wisdom and logic, he turned it into a daily operation. However, it took years for the paper to stand on its own. Nevertheless, a new and increasingly satisfying chapter had begun in Thomson's life. He continued to face major financial challenges, some of which seemed impossible to overcome. But even though there was no immediate hint of it at that time, he was on his way to success.

Thomson learned quickly that careful management of a local community newspaper in a market with potential could provide a good source of revenue. This would require vigorous sales promotion of advertising space in newspapers and of advertising time on radio stations. And rigorous control of expenditures would be essential.

In 1936, Thomson employed a young salesman, Jack Kent Cooke, to assist him in his radio business. Three years later he hired Sidney Chapman to assist him in the financial management of his newspaper business. The combined efforts of Thomson, Cooke, and Chapman produced increasingly satisfying results.

In the late 1940s the Thomson organization owned eight relatively small local newspapers in Ontario. The experience Thomson gained in the acquisition and publishing of these papers established the financial and editorial foundations on which much of the future development of the organization was based. Early in his career, as the owner of a number of newspapers, Thomson came to the conclusion that it would be in the best interests of the people served by particular newspapers if the editor of each respective Thomson newspaper were to manage its editorial and news activities. He refused to believe that he knew what was best editorially as well as the editor did. Thus each Thomson paper was managed on the basis of editorial freedom with control of financial matters retained by the Thomson organization. Such control was essential, in Thomson's view, because experience had taught him that he and his colleagues could run a paper better than those from whom he had bought it.

In 1949 the partnership between Roy Thomson and Jack Kent Cooke ended when Cooke, who had played a key role in the development of the radio side of Thomson's business, signed a contract to manage a major radio station, with the proviso that Thomson would not be involved. While this was a blow to Thomson at that time, it is likely that, in the long run, the break with Cooke was a blessing in disguise for both Thomson and Cooke.

In 1951 Thomson suffered deeply the death of his wife, Edna, who had been central in his life and in the lives of his two daughters and his son, Ken. He had shared his business hopes and plans with both his wife and Cooke. Now there was a void.

In his search for a new challenge, Thomson became a candidate in 1953 for election to the Canadian House of Commons but was unsuccessful. Before the election he learned that he could purchase a share in the

Lord Thomson of Fleet (left) shares humorous moment with rival Canadian Publisher, Lord Beaverbrook, on the occasion of the latter's 85th birthday in London, England, 1964.
[Photo, courtesy *The Toronto Star*]

Scotsman in Edinburgh, Scotland. This newspaper with an international reputation had interested him for some time. The unexpected opportunity provided precisely the type of challenge for which he was searching.

Initially Thomson's media concerns had been confined to Ontario, but in 1949 he purchased his first Canadian newspaper outside Ontario. He followed this three years later with the purchase of his first paper in the United States. By 1953 management of Thomson's North American operations, which then comprised sixteen newspapers and a small string of local radio stations, was being taken over by his son, Ken, and a small group led by St. Clair McCabe who had demonstrated outstanding expertise in the development of advertising techniques. Thus Thomson was free to consider carefully the purchase of the *Scotsman*. With Sid Chapman, he went to Scotland following the election of August 1953 and, after two days of hard bargaining, purchased it.

Touched by the magic of Edinburgh and stimulated, perhaps, by the spirit of his enterprising great-great-grandfather who had emigrated to Canada in 1773 from Westerkirk in Dumfriesshire, Thomson moved to Edinburgh in 1954 "to do some interesting but not too strenuous work." He was then 60 years of age. In the 22 years which remained to him he enjoyed astonishing success. A remarkable series of opportunities came to him and he seized them.

A decade of hard work revitalized the financial health of the *Scotsman*. Four years into that decade he secured the franchise for Scotland's first commercial television station. He described that franchise as a "licence to print money," a remark that, he admitted, might have been injudicious "but it was certainly right." Other acquisitions followed.

In 1959 he acquired the Kemsley chain of 18 newspapers in the United Kingdom including *The Sunday Times,* Britain's leading Sunday newspaper. Subsequently he entered the book and magazine publishing business and in 1967 acquired *The Times*, the most prestigious newspaper in the United Kingdom. Four years later he joined a North Sea oil consortium and in due course his organization and his shareholders benefited handsomely as a result of the carefully considered risk he had taken.

That was the last great risk Roy Thomson took before he died in August 1976. Fortunately he had written and published, a year earlier, his recollections of his work in Britain from 1954 onwards. His book, *After I Was Sixty*, is a most remarkable, highly stimulating, and open account by this most extraordinary man. This relatively brief, two-hundred-page volume is filled with information and insights from the man who, perhaps more than any other single individual, demonstrated how to develop and manage a global information and publishing corporation with amazing success.

In his lifetime, Roy Thomson's outstanding abilities and achievements as a businessman were never adequately recognised in Canada. In Britain his unique qualities and accomplishments led to his appointment to the House of Lords as a hereditary peer. His enduring memorial, however, resides in his life and work and in the influence of the great corporation to which he gave birth, which he nurtured, and which his spirit continues to inspire.

D. McCormack Smyth

THE PATRICKS
LESTER & FRANK
Hockey's Royal Family
1883-1960　　1885-1960

FOLLOWING Lester Patrick's death in 1960, sports columnist Jim Coleman wrote, "Lester Patrick didn't invent hockey but no other man has ever exerted such a lengthy and generally beneficial influence on any sport."

When Lester's younger brother, Frank, died four weeks later, another columnist claimed, "The modern rule book is a monument to Frank's invention: it still contains 22 of the rules he wrote."

While other hockey historians credit Lester with some of the rule changes, most agree that Lester and Frank created modern hockey and founded a hockey dynasty neatly described in a chapter of Trent Frayne's book, *The Mad Men of Hockey.* He wrote, "... for 15 years they organized and ran their own league, built and owned their own rinks, raided rival leagues and signed their own players, drew up their own schedules, made up their own rules, and owned, managed, coached and played on their own teams."

It was Frank who proposed the blue lines that divide the rink into three zones, the penalty shot, a penalty for checking into the boards, the assist for helping score a goal, the numbering of players, the forward pass, and the playoff system. Others give Lester credit for allowing defencemen to rush up the ice and goaltenders to

When the goalie of the New York Rangers was injured during the final round of the 1928 Stanley Cup finals, there was no one dressed to replace him. As manager of the team, Lester Patrick put on the pads and skated to the net, assuring a Rangers' victory by stopping 18 shots until Billy Boucher won the game in over-time. Forty-four at the time of this feat, Lester Patrick was called "the greatest name in hockey history" by "Cyclone" Taylor, hockey's first superstar. [Photo, courtesy Dean and Frank Miller]

stop a puck any way they can instead of being restricted to standing, and both are given credit for establishing the Pacific Coast Hockey Association that won the Stanley Cup for such teams as the Vancouver Millionaires, the Victoria Cougars, and the Seattle Metropolitans.

Lester was born in Drummondville, Quebec, in 1883, and Frank, in Ottawa, two years later. They were the sons of Joe Patrick, a successful lumberman who settled in Nelson, British Columbia, in 1907. By then, Lester had already established himself as an outstanding defenceman in Brandon, Manitoba, where he broke the tradition of playing only a defensive role when he rushed up the ice to score a goal. With the Montreal Wanderers in 1906, he scored the final two goals in a 12-10 total point two-game Stanley Cup victory over the Ottawa Silver Seven.

Lester stayed with the Wanderers as captain for another year and then joined his father at Nelson as did Frank. Frank had been a star defenceman with McGill University while obtaining a BA and, at age 20, he had refereed a Stanley Cup game. At Nelson the Patricks built a small covered arena and their team won the BC championship before the boys turned professional in December 1909 when mining magnate, M.J. O'Brien, bankrolled the Renfrew Millionaires. O'Brien paid Lester and Frank the unheard-of sum of $3,000 and $2,000 respectively to play 12 games in the winter of 1910. Another high-priced Millionaire player was Frank ("Cyclone") Taylor, but, despite the high-priced talent, the Millionaires failed to win the Stanley Cup.

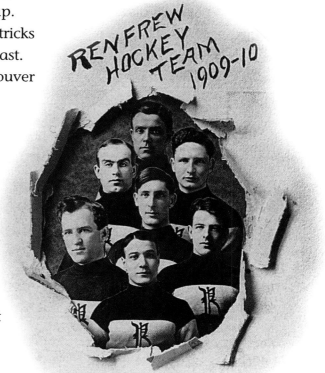

When Joe Patrick sold his business in 1911, the Patricks decided to launch professional hockey on the west coast. They built Canada's first artificial ice arenas at Vancouver and Victoria and raided eastern clubs for 16 players, among them Cyclone Taylor, Newsy Lalonde, Moose Johnson, and goaltender Bert Lindsay, father of "Terrible Ted" of Detroit Red Wings fame.

Some local players were added to make a total of 23 – carefully divided among Vancouver, Victoria, and New Westminster. In Vancouver, they played in what was described as the world's largest sports emporium, a 10,000-seat building. Here Frank not only owned, coached, and played for Vancouver but also served as president of the three-team league that played seven-man hockey until 1922 – instead of the six-man game already adopted in the east – while

In its brief history, the Renfrew Millionaires (1907-1911) were arguably the best amateur hockey team ever fielded. Fifty percent of the 1908 squad of eight players fielded four future Hockey Hall of Famers: Newsy Lalonde, bottom; "Cyclone" Taylor, upper left; Frank Patrick, upper right; and Lester Patrick, center. At top is Bert Lindsay, father of "Terrible Ted", another Hall of Famer, who skated on the same line in the 1940s and '50s with Gordie Howe and Sid Abel of the Detroit Red Wings. [Photo, courtesy Dean and Frank Miller]

Lester owned, coached, and played for Victoria.

The East laughed at the three-team league until, at the end of the season, the West won two of the three all-star games by scores of 5-1 and 10-4. It was an even bigger shock in 1915 when Frank's Vancouver Millionaires won the Stanley Cup, beating Ottawa in three straight games and, in 1917, the Seattle Metropolitans became the first U.S. city to win the Cup. Lester's Victoria Cougars also won it in 1925.

By then Patrick's Western league included teams in Saskatoon, Regina, Edmonton, and Calgary and had such future Hall of Fame players as George Hainsworth, Dick Irvin, Eddie Shore, Newsy Lalonde, and Bill Cook. Expansion plans in the East, however,with some owners willing "to throw money around like confetti" doomed the Western clubs that were losing money. After Saskatoon optioned itself to the Montreal Maroons, Frank, representing the three clubs they owned as well as Calgary and Edmonton, sold the teams to the Chicago, Detroit, and New York franchises for $250,000, making it possible for the Patricks almost to break even after operating the PCHA for 15 years. At the same time, Lester joined the newly established New York Rangers.

New York was a perfect match for the Ranger management. Lester not only produced a winning team but sold the game to skeptical sports editors like Ed Daley of the *Herald Tribune*, who created Lester's best-known nickname when he wrote, "Yesterday, I spent a fascinating half hour in the lair of the Silver Fox." Hall of Famer King Clancy once declared, "Lester fit the New York scene like a glove ... immaculately dressed, silver-haired, and with that elegant bearing, he oozed class and the Garden fans loved him for it."

Fans were even more adoring after the second game of the Stanley Cup playoffs with the Maroons in 1928 when the Ranger goaltender, Lorne Chabot, stopped a shot with his left eye and had to leave the game in the second period. The Rangers had no substitute goalie and the Maroons refused to let a goaltender in the stands replace Chabot; so Lester strapped on the pads. He allowed one goal that tied the game, but the Rangers won in overtime and went on to win the Stanley Cup.

Lester spent 13 years behind the Ranger bench as, every year but one, the team made the playoffs and won another Stanley Cup in 1933. With the inauguration of all-star selections in 1930, Lester was selected as the outstanding coach seven of the first eight years but was criticized for nepotism by fans when his sons, Lynn and Muzz, first joined the team in the mid-'30s. Both had reached star status, however, when the Rangers won the Stanley Cup in 1940, the last time until the spring of 1995.

After consummating the deal to sell the teams, Frank opted to stay in British Columbia, speculating in mining and oil claims and set up the Western (minor) Hockey League and managed the Vancouver club until turning it over to his younger brother Guy when he became managing director of the NHL in 1933. A year later, he joined the Boston Bruins as coach, returning to Vancouver in 1936. After the 1936 season he returned to Vancouver. In 1940, when Frank went to the Montreal Canadiens as top aide to Tommy Gorman, this caused Jim Coleman to write, "Frank Patrick, one of the great brains of hockey, has shouldered his way back into the

At the family home, Cyndomyr, Victoria, B.C., 1911, gather the Joseph and Grace Patrick family. From left, front row, sit Ted, Cynda, Myrtle, and Guy. At back, seated, are Lester, Dora, Stan, Grace and Joe, and Frank. Lester's two sons, Lynn and Muzz, not only played for the Rangers and became managers of NHL teams, but two of Lester's grandsons are active in the NHL today. They are Lynn's son Craig, manager of the Pittsburg Penguins and Muzz's son Richard (Dick), president and part owner of the Washington Capitals. [Photo, courtesy Dean and Frank Miller]

Visionary Frank Patrick's dream of a west coast hockey league was fulfilled in 1911 when he and brother Lester established the Pacific Coast Hockey Association. He not only built Canada's first artificial ice arena in Vancouver, but owned, managed, coached, and played defence for the Vancouver Millionaires leading them to the Stanley Cup in 1915. [Photo, courtesy Dean and Frank Miller]

game's high society." Over the next two years he signed such players as Elmer Lach, Kenny Reardon, and Butch Bouchard but then accepted a position with an industrial firm in Montreal in 1942 and, following the war, returned to British Columbia and semi-retirement.

Lester continued with the Rangers until December 1947. When he was feted as a retiring vice president, a New York columnist humorously observed, "It finally happened to Lester Patrick; he found himself at a loss for words." Another wrote, "Lester Patrick, the man known as the Silver Fox and Mr. Hockey, was heaped with words of praise and with gifts, which, when all stacked together, failed by far to measure up to what he himself has contributed to the game of hockey." The Ranger organization honoured Lester as late as 1966 when it created the Lester Patrick award, presented annually "for outstanding service to hockey in the United States."

"The Silver Fox" and his wife, Grace, returned to Victoria where he kept in touch with many of his old cronies and helped establish the Hockey Hall of Fame, originally located in Kingston, Ontario, and now magnificently housed at Front and Yonge Streets, Toronto. *Mel James*

Ernest MacMillan

1893 - 1973

Brilliant Musical Magician

MACMILLAN, the celebrated conductor of the internationally recognized Toronto Symphony Orchestra and leader of the no-less-acclaimed Toronto Mendelssohn Choir, was Canada's most influential musical figure in his time. Composer, organist, musical statesman and administrator, he was Principal of the Toronto Conservatory of Music in Toronto and Dean of Music at the University of Toronto. Knighted in 1935, Sir Ernest won many other honours such as the Order of Canada in 1969. But his honours were the result of hard productive work that elevated and enhanced the very world of music in Canada.

Sir Ernest MacMillan was the most versatile musical genius in Canadian history. He did his best to educate orchestra and audience in both the classics and twentieth century music, defending "modernism" in music much in the same way Eric Brown, Director of the National Gallery of Canada, defended the avant-garde Group of Seven in the 1920s. [Photo, courtesy Toronto Symphony Orchestra Association]

The son of a Scottish Presbyterian minister, Ernest MacMillan was born in 1893 at Mimico, then a small town just west of Toronto. He was a musical prodigy, writing songs and performing publicly on the organ at age 10; by age 15, in 1908, he was already a professional church organist. His studies in Toronto and Scotland were followed by advanced work in France. Caught in Germany at the outbreak of World War I, he was interned as an enemy alien. Nevertheless, he went on composing and performing concerts and theatricals in a civilian prison camp and, on the basis of his work composed while still in prison, he earned an Oxford doctorate in music. Back in Toronto in 1919, he soon became a church organist, choirmaster, and music teacher. In 1923 he directed the first complete performance in Canada of Bach's *St. Matthew Passion* and continued to give annual performances of it for over 30 years. From 1927 to 1931 he was also involved in Canadian Pacific Railway folk festivals while producing songbooks and essays on music, and touring Canada as a festival judge.

Then in 1931 came his appointment to conduct the Toronto Symphony. MacMillan raised its expertise to new heights, introduced contemporary Canadian music, and took the orchestra to the United States between 1952-1956. He, himself, served as a guest conductor with other orchestras in the U.S.A., Australia, and Brazil, but chiefly he made "the TSO" warmly popular at home where it performed regularly at downtown Massey Hall. He also conducted the Promenade Symphony Orchestra at summer "Promenade Concerts" on the University of Toronto campus in what in winter was the university's hockey arena. In 1942 Sir Ernest took charge of the Mendelssohn Choir, founded in 1895, already an august institution and heard not only with the TSO but with other symphonies like the Chicago and Philadelphia. Under MacMillan the choir certainly performed Bach or Beethoven but also present-day British composers such as William Walton and Ralph Vaughan Williams. When MacMillan retired from both the TSO in 1956 and the Mendelssohn Choir a year later, he had given each of these organizations fresh scope, appeal, and international stature.

His contributions had by no means ended. He continued to be heavily involved in conducting on the CBC, founding the Canadian Music Centre, and acting as president of the Canadian Music Council and CAPAC (Composers, Authors and Publishers Association of Canada). Music came of age in Canada thanks to Sir Ernest MacMillan.

J.M.S. Careless

The young Ernest MacMillan gave organ recitals at Toronto's Massey Hall when he was a 10-year-old child prodigy. [Photo, courtesy Keith MacMillan Fonds]

Beautiful Joe

by Marshall Saunders

Published in 1894, Beautiful Joe became the first book written by a Canadian author to sell more than a million copies!

Margaret Marshall Saunders

1861 - 1947

[Photo taken from Henry J. Morgan, ed., Types of Canadian Women (Toronto, 1901)]

THE FIRST CANADIAN AUTHOR to sell more than a million copies of a book was a woman who disguised her gender by calling herself Marshall Saunders. Her real name was Margaret, but she used the name Marshall because she believed there was more acceptance of stories written by men.

She also based most of her stories in the United States though the setting of her best-selling novel, based on a true story about a mistreated dog named Beautiful Joe, was Meaford, then a village on the historic shores of Georgian Bay, Ontario.

To mark the 100th anniversary of its original publication, volunteers, in conjunction with the Meadford Town Council, Chamber of Commerce, and Rotary Club, republished the original story in 1994, made "Beautiful Joe" a town symbol, and dedicated a park adjacent to a pink frame house that had become the dog's home following his rescue from a cruel, disgusting owner who had cut off his ears and tail.

Margaret Saunders wrote nine other children's books featuring animals, and, although all were successful, none matched the popularity of *Beautiful Joe*, the first American edition of which sold out in ten days. By 1900 sales in the United States totalled 650,000; in Canada, 558,000, and in Britain, 146,000. Eventually, the story was translated into 18 languages.

Saunders' nine other books are described as "adult romances" and "social problem fiction" by Elizabeth Waterston whose brief biography in 1992 reveals that Saunders' commitment was not to animal causes only but to such other issues as the abolition of child labour, slum clearance, better playgrounds, and greater recognition of the role of women in society.

The second of six children born to a Baptist minister in Nova Scotia and a mother whose family were successful West Indies traders, Margaret lived in the Annapolis Valley until she was six, then moved to Halifax in 1867. At age 15 she was sent to a boarding school in Scotland for further studies in conversational French and German as well as history and literature.

There her diaries and letters home showed no particular aptitude for writing but did reflect her loneliness. "I cry all the time," she wrote to her mother, "when it does not interfere with my lessons." She also studied in France before returning home at age 17. Over the next eight years she took some courses at Dalhousie University, taught school, became involved in numerous causes – at one point she belonged to 20 organizations – and helped around the house. She also "scribbled" and, when one of her short stories won a contest that paid $40, this stimulated a lifetime interest in writing.

Her first novel, a romance called *A Spanish Sailor*, was published in Britain in 1889. She submitted short stories to various magazines before learning through her brother's fiancée in Meaford about a dog that had been rescued from a cruel owner. Brought up in a home that housed numerous pets and aware that the American Humane Society (AHS) was offering a $200 prize for a novel that could repeat the success of *Black Beauty*, Margaret wrote *Beautiful Joe* and won the prize.

Her father, who gave up the ministry to become editor of a religious magazine and write tomes on such topics as the history of the Baptist Church in the Maritimes, suggested she retain the rights rather than turn them over to the AHS. *Beautiful Joe* was subsequently published with revised editions made to meet the needs of American and British readers (Canadian and British editions, for example, were endorsed by Lady Aberdeen, wife of the Canadian Governor General, while the U.S. edition had a letter written by the editor of the popular children's magazine called *Youth's Companion* which had published many of her short stories).

Written as an autobiography, *Beautiful Joe* illustrates not only that animals are cruel one to the other but also that many ordinary people can be malicious, evil, merciless, and self-destructive. Beautiful Joe's heroine is Laura whom he admires for trying to improve the world in ways that include stopping drunkards from their folly to adding mercy to the justice meted out to criminals.

After *Beautiful Joe's* enormous success, a number of short stories previously written by Saunders and published in Sunday magazines were produced in book form in 1896 under the title *For Other Boys' Sake*. Margaret by then was spending much of her time in Boston, attending Boston University and writing at least two novels, both published in 1897. She returned to Canada to spend five months among the Acadians to research her 1898 novel, *Rose à Charlitte*, and for the next five years her Boston publisher brought out a Saunders novel annually, the most popular of them in 1902 when she wrote *Beautiful Joe's Paradise*.

This sequel, prompted in part because the real "Joe" had died, explored the immortality of pets. Despite the topic, "which might make us expect ... a sad and sentimental book," Waterston writes that it was "lively, funny, and filled with inventiveness."

In 1908 Margaret suffered a breakdown. After rest in a home in Maine, however, she produced two more works in 1910, one of them her powerful work on how women might effectively confront social problems.

A year later, she was awarded an honorary degree by Acadia University and following the

Taken circa 1925 at Canadian Keswick, Lake Rosseau, Muskoka, Ontario, this photograph assembles four well-known Canadian authors at the peak of their careers: left to right, Sir Charles G. Roberts (1860-1943); Margaret Marshall Saunders (1861-1947); Wilson Pugsley Macdonald (1880-1967); and John M.Elson (1880-1966).
[Photo, courtesy Hugh P. MacMillan]

death of her mother in 1913, she and a sister with their father, then in his 80s, moved to Toronto where she published another autobiographical animal story, *Pussy Black Face.*

A further autobiographical dog story followed: *Boy: The Wandering Dog.* Set in New York City, it humorously describes the city as a bad place for dogs because of high licence fees, laws requiring muzzles, and rich owners giving "too many baths." But it also attacks fur merchants by describing "women walking about dressed in fur coats, thanks to the cruel seal traffic."

A revised edition of *Beautiful Joe* was published in 1918 by the Canadian firm then known as McClelland, Goodchild and Stewart. In 1919, Saunders published *Golden Dicky: The Story of a Canary* which Lucy Maud Montgomery described as so suspenseful when she read it to her son that "she had to read the ending to reassure him." On meeting Saunders, however, the author of *Anne of Green Gables* found Saunders "a clever woman but a bit of a bore – talks too much and overloads her conversation with irrelevant details."

Other animal stories followed: one about a pony, another about a monkey. In her final novel, *Esther de Warren,* she recalls her own experiences 50 years earlier. The heroine in this work is a Nova Scotia girl of 15 on board ship sailing to Edinburgh. While some critics find it a puzzling story with aspects of fantasy and fairy tale qualities, Saunders wrote to Lorne Pierce that "*Esther* is my favourite book."

When her writing career ended in 1927, Saunders carried on, giving lectures and illustrated talks to literary clubs and other groups. She also remained active in numerous clubs and societies. In 1934, the same year another edition of *Beautiful Joe* was published, she was awarded a Companion of the British Empire (CBE). In her 70s, she began suffering from bouts of mental confusion that, as a niece wrote, continued with greater "estrangement from reality" until her death at age 86 in 1947.

Mel James

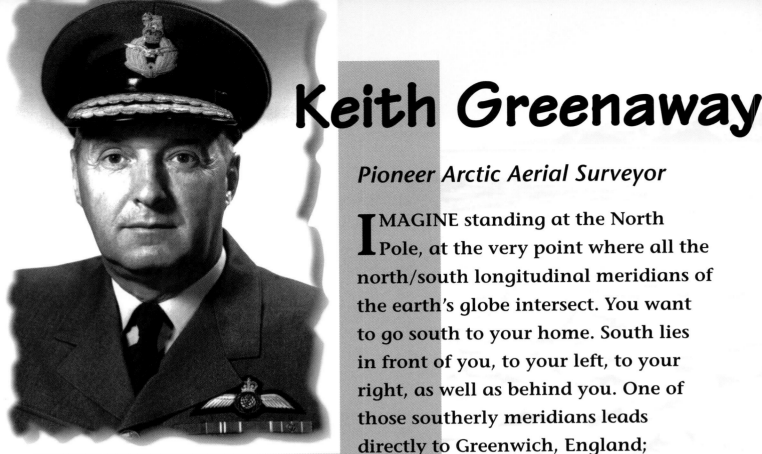

Keith Greenaway

Pioneer Arctic Aerial Surveyor

IMAGINE standing at the North Pole, at the very point where all the north/south longitudinal meridians of the earth's globe intersect. You want to go south to your home. South lies in front of you, to your left, to your right, as well as behind you. One of those southerly meridians leads directly to Greenwich, England; another leads to the middle of the Pacific Ocean; only one "south" will take you home.

At one time Keith Greenaway was the only aerial navigator in the world who could direct exactly how to get where you wanted to go from that imaginary geographical pinnacle. Today he is the acknowledged master of aerial navigation in the high polar regions. In actual fact, immediately following World War II Keith pioneered, developed, and refined Arctic air exploration.

Accurate navigation in the north is immensely complicated because the geographic pole (the place where you were imaginatively standing in the first paragraph) does not correspond exactly with the magnetic pole (the place to which the compass needle points). In 1995, for instance, the magnetic pole was in the Noice Peninsula on Ellef Ringnes Island, hundreds of miles from the geographic pole. In the year 2185, give or take 20 years, the meandering magnetic pole will actually bisect the geographic polar position.

Accordingly, a very large area of magnetic compass unreliability exists for aerial navigators throughout the entire magnetic pole region. For approximately 1,200 miles from east to west and 2,000 miles north to south, the magnetic compass is completely unreliable as a directional indicator, primarily because of very strong magnetic influences.

In the absence of a useful magnetic compass, the aerial navigator must determine an accurate method of assessing direction. Understandably, ability to establish headings is essential. No less important is the ability to maintain proper headings once they have been established.

Kenneth Maclure, Group Captain of the Royal Canadian Air Force, was a staff member of the Empire Air Navigation School in England. In April 1945, at the conclusion of a long-range polar flight in an *Aries* aircraft of the Royal Air Force, the EANS staff visited the RCAF Station at Rivers, Manitoba. It was there that Keith Greenaway, then attached to the RCAF's Central Navigation School, heard from Maclure of the difficulties involved in Arctic aerial navigation and of Maclure's early study of a grid system aimed at simplifying the plotting of navigational headings in the North.

Within a year following his encounter with Maclure, Greenaway was afforded a once-in-a-lifetime opportunity to develop and test his own modified grid system. He was posted to the Canadian section of the United States Air Force's *B29* Superfortress Detachment at Edmonton, Alberta. There he was involved with the USAF in modifying Maclure's pioneering grid system for practical use in the western hemisphere. Greenaway at the time was a navigator on board the first American military aircraft to cross the north geographic pole on May 9, 1946.

While creating a navigational polar grid for Arctic aerial navigation, Greenaway, in early 1947 discovered the wandering ice island later named T3. The huge ice mass was subsequently equipped with weather instruments that provided to Canada and the rest of the world valuable information about Arctic conditions.

The multi-talented Keith Greenaway was born in Victoria County, Ontario, in 1916. After attending the Canadian Electronics Institute in Toronto, he joined the RCAF in 1940. During World War II he trained navigators and wireless air gunners of the British Commonwealth Air Training Plan.

From the mid-forties into the sixties, Keith Greenaway continued to take advantage of the improving capabilities of directional gyroscopes to develop further an accurate and reliable system of aerial navigation in the polar regions of the Arctic. Thereafter until he retired from the Canadian Armed Forces in 1971, Brigadier-General Keith Greenaway served as Air Advisor to the Chief of the Air Staff of the Royal Malaysian Air Force.

Greenaway has received many awards and recognitions for his aerial navigational work in the Arctic. These include the Thurlow Award in 1951 from the United States Institute of Navigation for his contribution to navigational science, the McKee Trans-Canada Trophy in 1952 for contributions to Arctic flying, the Massey Medal in 1960 for outstanding personal achievement and contributions to the development of Canada, induction as a premier member in Canada's Aviation Hall of Fame in 1973, Companion of the Order of Icarus for contributions to manned flight.

This dedicated Canadian, who has made Arctic aerial transportation less complex, has been an editor, author, co-author and contributor to various international aerial publications. In 1956 with Moira Dunbar he co-authored the prominently important *Arctic Canada from the Air*.

A.J. Bauer

Photographed while recording a description of the flight to the geographic pole, March 29, 1954, for Leonard W. Brockington, right, first chairman of the Canadian Broadcasting Corporation. The Honourable Brooke Claxton, Minister of National Defence, centre, and Keith Greenaway are looking on. This was the first flight to the North Pole by a member of the Cabinet of the Government of Canada. The photograph was taken shortly after circling the Pole and on the way back to Resolute Bay.
[Photo, courtesy RCAF Archives]

Oronhyatekha

Peter Martin

1841 - 1907

Supreme Chief Ranger of the Independent Order of Foresters

ORONHYATEKHA was among the most visible persons of native heritage in Canada and, through his leadership of the Independent Order of Foresters, was widely known throughout North America as a visionary of fraternalism. Flamboyant and exciting, Oronhyatekha knew how to promote both himself and the ideas of his organization. He also maintained an almost mythical connection with the Royal family, with prime ministers as well as presidents.

Baptized Peter Martin when born in 1841 on the Six Nations Reserve on the Grand River near Brantford, Ontario, he was a grandson of the Mohawk warrior and chieftain George Martin, who had been a soldier in both the American Revolutionary War and the War of 1812. Oronhyatekha's gift of language resulted in part from preparation at the New England Company's industrial school, the Wesleyan Academy in Wilbraham, Massachusetts, and the Episcopal school, Kenyon College, Ohio. He returned to Canada in time to deliver an address in 1860 to the Prince of Wales who was visiting Canada West, evidently at 19 impressing the future Edward VII and regius professor Sir Henry Wentworth Ackland who invited him to attend Oxford University where Oronhyatekha's portrait hangs in St. Edmunds Hall to this day. He received his medical degree from the University of Toronto in 1867, having previously joined the Masonic Order and the Queen's Own Rifles. In 1871 he was part of the first Canadian Rifle team invited to compete at Wimbledon where he won no less than nine prizes.

Oronhyatekha was the first representative of first nation peoples to attend Oxford University and one of the first Iroquoians to become a practising physician in Canada.
[Photo, courtesy Independent Order of Foresters]

When the Duke and Duchess of Cornwall and York visited Canada in 1901, they paraded up Toronto's Bay Street and through the commemorative arch erected by the Independent Order of Foresters. At the time, Oronhyatekha was the Supreme Chief Ranger of the IOF whose headquarters acted as a backdrop for the Royal Arch. [Photo, courtesy Charles J. Humber Collection]

Oronhyatekha initially set up his medical practice at Frankford, Ontario, on the Trent River, and then at Stratford, Napanee, and London. In 1873 he was appointed by Sir John A. Macdonald as a consulting physician to the Tyendinaga Mohawks on the Bay of Quinte, nominally his home until death. He advertised himself as an Oxford physician who also practised "indian cures and herbal medicines." Although he was elected President of the Grand Council of Ontario in 1874 his career shifted away from native associations as he pro-moted self-help, mutual aid, and fraternal societies in the nation, on the continent, and around the world.

While practising in London, Ontario, in the 1870s, Oronhyatekha joined the Loyal Orange Lodge (L.O.L.). This allowed membership in a local branch of the United States based Independent Order of Foresters (IOF). After being appointed Chief Ranger of the Ontario high court in 1878, he crossed the province promoting the concept of brotherly love and insurance. Oronhyatekha was then elected the first Supreme Chief Ranger in a reconstituted international society in 1881. He so developed the society which, at that time, had only 369 members and a debt of $4,000, that, at his death in 1907, the IOF had 250,000 members worldwide and 11 million dollars in liquid assets. The society offered welfare benefits, weekly sick benefits, disability insurance, a pension plan and funeral costs. By 1897 the society headquarters was housed in the Temple Building on Toronto's Bay Street which formed an important backdrop to a promotional extravaganza around a visit by the Duke and Duchess of Cornwall and York in 1901.

Oronhyatekha associated himself with many organizations to promote himself (including Grand Templar, head of the International Good Templars of the World), his practice, and his

Holding a parasol, Dr. Oronhyatekha, shortly before his death in 1907, is seen in this view with orphans and staff of the orphanage he founded on Foresters Island on the Bay of Quinte. [Photo, courtesy Charles J. Humber Collection]

genuine concern for others. He was frequently criticized for his own excesses. In 1903 on an island he owned in the Bay of Quinte he built an extravagant orphans' home that called into question his judgment and intentions. Even at his death, a lavish funeral included his lying in state at Toronto's Massey Hall and his transport to Tyendinaga in a specially commissioned train.

Oronhyatekha led an organization that paid out more benefits than any other private or public institution over the same period of time. As one of the greatest builders of the fraternal movement in North America, he was widely accepted as a distinguished leader in Canada at a time when government policy still treated native peoples in a condescending and arbitrary manner. Married to Ellen Hill, the great-granddaughter of both Chief Joseph Brant and Chief John Deserontyou, Oronhyatekha successfully bridged a gap of perception and communication that challenged stereotypes and led to a wider understanding of the contribution of the First Nations when accepted for who they are.

Larry Turner

In 1907, mourners gathered at the Desoronto home of Dr. Oronhyatekha whose international reputation as the Supreme Chief Ranger of the Independent Order of Foresters made him the most famous Iroquoian of his day. [Photo, courtesy Charles J. Humber Collection]

Barbara Ann Scott

As Good as Gold

AFTER BARBARA ANN SCOTT won gold in 1948 at the European, Olympic, and World Figure Skating Championships, the Ottawa-born (1928) skater told the press, "I want to get married and live in a house with a white picket fence." This prompted the *New York Daily News* to headline its story, "Great Scott – She'd Rather Cook." The article, that followed however, described her accomplishment in glowing terms: "Beauteous Barbara Ann Scott, Canada's sparkling ballerina on the ice, won the women's figure skating championships ... before 7,000 dazzled admirers who hailed her performance as superior to Sonja Henie's best as an amateur."

That was only one of the lavish descriptions accorded Barbara Ann from the moment she won the European and World Championship a year earlier. On that occasion she returned home to a tumultuous welcome in Ottawa. Children were let out of school, a 32-piece band struck up "Let Me Call You Sweetheart," and the Mayor presented her with a new car and the freedom of the city.

The car, however, caused controversy because a fusty Avery Brundage, President of the American Olympic Association and President-elect of the International Olympic Committee, thundered that accepting the vehicle made her ineligible to compete in the 1948 Winter Olympics taking place the next year in Switzerland. Barbara Ann tearfully returned the car and

As European, World, and Olympic Champion, Barbara Ann Scott returned home to Ottawa in 1948 to face exuberant crowds exceeding 70,000 admirers. She was grateful upon being given the key to the city and a brand new convertible. [Photo, courtesy Charles J. Humber Collection]

Opposite: When Barbara Ann Scott won gold at the European, World, and Olympic Championships – all within six weeks – Canada's love affair with the blonde charmer blossomed into adoration. Her dazzling performances generated celebrity status for the first Canadian female skater ever to capture gold at the Olympics. [Photo, courtesy National Archives of Canada/PA-49893]

spent the rest of that winter performing at local charity carnivals and exhibitions besides practising eight hours a day to prepare for the three major championships of 1948: defence of both her European and World crowns, in addition to her quest for Olympic gold!

Some felt she should skip the European title being held at Prague, but her coach, Sheldon Galbraith, who described her as "a perfectionist with phenomenal balance," believed she could outskate not only all of the other women competitors but most of the men as well.

He proved correct. Before 12,000 Czech admirers, she earned the highest marks ever given to a figure skater in that country. Moving on to the Olympics at St. Moritz, Barbara Ann was greeted by warm weather that delayed the start of the ice skating competitions and added to the overall tension. The ice was still poor three days later when 25 women from seven countries competed in the compulsory figures. Barbara Ann won with 858.1 points.

The next day the ice was even worse as a result of two hockey games played that morning, but Barbara Ann's coach realized that during the games, when the boards for hockey were removed, a narrow strip of clear ice was left. They quickly worked out a variation of her planned four-minute program. She did one double loop instead of three at the beginning and ended with three double salchows instead of the double loops she had intended. A standing ovation followed and, though there were 12 other skaters to follow, few doubted she had won. And she did, scoring 166.077 points for the gold medal.

When standing on the podium the next day, she fondly remembered her father and "felt happy, sad and proud all at the same time." Her late father, a former army colonel and senior civil servant, had been the first to encourage her to skate. Her mother had been equally encouraging. At age nine, Barbara Ann trained seven hours daily while being tutored at home in school subjects. At 10 she became the youngest Canadian ever to win a national gold medal. She was Canadian senior women's champion between 1944 and 1948, North American champion 1945-48, and won the European and World titles in 1947. But her dream came true with the 1948 Olympic gold medal.

Two weeks later, at the age of twenty, she again captured the World Championship at Davos, Switzerland, and returned home to a thunderous welcome of 70,000 well-wishers. There was added pressure when she turned professional. This time, however, she was represented with a convertible with a personalized licence plate reading 48-VI, signifying her triumph at the 1948 sixth Winter Olympics. Her professional contract stipulated that a percentage of all her future earnings be given to aid crippled children.

Barbara Ann, however, did not enjoy the experience of living out of a suitcase or skating on smaller ice surfaces (in Hollywood a 30' by 40' tank and in Chicago, 20' by 24'), or audiences unable to appreciate the finer points of her figure skating abilities. Nevertheless, she carried on for a five-year stint with ice shows before quitting to marry, in 1955, Tom King, the publicity director of the revue in which she was the star. They settled near Chicago where her white picket fence became a white post corral as she turned her attention to raising show horses and became one of the top-rated equestriennes in the USA.

Mel James

LAURENCE J. PETER

Peter's Principle **1919 - 1990**

*T*HE PETER PRINCIPLE was first
published in 1969. Within a year,
the hard-bound version was being
printed for the fifteenth time and the
first pocketbook edition was on the
press. Laurence J. Peter, a native of
Vancouver, British Columbia, for
advocating a theory claiming that
"In a hierarchy, every employee
tends to rise to his level of incompetence," had become one of the most
talked about non-fiction authors of the decade. This maxim was his
response to the universal question of "why things go wrong."

The eagerly read book was prompted by Raymond Hull, who, after his arrival in
Vancouver from England in 1947, had become a successful stage and TV playwright.
Following a chance meeting in which they discussed a theatre production both were
attending, Peter briefly touched on his research about hierarchies and incompetence and
they ended up discussing the subject late into the night.

The Peter Principle, first published in 1969, claims that everywhere people tend to rise to the level of their incompetence. Laurence J. Peter, provocative author of this horripilatingly valid, ruefully charming and excruciatingly
applicable exposé, was convinced his message could revolutionize one's life. His global bestseller is deemed by some
to be one of the most penetrating social and intriguing psychological discoveries of the 20th century. The term "the
Peter Principle" is, today, as much a part of our everyday speech as are "Parkinson's Law" and "Murphy's Law" still
other slogans that have passed into common, everyday language. [Photo, courtesy The Toronto Star/ A. Dunlop]

Dr. Laurence J. Peter and Raymond Hull

THE PETER PRINCIPLE

WHY THINGS ALWAYS GO WRONG

With a Special Foreword for this Edition by Dr. Peter

Exposing the Age of Incompetence

In his introduction to the book that he described as "the most penetrating social and psychological discovery of the century," Hull wrote that "...[Peter] had so far been satisfied to discuss his discovery with a few friends and colleagues and give an occasional lecture on his research.... I stressed the dangers of procrastination and Peter agreed on a collaboration."

Peter was 50 when *The Peter Principle* was first published and an Associate Professor of Education, Director of the Evelyn Frieden Centre for Prescriptive Teaching, and Coordinator of Programs for Emotionally Disturbed Children at the University of Southern California. He had begun his career as a teacher in Vancouver in 1941 and he had later also been employed as a counsellor, school psychologist, and prison instructor. He eventually received his Ed.D. from Washington State University in 1963.

After teaching briefly at the University of British Columbia in 1964, he moved to California where in 1965 he wrote his first academic text to help teachers improve their skills in coping with the disparity between the physical and social sciences. "I became convinced of a long-deferred need for substantive improvements in public education that would help children become the kind of caring, intelligent, rational beings that could live in peace with their fellow residents on the planet, live in harmony with their natural environment, and live satisfying personal lives in a technological world," observed Peter in *The Peter Plan*, a 1976 publication advocating "ways to avoid falling victim of the Peter Principle."

By then he had also written in 1972 a follow-up to *The Peter Principle*, entitled *The Peter Prescription*, and a four-volume academic text, *Competencies for Teaching*. His "Prescription" book was another overwhelming bestseller, going through seven printings in the first six months of publication. As a result, he was in constant demand as a speaker at teacher conventions as well as at business and professional conferences across North America.

In *The Peter Prescription* Peter again used numerous quotations and witticisms to illustrate

65 remedies for a better life. The book was divided into three sections: the first re-enforced the evils wrought by "The Peter Principle," the second suggested how to be creative, confident and competent in order "to prevent yourself from becoming a tragic victim of mindless escalation," and the third demonstrated "how to be successful in dealing with others and how to increase your efficiency and competency as a manager."

The publication of *The Peter Plan* in 1976 completed Peter's "trilogy." This last volume aimed to show "...ways by which we can protect our planet while civilization moves confidently forward to new achievements to secure the future of the human race." In it he recalled his ancestry – pioneer farmers on the outskirts of Vancouver – but did not advocate going back to the "Good Old Days." "The only successful way out of the present crisis," he wrote, "is to break through to a new and more advanced civilization," and he suggested that "escalating pleasure, love, knowledge, skill, and actualization of human potential for concern and creativity in the service and protection of the only planet we have is the challenge of progress today."

While not claiming his "Plan" perfect, he recommended that "we develop conversion strategies based on new rules and new priorities so that progress toward a new level of civilization is accomplished with attention to the long range effects of what we do." The popularity of his three books led to an invitation to write a column called "Peter's People" for *Human Behaviour* magazine. The columns were reprinted in a 1979 book of the same name. Everything from one-line assessments of a number of United States presidents to features on comedians George Carlin and Johnny Carson, on whose show he appeared four times, is humorously explored. It includes insight into his own lifestyle after achieving fame and financial success. "We decided that if we were going to bypass the materialistic corruption of our lives, we would have to avoid the fashionable preoccupation with money, status and possessions" for a lifestyle "of deliberate simplicity – one that was outwardly simple and inwardly rich."

Peter returned to the theme of his first best-seller in 1984 with a book entitled, *Why Things Go Wrong – The Peter Principle Revisited* and again a year later with *The Peter Pyramid – Or Will We Ever Get to the Point*. He had earlier written another prescription book on humour published in 1982 – a collaborative effort with Bill Dana entitled *The Laughter Prescription*. In it he prescribed "humour as a useful treatment of our illnesses and woes" and described Bill Dana as "the pharmacist who fills this prescription."

A heart condition, however could not respond to that particular prescription as Peter experienced failing health and a stroke, while carrying on with what he considered his true life's work – improving teacher education. Following his death in 1990, a former student and friend, W.H. New, wrote, "I was lucky enough when I was 12 years old to have had him as a teacher and in my memory he stands out not just because he was a big man, but because he was large of mind and heart."

Mel James

WHEN Eddie Johnson as a boy stood on a picnic table in Guelph and sang "Annie Rooney," a popular tune of the day, the crowd knew that they were hearing an unusual voice, but no one could imagine that he would become one of the world's great tenors and, later, general manager of the world's largest opera house, the Metropolitan in New York.

Born in Guelph in 1878, the son of a father who was active in local musical groups, Edward established a name for himself as a soloist in various church choirs and, at 16, became conductor of a Sunday school choir at one church and soloist at another.

He first considered becoming a missionary. His father wanted him to study law, but at age 20, Edward decided to go to New York to study music. He sang in churches, synagogues, clubs, and anywhere else he could make a dollar to keep him in room, board, a few clothes and permit him to attend recitals, symphonies, and operas. Opera quickly became his true interest. Always practical, he knew he would have to study in Europe, so he carefully saved his money.

His "break" that enabled him to study in Europe came when Oscar Straus wrote *A Waltz Dream*, an operetta that required a slim and handsome naval lieutenant to play the lead. Johnson won the part. It provided him with $600 a week in salary, star billing, and rave reviews.

After one season, he had saved enough money for Europe. In Paris he was met by a young man known to him in Guelph who introduced him to a brilliant and sophisticated Portuguese aristocrat, Beatrix da Veiga, known to friends as "Bebe." She heard him sing and commented, "Yes, the voice is beautiful. He may go far if he works."

With Bebe's help in languages (she spoke several), he studied until his money ran out. He returned to New York for yet another year of concerts and choir appearances. On his return to Paris, Bebe arranged a recital for him which proved successful. The decision was made that he should study opera in Italy. This required more money, so Johnson returned to New York in 1907 and spent two years there to earn enough to marry Bebe, move to Florence, and study under Vincenzo Lombardi who had earlier taught Enrico Caruso.

In the next three years Edward and Bebe had their only daughter, Fiorenza, and Bebe continued to give Edward language instruction while Lombardi perfected his protégé's singing skills. His teacher insisted he would not allow Johnson to appear until he was ready. This happened in 1912 when he appeared in *Andrea Chénier* as Edoardo di Giovanni, not as Edward Johnson since Europeans of that time could not imagine an opera star with an English name.

As the curtain fell on his first performance, there were shouts of approval from the audience followed by high praise from the critics. This led to invitations to perform in other operas. He was approached to sing at the Costanzi in Rome, then starred in *Isabeau* and other roles that won critical acclaim and prompted La Scala to make him the lead tenor in Wagner's *Parsifal*,

Edward Johnson

1878-1959

The Tenor from Guelph who "Saved the Met"

Edward Johnson's debut as Nikki in Oscar Straus' A Waltz Dream at New York's Broadway Theater in 1908 made him an overnight star. [Photo, courtesy Guelph Museums/Photographer, Hall]

which he sang 25 times over the next three months. In 1916 La Scala sent the entire ensemble to Argentina and Brazil for six months and his stardom continued. In 1918, Puccini asked him to create the leading roles in two of his three one-act operas, titled *Il Trittico*. These were to be performed in the spring of 1919, one of the most devastating periods of Johnson's life as Bebe died in May after a brief illness.

Later that year Johnson joined the Chicago Opera Company where he was talked into using his own name and watched his years of European stardom slip into oblivion as the company was dominated by a backer who had her favourite singers and he was not among them. He managed to fulfil his contract, however, and, at the end of this period, New York's famed Metropolitan Opera Company beckoned. He joined it for the 1921 season, but illness threatened his career when he was forced to miss several performances.

That summer both he and Fiorenza went to Europe where he regained his health and returned to the Met not only to sing leads in many of the grand operas but also to play Pelléas in Debussy's *Pelléas and Mélisande* opposite Lucrezia Bori as well as the lead in the first opera to be written in English, *The King's Henchman*. The libretto was written by Edna St. Vincent Millay and the music by Deems Taylor who wrote, after the opening, "Dear God, thank you for thinking up Eddie Johnson when you were making tenors."

In the years that followed, Johnson toured in Japan and China, spent five summer seasons at Chicago's Ravinia Park and winters at the Met where he starred in numerous productions. Among them was the role of Peter in another Taylor opera, *Peter Ibbetson*.

The depression and the death of multi-millionaire backer Otto Kahn caused financial havoc for the Met in the early 1930s. Johnson took on an additional role, that of fund raiser, sometimes making several speeches a week to service clubs and other groups, appealing to audiences from the stage, and even visiting upscale bars and salons along Park Avenue to enlist support. As a result, he became the Met's assistant general manager in 1934, and general manager a year later when Hubert Witherspoon, who had recommended him for Nikki in *A Waltz Dream*, died of a heart attack.

For the next 15 years Johnson worked prodigiously to "Save the Met" as well as introduce many new stars and operas. H. Napier Moore spelled out the enormity of the job in a *Maclean's* magazine article in 1939; he reported that Johnson not only dealt with the performers and conductors but was responsible for a staff of 750 people backstage and another 110 for box office, secretarial, and janitorial services.

As an administrator, Johnson carefully revitalized the Met. He was largely responsible for getting NBC to broadcast the Saturday afternoon performances live during the season to expose grand opera to millions of people across the continent. He extended the company's repertory to include the works of Mozart and expanded its road trip itinerary. He got a sponsor for his "Metropolitan Auditions of the Air" program, and this led to the discovery of dozens of new stars, among them America's Risë Stevens, Patrice Munsel, Robert Merrill, Richard Tucker, Canada's Raoul Jobin, and France's Martial Singher.

To mark his farewell in 1950, a grateful Metropolitan Board held a pageant with many of the famous opera stars taking part. Johnson was presented with the evening's proceeds of $46,000. He promptly turned this back to the Met as a fund to be used to assist needy artists.

This was not his first financial contribution to music. In the 1930s he donated $25,000 to make possible the teaching of music in Guelph schools. Despite his world fame, the city of Guelph always remained an important centre in his life, a fact that was reinforced when his daughter married a rising young political figure of the community, George Drew, who later became Premier of Ontario and leader of the Federal Conservative Party.

Returning to Guelph in 1950, Johnson did anything but retire. He became involved with the Toronto Conservatory of Music, worked with others to have some of the best works of Canadian composers played in Carnegie Hall, adjudicated various competitions and concerts and visited New York and Europe often. In 1953, he became the fourth person in the 50-year history of the Canadian Club of New York to receive its gold medal. Two years later, Guelph also paid tribute to him, naming a public school in his honour.

Then 77, Johnson still continued to be involved in musical education and appreciation until the evening he died four years later. On April 20, 1959, the internationally acclaimed tenor, dressed in his familiar white tie and tails for a National Ballet recital at the Guelph arena, suffered a fatal heart attack on entering the building.

Mel James

Peterborough Lift Lock

World's Highest Hydraulic Lift Lock

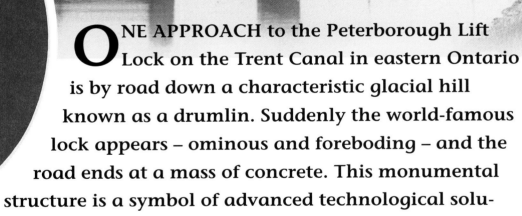

ONE APPROACH to the Peterborough Lift Lock on the Trent Canal in eastern Ontario is by road down a characteristic glacial hill known as a drumlin. Suddenly the world-famous lock appears – ominous and foreboding – and the road ends at a mass of concrete. This monumental structure is a symbol of advanced technological solutions in an era when steel and concrete shaped the new dimensions of progress. Like the larger celebrations of technology represented by London's Crystal Palace in 1851 or the Chicago World's Fair of 1893, the Peterborough Lift Lock was another example of problem solving by means of contemporary applications of new technology.

A civil and mechanical engineer from McGill University, the visionary R.B. Rogers oversaw the construction of the world-famous Peterborough, Ontario, Hydraulic Lift Lock. [Photo, courtesy Friends of the Trent-Severn Waterway]

When the challenging engineering project was completed and officially opened on July 9, 1904, as viewed here, the Peterborough Lift Lock had the capacity to raise or lower a water vessel 70 feet making it the largest hydraulic lift lock in the world even to this day. [Photo, courtesy Charles J. Humber Collection]

The first hydraulic balance lock built by Edwin Clark in 1874 at Anderton, on the River Weaver, in Cheshire, England, was followed by similar locks built in Belgium and France. Engineer Frank Turner recommended such locks for the ill-fated Huron and Ontario ship canal in 1879 and raised the notion again as a member of the Trent Valley Canal Commission. The challenge at Peterborough was to create a device for lifting a vessel from one level to another without wasting water and with one efficient mechanical lock replacing a bottleneck series of standard locks that resembled giant steps.

Richard B. Rogers, as superintendent of the Trent Canal, latched on to the hydraulic lock concept and greatly expanded its possibilities, suggesting that a hydraulic lock could raise or lower a vessel 70 feet in the same time as a typical lock could raise or lower one a mere 7 feet. He figured such a lock would reduce construction costs, alleviate concerns over water supply on the canal, and be more efficient. Rogers actually designed the lock before he travelled to Belgium and France to see how existing models worked.

Behind the scenes, the Peterborough Lift Lock story is one of intrigue and political manipulation. The hydraulic lock was approved in 1896 by an anxious government that feared defeat at the polls, and contractors signed deals to build the lock without actually seeing the specifications. The rushed deal did not save the government and Richard Rogers, as a practical civil servant who feared for his job as a result of lost government patronage, released portions of his design only when necessary. Having made himself indispensable, Rogers protected his own interests at the expense of contractors and government who haggled over unexpected expenses.

Contractors Corry and Laverdure of Peterborough, responsible for the concrete and the embankments, and the Dominion Bridge Company of Montreal, responsible for the design of the mechanical systems, were challenged by the sheer magnitude of the project and the innovations that it required. Rogers himself experimented with the new technology of cement mixing, recommending a dry mix he actually developed in the basement of the Trent Canal office. It was an extraordinary risk that made Rogers an international celebrity among engineers designing new uses for cement.

Opening day for the lift lock was one of the most dazzling celebrations in Canadian history. Thousands of citizens came to Peterborough on July 9, 1904, to witness the spectacle. In the words of historian James T. Angus, "From this day onwards every schoolchild in Canada would know about Peterborough, with its `highest lift lock' in the world."

Richard Rogers did not witness the opening of the smaller but similar lift lock at Kirkfield between Balsam Lake and Lake Simcoe at the summit of the Trent-Severn Canal (49ft or 14.9m lift compared to Peterborough's 65ft or 19.8m lift). As Rogers had feared, the government had replaced him a year before its opening in 1907.

The Peterborough Lift Lock was a triumph of engineering over the challenges of land and geography. Along with other emerging hydroelectric stations, it is a monument to the ingenuity of Canadian engineers, architects, and construction workers in the transformation of landscapes for human efficiency.

Larry Turner

C. Miller Fisher

Neurologist Preventing Strokes

WHILE IN MONTREAL C. Miller Fisher made a discovery regarding the carotid artery as a cause of strokes. This was of such great importance that he was invited to Harvard in 1954 where he remained as professor of neurology. He had earlier endured some challenging experiences that included his years as a prisoner of war in Germany after the ship on which he was medical officer was sunk in the south Atlantic.

Born in Waterloo, Ontario, in 1913, Fisher received all his pre-university education in that part of southwestern Ontario. He then studied medicine at the University of Toronto, graduating in 1938, and interning at Henry Ford Hospital in Detroit until the fateful summer of 1939. Then, along with thousands of fellow members of the Canadian militia, he was called to service. He reported to Montreal and worked at the Royal Victoria Hospital until the navy required his medical assistance.

In the summer of 1940, he was sent to England as one of 12 naval surgeons seconded to the Royal Navy. After his training, Surg.Lt. Cmdr. Fisher was assigned to an armed merchant cruiser, *HMS Letitia*, that was patrolling in the North Atlantic. Then, while in Halifax being refitted, the *Letitia* was damaged and Fisher found himself on *HMS Voltaire* en route to West Africa, via Trinidad, to join an inbound convoy. The *Voltaire* was not a lucky ship. On April 4, 1941, a German surface raider appeared, undetected until far too late.

The sick bay, fortunately empty, was obliterated in one broadside. The ship sank. The survivors, about half the crew, were transferred to a German prison ship that took them to Bordeaux. Fisher then found himself in Marlag-und-Milag Nord – bleak, wind-blown country in northwestern Germany. He was transferred later to Sandbostel.

When repatriated in the autumn of 1944, Fisher had been a POW for three years. He returned to the Royal Victoria Hospital and, after several refresher courses, began studying at the Montreal Neurological Institute. There he came under the influence of Dr. Wilder Penfield. In 1947 he received his Fellowship in the Royal College of Physicians and Surgeons of Canada, and five years later this same college awarded him its Prize in Medicine.

Fisher's first major contribution to world medical knowledge came when he was still a medical resident. He was becoming more and more interested in the neurological components of cerebrovascular disease, including hypertension. While dissecting the brains of patients dying after suffering strokes, he noted a relationship between embolism from the heart and infarction of brain tissue, a fundamental observation that now is part of the standard understanding of the disease process.

His major contribution came after 1947 while in Montreal. In his studies of stroke victims he began to suspect that many of these emboli might have a source other than the heart and he suspected the carotid artery. This was difficult to prove because at this time autopsies did not allow dissection of the neck for cosmetic reasons.

By private arrangements with funeral homes, he explored this artery and to his amazement he found a rough calcified nodule covered with thrombus (blood clot) where the artery divides – an obvious source of emboli of all sizes. Such patients had an auditory murmur and a palpable vibration felt over this section of the artery.

Thus was born the concept that the carotid artery was indeed the chief offender in strokes and surgeons quickly responded by opening the artery and carefully removing the offending plaque.

A major neurological study for forty years has been: which cases should be treated by long-term anticoagulants and which should receive surgery.

This was such an important discovery that Harvard University and the Massachusetts General Hospital induced him to leave Canada. He accepted and has remained in Boston ever since 1954 as an esteemed professor of neurology.

From Fisher came the concept of transient ischemic attacks, or TIAs, now widely recognized as a common and important disorder for those about to suffer strokes. Fisher proposed the use of anticoagulant drugs to prevent strokes in patients who were experiencing TIAs.

Fisher has been a compassionate clinician, a dedicated and innovative pathologist, a talented teacher and researcher, and a distinguished contributor to the literature of science. He has coined many terms that have become part of the day-to-day vocabulary of medicine: these include not only the TIA but also "subclavian steal," "transient monocular blindness" (TMB), and "ataxic hemiparesis." By describing in the autopsy room what is known as Creutzfeldt-Jakob disease (also known as spastic pseudosclerosis) he made it possible to diagnose the disease in the living patient.

Many former students now run laboratories and clinical programs throughout the world. These men and women have extended their teacher's work and proselytized his teaching principles, which are sometimes referred to as "Fisher's Rules" and have a distinct Oslerian ring to them. Examples are "The bedside can be your laboratory; study the patients seriously," and "Fully accept what you have heard or read only when you have verified it yourself." By his own adherence to these and similar "rules," Fisher has improved the life-style and life expectancy of millions of human beings around the world.

Charles Roland

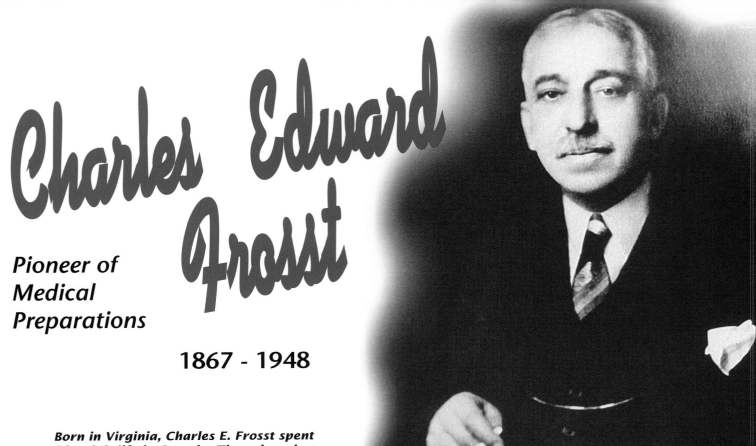

Charles Edward Frosst

Pioneer of Medical Preparations

1867 - 1948

Born in Virginia, Charles E. Frosst spent his adult life in Canada. The axiom that says "all successful businesses start with personality" certainly held true for Mr. Frosst whose soft, southern accent and straight thinking as a salesman wowed potential clients and engendered close friendships. Today the Montreal-based company he founded in 1899 is an integral part of one of the world's largest pharmaceutical companies. [Photo, courtesy Merck Frosst Canada Inc.]

CHARLES EDWARD FROSST, born in 1867 in Richmond, Virginia, came to Canada as a salesman for Henry Wampole & Company at the age of 25. Seven years later, he established his own company that became the widely known and highly respected Charles E. Frosst & Co., developer of such painkillers as 217®s and 222®s and the first Canadian company to be licensed to produce Vitamin B₂.

The Wampole Company sent Frosst all over Canada to sell and in the seven years he spent with them, he proved an accomplished and knowledgeable salesman of pharmaceuticals and he befriended a network of people in the medical establishment. By 1899, he was encouraged to strike out on his own and elected to do so in Montreal because he had an excellent relationship with McGill University's Department of Medicine and because

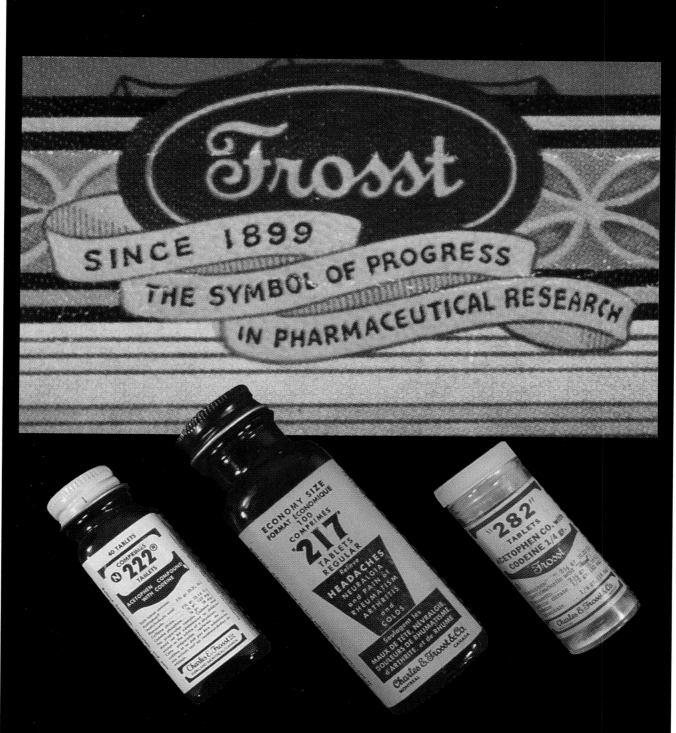

The 222®, 217®, and 282® pain killer tablets known and sold worldwide since World War I made the Charles E. Frosst & Co. a household name marketing products, all relieving hurt and ache for millions of sufferers. [Photo, courtesy Charles E. Frosst Jr.]

Montreal was then the business centre of Canada.

His first laboratory was a modest one, a 2,000 square foot space on Dufferin Square where he researched and developed his own formulas. On occasion he also built his own machinery to manufacture his carefully tested products and initially he was also his own salesman. Frosst made a point of selling to licensed druggists only, avoiding those who continued to rely on old-time remedies and hypnotic compounds. This policy encouraged hospitals to deal directly with his company and they soon became his biggest customers.

By the beginning of World War I, Frosst had developed and manufactured two famous painkillers that are still available. They were labelled Frosst 217®s and 222®s: a common way of identifying product lines at the time. After the war, his oldest son Eliot, who had served in the military overseas, joined the firm that grew rapidly in the postwar years. By 1927, the Frosst business establishment was listed in the Canadian Medical Directory as a "chemist and chemical company in Canada and Newfoundland" dealing in wholesale drugs as well as supplies to hospitals, physicians, and surgeons. The original "lab" had long since moved to a 50,000 square foot building on St. Antoine Street.

By then, two sons, John and Charles Jr., had also joined the firm and, with its expanded research, the company had successfully developed drugs to fight bacterial infections. In the early 1940s, it obtained a licence to produce Vitamin B_2 and branched out to develop a line of veterinary drugs for the treatment of small animals.

The senior Frosst had a management style that is today described as "management by walking around." Although he presented a stern image, he made a point of knowing what the names were of all employees, how many children they had, and what their interests were. Employees were encouraged to take pride in their work and learned that they could always approach him if they had a problem. He was also known for his sense of humour as evidenced by his annual sponsorship of the "dingbat" calendars, waggish cartoons facetiously caricaturing the medical and pharmaceutical professions.

His major managerial commitment, however, was insistence on thorough research and extensive testing before any product was put on the market: in fact the Frosst Company was known for setting a North American industry standard in the percentage of research to sales. He was also a major supporter of hospital research and provided numerous scholarships to medical and health care students.

In 1943, Charles, then 76, stepped down from the day-to-day running of the still family-owned company, leaving his three sons in charge. He retained, however, the role of chairman and, from time to time until his death in 1948, made a visit from his home in Westmount or his country home at Ste. Agathe, Quebec (easily identified because of the large Union Jack that flew from it), to the St. Antoine Street headquarters.

In 1959 the company went public and in 1965 was acquired by Merck & Co. Inc. to become Merck Frosst Canada Inc.

Mel James

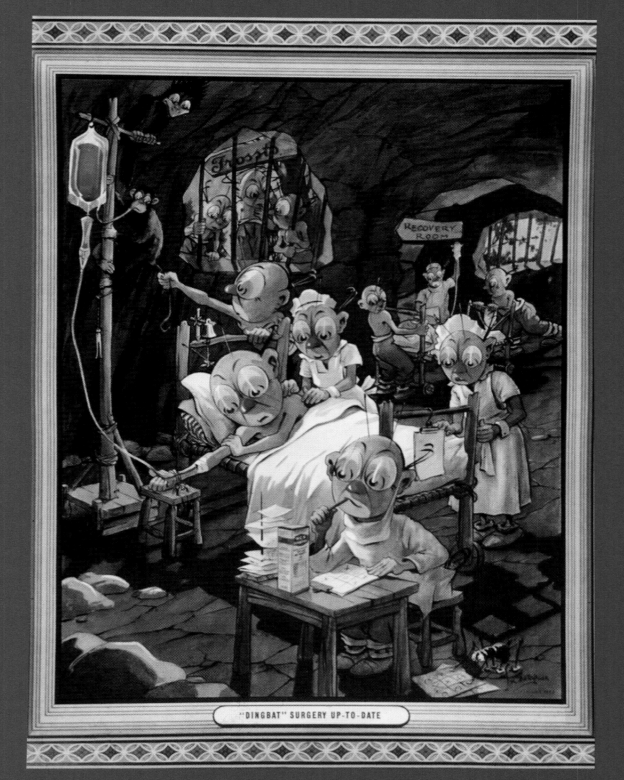

"DINGBAT" SURGERY UP-TO-DATE

With stirred imaginations, thousands and thousands of children thrillingly anticipated "Dingbat" calendars, those annual cartoons hanging for nearly half a century in the waiting rooms of just about every doctor and dental office across Canada. This one, published in 1957, was rendered by L.R. Batchelor. [Photo, courtesy Charles E. Frosst Jr.]

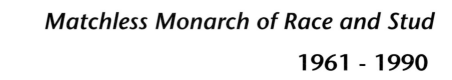

Northern Dancer

CANADIAN SPORTSWRITER Trent Frayne recalled that standing on the roof of the old wooden grandstand at Louisville, Kentucky, in 1964, he found himself pounding his fists repeatedly into the restraining railing on the roof and shouting over and over, "He's going to make it! He's going to make it!" Frayne was describing his own reaction to writer Peter Gzowski as Northern Dancer held the lead in the Kentucky Derby – the first Canadian-bred horse to win the premier leg of the American *Triple Crown*. Not only that but it had been done in the record time of two minutes flat! When Northern Dancer won the Preakness in Baltimore, Canadian hopes soared: perhaps E.P. Taylor's colt would become the first horse since Citation in 1948 to win the Triple Crown.

The most successful thoroughbred in Canadian racing history, Northern Dancer was the first Canadian-bred horse to win the Kentucky Derby, doing so in record time. That same year, 1964, he went on to win the Preakness, finished third in the Belmont and won Canada's own Queen's Plate, his last race.
[Photo, courtesy Michael Burns Photography]

That didn't happen: the Dancer placed third at the Belmont Stakes in New York. He did, however, return home to Toronto late in June to win North America's oldest continuously-run sweepstakes, the Queen's Plate. Peter Gzowski described the event in his 1983 book, *An Unbroken Line*. "For a while, as he loped around the first turn dead last, we gulped in disbelief. But when he began his Lamborghini move past the field we cheered him again, and we kept cheering as he swept up the homestretch, the race now convincingly won … he was still tearing up the dirt in that unforgettable choppy, driving run."

It was his last race: he suffered a bowed tendon shortly after winning the Queen's Plate and as a three-year-old had to be retired after only one short year in which he had won seven of his nine starts for a total of $490,171. He then went on to make millions over the next 25 years as the father of a string of champions in both the United States and Europe.

Despite impressive bloodlines – he was sired by the stallion Nearctic out of Natalma – Northern Dancer so unimpressed potential buyers at E.P. Taylor's Windfields Farm yearling sale in 1962 that no one bought him for the $25,000 asking price. As a result, Taylor kept the colt which some described as "chunky" and "little." (When fully grown, at 15 hands and two inches, he was still small.) His stride was also described as short and choppy and his disposition "ornery and mischievous," but, as a two-year-old, he quickly established himself by winning five times in Ontario and also winning the Remsen Stakes at Aqueduct in New York. From there he was shipped to Florida where, in the spring of 1964, he won two major races, both with the famed Willie Shoemaker in the saddle.

Shoemaker, however, had doubts about the Dancer's chances in the Kentucky Derby in 1964 and chose, instead, Hill Rise. Jockey Bill Hartack was hired for Northern Dancer and Hartack rode him to a victory in the Blue Grass Stakes two weeks before the 90th running of the Derby where he was to challenge the unbeaten Hill Rise. The Dancer not only won over the favourite but set a new record of two minutes flat for the mile and a quarter distance where such previous immortals as Whirlaway, Count Fleet and Citation had won.

In 1965, after he was named Canadian horse of the year, Northern Dancer's legendary stud career began. In 1981, the syndicate that owned Northern Dancer rejected a $40 million offer for the champion. Ultimately, 146 stakes winners and 26 champions, including Epsom Derby winners Nijinsky and The Minstrel, inherited his prepotent genes.

Mel James

CLARENCE DECATUR
HOWE

1886-1960

*Transforming
Canada into a
Modern
Industrial Nation*

*Before his election to
Parliament in 1935, C.D.
Howe was Canada's
foremost grain elevator
builder. A Cabinet
member for 22 years
representing Port Arthur
(Thunder Bay), Howe's
political energy helped
turn Canada into a
modern industrial nation.
Industry Canada is mainly
centered in the
C.D. Howe Building,
background, in Ottawa,
and his office desk, to this
day, is used by the
current minister.*

CLARENCE DECATUR HOWE, widely known as the "Minister of Everything" in the government of Prime Ministers Mackenzie King and Louis St. Laurent, organized and managed Canada's industrial war effort throughout World War II. With foresight and determination, he forged an industrial powerhouse that mobilized millions of Canadians and established Canada as a leading industrial power. He set the stage for a postwar economic boom that propelled Canada into becoming one of the leading industrialized nations.

Born in Waltham, Massachusetts, in 1886, Howe graduated from the Massachusetts Institute of Technology in 1907 with a Bachelor of Science. In 1908 he moved to Canada to become the first professor of engineering at Dalhousie University in Halifax. From 1913-1916, during which time Howe was the chief engineer for the Board of Grain Commissioners, he resided at Fort William (now Thunder Bay), Ontario.

In 1916, C.D., as he was colloquially known, started his own engineering and construction firm that specialized in designing and building concrete grain elevators. It soon expanded into building all types of structures including docks, bridges, and factories. By 1935 his firm had built over $100 million worth of infrastructure. His reputation for quality construction was unsurpassed.

In 1935, Howe was talked into running for Parliament as the Liberal member for Port Arthur. With no prior political experience, he won his seat in a Liberal sweep of the country and was given a dual Cabinet position as Minister of Railways and Canals and as Minister of Marine, but these ministries were soon combined into the Ministry of Transport.

In his first term he reorganized both the Canadian Broadcasting Corporation and Canadian National Railways, created a National Harbours Board, and set up Trans-Canada Airlines. During this period he established a reputation as a man who could talk sense with businessmen and industrialists. He scorned red tape and long circuitous conferences as much as they did – because at heart he was one of them.

Howe believed firmly that, in many sectors, Canada was too small a country to support more than one company. He preferred a system of either private monopoly regulated by government controls or Crown-owned corporations. In crafting the economic system and companies that are still evident today, he developed a personal style that was described as no-nonsense, even authoritarian in its pursuit of industrial development. This style carried over into the House of Commons where he would not speak on a subject until he had thoroughly researched it and decided what needed doing, after which he rarely deviated from his position.

Canada entered World War II in September 1939 unprepared both militarily and industrially. In the next few weeks legislation was rushed through Parliament creating a War Supply Board headed by C.D. Howe that was given wide-ranging powers over private industry to direct arms production. During the "phony war" that winter, Howe started a massive rearm-ament program that involved the manufacture of ships, aeroplanes, small and large arms, clothing, vehicles, and other items required by the allied armed forces. To manage this effort, Howe hired his famous dollar-a-year men, corporate executives with solid management skills who were called to Ottawa to organize the economy as efficiently as possible. As Canadian author Peter C. Newman concluded, "It was the network of connections and interconnections between business and government, fathered by Clarence Decatur Howe, that became the Canadian Establishment – its great dynasties spreading into every form of commercial enterprise across the country."

The war mobilization involved transforming Canada, in just a few years, from a country with an agricultural economy to one with a modern industrial economy. Canada's GNP grew from five billion dollars in 1939 to twelve billion dollars in 1945 as Howe and his staff from the new Department of Munitions and Supply directed 1.1 million Canadian workers. The volume of war material produced by Canadian industry was staggering. In a few short years, over 500,000 vehicles, 600 ships, 85,000 heavy guns, and millions of tons of military supplies were manufactured and shipped overseas. By the end of World War II, Canada had the second largest navy in the world, produced 40 per cent of the world's aluminum, and was a leading producer in many sectors of the world economy.

The Joint Air Training Program was the most visible war program that Howe's team managed. It involved the construction of 120 airports run by 40,000 staff who trained 131,000 Commonwealth aircrew. Howe experienced the war first-hand on a visit to Britain to co-ordinate this Canadian effort when his ship, the *Western Prince*, was torpedoed and sunk on December 14, 1940. After being picked up by a passing collier and taken to London, he negotiated not only the training program for pilots but an aircraft production program as well. By the end of the war, Canada had produced over 12,000 aircraft.

During the war, Howe's great foresight became evident as he worked with Dr. C.J. Mackenzie, the head of the National Research Council (and one of his former students at Dalhousie University), to establish Canada's nuclear industry. Starting with the Eldorado Mine in the Northwest Territories, which the Federal government purchased in 1944, Howe initiated a Canada-wide search for uranium and established a nuclear research program

The Honourable C.D. Howe presents the 1955 Design Award Certificate to W.C. Wood, President of W.C. Wood Co., Limited of Guelph, Ontario. As the Minister of Trade and Commerce in the 1950s, Howe oversaw the emergence of an industrial power from what was an agricultural nation in 1900. [Photo, courtesy John F. Wood]

that evolved, after the war, into the CANDU reactor program and the construction of Canada's first nuclear reactor at Chalk River. He was also instrumental in supporting the National Research Council in its efforts to establish Canada's scientific research capabilities in other fields.

Following the war, Howe established the Department of Reconstruction and became its first minister. His efforts now were focused on changing production from guns to butter and producing hundreds of thousands of new houses and a consumer economy for returning veterans. By 1948 this was accomplished, and Canada was well on the way to an economic boom unsurpassed in its history.

The Korean War gave Howe his old powers back as chief organizer of the Canadian economy, but rather than launching an all-out effort, he managed a controlled response so as not to disrupt the boom at home. In an era of rising expectations, he produced the war material that was required, kept the Canadian economy rolling, and held down rising prices – a rare achievement in any industrialized country. He also initiated, with the construction of the Trans-Canada Pipeline, the first of many Canadian megaprojects.

C.D. Howe's competence as a national industrialist was unsurpassed; in the 22 years he was a cabinet minister, he transformed Canada from an agricultural society to an industrial and financial power. The Parliament of the day clearly recognized his talent and bestowed on him legislative powers that gave him *de facto* control of the Canadian economy not only during the war but until he left office in 1957. Many of the companies he was instrumental in founding such as Air Canada and the Canadian Broadcasting Corporation are household names. What is most impressive, however, was his management and direction of the Canadian economy that transformed Canada into a world-leading economic power.

Art Bailey

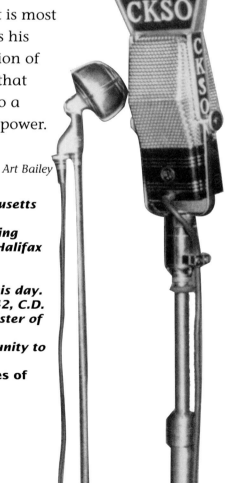

A graduate of the Massachusetts Institute of Technology, C.D. Howe taught engineering at Dalhousie University in Halifax before becoming the most successful businessman politician of his day. In Sudbury, Ontario, in 1942, C.D. Howe, viewed here, as Minister of Munition & Supply, exhorts Canada's nickel belt community to buy Victory Loan Bonds.
[Courtesy, National Archives of Canada/C-19380]

JOHN MOLSON

1763-1836

Strength Through Diversity

An orphan from Lincolnshire, England, John Molson (1763-1836) settled in Montreal, Quebec, in 1782. By 1786, the young entrepreneur had established a small brewery in Montreal that is today one of Canada's oldest companies and one of the most widely recognized Canadian corporate names around the world.

FOUNDER OF a noted Canadian brewing enterprise that is now over two centuries old, John Molson was also a steamboat builder and railway financier in early nineteenth century Canada in addition to being a member of the Assembly for Lower Canada (later Quebec) in the 1820s, a member of its Legislative Council in the 1830s, and president of the powerful Bank of Montreal from 1826 to 1834. In short, he was a highly significant figure in the development of Montreal – Canada's first real metropolitan city.

Aside from his personal capacities – considerable – his basic role as a brewer was important. In a still rather primitive Canadian economy, barter and unsecured, risky credit played all too large a part. Molson's product, however, since it was purveyed for cash, enabled him to provide valuable capital for entrepreneurial ventures. When he created a new "steam" technology to pump his vats and grind his grain, brewers (who also became distillers) welcomed the industrial revolution that was extending from a manufacturing Britain to an agrarian Canada. Thus not just Molsons but Gooderhams (brewer-distillers in Toronto) and others elsewhere would take up new productive enterprises. Yet it was John Molson who was the first to seize the business initiatives that grew out of brewing.

Born in Spalding, England, in 1763, orphaned and privately schooled, John Molson came to Canada in 1782 and, four years later, used his parents' legacy to become sole proprietor of a brewery in Montreal. It prospered, as did Montreal, with trade expanding into a fast-settling Upper Canada further west up the St. Lawrence. Molson used income from brewing to enlarge his operations: to apply steam power at his works with a new engine brought from England, and then to start a steamboat line on the St. Lawrence between Montreal and Quebec. Moreover, in 1809, he put a Montreal-built steamboat, the *Accommodation*, into service on his line with an engine now made at the Forges Saint-Maurice that, dating from French times, was Canada's earliest iron foundry. The *Accommodation* was the first successful steamboat built entirely in North America.

His steamboat line prospered markedly during the War of 1812 by carrying British troops and munitions from the port of Quebec to assist in the conflicts against the United States that were taking place in Upper Canada. And after the war, this Molson enterprise once again prospered by transporting British immigrants and their goods up the St. Lawrence for settlement.

A highly prominent Montreal business figure, John Molson became president of the Bank of Montreal in 1826 and kept that office until two years before his death in 1836. While still the entrepreneur of new modes and projects, he put his financial weight behind Canada's first railway, the Champlain and St. Lawrence Railroad that was built to run 16 miles from the St. Lawrence shore across from Montreal to Saint Jean, where the Richelieu River flows into Lake Champlain. This railroad thus provided a link between two great water routes: the St. Lawrence River up to the Great Lakes and the Hudson River down to New York.

Molson died early in 1836, just months before the new rail line was opened to traffic. His enterprises, however, continued. His son, John Junior, was first president of the Champlain and St. Lawrence Railroad; son William became first president of Molson's Bank – a power for many decades – that he and his brother established in the early 1850s.

The original John Molson would endure in history for good reasons; as founder and builder of a great Canadian brewing and distilling house and as an initiator of both the steamboat and the railway age, he embodied a popular motto of the Molson companies today – "Strength through Diversity."

J.M.S. Careless

Samuel I. Hayakawa

Samurai Scholar

1906 - 1992

A CONFRONTATION with striking students at San Francisco State College in 1968 propelled Vancouver-born Samuel I. Hayakawa, already recognized as a world-renowned semantics expert, into a college presidency and later, to the U.S. Senate.

Dr. Hayakawa was a professor at the college when some 500 students went on strike to force their demands for changes to several of the college's policies, particularly to those with regard to minority groups and black studies. When a second president resigned because of the protests that year, the famed semantics professor was appointed acting president and became headline news days later when rioting students refused to turn off blaring loud speakers on a van so that he could be heard. Hayakawa, then 62, strode through the protestors, nimbly scrambled to the roof of the vehicle and yanked the wires from the speakers, all of this action recorded on TV and shown that night to millions of people.

As one of the world's great semanticists, Vancouver-born S.I. Hayakawa, viewed here wearing his signature tam, instantly became world famous when he, acting president of San Jose State University, confronted striking students determined to shut down the university at the height of the Vietnam War in 1968. [Photo, courtesy San Jose State University]

His determination to quell the riots and his efforts to bring law and order to the campus over the next few months earned him the epithet, "the Samurai Scholar." By June, grateful trustees confirmed his presidency – a position he held until 1973.

The son of Ichiro and Toro Hayakawa, Samuel Ichiye was born in Vancouver, British Columbia, in 1906. His father was a Japanese import/export dealer who moved the family of four children to Winnipeg where Samuel completed high school and, in 1927, obtained a BA at the University of Manitoba. A year later he was awarded an MA in English at Montreal's McGill University and in 1930 began teaching as a graduate assistant at the University of Wisconsin. He received his PhD there in 1935 and, in 1939, joined the staff of Illinois Institute of Technology, first as an assistant, then as associate professor of English.

By then Dr. Hayakawa was already working on his first book dealing with the theories of general semantics advanced by Alfred Korzybski, a Polish scholar whom he met in 1938. The book, entitled *Language in Action*, became a best-seller when it was published and selected by a book club in 1941. For the next eight years it was the basic text for his lively and incisive lectures on semantics. He also became the founder and editor of *ETC*, a journal published by the International Society for General Semantics. In 1949 he made major revisions to his original book, calling the new volume *Language in Thought and Action*. Like its predecessor, it was translated into a number of languages.

Dr. Hayakawa moved to the University of Chicago as a lecturer in 1950 and his popularity on the lecture circuit grew when he produced a series of 13 half-hour shows on general semantics for National Education Television and also conducted, over a Chicago radio station, a series of informal lecture demonstrations on another major interest of his – jazz.

In 1955 he moved to San Francisco State College as a professor with a growing worldwide reputation as lecturer, writer, and editor. He returned to Montreal in 1959 to become the first non-physical scientist to give the prestigious Claude Bernard Lecture at the University of Montreal's Institute of Experimental Medicine and Surgery, his topic being the semantic causes of stress. By then, Dr. Hayakawa had also edited *Language, Meaning and Maturity* and later, in 1959, *Our Language and Our World*, both books comprised of essays published initially in *ETC*.

Another book was published in 1963 and, in 1968, his *Modern Guide to Synonyms and Related Works* concentrated on the development of slang in American English. At the height of the Vietnam War he was teaching only one evening seminar on advanced problems in communication at San Francisco State College when all classes were cancelled in November 1968 following a strike by some 500 students and clashes with city police.

Dr. Hayakawa, sympathetic to some of the demands made by the protesters, felt, however, it was more important to keep the college open. "What my colleagues seem to forget," he observed during the uprising, "is that we have a standing obligation to the 17,500 or more students – white, black, yellow or brown – who are not on strike and have every right to expect continuation of their education." It was this stance that prompted the trustees and Ronald Reagan, as governor of California, to appoint him acting president on November 26.

On December 2, he called for the resumption of classes and, when the striking students tried to drown out his remarks that day, his quick reaction as seen on TV screens around the world created a new image for the heretofore humorous, off-beat professor – that of a hard-nosed college administrator. While some faculty and protesting students continued to criticize him, his no-nonsense stance won overwhelming support of the public and enabled him to win confirmation as college president.

His involvement with Congressional committees investigating causes for student unrest and a meeting with President Nixon prompted a number of people to suggest that he enter California politics, but he put aside the idea until the 1976 senatorial race three years later. Then, at age 70, sensing the public's negative attitude towards politicians in the post-Watergate era, he ran on the Republican ticket and won by more than 250,000 votes. He did not, however, seek a second six-year term but chose to become special advisor to the Secretary of State making trips to such countries as Laos, Thailand, and New Guinea.

He also became chairman of a group called U.S. English, bent on pressing for a constitutional amendment to make English the nation's official language. "Bilingualism for the individual is fine," he argued, "but not for a country." He marked his 50th wedding anniversary in 1987 having married Margedant Peters whom he had met at the University of Wisconsin. He predeceased her at age 85 in 1992.

Mel James

Mavis Gallant

Story Teller International

MAVIS GALLANT, an only child, was born in Montreal in 1922. Her parents died when she was young, and she was educated in a mind-boggling series of 17 public, convent, and boarding schools. In her twenties, she worked as a reporter for the *Montreal Standard* (1944-1950), leaving journalism in 1950 to pursue her true love and vocation – fiction writing.

Because of her fluency in both French and English, she selected Paris as her home base. Although she maintains her Canadian citizenship, Gallant enjoys a life of independence, cultural stimulation, and "marvellous peace and quiet."

In interviews and descriptions of her lifestyle, Gallant is forthright about the protectiveness she feels towards her independence and privacy. In an interview with Geoff Hancock in *Canadian Fiction Magazine* in 1978, she discussed her "life project" and her deliberate move to France to write by saying, "I have arranged matters so that I would be free to write. It's what I like doing." In the preface to her collection of stories, *Home Truths: Selected Canadian Stories* (1981), she uses the words of Pasternak as her epigraph: "Only personal independence matters."

This view of Mavis Gallant was taken at Chibougamau, Quebec, while reporting for the Montréal Gazette in the mid 1940s. Finally recognized by her homeland when she was appointed Officer of the Order of Canada in 1981, Mavis Gallant has lived mainly in Paris since 1950. Not widely read in Canada until publication of Far from the Fifteenth District (1979), Home Truths (1981), and Overhead in a Balloon (1985), Mavis Gallant, today, is one of Canada's best-known authors read internationally. [Photo, courtesy National Archives of Canada/PA-114591]

Mavis Gallant has the esteemed privilege of being, along with Alice Munroe, one of the few Canadian authors whose works regularly appear in *The New Yorker*. Many of Gallant's stories appear there first and are subsequently brought under one cover to form a collection.

Grazia Merler observes in her book, *Mavis Gallant: Narrative Patterns and Devices*, that "Psychological character development is not the heart of Mavis Gallant's stories, nor is plot. Specific situation development and reconstruction of the state of mind or of heart is, however, the main objective." Frequently, Gallant's stories focus on expatriate men and women who have come to feel lost or isolated; marriages that have grown flimsy or shabby; lives that have faltered and now hover in the shadowy area between illusion, self-delusion, and reality. As well, because of her heritage and understanding of Acadian history, she is often compared to Antonine Maillet, considered to be spokesperson for Acadian culture in Canada.

In a critical book, *Reading Mavis Gallant*, Janice Kulyk Keefer says, "Gallant is a writer who dazzles us with her command of the language, her innovative use of narrative forms, the acuity of her intelligence, and the incisiveness of her wit. Yet she also disconcerts us with her insistence on the constrictions and limitations that dominate human experience."

Gallant has written two novels, *Green Water, Green Sky* (1969) and *A Fairly Good Time* (1970); a play, *What is to be Done?* (1984); numerous celebrated collections of stories, *The Other Paris* (1956), *My Heart is Broken* (1964), *The Pegnitz Junction* (1973), *The End of the World and Other Stories* (1974), *From the Fifteenth District* (1978), *Home Truths: Selected Canadian Stories* (1981), *Overhead in a Balloon: Stories of Paris* (1985), and *In Transit* (1988); and a non-fiction work, *Paris Journals: Selected Essays and Reviews* (1986).

In 1981, Gallant was honoured by her native country and made an Officer of the Order of Canada for her contribution to literature; that year, she received the Governor General's award for literature for her collection of stories, *Home Truths*. In 1983-84, she returned to Canada to be the writer-in-residence at the University of Toronto. Queen's University bestowed an LL.D. upon this famous short story writer in 1991.

Mavis Gallant's life in Paris is spent writing her internationally acclaimed stories and in participating in the occasional gallery opening and gala opening night exhibits. She assiduously reads daily newspapers in German, Italian, French, and English and occasionally (and reluctantly) grants an interview.

In a review of her work in *Books in Canada* in 1978, Geoff Hancock asserts that "Mavis Gallant's fiction is among the finest ever written by a Canadian. But, like buried treasure, both the author and her writing are to discover."

Speaking of Gallant in *Canadian Reader*, Robert Fulford has said, "One begins comparing her best moments to those of major figures in literary history. Names like Henry James, Chekhov, and George Eliot dance across the mind."

Patricia Stone

Robert MacNeil

Paradigm of
Public Broadcasting Credibilty

ROBERT MACNEIL heard three shots. He stopped the press bus, jumped out, and raced towards the nearest building looking for a telephone. A man leaving the Texas Book Depository pointed to another man inside the building and said, "Better ask him." Later it was confirmed that MacNeil had spoken to Lee Harvey Oswald, who was leaving the building minutes after shooting President John F. Kennedy in Dallas, Texas, November 22, 1963.

Robert MacNeil, arguably, had more credibility and broadcast integrity than any other telejournalist in recent memory. The program which he either anchored or co-hosted with Jim Lehrer for twenty years generated informed public opinion. [Photo, courtesy MacNeil/Lehrer Productions]

This is one of the incidents that illustrates why Montreal-born, Halifax-raised, MacNeil titled a book on his 40-year journalistic career *The Right Place at the Right Time*. It was written while he was serving as executive editor of *The MacNeil/Lehrer NewsHour*, the TV show seen on some 300 PBS stations that has won more than 30 awards for journalistic excellence. After 20 years of sharing the program with Jim Lehrer, Robert – better known to friends and associates as Robin – retired from *NewsHour* in October 1995 to spend more time writing fiction instead of fact. His first novel, also written while MacNeil was still with the program was a Canadian best-seller, and a second, *The Voyage*, came out at the time of his retirement. He is now writing a third novel and possibly another non-fiction book to go with the five he has already written.

MacNeil has worked in radio and TV newsrooms in Canada, Great Britain, and the United States and, as an international correspondent, has covered events such as the Belgian Congo uprising, the civil war in Algeria, the building of the Berlin Wall, and the Cuban missile crisis. There were also stints as NBC's Washington correspondent reporting on civil rights and the White House, and later, for PBS, the Senate Watergate hearings.

MacNeil had no burning desire to be a newsman. "I stumbled into it," he wrote in his autobiography. "I was not pushed. I did not choose it." His first choice was to be a naval officer. He enrolled in the Navel Training Division at Dalhousie University in Halifax but gave that up in 1950 to become an actor. While with a New York summer stock company, he realized he "wasn't meant to be an actor." This experience, however, led to his acting on a local radio station and this, in turn, led to a summer job in 1951 as well as a stint as an overnight disc jockey before he moved to Ottawa to study at Carleton University.

In Ottawa he got other radio jobs and, in 1954, moved from CBC radio to its TV station where he hosted 26 episodes of a children's program, *Let's Go To a Museum*, before graduating in 1955. Determined to go to England, he quit the CBC and got a job as a writer with London's independent television network, ITV, on the basis of his experience in Ottawa, "embroidered," he admits, "with a little delicate exaggeration."

A year later he joined Reuters, a newswire agency that taught him "to write fast, simple, yet graceful English leaving no ambiguities." After five years there, NBC hired him as its roving correspondent and sent him to the Congo, Algeria, Berlin, and Cuba before bringing him back to Washington as its White House correspondent in 1963.

Most of 1964 was spent covering the U.S. presidential campaign and, in 1965, he was named anchor of a nightly newscast in New York. Later he teamed up with Ray Scherer for a Saturday evening network news roundup and developed a number of TV documentaries on such subjects as electronic surveillance and gun control legislation. By 1966, however, he grew tired of being "a commodity" on commercial TV and returned to London to be a reporter for *Panorama*, the prestigious BBC show that, he claimed, "makes CBS's *60 Minutes* look like a pale grandchild."

For the next four years he flew from story to story, covering such events as the resignation of President Charles de Gaulle, the student riots in Paris, the police violence at the Chicago

Democratic Convention in 1968 (later developed into a 90-minute documentary "The Whole World is Watching") and the assassinations and funerals of Dr. Martin Luther King and Robert F. Kennedy.

Despite his life of jet lag and the anxiety of covering headline events, he wrote his first book, *The People Machine: The Flame of Television on American Politics*, which *Current Biography* called "a blistering indictment of commercial television's preoccupation with entertainment." In 1971, he left the BBC to return to the USA to become with Sandy Vanocur a senior correspondent for the National Public Affairs Center (NPAC), later adding the role of host on the PBS program *Washington Week in Review*. In 1973, while at the NPAC, he met and co-anchored with Jim Lehrer the Senate Watergate hearings, coverage that won an Emmy award.

MacNeil rejoined the BBC *Panorama* program in 1973 but spent much of his time in the U.S. covering the impeachment hearings of President Nixon. Later he interviewed President Gerald Ford, a television interview shown in 19 countries.

Produced in 1994 by MacNeil/Lehrer Productions in association with Thirteen/WNET, New York, Robert MacNeil hosted Bah! Humbug!, *a television Christmas special from the east room of the Pierpont Morgan Building, New York, with special guests James Earl Jones, left, and Martin Sheen, right, reading selections from the Charles Dickens classic* A Christmas Carol. *[Photo, courtesy MacNeil/Lehrer Productions]*

In 1975 he was "lured by the promise of his own news analysis program" to join WNET-TV in New York City with Jim Lehrer in Washington. Within a year a number of PBS and educational stations signed on and a *Saturday Review* critic wrote, "I have been watching with mounting admiration the *Robert MacNeil Report*, for my money this year's most exhilarating innovation on public TV."

On Labour Day, 1976, the title of the half-hour show was changed to the *MacNeil/Lehrer Report* and, after 1,000 shows, MacNeil conceded in a 1979 magazine article that, while the show didn't give anyone sleepless nights, it was proving that "in-depth journalism has a place on TV." That was reinforced in 1983 when it became the hour-long program, *NewsHour*.

Besides his five days a week editing and co-hosting *NewsHour*, MacNeil has written or co-authored and hosted numerous other documentaries including the nine-part TV mini-series, *The Story of English*, first shown on the BBC and then PBS in 1986. In 1987 it won TV's Peabody and Emmy Award for excellence in writing and was published later in book form by Viking Press. In 1989 his on-going love of the English language resulted in another successful book, *Wordstruck*, and in 1992 he produced his first novel, *Burden of Desire,* set in Halifax at the time of the explosion in 1917.

When Robert Breckenridge Ware MacNeil announced his intention to retire from *NewsHour*, Lehrer, his partner of 20 years, told *The Toronto Star's* Robert Crew, "It's a bit like a death in the family for me. He is responsible for what's left of serious news reporting on television. He led the way; I follow in his wake."

Mel James

Prime Minister Golda Meir of Israel was interviewed by Robert MacNeil in 1973. In a 40-year career of public telebroadcast journalism, MacNeil's honesty and leadership generated widespread audience loyalty. [Photo, courtesy MacNeil/Lehrer Productions]

In 1957, at the height of the Cold War, Bertrand Russell invited Canadian tycoon Cyrus Eaton to organize a conference bringing together, from East to West, scientists, scholars, and public figures whose collective desire was to diminish the part played by nuclear arms in international politics. A strong advocate for friendly relations with the communist world, the multi-millionaire industrialist Eaton not only agreed to bankroll the conference but offered his summer home in Pugwash, Nova Scotia, to act as an ongoing international base for discussions on nuclear and other security issues. In 1995, this same conference, which traces its origins to a 1955 anti-war manifesto signed, among others, by Albert Einstein, shared the 1995 Nobel Peace Prize with noted British physicist Joseph Rotblat, member of the 1957 Pugwash Conference originally hosted by Cyrus Eaton in a fishing village in Nova Scotia. [Photo, courtesy John Sebert Photography]

Sowing Seeds for Nobel Peace Prize

CYRUS S. EATON

1883 - 1979

THE TOWN OF PUGWASH, Nova Scotia, became a world-famous community because a business tycoon, born there in 1883, volunteered funds and hosted a group of 22 scientists from around the world at his Pugwash summer home in 1957. The host was Cyrus S. Eaton, one of North America's most successful businessmen, but controversial because of his friendship with Russian and Cuban Communist leaders.

Eaton became the sponsor of the Pugwash Conferences on Science and World Affairs when British philosopher Bertrand Russell encouraged a meeting of scientists from around the world to speak out on the proliferation of the atomic bomb. Funds were needed to make such a meeting possible. When a proposal to meet in India fell through, Russell had two other options: to accept an offer made by Aristotle Onassis, the Greek shipping magnate, or one by Cyrus Eaton, the Cleveland businessman who had already held a number of conferences at his summer home in Pugwash. Russell chose Eaton's offer to pay travel expenses and host the event.

After a three-day meeting in July 1957 that brought together scientists from the U.S.A., China, Russia, Great Britain, France, and several other countries, the name Pugwash was adopted in the title for future conferences with Eaton readily agreeing to sponsor a second

session the following year at Lac Beauport, Quebec.

Eaton's willingness to bankroll such a conference stemmed from a lifelong interest in being in the company of intellectuals. The fifth of nine children born to a farmer and general store owner in Pugwash, he studied to be a minister at McMaster University (then located in Toronto), graduated in philosophy in 1905, and moved to Cleveland, Ohio.

His association with Cleveland started in 1901 when young Cyrus visited his uncle Charles, a Baptist minister there, and met one of the parishioners, John D. Rockefeller Sr. Eaton spent his summer vacations working at Rockefeller's estate and returned to Cleveland upon graduation. By 1906, however, he decided that being a Baptist minister was too restricting for his interests. Rockefeller offered him full-time employment. An early assignment was to placate property owners whose lawns were being torn up by the East Ohio Gas Company.

In 1907, Eaton married a Cleveland girl and managed to get a loan from a neighbour to buy utilities franchises in western Canada. These he later organized into the Canadian Gas and Electric Corporation. By 1912, he was a millionaire. Before World War I, he bought a substantial interest in Otis and Company, one of the largest investment bankers and stockbrokers outside of New York, and, during the 1920s, "he was into everything, buying, selling, swapping, manoeuvring, manipulating. His touch was of the purist gold," wrote E.J. Kahn Jr. in a two-part article in *New Yorker* magazine in 1977. His innumerable holding companies owned utilities, steel mills, a major portion of Goodyear Tire, and numerous other businesses until the crash of 1929 virtually wiped him out.

Throughout the 1930s and '40s, however, from his offices in Cleveland's Tower Building Eaton sold, bought, traded, and swapped his way back into America's business establishment, eventually adding railroads, coal mines, and the Steep Rock Iron Mines of Ontario to his acquisitions. His interest in world affairs also grew. It became his custom to invite people from the academic world to spend their vacations at his various residences in either Canada or the United States not only to enjoy sporting activities but also to engage in stimulating discussions of world affairs.

By the early 1950s, these earlier vacation sessions had turned into conferences at his Pugwash home and this led to Russell's choice of Pugwash for the first meeting of scientists.

After a second conference with Eaton's backing was held in Lac Beauport in 1958, Austria played host to a third later that year, and another was held in Baden, Germany, in 1959 before Eaton sponsored a fifth at Pugwash, also in 1959. By then, however, Eaton's outspoken views on *detente* with Russia and his controversial relationship with Nikita Kruschev – they exchanged gifts and Eaton was given the red carpet treatment when he visited Moscow in 1958 – led the scientists to consider his sponsorship a liability.

In 1960, when Eaton was awarded the Lenin Peace Prize, this prompted Lord Russell to write to British physicist Joseph Rotblat, coordinator of the Pugwash conferences, "I trust your thoughts about Cyrus have remained Christian." They did, for Eaton attended many future meetings as a guest, no doubt in part because of his close association with political leaders in the United States, Russia, and other capitals on both sides of the Iron Curtain.

As early as the 1920s he was Herbert Hoover's guest at the White House on several occasions, and his White House connections continued when he openly opposed an Ohio lawyer who sought the Democratic nomination against Roosevelt in 1932. Roosevelt later enlisted Eaton's aid to explore such things as Ontario Premier Mitch Hepburn's opposition to the building of the St. Lawrence Seaway. Eaton also publicly backed Roosevelt's bid for a third term and claims he was one of the intermediaries responsible for the lend-lease arrangement that provided 50 old U.S. destroyers to Great Britain in 1940. When Harry Truman became president in 1945 Eaton had known Truman for more than two decades and had supported his bid for reelection in 1948.

By the 1950s, however, his outspoken support for *detente* with Russia and his friendship with Kruschev and other Russian leaders and his vocal criticisms of such agencies at home as the FBI and the CIA prompted angry outbursts from the press, politicians, and the public in the U.S. despite his assurances that he was a staunch capitalist and not a supporter of Communist doctrine.

Although Eaton's career centred in Cleveland and he became an American citizen in 1913, his ties with Canada remained strong. As early as 1929 he generously supported the town of Pugwash when a fire destroyed much of the village and later he established a farm at Upper Blandford, Nova Scotia, where he made a point of spending a month each summer with his grandchildren without their parents. The month was devoted to participating with the children from age two and up in everything from household chores to spotting birds and identifying trees (it was claimed he knew the names of every bird and tree in North America), to riding horses and picnicing – one of his favourite year-round pastimes.

Eaton's hospitality was also cited in Lord Russell's autobiography when he attributed some of the success of the Pugwash Conference group to the fact that the scientists were able to get to know each other as human beings as well as scientists. "This most remarkable, important characteristic," he wrote, "was in large part made possible by the astute understanding by Cyrus Eaton of the situation and what we wished to accomplish and by his tactful hospitality."

Eaton, who achieved the ambition of being the oldest living board member of the University of Chicago, was also the recipient of nine honorary degrees: four from Canadian universities including Dalhousie and Acadia of his native Nova Scotia, two from U.S. institutions, and three from universities in Bulgaria, Budapest, and Prague. The capitalist from Nova Scotia did not, however, achieve the goal of living to be 100, falling short of that mark by four years.

In 1995, 16 years after Eaton's death in 1979, and 35 years after he had won the Lenin Peace Prize, the Pugwash Conference shared the prestigious Nobel Prize with Joseph Rotblat, the last surviving scientist of the original 11 who had, in 1957, co-founded "the thinkers' conferences" bankrolled by a Bluenoser.

Mel James

Ernest Thompson Seton

1860 - 1946

Literary Audubon

ERNEST THOMPSON SETON is best known for his extraordinary animal stories, popularized originally in magazines before being reintroduced in book form as *Wild Animals I Have Known* (1898). In fact, the fame of these stories was so widespread they even inspired Rudyard Kipling's *Jungle Books* (1894-1895). Seton's particular brand of eccentricity, inner drive, and self-conviction, however, led him to pursue many other occupations during his lifetime: naturalist, writer, artist, educator, and explorer. As well, he was, in 1910, co-founder of the Boy Scouts of America.

Seton was a descendant of the Scottish Setons who fought for the Stuarts in 1745 and then fled to England under the name of Thompson. Ernest Thompson Seton (he assumed his family's historical identity in his twenties) was born in southern England in August 1860, the ninth son in a family of ten boys.

When he was six years old, Seton's family emigrated to Canada, and for several years they resided on a farm near Lindsay, Ontario, where Seton began his lifelong study of birds – often catching and dissecting wildlife to assure that his drawings were realistic.

Falling onto hard times, the family moved to Toronto in 1870, but Seton found rural sustenance in the wilds of the Don Valley, the Toronto Marsh, and Queen's Park, all of which, at that time, teemed with wildlife. His forays into the wilderness did not, however, interfere with his studies: his brilliance as a pupil was soon recognized, and he continued his schooling at Jarvis Street Collegiate. Later, he was apprenticed to a Toronto portrait artist and then studied at the Ontario College of Art where he took the Gold Medal in 1879.

For a while he lived with his brother on their farm in Carberry, Manitoba, and his experience there intensified an interest in animal life, particularly in coyotes, bears, and wolves.

Through self-discipline and a honing of his artistic ability, he gained entrance in 1881 to the Royal Academy of Arts in London, England. Following that experience, he went to New York City and joined the Art Student League of New York. His painting, "The Sleeping Wolf," won first prize at the Paris Salon in 1891. He also finished his illustrated work, *Birds of Manitoba* (1891), for Washington's Smithsonian Institute.

An experience of witnessing the capture of a legendary old wolf, Lobo, in New Mexico affected Seton for the rest of his life. Although he continued to dissect animals and to produce books such as *Studies in the Art Anatomy of Animals*, he increasingly turned to writing stories including the four-volume *Lives of Game Animals* for which he was awarded the John Burroughs and Elliot Gold Medals.

It is Seton's books and stories on animals that have ensured his place in history and, particularly, in the affection of many North American children. His animal stories are often taken from the animal's point of view and invest the animals with such human qualities as curiosity, desire, and sympathy. Many of these protagonists have become household names – "Lobo, the King of Currumpaw"; "Raggylug, the Story of a Cottontail Rabbit"; "Redruff, the Story of the Don Valley Partridge." In a preface to his collected works, Seton says:

> *These stories are true. Although I have left the line of historical truth in many places, the animals in this book were all real characters. They lived the lives I have depicted, and showed the stamp of heroism and personality more strongly by far than it has been the power of my pen to tell.*

The many aspects of life with which Seton was involved – art, anatomy, wildlife, folklore, exploration, Boy Scouts, Amerindian history – were pursued with a singular determination that made him stand apart and win notice, but notice that was not always favourable. In particular, his custom of investing animal characters with human qualities gained him the negative and vocal criticism of such influential personalities as Theodore Roosevelt and John Burroughs.

Because of his keen sense of affinity with the wolf, especially, Seton began to refer to himself as "Wolf" or "Black Wolf" Seton.

He married twice – in 1896 to Grace Gallatin with whom he had one daughter (Anya Seton who later wrote historical novels) – and again in 1935 to Julie Moss Buttree who was 29 years his junior. In the last few years of his life, he and his second wife established The Seton Institute of Indian Lore in Cimmaron, New Mexico, which is still open today as a museum and run successfully by his adopted daughter, Dee.

Patricia Stone

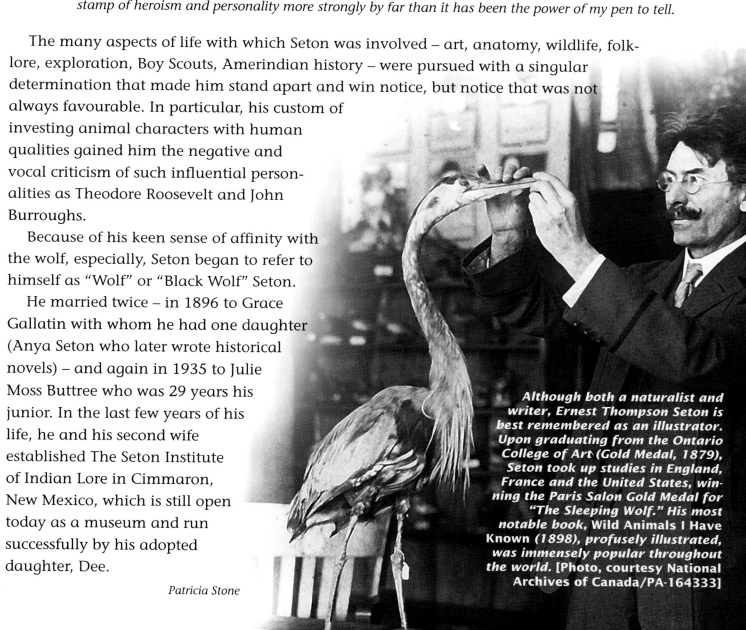

Although both a naturalist and writer, Ernest Thompson Seton is best remembered as an illustrator. Upon graduating from the Ontario College of Art (Gold Medal, 1879), Seton took up studies in England, France and the United States, winning the Paris Salon Gold Medal for "The Sleeping Wolf." His most notable book, Wild Animals I Have Known (1898), profusely illustrated, was immensely popular throughout the world. [Photo, courtesy National Archives of Canada/PA-164333]

CHIEF DAN GEORGE was over 60 when he became a movie actor. At 71 he won the prestigious New York Film Critics award and an Academy Award nomination for best supporting actor. This success catapulted him into the position of spokesman for the people of Canada's first nations – a role he performed with dignity in speaking about the past and present plight of North America's first peoples.

CHIEF DAN GEORGE

1899 - 1981
Sagacious Sachem

He knew those circumstances well. The son of a tribal chief, born on Burrard Reserve No.3 on Vancouver's north shore in 1899 and given the native name of "Tes-wah-no" but known in English as Dan Slaholt. When he entered a mission boarding school at age five, his surname was changed to "George" and he, along with the other Indians at the school, was forbidden to speak their native language.

At 17 he left the school to work in the bush. In 1923, his father-in-law secured him a job as a longshoreman that lasted off and on until 1947 when a swingload of lumber smashed into him. No bones were broken, but "my leg and hip muscles were smashed to hamburger," he later recalled.

After overcoming these injuries, he began working in construction, and, later, while he was a school bus driver, he was asked to try out for the role of the aging Indian, "Old Antoine," in the CBC series, *Cariboo Country*. The actor previously playing the role had become seriously ill and a replacement was needed within a week. Dan got the part and soon critics were describing him as one of the "finest natural actors anywhere." One episode entitled "How to Break a Quarterhorse" won the Canadian Film Award for best entertainment film of 1965 and Walt Disney studios adapted another of the series into a movie named *Smith* starring Glen Ford and Keenan Wynn. A critic wrote that Dan George as Old Antoine played the role to "ultimate perfection."

His performance in *Smith* led to an invitation to be Old Lodge Skins in the 1970 movie, *Little Big Man*, starring Dustin Hoffman. Chief Dan's performance was singled out by Judith Crist of the *New York Times* who wrote, "This Indian will not vanish from your memory." He won the New York Film Critics Award and the National Society of Film Critics Award for that role and was nominated for an Oscar as best supporting actor only to lose to actor John Mills for his performance as the wordless sage in *Ryan's Daughter*.

By then he was also a noted stage actor. His stage career began when Dan met playwright George Ryga who was so impressed by him that he enlarged the part of the father in his play, *The Ecstasy of Rita Joe*, first staged at the Vancouver Playhouse and selected for the opening of the National Arts Centre in Ottawa where it won rave reviews. In 1973 a theatre in Washington, D.C., staged it and a critic wrote, "Chief George's scene with Rita Joe (his daughter acted by Frances Hyland) when he recalls a story from her childhood ... is a perfect and probably indelible moment of theatre."

These successes thrust him into another spotlight: he became spokesman for native people throughout North America. One of his first appearances in that role was at Empire Stadium in Vancouver for that city's centennial celebrations in 1967. He recited his much publicized "A Lament for Confederation," which, recalling past injustices of first nation peoples, promised the crowd of 35,000, "I shall grab the instruments of the white man's success – his education, his skills, and with these new tools I shall build my race into the proudest segment of your society."

His message of calling for understanding and integration of native peoples continued during his term as national chairman of Brotherhood Week in 1972. While active in *Rita Joe* in Washington in 1973, a native group of first nation peoples tried to enlist his support for the militant action taking place at Wounded Knee, South Dakota, but he quietly responded, "We buried the hatchet in Canada long ago, and although treaty after treaty has been broken we have never dug it up. We have troubles but we have our council of chiefs to work on them."

Honoured with a Doctor of Laws degree from Simon Fraser University (1972) and a Doctor of Letters from the University of Brandon the following year, Chief Dan continued to play minor roles in several other movies such as *Cancel My Reservation* starring Bob Hope. This was criticised by some of the press and public but his reply reflected the words of George C. Scott, "The business of an actor is to act." He would not, however, play a role that demeaned his race and until his death in 1981, he remained on the reservation where he had been born.

Mel James

Opposite: *A man of considerable dignity and a noble spokesperson for his race, Chief Dan George (1899-1981) was 60 when he became a movie actor. At 71, he won an Oscar nomination for his role as an old Cheyenne Chief in* Little Big Man *(1970), losing to John Mills who won best supporting actor for playing the crippled village idiot in* Ryan's Daughter. [Photo, courtesy *The Toronto Star*/Frank Lennon]

William Boyd

1885 - 1979

WILLIAM BOYD must have inspired as many students as any other physician in the world, perhaps even rivalling Sir William Osler. Textbooks were the principal reason for this global impact: Boyd's extraordinary gift of direct and colourful prose enlivened the usually dead pages of pathology texts.

Pathologist with Silver Tongue and Golden Pen

Born in Scotland, Boyd developed a taste for rock climbing, and spent many days, in his youth, clambering about native hills and crags. He completed his formative education in Glasgow and, by 1902, was enrolled at the University of Edinburgh to study medicine. He was gold medalist upon graduation. His first professional work was as assistant physician in the Derby Borough Asylum, a career chosen, perhaps, after he saw his sister suffer a psychiatric illness. The separation of this from his future work as a pathologist was less than it might seem, however, as his major responsibility at the asylum was performing autopsies.

When war broke out in 1914, Boyd entered the Royal Army Medical Corps, serving in Flanders in 1914 and 1915. One result was a fascinating but largely forgotten little book, *With a Field Ambulance at Ypres*. While he was serving in the field, he was appointed to his first Canadian post, Professor of Pathology in the Manitoba Medical College in Winnipeg.

During his two decades in Winnipeg, Boyd wrote medical textbooks that made him a household name in the medical profession. Devoted entirely to pathology, his textbooks combined skillful, meticulous observations with an unusual, inventive prose style that encompassed clarity and wit. The result was the best of all teaching methods: statements that his readers would remember. For example, he wrote about pathologic processes that made "bones look as if they have been twisted by a giant hand."

The same character traits that inspired William Boyd's rock climbing were parlayed into his spontaneous lectures and animated medical texts. His unrestricted prose was ingurgitated by medical students around the world for nearly half a century.
[Photo, courtesy Charles G. Roland]

In the beginning, some criticized his lively style, perhaps in the misguided belief that difficult, convoluted prose is more "scientific," thus more desirable. Boyd rejected this approach, knowing the equation between good writing and memorable reading. Readers found it easy to remember colourful passages such as:

> When we think of cancer in general terms we are apt to conjure up a process characterized by a steady, remorseless and inexorable progress in which the disease is all-conquering, and none of the immunological and other defensive forces which help us to survive the onslaught of bacterial and viral infections can serve to halt the faltering footsteps to the grave.

A master of arresting phraseology, Boyd knew the necessity of getting his readers' attention. His best-known aphorism, "Of all the ailments which may blow out life's little candle, heart disease is the chief," epitomizes this colourful diction.

The problem that besieges well-written scientific books is that science advances, and no matter how readable a text may be, it is almost always set aside in favour of the more modern works or the next generation of texts. This, though inevitable, is unfortunate. Boyd's descriptive pathology, though it may today be incomplete, is not invalid. Today's students not exposed to the writings of this fluent interpreter of the faltering human body risk missing such sparkling gems as:

> It would indeed be rash for a mere pathologist to venture forth on the uncharted sea of the endocrines, strewn as it is with the wrecks of shattered hypotheses where even the most wary mariner may easily lose his way as he seeks to steer his bark amid the glandular temptations whose siren voices have proved the downfall of many who have gone before.

Such textbooks as *Surgical Pathology* (1925), *Pathology of Internal Disease* (1931), *Textbook of Pathology* (1932), and *Introduction to Medical Science* (1937) have been read and referred to by tens of thousands of physicians and students from around the world. Translated into many languages, they became international best-sellers. He wrote some books for pathologists, but most of his books were for wider audiences: surgeons, medical students, interns, and residents. One who knew Boyd only later recalls an older colleague telling him, "It doesn't matter what textbook you recommend, they will all read Boyd."

Boyd kept "a commonplace book," a notebook (or many notebooks) into which one records especially appealing quotations from works one is reading. Usually one's own high thoughts – often expunged later – are included. Boyd's book certainly tells us much about him. As a young man he noted down an aphorism from Milton: "There is no misery in being blind. It would be miserable not to be able to bear blindness." Six decades later, Boyd himself was blind. But there is no evidence that he was miserable.

William Boyd died peacefully in his sleep in Toronto on March 10, 1979, a much honoured and globally respected pathologist.

Charles Roland

CANADA'S LIFE INSURANCE INDUSTRY

Exporting an Invisible Giant

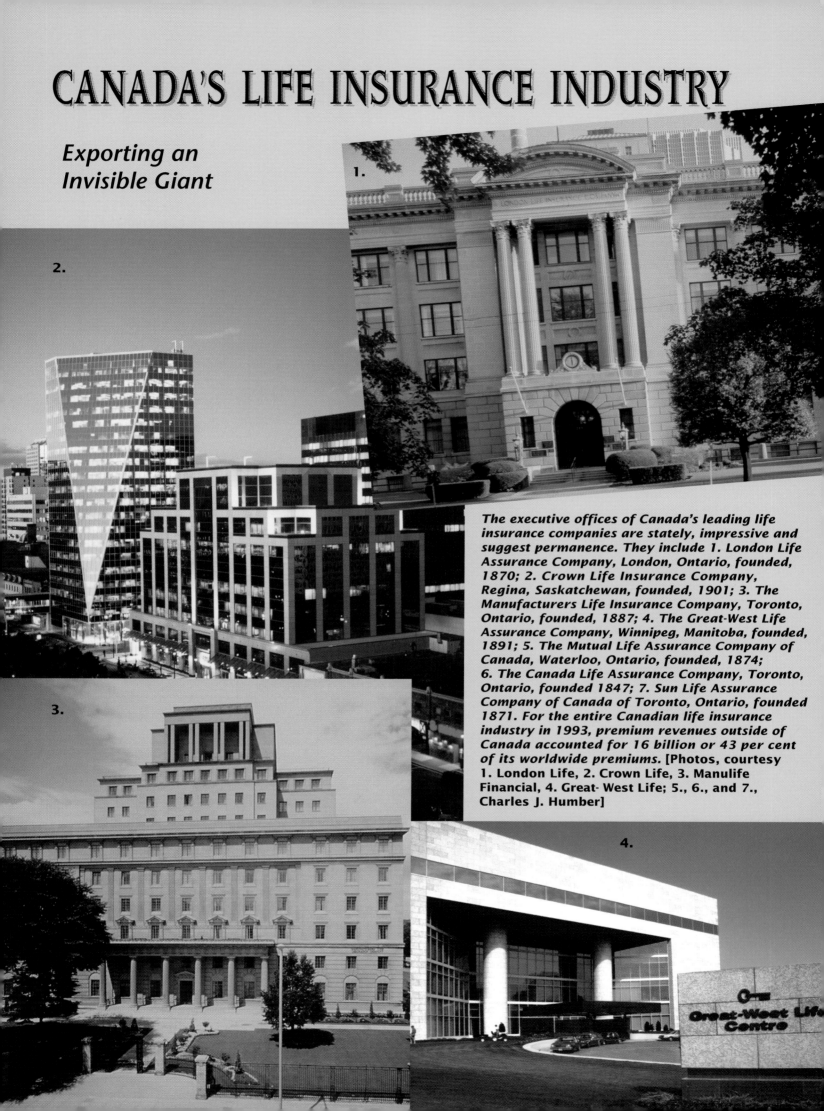

The executive offices of Canada's leading life insurance companies are stately, impressive and suggest permanence. They include 1. London Life Assurance Company, London, Ontario, founded, 1870; 2. Crown Life Insurance Company, Regina, Saskatchewan, founded, 1901; 3. The Manufacturers Life Insurance Company, Toronto, Ontario, founded, 1887; 4. The Great-West Life Assurance Company, Winnipeg, Manitoba, founded, 1891; 5. The Mutual Life Assurance Company of Canada, Waterloo, Ontario, founded, 1874; 6. The Canada Life Assurance Company, Toronto, Ontario, founded 1847; 7. Sun Life Assurance Company of Canada of Toronto, Ontario, founded 1871. For the entire Canadian life insurance industry in 1993, premium revenues outside of Canada accounted for 16 billion or 43 per cent of its worldwide premiums. [Photos, courtesy 1. London Life, 2. Crown Life, 3. Manulife Financial, 4. Great-West Life; 5., 6., and 7., Charles J. Humber]

CANADA'S EARLY ECONOMY relied almost entirely on the exploitation of its abundant natural resources. For a long time, in fact, Canada was one of the world's leading suppliers of raw materials. This gave way, in time, to a

5.

6.

7.

very successful and highly integrated manufacturing sector exporting processed goods. More recently, and almost unnoticed, Canada has become a major exporter of services. The largest service exported by Canadians today is the insurance of persons by Canadian life insurance companies.

The size of this Canadian export industry and its related products is staggering. In direct life insurance alone in 1993, Canadian companies insured more than five million non-residents located in over 20 countries. The insurance industry expresses its gross sales as "premiums," which is the aggregate of the prices paid by consumers for their insurance protection. For the entire Canadian life insurance industry in 1993, premium revenues outside of Canada accounted for $16 billion or 43 per cent of its worldwide premiums. Assets invested abroad to protect the security of lives insured by branches and subsidiaries of Canadian life insurers exceeded $111 billion, an amount comparable to the revenues of the Federal government of Canada in the 1993/94 year, and more than 20 per cent of the entire government debt. These numbers do not include direct foreign sales of health insurance, sold mainly by life insurers, or revenues derived from assuming life and health risks originally accepted by foreign insurance companies, normally termed "reinsurance."

In what parts of the world do Canadian life insurers do business? Easily their most important export market is the United States which accounts for about 75 per cent of the direct life insurance sold abroad. The recent Free Trade Agreement only served to increase the importance of the U.S. market to Canadian life insurers. Other important markets are the U.K. and Ireland, which together account for 18 per cent of insurance placed abroad. Bermuda was one of the earliest foreign markets entered by major Canadian companies and, today, companies operate directly as branch operations or through subsidiaries in Latin America, the Caribbean, and the Far East, especially Hong Kong.

The early entry of Canadian life insurers targeting an international market is one reason life insurance and health insurance have been successful service exports for Canadian companies. For example, Canada Life entered the U.S. market as early as 1889 and both the U.K. and Ireland by 1903. Canada Life today is a major player in both the individual and group insurance markets with each of these countries. As well, Sun Life of Canada entered the U.S. in 1895 and Bermuda almost as early. Manulife (formerly Manufacturers Life) began selling insurance in Bermuda in 1898 and in the U.S. in 1903. Sixty per cent of Manulife's revenues are now derived from operations outside Canada. The company, moreover, is the largest Canadian employer in Hong Kong. More recently, but still long enough ago to have now become well established, Crown Life entered the U.S. in 1924; it has since expanded to Hong Kong, Bermuda, and the Bahamas. Great-West Life has long been a player in the U.S. and in 1994 derived more than twice as much premium revenues in the U.S. (almost seven billion dollars) as in Canada (almost three billion dollars). And veteran Canadian mutual company, Mutual Life, which was founded in 1870, now has an important presence in the U.S. and is planning entry into the Asian-Pacific arena.

Because Canadians traditionally have had the highest per capita value of life insurance in the world (a record only recently overtaken by the Japanese), Canadian insurers, by the late nineteenth century, were forced to look abroad to sustain growth in an ever-competitive market.

Still another reason Canadian life insurers expanded globally at the turn of this century is directly related to the Canadian government regulators who put financial security well ahead of other concerns in overseeing the life insurance industry in Canada. Thus, the financial security of Canadian insurers quickly became a watchword throughout the world.

The geographical terrain of Canada itself contributed to worldwide growth of specialized classes of insurance and reinsurance. Our dependence on transportation over long distances and into remote areas made aviation a high priority for Canadian insurers. Insuring bush pilots and the like gave Canadian life insurers an insight into high-risk insurance requirements worldwide.

The reinsurance business is little known to the general public. In fact, reinsurance plays a crucial part today in the worldwide business of insurance. It supports the financial security of companies since, by allowing them to accept amounts of insurance coverage larger than they could retain on their own books, it thus shields them from the impacts of catastrophic events ranging from hurricanes and earthquakes to airline crashes and mining disasters. Although most of Canada's life insurance companies have active reinsurance operations in their own name, they also have banded together to participate in one or more reinsurance pools that collectively accept risks larger than any one of the companies, even the largest, is prepared to retain for itself. Reinsurance business is very cost effective because large blocks of business can be handled by a small number of staff. Because of this, the reinsurance business of Canadian life insurers is even more widely distributed geographically than their direct insurance business.

One Canadian-based reinsurance pool is the Canadian Accident Reinsurance Facility (CARF) which is managed out of Toronto by Tri-Can Reinsurance Inc. Although this pool only negotiates reinsurance business in North America, many of the same Canadian companies are also members of an international pool called CARF International which is managed by Tri-Can International Ltd. of Bermuda, an associated company of Tri-Can Reinsurance Inc. CARF International specializes in reinsuring accident risks on a worldwide basis. Thus, while the man in the street thinks of international accident insurance as being the natural province of Lloyd's of London, in fact the CARF International pool and many of the individual Canadian companies which participate in it reinsure Lloyd's itself.

Canada's life insurance industry has not only a strong international presence but also an extensive network of reinsurance connections with the world's insurance industry. With its developed base of traditional expertise in world markets reinforced by financial strength, there is little doubt that this service will sustain its success well into the twenty-first century.

Derrick Crawley

Marketing Pulp Fiction Sizzle

HARLEQUIN Romances

ROMANCE SELLS ... and pays millions! At least it does for Harlequin Enterprises, the world's largest publisher of series romance fiction. From its headquarters in Don Mills, a suburb of Toronto, Ontario, Harlequin directs its publishing empire to produce approximately 180 million paperbacks a year in 23 languages. Marketed to more than 100 countries, this pulp fiction sizzle provides its parent company, Torstar, publisher of Canada's largest newspaper, *The Toronto Star*, with more than 80 per cent of its operating profits annually.

After the fall of the communist regime in Poland which, prior to 1990, had made the Palace of Culture and Science building in Warsaw their national headquarters, Harlequin enthusiasts successfully unfurled a huge flag near the building's top, as viewed here. This "banner with a heart," a universal symbol of love and passion, in an unprecedented coup, was prominently displayed on Valentine's Day, 1990. [Photo, courtesy Harlequin Enterprises]

Harlequin executives, however, don't feel they have exhausted their growth potential by any means! They are now extending their successful editorial and sales techniques to Eastern Europe, Russia, China, India, South East Asia, and Central and South America because, as Brian Hickey, president and CEO of Harlequin said in a 1993 *Canadian Business* article, "We have yet to come across a culture that has rejected us."

Worldwide sales indicate that Hickey's claim is justified. Countries with more than a million Harlequin readers who are over 15 years of age include the United States with 23 million; Poland, 6.6; Germany, 5.9; Great Britain, 3.2; Italy, 2.5. Even Austria, the former

Opposite: *The marketing of romance is Harlequin Enterprises' niche. By meeting the needs of pulp fiction aficionados worldwide, Harlequin publishes 180 million paperbacks each year in no less than 23 foreign languages. [Photo, courtesy Harlequin Enterprises]*

Czechoslovakia, Holland, Hungary, Japan, and Spain all have a million or more readers.

It's a giant leap from the original private company incorporated as Harlequin Books in Winnipeg, Manitoba, in 1949, to publish pocketbook reprints. Originally interested in mysteries, westerns, romances, thrillers, and cookbooks, Harlequin listed such popular authors as Agatha Christie, Somerset Maugham, and Jean Plaidy, who also writes as Virginia Holt. The company was still struggling in 1958 when Richard and Mary Bonnycastle, also of Winnipeg, bought it. Over the next ten years they changed the name to Harlequin Enterprises, went public and moved to Toronto. The most significant decision, however, was Mary's determination, as editor, to print more "romance fiction in good taste," most of it purchased from the British publishing house of Mills and Boon.

In 1971 the Bonnycastles bought their British supplier and turned the company over to their son, Richard, who hired a management team headed by W. Lawrence Heisey, a Toronto graduate of Harvard's Business School with thirteen years' experience at Procter & Gamble. Heisey applied packaged goods marketing techniques to publishing, launching a research program to find out what typical readers wanted in terms of settings, characters, and plots. He also arranged for the sale of books in supermarkets and drug stores, created a subscriber division, participated in giveaway promotions with feminine products, and provided coupons in women's magazines that could be exchanged for a free book. Television advertising aimed at soap opera listeners also dramatically increased market awareness and sales, giving Harlequin almost total dominance in the romance publishing business by the mid-1970s.

Such success, however, prompted others to enter the field. Publishing giant Simon & Schuster, having lost its contract with Harlequin as its U.S. distributor, launched its own Silhouette romance series and soon gained 30 per cent of the market. Dell Books and Bantam also entered the field to further reduce Harlequin's share of the market and cause profits to plummet dramatically in the first few years of Torstar's total ownership which took place in 1981.

While some believed the decline was due to the changing life-styles and interests of women, Torstar felt another type of marketing expert was needed and hired Brian Hickey, director of strategic planning of S.C.Johnson and Son in Racine, Wisconsin. "I was shocked by the offer," he told Gina Mallet in a *Canadian Business* article but said that, on reading a Harlequin, "I found it to be one of the most relaxing things I could have done," and decided that selling Harlequins was not all that different than selling Johnson's wax. "It's marketing nice things to women," he told Ms. Mallet.

Under Hickey's stewardship, Harlequin downsized its staff nearly 20 per cent but kept its author base of roughly 1,000 writers, each of whom is guided by additional market research findings conducted to determine what readers want. As women's sexual attitudes changed in the 1980s, Harlequin introduced more sophisticated stories in different series. The traditional Harlequin Romance was retained, but new series were added and described in such terms as: Harlequin Presents – "Intense passionate romances that take readers around the world" ;

Harlequin Historicals – "Love and passion bring the past to life" ; Harlequin Superromance – "Provocative, passionate, contemporary stories that celebrate life and love" ; Harlequin Intrigue – "The perfect combination of danger and desire"; and Harlequin Temptation – "The sensual passionate face of romantic fantasy about men and women living and loving in the 1990s."

The resurgence of Harlequin in the 1980s as a more competitive publisher enabled Harlequin to purchase Silhoutte in 1984 and to keep its editorial division separate from its own brand of romantic novel. Harlequin also re-established Simon & Schuster as its distributing agent in the U.S., while its worldwide expansion included the establishment of direct mail-order houses in Great Britain, Scandinavia, France, the Netherlands, and Australia and it is at present adding Germany and Italy to that list.

The 23 languages presently in use include Arabic and Turkish. Other languages will be added as the company succeeds in such countries as China, where revenue could far exceed the 1994 operating profit level of $70.7 million and vastly increase the present annual sales of approximately 180 million books that equate to the sale of 5.7 Harlequin paperbacks every second of the day.

Mel James

Brian Hickey, president and chief executive officer of Harlequin Enterprises, oversees a publishing empire meeting the needs of a worldwide reading audience revolutionized by sexual attitudes and changing mores. [Photo, courtesy Harlequin Enterprises]

The godfather of pulp fiction sizzle is William Lawrence Heisey who turned Harlequin Enterprises into a global publishing house. [Photo, courtesy Harlequin Enterprises]

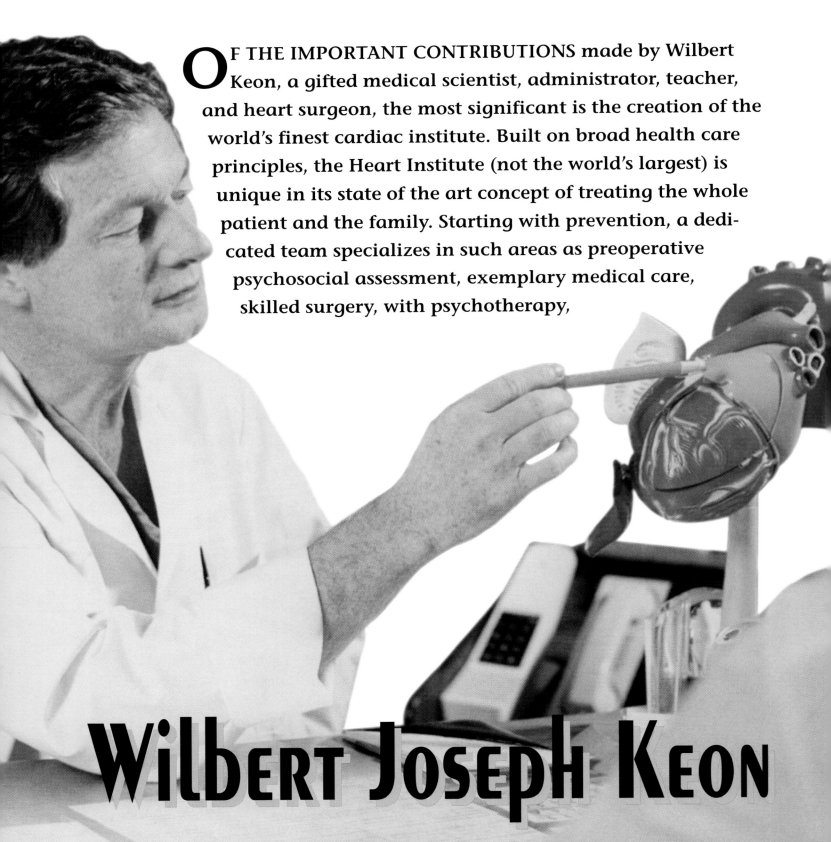

Creating the World's Finest Cardiac Institute

O F THE IMPORTANT CONTRIBUTIONS made by Wilbert Keon, a gifted medical scientist, administrator, teacher, and heart surgeon, the most significant is the creation of the world's finest cardiac institute. Built on broad health care principles, the Heart Institute (not the world's largest) is unique in its state of the art concept of treating the whole patient and the family. Starting with prevention, a dedicated team specializes in such areas as preoperative psychosocial assessment, exemplary medical care, skilled surgery, with psychotherapy,

Wilbert Joseph Keon

Dr. Wilbert Joseph Keon operates each year on the hearts of nearly 300 patients. Known as "the consummate surgeon" by his peers, this pioneering heart surgeon is involved in life and death decisions daily. Esteemed by a dedicated cardiac team of specialists, this exceptional doctor has made Ottawa's honoured Heart Institute internationally famous and globally respected. [Photo, courtesy Dr. Wilfred G. Bigelow via the University of Ottawa Heart Institute, Ottawa Civic Hospital]

dietetics, physiology and a rehabilitation program. It also offers a wide range of services from physical and vocational activity to spousal support groups. Since the early 1990s, multidisciplinary clinics have been created for the control of major risk factors including hypertension, hyperlipidaemia and stress.

The University of Ottawa Heart Institute today is known for its clinical and surgical expertise. It has developed an excellent teaching program for cardiovascular surgery and has strategically placed graduates worldwide. It has also continued its research into devices to assist a failing circulation, parallel arts and cardiac transplantation. Its founder, Dr. Keon, the first Canadian surgeon to implant a total artificial heart as a bridge to a homograft transplant, was a medical pioneer of the now-accepted treatment of emergency revascularization in acute heart attacks. Dr. Keon's current research involves a fifteen-member team perfecting a truly implantable artificial heart.

Of course, the Heart Institute is primarily designed to care for patients with heart disease and with Donald Beanlands, head of the medical section and Wilbert Keon in charge of surgery, this priority is respected. There is a special wing for experimental and clinical research.

The team has an interesting approach to "prevention." There is a no cost "Heart Check Centre" on a walk-in basis with no appointment required. For anyone with a long-term or recent concern regarding the status of his or her heart, this is an easy way to start.

Some years ago, the University of Hamburg, a leading German cardiovascular centre, sent a fact-finding team to Dr. Keon to study the Heart Institute with plans for a similar one in Hamburg. The team included financial and architectural experts. After five days of thorough browsing, they held a meeting with Keon. He walked in, sat down, looked at the group and said, "Well, I guess you gentlemen know more about the Institute than I do." Not exactly an austere *Herr Direktor.*

When challenged regarding the cost of the Heart Institute's hi-tech procedures, Dr. Keon makes no apologies. "I haven't the slightest problem rationalizing what we do here considering the demonstrable benefits."

In setting up the Institute's research wing, Dr. Keon was able to attract Dr. Adolpho de Bold to be Director. Dr. de Bold's discovery of cardio-natrin, a natural diuretic produced by heart muscle, had attracted worldwide attention.

In acknowledgement of the Institute's excellence in clinical work as well as of its superb research, the Institute received, in 1994/95, $2.6 million in peer-reviewed grants, and $6.5 million in research contracts jointly with a well-known transplant centre in the United States. This total of $9.1 million in 1994/95 for use by the Institute is remarkable considering the relatively small specialized staff. The Institute will likely be the first to use an implantable artificial heart – the goal of many University centres worldwide.

The creator of Ottawa's Heart Institute was born in Sheenboro, Quebec, in 1935, the youngest in a family of 13 and it was his good fortune that he had a most remarkable widowed mother. She launched all her children into successful careers. Wilbert Keon was not obsessed at an early age with becoming a heart surgeon. As a late teenager he had plans to be a hockey player until his mother intervened, without consultation, sending him to college in preparation for medicine. He received his medical degree in Ottawa, surgical training at McGill, cardiovascular surgical training at the University of Toronto and surgical research experience at Harvard. In 1969 he returned to Ottawa and, besides directing the newly formed Heart Institute, was appointed professor and chairman of the Department of Surgery, University of Ottawa, 1976 to 1991.

The people of Ottawa are extremely proud of "their" Institute. And they adore its director/founder, Wilbert Keon. His qualities of humanity, humour, and special caring for the patient have become legendary and he is admired by both the professional and non-medical population of Ottawa. As an example of the community's goodwill, $50 million has been raised for the Heart Institute. The first building, built in two phases, cost $17 million, $10 million of which Keon was primarily responsible for obtaining and $5 million came from the Progressive Conservative government of Ontario.

When the research wing was built for a further $17 million, Dr. Keon raised an additional $10 million, $5 million this time coming from the Liberal government. He played no favourites! In December 1991, in spite of contrary advice because of the recession, he personally sponsored a 24-hour telethon and raised $1.8 million! The Institute continues to raise over $2 million per year from the community for Research & Development.

Dr. Wilbert Keon has been honoured by the medical profession with numerous awards; by his church as a Knight of St. Gregory the Great, by Pope John Paul II, and as an Officer of the Order of Malta; by his province with the Order of Ontario; by his country as an Officer of the Order of Canada and by his appointment to the Senate of Canada. This latter appointment, a surprise to his colleagues, followed a long, late-evening phone call from Prime Minister Brian Mulroney, who emphasized the government's need for someone of Keon's calibre to contribute to a joint Senate-Commons health committee.

Wilbert Keon is a COMPLEAT surgeon. Fishermen will recognize this word, first used in 1653 by Izaac Walton. It indicates that there is nothing missing. Willie Keon has it all, including the association, love and devotion of his wife Anne and their three successful children.

What is most striking about Dr. Keon is his unstinting dedication to academic excellence and the improvement of health care of all Canadians. Throughout his career he has chosen to work for a modest salary as a full-time academic while returning several million dollars from his clinical earnings to the University and the Heart Institute for academic development. Through his leadership and humanity, this pre-eminent, world-famous doctor has produced a *milieu* where all clinicians at the Ottawa-based Heart Institute work under full-time arrangements in harmony with basic scientists.   *Wilfred Bigelow*

The Living Section

People

The Citizen, Ottawa, Monday, July 9, 1984, Page 45

Pages 39-56
• Comics
• Living
• Entertainment

4

Keon's humanity inspires devotion

By Laura Robin
Citizen staff writer

Keon stands in front of Civic Hospital heart institute

Surgical team during a heart transplant operation

Heart-transplant patient's life returning to normal

By Laura Robin
Citizen staff writer

Jean-Guy Villeneuve

The pride of Canada's capital is the University of Ottawa Heart Institute at the Ottawa Civic Hospital. The Ottawa Citizen's salute to the Institute's founder warmly describes Dr. Keon's humanity outshining all his other accomplishments. [Reproduced from The Ottawa Citizen, July 9, 1984]

Emily Carr

Searching for Primal Energies
1871 -1945

EMILY CARR once wrote, "I could not paint in the old way – it is dead – meaningless – empty." Because of these strong views, she was ostracized for years by her family and the people of British Columbia. Now, 50 years after her death, she is recognized as one of Canada's greatest painters – male or female – and numerous books, besides her own autobiography, have been written about her work and about her personal life-style that differed greatly from expectations for a woman in Victorian times.

Born in 1871 in Victoria, British Columbia, Emily had four older sisters and a younger brother. She was 12 when her mother died and, on the death of her domineering father two years later, her eldest sister ruled in similar fashion, even, on occasion, whipping her rebellious youngest sister.

To escape such tyranny, Emily rode her pony to nearby Beacon Hill Park where she first sensed the joy of the forest. Like many young women of the era, she took art lessons and, while still in her teens, enrolled at the California School of Design in San Francisco. There she painted the basics: antiques, still life, and scenery, but was too shy to take the "life" class that posed nude females.

In 1893 she returned to Vancouver and opened a studio in the loft of the cow barn on the family property. She happily taught children and painted, spending the summer of 1898 at Ucluelet, an Indian village on the northwest coast of the island where she met the native peoples and experienced their day-to-day culture. Because she could not speak their language, she resorted to pantomime. The ensuing laughter caused them to call her "Klee Wyck" or Laughing One.

Emily, realizing that she needed more training, enrolled the following year at the Westminster School of Art in London, England. She did not enjoy the city and found the countryside too manicured, but she studied and worked hard for four years until illness forced her into a sanitarium for 18 months.

Back in Canada in 1905, she opened a studio in Vancouver – again gave art lessons and spent summers with the native people, often sleeping "in tents, in roadmaker's tool sheds, in missions, and Indian houses." Her friendship with the native people gave her new insights into their creativity, but again she felt more training was needed and, in 1910, went to Paris to study at the Académie Colarossi.

Once more, however, Emily became ill and spent "three hellish months" in hospital. A doctor advised her to stay out of large cities and, since Harry Gibb, her teacher, held "new school" classes at Crécy – a two-hour trip from Paris – she went there. Gibb was supportive, once predicting, "You will one day be one of the women painters of your day." Before she left to return to Vancouver in 1911, two of her paintings were shown at a Paris salon.

On her return, Emily refused to paint the fashionable pretty scenery then in vogue but, instead, created sweeping scenes with bold and vivid colours. These embarrassed her sisters and caused the public to laugh at her work. The art school did not rehire her and parents stopped sending their children for private lessons. Despite this, she carried on and, in the summer of 1912, travelling with only a sheepdog for a companion, sketched and painted other remote villages on the Queen Charlotte Islands and Skeena River.

With no money coming in, Emily was forced to return to Victoria where the family property was divided among the sisters (her sickly brother had died). With her share, Emily, now over 40, decided to build and run a boarding house.

For the next 15 years she cooked, cleaned, and did most of the repair work. To earn extra money, she also raised and sold sheepdogs, hooked rugs, and created pottery based on native designs to sell to tourists while most of her paintings remained in the attic. Her eccentricities were a source of amusement for she surrounded herself with pets – dogs, birds that included a parrot and a cockatoo, a white rat, and a monkey named Woo that she often wheeled about in a baby carriage.

In 1927, however, her life changed dramatically. In 1926, Ottawa's National Gallery decided to exhibit "Canadian West Coast Art, Native and Modern," and asked Marius Barbeau, an anthropologist, to help find exhibits. Barbeau, who had learned of Emily

Following her 1910 visit to France, an invigorated Emily Carr returned to British Columbia, bringing with her a postimpressionist style that marked the end of her earlier anachronistic English watercolour mode. By 1932, after encouragement from the likes of Lawren Harris and still other Group of Seven members, Emily Carr's canvases began stressing themes of nature rather than recording the vanishing villages, houses and totem poles of First Nation Peoples of the northwest, themes which earlier had predominated her canvases for 20 years. [Photo, courtesy The Art Gallery of Ontario]

through the Indians, visited her and recommended her work to Eric Brown, the gallery's director. He, too, visited her, was impressed with the power and originality of her work, and asked her to send 50 paintings as well as some of her rugs and pottery to Ottawa. He also arranged a rail pass for her to see the show and suggested she read a book about a Toronto-based group of artists known as the Group of Seven.

She had never heard of them but obtained Fred Housser's *A Canadian Art Movement* and, before heading east, visited Frederick Varley, then teaching in Vancouver. He wired his colleagues and she met A.Y. Jackson, Arthur Lismer, J.E.H. MacDonald, and, finally, Lawren Harris, whose work so excited her that after the opening of the Ottawa show – at which 26 of her paintings were exhibited and praised – she returned to Toronto to revisit Harris who became one of her staunchest supporters.

On her return to Victoria she immediately resumed painting. Within weeks she was encouraged when Harris, after seeing her work in Toronto, wrote, "I really have, nor can have, nothing to say by way of criticism.... The pictures are works of art in their own right."

Emily worked with renewed energy and skill, repainting many of her previous pieces and revisiting some of the Indian villages to paint them afresh. She was invited to exhibit paintings in a Group of Seven show where further praise was lavished on the improvement and greater freedom of her work. "I am astonished," A.Y. Jackson wrote. Harris went further and, by suggesting she broaden her scope "to create forms for yourself, direct from nature," he thereby stimulated her to paint the forests and vast scenery of British Columbia with greater verve and creativity.

Over the next decade her work was exhibited in numerous shows in Victoria, Vancouver, Eastern Canada, the USA, and at a Commonwealth exhibit at the Tate Gallery in London where the *Times* critic considered her *Indian Church* "one of the most interesting pictures in the exhibit."

By then she had sold the boarding house and moved into a cottage, where she suffered her first heart attack in 1937. When her doctor insisted she live more quietly, she turned to writing stories about Indians she had visited over the years. Her first book she called *Klee Wyck*. When a publisher rejected it, she put it aside until a friend, a previous student boarder who had become a math professor, showed it to Garnett Sedgewick, professor of English at the University of British Columbia. He read some of the stories to his classes and to a wider audience over CBC Radio.

Ira Dilworth, then head of CBC's Western region, also read her stories over the air and sent *Klee Wyck* to Clarke, Irwin & Company in Toronto where it was soon published and became an instant success. Suddenly Victoria was proud of her. A local woman's club celebrated her 70th birthday in December 1941 with a huge tea party with messages from various dignitaries. *Klee Wyck* also won the Governor General's Award for Literature for that year. She made light of the newfound success but enjoyed it.

Like Harris, Dilworth also became one of her trusted friends and supporters. He edited her subsequent books: *The Book of Small* (1942) about her childhood published a year after *Klee*

Wyck; and *The House of All Sorts* (1944) about her boardinghouse experiences. After her death, there were four more volumes including *Growing Pains*, an autobiography she had started at Lawren Harris' suggestion.

Before she died in March 1945 – after several heart attacks and two strokes – she created an Emily Carr Trust – naming Harris and Dilworth to select 45 of her paintings for the Vancouver Art Gallery. The rest of her work was to be sold as needed for the upkeep of the Trust. Any leftover money was to be used for the education of Canadian artists. The Trust remained in effect until 1969. The Vancouver Art Gallery now exhibits in a special room almost 200 pieces of her work. Many thousands of residents and tourists visit annually to admire – not laugh at – her remarkable talent as an artist.

Mel James

Fascinated by nature's pulsating energy, Emily Carr's later career examines the mysterious, undulating vibration of nature as portrayed in "Sombreness Sunlit," circa 1937-40. [Photo, courtesy The Province of British Columbia Archives]

From an earlier period in the career of Emily Carr, "Indian Village with Totem Poles," oil on canvas, documents her passion to record the vanishing visual history of British Columbia's westcoast First Nation Peoples. [Photo, courtesy The Collection of Power Corporation of Canada]

"The Expulsion of the Acadians" (1893) by George Craig captures the tragic events at Grand Pré, Nova Scotia, nearly 250 years ago when Col. John Winslow, viewed here on a horse surrounded by nearly 2,000 New England militiamen, read a decree proclaiming the expulsion of all Acadians living in what today is called Nova Scotia and New Brunswick. **[Photo, courtesy Musée acadien, Université de Moncton]**

LES ACADIENS

Resilient Settlers of the New World

THE ACADIANS from France are the original North American settlers. Today they form pockets of distinct communities in Canada's Maritime Provinces, Québec, and Louisiana. The first true Acadian families trace their origins to approximately 300 people who settled Port-Royal and the fertile Annapolis Valley as early as the 1630s;

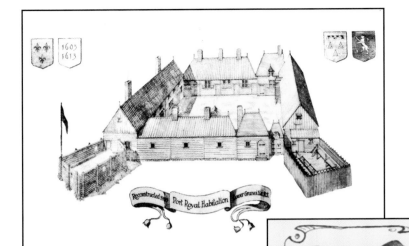

Established near the mouth of the Annapolis River in Nova Scotia, Port-Royal Habitation was meant to be a permanent French colony created by Pierre Du Gua de Monts and Samuel de Champlain in the summer of 1605. The habitation consisted of a courtyard encircled by wooden buildings suggesting a fortification. Its garden became the first experimental seed plot in North America. Here the **Ordre de Bon Temps** was organized in 1606, the first social club in North America. It was here, as well, that the first theatre production in Canadian history took place (1606). Port-Royal was destroyed in 1613 by English freebooter Samuel Argall.

Some tools and early French artifacts archaeologically dug up at the site of Port-Royal earlier this century.

small numbers subsequently settled the Minas Basin, Cape Sable, and the Canso areas of present-day Nova Scotia – peninsular lands formerly called Acadia.

Unlike the fishermen who were often temporary or intermittent settlers in the Gulf of the St. Lawrence the Acadians were essentially farmers. They were capable of cultivating uplands but with their ingenuity they accepted the challenge of building and maintaining dykes in fertile wetlands. The Acadian dykes were made from sods of marsh grasses, were equipped with sluices and clappers to keep out salt water, and were reinforced by logs and branches. These marshland farms, supplemented with resources from the forest and ocean, provided most of their subsistence needs.

At their original settlement in Port-Royal and elsewhere, Acadians, mercilessly victimized by external forces, had little in the way of defensive support. Port-Royal was attacked several times in the 1600s, including 1613 by Argall, 1654 by Sedgwick, and 1690 by New England adventurer Sir William Phips. A fort built at Port-Royal repelled two British attacks in 1707 but, in 1710, it fell again before Nicholson with his 36 ships and 3,500 men. The treaties of St. Germain-en-Laye (1632), Breda (1667), and Ryswick (1697) all confirmed French control of Acadia, but French neglect made the communities vulnerable particularly to aggressive New Englanders. Finally, in 1713, the French ceded the ancient boundaries of Acadia to the English in the Treaty of Utrecht. The Acadians refused to take an oath of allegiance but maintained neutrality and were ostensibly a peaceful, pastoral community. With the rise of the French fortress of Louisbourg as well as the French defenses at Fort Beauséjour and other Chignecto posts, however, the British began to be uncomfortable with their existence. After Halifax was established in 1749, in the midst of ongoing hostilities between French and English, the British regarded the Acadians' persistent refusal to take an oath as a form of treason, despite their neutrality. Just prior to the beginning of the Seven Years War with France in 1756, the expulsion of nearly 14,000 Acadians from Acadia was begun at Grand Pré on September 10, 1755.

Expulsion occurred without consultation with the British government or notification to colonial officials where Les Acadiens were being sent. Approximately 2,000 Acadians fled to Île Saint-Jean (Prince Edward Island), 1,500 to New France (Québec) on the St. Lawrence, over 1,000 to the Baie des Chaleurs and the Gaspé Peninsula. Temporary settlements sprouted on the Miramichi and St. John Rivers in present-day New Brunswick and on the Magdalen Islands. Another 1,000 were deported to Massachusetts, 800 to Maryland, 600 to Connecticut, and hundreds of others to other American colonies such as New York, Pennsylvania, Georgia, and South Carolina. Those arriving in Virginia were dispatched to England and another 3,500 Acadians were sent back to France, a faraway homeland they had not seen for a century and a half. During the American Revolution, the settlement on the islands of St. Pierre and Miquelon, made up of many who had originally left Acadia, was dispersed again, most being transported to France. In 1785, some 1,500 of these Acadian refugees embarked for the territory of Louisiana which had already received about 1,500 people from the original evacuation. Throughout the diaspora, the hardiest returned to Nova Scotia and reconnected with scattered families who had avoided deportation. There the returnees discovered that the most fertile areas had been taken over by the English. By 1800, some 8,000 resilient Acadians were eking out a living in the Maritime provinces, 8,000 were surviving in Québec, and some 10,000 in Louisiana, the latter giving rise to "Cajun culture."

Building dykes in fertile wetlands was a priorty for Acadians not living in uplands. Acadian dykes were made from sods of marsh grasses, were equipped with sluices and clappers to keep out salt water, and were reinforced with logs and branches. Marshland farms provided Acadians with most of their subsistence needs. [Photo, courtesy Dept. of Education, Nova Scotia Museum Complex]

British institutions, New England settlers, Loyalist refugees, English, Irish, and Scottish immigration could not suppress or expunge the many cloistered, cohesive Acadian maritime communities. The topography of the coastline and the nature of distinct pockets of settlement permitted an adamantine Acadian culture to thrive during the nineteenth century in Nova Scotia, Prince Edward Island, and especially New Brunswick. In the twentieth century, however, the English-speaking cultural invasion of radio, television, and other media has dealt a blow to many steadfast Acadian communities. Nonetheless, through its folklore, literature and music, Acadian culture and its unique voice has been sustained, even revived. The Université de Moncton (1963) in New Brunswick and the Université Sainte-Anne in Nova Scotia have greatly assisted in sustaining a viable, essential, and exciting Acadian character.

The Acadian community in New Brunswick, with its majority status in eastern parts of the province and the bilingual character of its government, has been the most successful in staking a political, economic, and cultural presence. The first elected Acadian premier of New Brunswick, Louis J. Robichaud who governed from 1960 to 1970, passed the Official Languages Act and did much to raise the esteem of his people and encourage a cultural revival. Acadians, as a founding people that is neither Aboriginal, Anglophone or Quebecois, have a distinctive role in Canadian life.

Communities such as Arichat and Cheticamp on Cape Breton Island, Meteghan, Pomquet, and Beliveau Cove on mainland Nova Scotia, Tignish, and Miscouche on Prince Edward Island, and Moncton, Shediac, Bouctouche, Caraquet, Petit-Rocher, Bathurst, and the

Five-generation portrait of the Piorier family, Acadians from the fishing village of Tignish, P.E.I., circa 1900. Well-known descendants of pioneering Acadians include Maurice and Henri Richard, Jean Beliveau, Ray Bourque, and Patrick Roy, all of National Hockey League fame. Rock superstar, Rock Voisine, has Acadian roots as do such literary figures as Antonine Maillet and Mavis Gallant.
[Photo, courtesy Charles J. Humber Collection]

The Evangeline statue, a work completed by Louis-Philippe and Henri Hébert, sculptors of Acadian descent, was unveiled in 1920 near Grand Pré, Nova Scotia. Interest in the site no doubt was inspired by William Wordsworth Longfellow whose poem "Evangeline" did much to generate worldwide interest in the tragic story of Acadian expulsion from Nova Scotia in 1755. The chapel in the background was built on the site of the original Acadian church and is but a reconstruction of an early eighteenth century French chapel. It was opened in 1923. In 1956 it was acquired by the Canadian government and turned into a National Historic Site. [Photo, courtesy Musée acadien/Université de Moncton]

Madawaska Valley among others offer an Acadian flair to the Canadian experience. Although much of the geography of original Acadia is lost, a spiritual Acadia is reinforced by the literature of Antonine Maillet, the historicism of Claude Leboutillier and Alphonse Deveau, and the many works of other writers and interpreters of the Acadian experience. In 1994 the Acadians celebrated their 390th year as a distinct North American culture, and, in 1995, the Rt. Hon. Roméo LeBlanc was appointed Governor General of Canada, the first Acadian to hold the position.

Historian N.E.S. Griffiths has written, "Whatever else the deportation had brought to the Acadians it had also instilled into them a conviction of their own capacity for survival. It is a conviction that has not yet been proven false."

Larry Turner

Lynn Johnston

Far Better Than Worse

CANADIANS have a wonderful sense of humour. They love laughing at themselves and the traditions of everyday life provide a rich source. Perhaps no Canadian humorist has ever reached such heights of international acclaim as Lynn Johnston, the creator, writer, and artist behind the comic strip "For Better or For Worse." Syndicated in 23 countries and translated into 5 languages, this probing comic strip is today read by millions of faithful followers.

Lynn Johnston's cartoons and comic strips are based on her own family, a typical nuclear family in the sprawling suburbs of everywhere. Both serious and comic situations are rooted in real experience. Her cartoon characters are Elly and John Patterson, their children – Michael, Elizabeth, April – and their dog, Farley.

Elly is named after a best friend who died of brain cancer in high school; John, Michael, and Elizabeth are the middle names of husband Roderick, and children Aaron and Katherine, and Farley actually existed.

Lynn's favourite moments with her maternal grandfather were reading the comics together.

Cartoonist Lynn Johnston's sterling eye for detail and her uncanny sense of what parents and children struggle with daily are a big part of the worldwide success of For Better or For Worse, *the syndicated cartoon strip launched in 1979. [Photo, courtesy Lynn Johnston]*

"He took them seriously. These were not merely vacuous fillers of space but bright social commentary, and he had an opinion reserved for each one of them." She became enamoured with such comic strips as "Peanuts" where stories and pictures came alive "with expressions [that] had me literally on the floor. I wanted to be able to make someone laugh like that. I wanted to be able to draw like that." Somehow her father knew the path she would take. He used to tuck her in at night and say, "See you in the funny papers."

She describes herself as a born artist. From the age of four, "I would see images appear, my imagination come to life, my right hand drawing my thoughts on paper. Even to me, the gift was magic." Her mother used to do illustrations and calligraphy that went into the stamp collections organized by her grandfather. "My mother would draw fine lines around each stamp, framing them like miniature paintings.... From as early as I can recall I drew tiny pictures in boxes, row on row, bringing thoughts and fantasies to life."

When Lynn entered high school she found her own "signature" drawing style. She also discovered the radical, comic humour of *Mad* magazine. While her mother did not approve of this "absolutely dreadful" rag, she and her artist friends yearned "to be part of the magic circle that produced this great, sarcastic wit." She attended the Vancouver School of Art, became interested in the commercial application of her field of interest, and began a job with Canawest as a cartoonist.

During her first marriage, Lynn moved to Hamilton where she got a job at McMaster University's prestigious medical school illustrating multimedia educational tools. While pregnant with her first child, she created, for her physician, a series of cartoons to decorate ceilings in the clinic to amuse women waiting impatiently for tests. He realized her special talent and found the contacts who knew how to showcase her skills. Her book, *Dave, I'm Pregnant*, launched her as a cartoonist.

When Universal Press Syndicate showed interest in her work in 1977, she was heading to Lynn Lake in northern Manitoba with her second husband, the flying dentist Roderick Johnston. "For Better or For Worse" was launched in 1979, and by 1984 she and her family had moved to Corbeil near North Bay. While her home-based work has involved relatively isolated locations, her drawings could take place in any urban and suburban setting around the world. Her art is about typical situations, family humour, domestic ironies, and everyday incidents with children, adults, and dogs. Her comic strips can cause laughter, or sometimes even tears, and she has dealt honestly with such issues as abuse in the home, homosexuality, and family adversity.

In a 17,000 reader survey conducted by the Detroit *Free Press* in 1993, "For Better or For Worse" was rated first overall in the comic strip survey. She was first choice among females and the elderly, second among males, and fourth among age 17 and younger. Her comic strip was the only one in the first five of each category. In 1985 she was the first female winner of the Reuben Award and honoured as Cartoonist of the Year by the National Cartoonist Society in the United States, which also recognized her work in 1992 as the Best Syndicated Comic Strip. She received the Order of Canada in 1992 and was nominated for a Pulitzer Prize in 1994.

Larry Turner

On March 26, 1847, Paul Kane recorded the eruption of Mount St. Helens from the mouth of the Lewis River in the Oregon Territory. [Painting, courtesy Royal Ontario Museum/912.1.78]

WHEN A BRITISH ARMY OFFICER recommended Paul Kane to Hudson Bay governor Sir George Simpson, he wrote that Kane "would return from the west with a portfolio of sketches not much inferior to [George] Catlin's in variety and greatly superior in truth." Simpson also received a letter from his Hudson Bay agent at Sault Ste. Marie praising Kane's work and assuring him that the artist "was prepared for the hardships of travel in the west."

Wandering Frontier Artist

PAUL KANE

1810 - 1871

After he met Kane in 1846, Sir George issued instructions to Hudson Bay officers "in Rupert's Land and Elsewhere" that Kane be given free transportation on company boats and "hospitalities" at all posts.

Kane was in his 36th year when Simpson wrote those orders. For the next two years Kane made several hundred sketches of voyageurs, buffalo hunts, Indian settlements from Fort William to Oregon Territory on the Pacific coast, and portraits of first nation peoples that reflected, as a later article declared, the life and times of "American Indians at the point of fatal contact with the white man's culture."

Born in Mallow, Ireland, in 1810, Kane came to the town of York (later Toronto) in Upper Canada with his family between 1819 and 1822. Although little is known of his early life, it is known that he studied art with Thomas Drury, the drawing master of Upper Canada College. In 1834, a local newsletter, *The Patriot*, praised Kane, concluding that "practice and study should make Mr. Kane an artist of name."

At the time, however, according to the *York Directory* of 1833-34, Kane was "a coach, sign and house

In his lifetime, Paul Kane (1810-1871) was well known throughout North America and Europe as the most famous of all Canadian artist-explorers. This likeness of Kane was probably taken shortly after Wanderings of an Artist among the Indians of North America *was published in 1859. It is an illustration from E.C. Guillet's* The Valley of the Trent, *published by the Champlain Society in 1957.*

A prairie fire probably seen from Fort Edmonton on September 26, 1846, this dramatic Paul Kane oil on canvas records a scene of impending disaster and suggests the imminent risk travellers faced when crossing Canada's vast prairies. [Painting, courtesy Royal Ontario Museum/912.1.39]

painter." When he later moved to the A.W. Conger Furniture factory in Cobourg, Ontario as a decorative painter, he began to do portraits. In 1836, he went to Detroit and for the next five years painted portraits in various cities including St. Louis and New Orleans. From there he sailed to Europe in 1841.

He arrived at Marseilles, went to Genoa and Rome where he spent time studying and copying paintings by Murillo, del Sarto, and Raphael, and made some money selling copies of the old masters. By October 1842, he was in London and there met the artist with whom he is often compared, the American George Catlin, whose work and book had been a huge success in England in 1841 and who was holding an exhibition at Piccadilly. The exhibition and subsequent friendship peaked Kane's interest in painting indigenous Canadians, but he first spent time at Mobile, Alabama, to earn money to pay the debt incurred for his return trip.

Arriving in Toronto in the spring of 1845, Kane left almost immediately for the Great Lakes area, convinced, as was Catlin, that "the red man was disappearing everywhere as a result of disease and dislocation caused by the incursion of whites." His first summer was mainly spent with the Ojibway around the Great Lakes. Among the chiefs he painted was Oscosh, descendant of the great warrior chief, Tecumseh.

On this trip he also met the Hudson Bay Company's agent at Sault Ste. Marie, the same agent who had earlier suggested that Governor Simpson see him. Simpson's subsequent letter enabled Kane to travel in the canoes of the voyageurs and, after reaching Fort Garry, to take up Simpson's suggestion of buffalo hunting with the Metis. Kane not only sketched on that hunt but also shot two of the estimated 500 bulls that were killed. That summer he made numerous sketches of the buffalo on hunts and in compounds.

Portraits, however, continued to be his major interest. His approach was to walk up to an Indian, sit down, and begin a portrait. If the Indian objected, he sometimes used flattery – telling his subject he intended showing the picture to the Great White mother, Queen Victoria. Others were fearful that his ability to draw a "second self" would put them in his power, but generally he successfully painted hundreds of first nation peoples and among them some notable chiefs.

According to J. Russell Harper's biographical sketch for the book, *Paul Kane's Frontier* (1971), his portraits reflected the changing appearance and dress of the indigenous population as he moved westward. "On the prairies they are no longer pictured wearing clothing with European additions or with government medals around their necks" but are pictured more as "noble beings." Kane also made a point of drawing the various forts he visited, from Fort Francis to Fort Victoria and Fort Vancouver in what was then The Oregon Territory. He painted them in their natural surroundings and won the praise of James Douglas, the Hudson Bay Factor there for 20 years, who later became first Governor of British Columbia. "I have seen Mr. Kane's faithful and spirited sketches of Oregon scenery and have been perfectly delighted with these masterly delineations of places," Douglas wrote.

On returning to Toronto in 1848, Kane painted 14 canvases for Sir George but did not exhibit until 1851, when a critic wrote, "It is hoped that Canada may at some future day possess the entire collection of this great artist," a sentiment later echoed by Egerton Ryerson, founder of the provincial school system in Ontario. Governments seldom gave substantial support to artists, and, although he and his work were praised for more than two hours in the Ontario Legislature, only 12 paintings for $500 were commissioned. Kane did, however, later sell a wealthy Torontonian, George W. Allan, 100 paintings for $20,000. This enabled him to marry the daughter of his Cobourg employer and settle for good in Toronto.

For the Paris World's Fair in 1853, the government borrowed some of the paintings done for Allan to exhibit – he had not completed the 12 they had ordered – and his paintings were the only Canadian work to win praise. One critic wrote, "He is almost the only artist, in the proper sense of the word, that Canada boasts of, and I cherish strong hopes that he is destined at once to immortalize himself."

The interior of 19th century British Columbia was extensively occupied by Salish native people. When Paul Kane wandered through this part of Canada in 1847, his journey followed the Columbia River watershed, taking him to southwestern Washington in the newly created Oregon Territory. Here he encountered Flatheads whose custom it was to bind the heads of young children in such a way that upon reaching a certain state of maturity their heads would be "flattened." This Paul Kane oil on canvas poignantly portrays a young child enduring this uncomfortable procedure. [Painting, courtesy Royal Ontario Museum/912.1.80]

Kane had considered a book when he first returned to Toronto but it was 1859 before his *Wanderings of an Artist among the Indians of North America* was finally published. It contains more than 100 reproductions of his work and, written in diary form, vividly describes the people he met, the way they lived, and his own adventures among them. It was well received but Kane had by then lost interest in painting.

His eyesight was deteriorating, due partly to the snow blindness he had experienced while

Whether he was an Ojibwa chief from Fort William or the Ojibwa chief of Michipicoten Island in Lake Superior, this colourful portrait of Indian chief Maydoc-gan-Kinungee proudly holding his King George III medal, depicts Kane's stunning ability to chronicle visually the history of Canada's first nation peoples. [Painting, courtesy Royal Ontario Museum/12.1.16]

on his "wanderings" in the Rockies. He gave up his studio in the 1860s and lived quietly until his sudden death on February 20, 1871. An obituary noted that "he will be long remembered not only on account of his great talents as an artist, but on account of his goodness of heart and upright character as a man." It added, "he was only a few hours ill – having been out of the city on the morning of the day he died."

Mel James

Corporate Visionary

Frank Dottori

THE YEAR WAS 1972. A major international paper company decided to close its Canadian pulp mill in the single-industry town of Temiscaming, Quebec. Within 90 days some 500 employees (average age 48 with 25 years seniority) were laid off. The town was devastated, for the mill had been its lifeblood for 50 years of strike-free operation. Some employees accepted the fact, others vented their anger in demonstrations and shouting matches, but four men decided on a new course: to keep the company going as an employee-owned industry.

Spearheading that drive was Frank Dottori, who, today, serves as president and CEO of both Tembec Inc. in Temiscaming and Spruce Falls Inc. at Kapuskasing, Ontario – a victim in 1991 of an international company's decision to downsize another newsprint mill. Today, both business establishments are successful employee-owned companies with combined sales in 50 countries around the world totalling more than $1.2-billion.

Dottori was a 33-year-old technical expert at the Temiscaming mill when it closed. A native of Timmins, Ontario, after graduating in chemical engineering from the University of Toronto, he joined the Canadian International Paper Company (CIP) in 1963.

He left CIP in 1966 to work for Texas Gulf Sulphur but returned to the Temiscaming pulp mill in 1969 to serve in several technical and operating posts before the shutdown was announced.

At a 1994 symposium, Dottori outlined the steps taken to "organize the employees as partners and make a bid to take over the mill. We developed a vision: a company of people building their own future," he said, and outlined the four key principles required: employee ownership, profit sharing, a participative/flexible management, and open communication.

In the early 1970s, however, employee takeovers were unheard-of. The owners wanted to demolish the plant on the shores of the Ottawa River, not sell it. Battles and demonstrations stretched into 1973 before, with the support of the Quebec government, an agreement was reached to sell the company to the employees for $2.5 million. The labour act was changed to allow union members to serve on the board of directors of the new company.

Dottori became production manager of the newly named Tembec Inc., was named mill manager the next year, and was appointed executive vice-president in charge of operations in 1977. He became president and CEO two years later, a position he still holds today but over a much larger enterprise that includes the mill at Kapuskasing, Ontario.

With Tembec established as the industry model of a successful employee-owned company, Dottori became involved in negotiations taking place in 1991 between the 1,200 employees at Kapuskasing and joint owners Kimberly-Clark Corporation and the New York Times Co. to acquire the mill slated for major downsizing. The Ontario government acted as facilitator during these negotiations, and Dottori provided the leadership that would define the philosophy and structure of the new venture. The result was that Tembec would own 41 percent of the company, employees 52 percent, with other investors in the community and region holding the rest. The same vision and principles used to create Tembec were established at Spruce Falls.

The results at Spruce Falls Inc. proved spectacular. By December 1992, production was up 40 percent and a profit of $4.5 million was declared. In 1993 that jumped to $15.7 million and year-end results for 1995 were net earnings of $50.9 million. At the same time, a $360-million-dollar modernization program was well under way. This included a thermomechanical pulp plant which required 50 percent less trees than conventional chemical pulp processes.

"Employee ownership," Dottori asserts, "doesn't make us socialists, but rather small 'c' capitalists. Every employee must be a shareholder and ownership must be significant enough to give employees a real sense of ownership and responsibility." Profit sharing at Spruce Falls is based on six percent of adjusted gross profits.

"Management style must also be different in such an employee enterprise," says Dottori. "Management doesn't have rights in our companies. We have responsibilities." Senior management and union executives meet frequently to discuss everything from plant operations to marketing. Other meetings between division managers and employee representatives are conducted to keep employees informed and get feedback. At the same time the two companies provide up to 80 hours a year per employee on training or retraining programs.

Now approaching two decades as president of the two employee-owned companies and numerous subsidiaries with plants in eastern Canada and France and trade with more than 50 nations worldwide, Dottori admits to being a workaholic, enjoying being on the job an average of 70 to 80 hours a week.

Married in 1964, with a family of three children, Frank Dottori received the Order of Canada in 1989 and was named "Businessman of the Year" for Northern Ontario in 1992, admitting on that occasion, "I admire anyone who sets his mind to accomplishing and achieving a goal that is good for themselves and good for society." *Mel James*

MAZO DE LA ROCHE

Mistress of Jalna

1879 - 1961

MAZO DE LA ROCHE is an enigma to anyone wishing to learn about her life. Information that she gave altered the facts: she changed her date and place of birth, changed her surname, and rewrote her family's history. Her first biographers faced much detective work to establish the details of her life. Yet her fiction writing was different. The 16 *Jalna* books deal with many people and cover more than a century of time. Written over 33 years and not in chronological order, they are faithful to the larger historical record and inwardly consistent. A family tree, updated in every volume, shows that Mazo adhered to a strict time frame. One must conclude that she created historical fiction and fictional history. She herself said, "I have put myself into my books." Perhaps that is ultimately where one can find her.

Born in Newmarket, Ontario, in 1879, Mazo was the daughter of William and Alberta Roche. Her mother's ill health and her father's many jobs – in stores, in a hotel, and, lastly, on a farm – resulted in frequent family moves. Mazo drew on these experiences for her later writing. A high-strung and expressive child attuned to tragedies and changes around her, she developed a complex fantasy world that she called "The Play." This interested and sustained her throughout her life as she created imaginary scenes and characters, often with her younger cousin and lifelong companion,

By the time **Variable Winds at Jalna** *(1954) was published, more than 1.6 million copies of the Jalna series had been sold to Americans. "Mazo de la Roche's achievement as a novelist," exclaimed Edward Weeks, editor of the* **Atlantic Monthly,** *"makes me think of* **Trollope** *and* **Galsworthy.**" *In Europe where her books were translated into 15 languages, the European readership corresponded directly by the hundreds with the author through her publisher. They wanted to share with her emotionally how they identified with and were enthralled by their beloved Whiteoak clan of Jalna.* [Dustjacket photo, courtesy Little, Brown and Company]

Caroline Clement. It too was a rich source for her writing.

Mazo's education combined formal schooling with extensive reading at home and music and art classes. In 1902, she published her first magazine story and continued writing as much as she could after that. When in 1927 her *Jalna* won the American magazine *Atlantic Monthly*'s prize of $10,000, she became immediately famous. The prestigious prize gave her the financial freedom to pursue writing full-time and to move to Europe. There she lived, mainly in England, until 1939. Then, with war coming, she returned to North America with her two adopted children. She spent the rest of her life mostly in Toronto, where she died at age 82. She was buried at St. George's Church, at Sutton, Ontario, on the shore of Lake Simcoe, a place she knew and loved from summer holidays.

The *Jalna* series, her best-known work, chronicles the lives of the Whiteoak family. Jalna, their family house, was named for the station in India where the first Whiteoak served before settling with his wife in a community of retired British officers on Canada's Lake Ontario shore. The novels are full of lively, but not always likeable, characters and gripping, yet sometimes fantastic, plots. They present passionate people against a backdrop of intense loyalty to family and abiding love of home. They depict nature as well as people and reveal Mazo's sensitivity to animals, to changes of the seasons, and to the beauty of Ontario scenery. Her descriptions of Britain similarly show her strong relationship to her surroundings.

De la Roche wrote other books, short stories, and plays. One of these, *Growth of a Man* (1938), was about one of her cousins, British Columbia's lumber magnate, H.R. MacMillan. A stage version of her Whiteoak tales enjoyed a long run in London and won favour with, among others, George Bernard Shaw.

Her writing elicited various reactions. Some critics dismissed her novels as unrealistic romances; certain local ones objected to characters too British in style to be believable Ontarians. Yet scholars also noted her as one of Canada's few writers of worth between the two world wars and following. Her work has been included in anthologies and in university literature courses. The Canadian poetess and fellow author, Dorothy Livesay, has called her "our most productive, most imaginative novelist."

The public's response worldwide has been consistently more positive. By the time of Mazo's death in 1961, her *Jalna* series in English and in many other languages had sold 12 million copies. The novels have been adapted for theatre, radio, television, and a 1935 RKO movie called *Jalna,* directed by John Cromwell. Allied secret agents used a Jalna book as the basis for a code during World War II. A 1960 poll found Mazo, along with A. J. Cronin, the favourite of French school children. They, now older, are among those watching the current French television version of *Jalna*. It seems assured that not only present but future generations as well will continue to meet the Whiteoaks of Jalna. And there they may find Mazo too.

Virginia Careless

Opposite: *In her later years, Mazo de la Roche could look back on a career that included 16 novels – all domestic romances – in the Jalna series. When she submitted Finch's Fortune, the third novel of the series, to Ellery Sedgwick, editor of Atlantic Monthly, he wrote to her on September 19, 1930, from his Boston office: "There can be no doubt that you have written another first-rate novel.... Each episode is treated masterfully.... Nothing you have ever done is better.... The whole book is full of living beings." Her novels were translated into dozens of languages, and adapted for stage, screen and television. She was awarded the Lorne Pierce Medal by the Royal Society of Canada in 1938. [Photo, courtesy Thomas Fisher Rare Book Library]*

Charles Marius
BARBEAU

Erudite Folklorist   **1883 - 1969**

AN ESTEEMED FOUNDER of Canadian cultural anthropology –
ethnologist, folklorist, and ceaseless collector – Marius Barbeau
made outstanding contributions to the understanding and preservation
of both Quebec and first peoples' heritages in Canada. His work on
Quebec folk traditions, songs, and texts, however, would loom larger.
He was born in 1883 at Ste-Marie-de-Beauce on the Chaudière, across
the St. Lawrence from Quebec City, in what was certainly a bastion of
rural French-Canadian culture and, like many another academically
promising *Canadien* of that era, he studied for the Catholic priesthood
but later switched into law.

He excelled in law at Quebec's Laval University; in fact, he was chosen as a Rhodes
Scholar to attend Oxford University in the Anglo heart of the British Empire. As an Oxford
student in the early twentieth century, Barbeau was powerfully attracted by the emerging
discipline of anthropology and thereafter, with a highly successful degree in anthropology,
he was recommended to the young National Museum of Canada which became his home
base from 1911 to the late 1960s. In sum, over the half century that followed his return to
Canada, Marius Barbeau, with close to a thousand publications along with many more ren-
derings of folk songs permanently preserved at the Museum, was the dominant figure in the
recording of Quebec social and cultural traditions. While sharing his own treasured store of
artifacts and knowledge with the people through books, popular lectures, and scholarly
teachings, he also established the Archives de folklore at Laval University. In these various
ways, he preserved vital work on the *Canadien* past.

With perseverance, he examined as well the ethnoculture of Canada's first nations, especially in British Columbia where he gave particular attention to the Tsimshians of the northwest coast. Here, with William Benyon, a noted hereditary native chief, he built up an

Marius Barbeau worked at Canada's National Museum for over one half century. When he was a Rhodes Scholar at Oxford, he became interested in anthropology. Viewed in this scene examining an early Quebec wood sculpture, Barbeau was an enthusiastic collector of folk traditions germane both to rural Quebec as well as Canada's native peoples. A world-renowned ethnologist, his much-respected name was given to the highest mountain in the Canadian Arctic. Barbeau Peak rises to a height of 8,760 feet on Ellesmere Island. [Photo, courtesy National Archives of Canada/PA-149993]

invaluable, ethnographic census. Even though Barbeau's own interpretation of Tsimshian tribal myths depicting a journey within living memory from an ancient Asian homeland did not stand up to later anthropological science, his pioneering work in his field nonetheless proved invaluable in keeping alive old native memories of times long vanished.

Marius Barbeau – eager, eloquent, and deeply learned – was important as a Canadian ethnoscientist for well over half a century – in fact, until his death in 1969 when he received warm tributes and honour for his own tireless journeying across a widespread anthropological Canadian past. Today both academics and students worldwide are indebted to the poignant legacy left behind by this prodigious scholar of Canadian culture.

J.M.S. Careless

One of North America's most celebrated jockeys, Sandford Desmond Hawley, as a 21-year-old rookie, topped all North American jockeys in 1969 with 390 wins. In 1973, he became the first jockey ever to win more than 500 races in one year. It is no wonder that he eclipsed in 1993 Johnny Longden's world record of 6,032 wins. [Photo, courtesy *The Toronto Star*/G. Bezant]

AT AGE 47, SANDY HAWLEY (born, 1949) may keep riding for a few more years. He is not sure just when he will retire as a jockey. He has already eclipsed Johnny Longden's one-time record of 6,032 wins. On the other hand, Longden was 56 before he retired, and is one of only two Canadian jockeys to have captured the Triple Crown of American racing by winning the Kentucky Derby, the Preakness, and the Belmont Stakes in the same year.

Longden,

The other Canadian to win the American Triple Crown is Ron Turcotte. Born in 1941 at Grand Falls, New Brunswick, Ron did not get a chance to set a record number of wins because of a tragic spill in 1978 which crippled him.

What Hawley, Longden, and Turcotte do share in common is that they are three Canadians recognized as among the world's most accomplished riders and celebrated jockeys.

Longden, born in England in 1910, moved with his family to Taber, Alberta. At age 13, he joined his father in the coal mines there. He started earning money at 10 by riding herd on a neighbour's cows on the open prairie; at 14, while working in the mines from 7:00am to 4:00pm for $1.25 a day, he competed at local fairs on weekends. One of his favourite events was the Roman races (one foot on the bare back of each of two horses). One summer he won 14 such contests.

These victories and the half-mile races – bareback – are not part of what was his record 6,032 victories. Nor is his first victory in the U.S. in 1927 when, as the son of devout Mormons, he visited Salt Lake City during the racing season and was offered $5 to ride a difficult mount. Longden not only rode the horse but won the race and decided racing was better than coal mining.

A year later he met "Sleepy" Armstrong, a trainer who taught Longden "everything I know about riding." Longden toured the prairies and British Columbia in summer and went to California and Mexico in winter. As he won more races he got better mounts and, by the end of the decade, had won such top races as the Brooklyn Handicap, the Champagne Stakes, and the Louisiana Derby.

His love of horses and his expertise with them were the major factors in his riding Count Fleet to the U.S. Triple Crown in 1943. Considered an unpredictable – even dangerous – horse as a two-year-old, Count Fleet was put up for sale. Because Longden was not afraid to ride him, he telephoned the owner to ask that the colt be kept. John subsequently rode the two-year-old Count Fleet 15 times and six more times in 1943, winning, in all, 16 of 21 races that included the Triple Crown.

Turcotte, & Hawley

Champion Jockeys

In B.K. Beckworth's biography, *The Longden Legend* (1973), he quotes Longden on his riding style. "Good hands are essential. You use your voice ... to encourage him or perhaps quieten him down," but, with your hands, "you sense the mood of your mount ... whether he's giving his best or cheating on you a little." Longden also advocated using the whip sparingly, pointing out, "You'll always get more out of a horse by being kind to him rather than cruel. He needs confidence and encouragement just as humans do."

Longden's career took him worldwide. In England he met Winston Churchill, "who knew a surprising amount about my racing career." He was a jockey at numerous other tracks throughout the world, including tracks in Ireland, Australia, Hong Kong, and Japan, once riding three winners in three countries on two continents in less than a week. Victory 4,000 occurred in 1952; win 5,000, came five years later. In 1966, fellow jockeys had his friend, Bing Crosby, on hand at the race track to sing "Happy Birthday." Later that year, he won his last race as a jockey aboard George Royal at the Santa Anita Race Track in California before some 60,000 fans.

This was not, however, his last visit to a winner's circle. Johnny became a trainer and in 1969, when Majestic Prince won the Kentucky Derby, he became the only person to have appeared there as both jockey and trainer. Now in his eighties, Johnny is still training thoroughbreds around Santa Anita, California.

Ron Turcotte, the other Canadian winner of the American Triple Crown, has another distinction with respect to the Kentucky Derby: he was the first jockey in 70 years to win "the Run for the Roses" back to back. That happened in 1972 when he rode Riva Ridge to victory in both the Derby and the Preakness. The next year he won the Triple Crown on Secretariat. Like Longden, Turcotte in his teens built up his five-foot-tall body with hard, physical labour by working at a lumber camp in his native New Brunswick. When

Former top jockey and Hall of Famer, Johnny Longden, right, welcomes Ron Turcotte to Canada's Sports Hall of Fame in 1980. One of the most successful jockeys of all time, Turcotte was tragically injured in a 1973 racing accident which left him paralysed. [Photo, courtesy *The Toronto Star*/Boris Spremo]

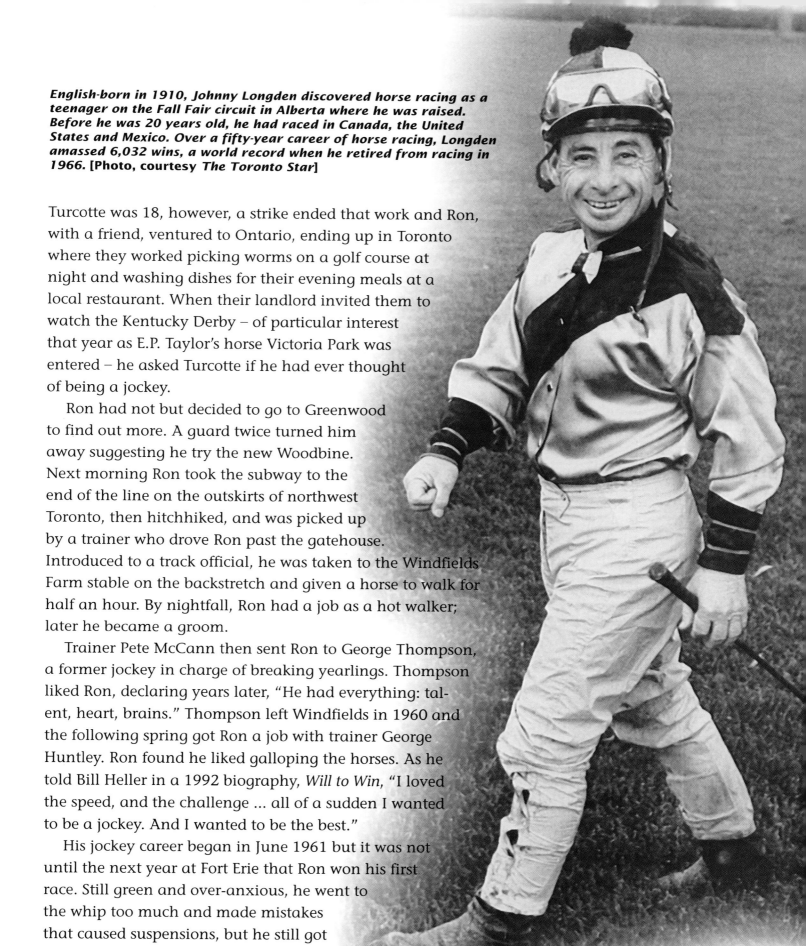

English-born in 1910, Johnny Longden discovered horse racing as a teenager on the Fall Fair circuit in Alberta where he was raised. Before he was 20 years old, he had raced in Canada, the United States and Mexico. Over a fifty-year career of horse racing, Longden amassed 6,032 wins, a world record when he retired from racing in 1966. [Photo, courtesy The Toronto Star*]*

Turcotte was 18, however, a strike ended that work and Ron, with a friend, ventured to Ontario, ending up in Toronto where they worked picking worms on a golf course at night and washing dishes for their evening meals at a local restaurant. When their landlord invited them to watch the Kentucky Derby – of particular interest that year as E.P. Taylor's horse Victoria Park was entered – he asked Turcotte if he had ever thought of being a jockey.

Ron had not but decided to go to Greenwood to find out more. A guard twice turned him away suggesting he try the new Woodbine. Next morning Ron took the subway to the end of the line on the outskirts of northwest Toronto, then hitchhiked, and was picked up by a trainer who drove Ron past the gatehouse. Introduced to a track official, he was taken to the Windfields Farm stable on the backstretch and given a horse to walk for half an hour. By nightfall, Ron had a job as a hot walker; later he became a groom.

Trainer Pete McCann then sent Ron to George Thompson, a former jockey in charge of breaking yearlings. Thompson liked Ron, declaring years later, "He had everything: talent, heart, brains." Thompson left Windfields in 1960 and the following spring got Ron a job with trainer George Huntley. Ron found he liked galloping the horses. As he told Bill Heller in a 1992 biography, *Will to Win*, "I loved the speed, and the challenge ... all of a sudden I wanted to be a jockey. And I wanted to be the best."

His jockey career began in June 1961 but it was not until the next year at Fort Erie that Ron won his first race. Still green and over-anxious, he went to the whip too much and made mistakes that caused suspensions, but he still got many mounts because trainer Huntley commented, "There was that something with him, that communication between him and a horse." At Woodbine that fall he won 72 races including his first stakes race and 88 at Greenwood to become the leading rider of the year. Ron won the title again in 1963. One of his victories that year was aboard Northern Dancer who was racing in his first event as a two-year-old.

In October he went to Maryland and, by the end of the 1963 season, had another 47 victories on 259 mounts. The following year he won 250 races and was the leading rider at five U.S. tracks including Pimlico and Delaware Park before moving on to New York, where he raced mainly at the Belmont and the Aqueduct, consistently winning major events over the next decade. These included the Triple Crown on Secretariat in 1973. In 1976, he matched the New York racing history record of six wins in a single day and, by mid-1978, had 3,032 victories.

All that came to an end, however, on July 13 when the horse ahead of him drifted into his path and Ron's horse clipped heels with the mount beside him and went down. "She just slinged me like a slingshot," Ron later recalled. He also realized that he had no feeling in his legs. He was paralysed and has remained so ever since.

Turcotte returned to Grand Falls, New Brunswick, where a rebuilt bridge had already been named in his honour. He had a home built for his wife and four daughters and from time to time made trips to take part in various ceremonies honouring him and other jockeys. He was unable to be present for his induction into the national Museum of Racing's Hall of Fame in 1979 but was in Toronto in 1980 when he was inducted into the Canadian Sports Hall of Fame.

A film company suggested a life story movie but fictionalized it so much that Ron, who had the right to approve the script, told them to forget it. In connection with his injury, he sued the New York Racing Commission because he felt the stewards had "failed to maintain compliance with the rules of racing," but the New York Court of Appeals judges dismissed the case in 1986 stating that a jockey's work is dangerous and has an "assumption of risk."

Like Turcotte, Hawley, a native of Oshawa, Ontario, also began his career in racing at Windfields Farm and, like all jockeys, Sandy Hawley has had his share of spills – more than a dozen of them – but the thrill of racing and winning is still with him. After being a groom he got his first mount at Woodbine in October 1968 and in 1969 as a jockey with rookie status – known as a bug boy – he topped all apprentice jockeys in North America with 390 victories.

The crucial test came the following year when the rookie advantage of carrying up to ten pounds less weight was removed. He became the world's top rider with 452 victories. In 1973 by winning 515 races he was the first jockey to win more than 500 races in one year. In 1976 he won the Eclipse Award as North America's outstanding jockey and, that same year, he received his second Lou Marsh Trophy as Canada's outstanding athlete. By then he had also won Canada's prestigious Queen's Plate three times and two years later became only the second jockey to win it a fourth time.

Yet, for all his success, his riding skills are considered awkward. Hawley sits further back than most jockeys so that when he pumps in rhythm with the horse, the horse, feeling the weight on his rump, is prompted to run, Sandy believes, at a slightly faster pace. For Bill Surface's article in the *Reader's Digest* trainer Lou Cavalaris had another explanation: "A lot of jockeys know they are good, but Hawley's confidence has horses thinking he and they are the best."

Confidence waned, however, in the early 1980s when Hawley did not win as many races as he had hoped at Santa Anita, his California home track, and when his long-time friend and agent, Colin Wick, elected to return to Canada, Hawley switched to the mid-west and by 1986 was top rider in Minnesota. Later that year, at Chicago's Arlington track, he won 23 races in 13 days before returning to California to check on a mole growing on his back. It proved to be malignant as did two more tumours that required surgery in 1986 and 1987. At the same time his second marriage to an aspiring actress ended in divorce. Sandy decided to return to Toronto and make Woodbine home base in April 1988.

Like Longden and Turcotte, Sandy rode worldwide. He competed against Turcotte in South Africa and raced in Australia, France, Great Britain, Trinidad, and Saudi Arabia. One of his favourite victories occurred in Barbados when he won that country's top race for Scobie Breasley who was entering his last horse as a trainer. "It was a great thrill to win that one for Mr. Breasley," he said in a 1995 interview.

In the same interview he said that doctors gave him a clean bill of health after they removed a tumour from his lung in 1991 and that, unlike many jockeys, he still has no weight problems as he is able to maintain his 110 pounds on a vegetarian diet. He has also become a father twice since his marriage to Lisa in 1991. Now living year-round in Mississauga, Ontario, he rides in California for roughly six weeks each winter but then hurries back to Woodbine. "I love riding there," says Sandy who hopes to stay close to racing as either a steward or colour commentator once he dismounts for good.

Mel James

Born in Grand Falls, New Brunswick, Ron Turcotte won the Triple Crown of American thoroughbred racing aboard Secretariat. He rode Northern Dancer in 1963, jockeying that Canadian-bred "big red" to his first ever victory as a two-year-old colt. [Photo, courtesy AP Wirephoto]

Samuel B. Steele

Scarlet Rider of the Frontier

1849 - 1919

WHEN SAMUEL BENFIELD STEELE became the third man to enlist in the North-West Mounted Police (N.W.M.P.) in 1873, he wrote, "Now I had the Great Lone Land before me where it is a man's own fault if he fails while he has health and strength." Steele, who had an abundance of both, became in time one of the most famous officers of the N.W.M.P., Colonel of Strathcona's Horse in the Boer War, and Canada's first major general in World War I.

Born in 1849 near Orillia, Ontario, Samuel was the fourth son of the second wife of Elmes Steele, who had been a captain in the Royal Navy before settling on crown lands in Ontario. As a youngster, Samuel learned to ride and "make gun powder and ball, using the heavy rifle or fowling piece as soon as we could carry them." When the Fenians invaded Canada in 1866, he won a commission and, while working as a clerk in Clarksburg, raised and trained the Clarksburg Company of the 31st Regiment so effectively that he was asked to take command of it even though he was just 17.

In 1870 he joined General Wolseley's Red River Expedition to Western Canada and demonstrated his amazing strength at a number of the portages by hoisting 300-pound barrels of flour onto his shoulders. He enlisted in Canada's first permanent force in 1871 but left it to become sergeant major of the North-West Mounted Police.

For the next 24 years he served the N.W.M.P. in numerous capacities and at numerous

Born at Purbrook, near Orillia, in 1849, Sam Steele was a man of enormous strength and endurance. Highly decorated as this photograph of him in late life demonstrates, he was enlisted in the militia during the Fenian Raids of 1866, he was a private in the Red River Expedition of 1870, he served in the Riel Rebellion of 1885, he was Colonel of Strathcona's Horse during the Boer War in South Africa and was a major general during World War I. [Photo, courtesy Western Canada Pictorial Index]

forts. Steele helped form the first N.W.M.P. band – the men paid for their instruments – and it was enthusiastically received by the pageantry-loving peoples of the first nations when they attended ceremonies to sign Treaty No. 7 at Fort Carleton in 1876. He served at Fort Macleod and moved to Fort Walsh in 1878 at the arrival of Chief Sitting Bull and thousands of Sioux Indians following the defeat of Custer at Little Bighorn, Montana.

In 1882, while CPR construction crews crossed the Canadian prairies, Steele was in charge of a small force sent to maintain order. He dealt with strikes, gunslingers, bootleggers, bar-room brawlers, card sharks, and prostitutes, sometimes using the back of a Red River wagon to serve as a courtroom bench. He meted out stiff penalties on those who fleeced the workers but was known to lock up drunks overnight to protect them from being robbed.

During the Riel Rebellion of 1885, he headed a group known as the Steele Scouts who eventually tracked down Chief Big Bear at Loon Lake, Saskatchewan, and, with just 40 men, attacked 500 Cree who refused to surrender. Later, he faced a different kind of confrontation when he and a newly appointed Commissioner tangled: Steele was shuffled off to Battleford and, later, Lethbridge. He also established Fort Steele in British Columbia. In January 1890 at Vaudreuil, Quebec, he married the daughter of a Conservative M.P.

Returning to Fort Macleod, Steele played host at musical soirees and other entertainments while carrying out his duties. He introduced the wearing of the Stetson, still worn today, to replace what had become a growing assortment of head gear that ranged from the original pillboxes to cowboy hats. He appeared to be quietly completing his career until retirement when the Klondike Gold Rush changed all that.

In 1894 the N.W.M.P., who had established small posts in the Yukon, were the first to alert the Canadian government to the strike at Bonanza Creek near Dawson City. Since the boundary line with Alaska was still in dispute, the N.W.M.P. were ordered to establish border posts at the peaks of both the White and Chilkoot passes. Log cabins were erected at the top of each pass to serve as a customhouse and officers' quarters. Steele arrived in mid-February "to maintain order on the Canadian side of the trail of '98."

While disorder and violence ruled supreme at Skagway where "Soapy" Smith and his gang of hoodlums ran the town, Steele established his office at Lake Bennett and policed the camps as he saw fit. No guns were allowed. He ordered the registration of the hundreds of boats that had been built on the ice-bound lake and were awaiting spring breakup, and of every man, woman, and child sailing in them, a move that enabled him to identify the nearly 150 boats lost and five people drowned on the first day's encounter with rapids on the Yukon River. Steele then made another law: boats had to be approved by one of his own corporals, "an experienced white water man," and the police would provide a list of experienced pilots to take the boats through at $5 per vessel. Those not complying would be fined $100. No further boats were lost.

In July Steele became head of the N.W.M.P. for both Yukon and British Columbia with the military rank of colonel. That September he visited what he called a "city of chaos" – Dawson. Built on a muskeg swamp two years earlier, this boom city, mainly American in population, had become "home" for some 20,000 stampeders. Saloons, gambling dens, dance halls, and brothels operated freely, some run by members of Soapy Smith's old gang after Smith was killed by vigilantes at Skagway in July.

Steele secured 70 army personnel serving at Fort Selkirk to act as guards at banks and perform routine duties while his own group of 13 men "policed" the community. Those arrested were forced to leave or fined or put to work collecting refuse, washing dishes, shovelling snow, or – the most dreaded sentence of all – cutting wood for the Mounted Police command post and other government buildings. "That wood pile was the talk of the town and kept 50 or more toughs of Dawson busy every day," he wrote, calculating that the work of each prisoner "saved the government at least $5 a day."

Steele, as chairman of the local Health Board and Licensing Commission, imposed heavy fees before he permitted the operation of a drinking place of any kind and used the funds to prop up the revenues of the territorial government. He let the gambling and the dance halls and even a red-light district operate so long as they abided by laws he established, one of which – Sunday closing – earned him a sort of affectionate respect in the community. "Big Sam was regarded as the stern *paterfamilias* of Dawson City, doing what was right for everybody," a later biographer wrote.

Steele, however, ran afoul of some of his fellow Yukon Territory council members who were receiving kickbacks, accepting bribes, and "fixing" cases through political influence. When one man was recommended as "issuer of liquor licenses," Steele, with the backing of Dawson's influential citizens, had the appointment quashed and this resulted in Steele's removal despite a public and press outcry. Protests were also expressed by the gamblers, dance hall girls, grizzled prospectors, ragtime piano players, and prostitutes who crowded the dock to give him, as the *Yukon Sun* reported, such a send-off "as no man

This photograph, circa 1894, shows Sam Steele, second row, third from left, as Superintendent of the North-West Mounted Police at Fort Macleod, Alberta. [Photo, courtesy RCMP Collection, Ottawa/Western Canada Pictorial Index]

has ever received from the Klondike gold seekers."

Steele had barely reached Montreal where his wife and family had gone during his Yukon service when the Boer War broke out in October 1899. He helped recruit a regiment to be known as the Canadian Mounted Rifles and was then asked to form a special corps of roughly 500 mounted riflemen being sponsored by his old friend from CPR days, Donald Smith, now known as Lord Strathcona, High Commissioner to Great Britain. Steele's first act was to name the unit Strathcona's Horse and within days he had recruited a number of officers and NCOs from the N.W.M.P. and had selected 537 from almost 2,000 volunteers.

The men sailed in March 1900 and saw their first action on July 1. From then until October they were almost constantly in battle, winning the praise of General Sir Redvers Buller. "It will be my privilege ... to tell Lord Strathcona what a magnificent body of men bear his name." Major General Robert Baden-Powell (future founder of the Boy Scouts) sought out Steele personally. Charged with organizing a police force to keep order after the war, Baden-Powell wanted to model it on the N.W.M.P. and asked Steele to command the South African constabulary in northern Transvaal.

Steele agreed but first returned home via England with Strathona's Horse who were paraded on the grounds of Buckingham Palace where King Edward VII presented the regiment its battle colours, made the first presentation of the South African medal to each man, and pinned the Victorian Order on Steele. The press raved about "Fighting Sam" and he was fêted at numerous luncheons and dinners before returning home with the regiment in March 1901.

Recalled to South Africa to serve in the Transvaal, Steele settled in Pretoria with his wife and two children. Shortly after his arrival, his Klondike expertise was used again when gold was discovered in the Labata Hills, but many of his recommendations were ignored by the colonial officials and by 1906, the role of the force was reduced and Steele returned home.

In 1914, he published his autobiography *Forty Years in Canada*, which sold even better in Britain than at home. Seven weeks after World War I was declared, Steele mobilized the western militia forces, thus enabling them to sail with the 1st Division. Promoted to major general in December – the first Canadian soldier to gain that rank – he later headed the 2nd Division but British War Officials who felt division commanders should be staff college graduates refused to let him lead it into battle. He was then made commander of the British-run army camp at Shorncliffe until his retirement on July 1, 1918. Knighted on the recommendation of Britain rather than Canada, he was waiting to sail home with his family in January 1919 when he became the victim of the flu epidemic that swept Europe and died at Putney on January 30.

World War I chaplain, Major the Reverend C.W. Gordon, better known by his pen name Ralph Connor preached the memorial service. Steele's body was eventually returned to Winnipeg, and, on the morning of his burial, it brought a temporary lull to the Winnipeg General Strike, as even the strikers bowed their heads while the cortege passed by in what was described as "the largest funeral western Canada had ever seen."   *Mel James*

GEORGE MONRO GRANT

On the Cusp of Nation Building

1835 - 1902

THE EMERGENCE OF A NEW NATION in 1867 required leaders to forge consensus and unity across a diverse landscape. Having such men as the eminent George Monro Grant, Canada was well provided. Best known for inspiring Queen's University of Kingston to become one of North America's most prominent and respected institutions, he also reflected, through public service and national promotion, the concept of Canada as more than a series of colonies gathered together under imperial unity.

Born in 1835 in the Scottish enclave that was Pictou County, Nova Scotia, George attended two of the colony's most dynamic educational institutions: Thomas McCulloch's Pictou Academy and James Ross's West River Seminary and then graduated from the University of Glasgow with degrees in theology. As a Presbyterian, he espoused a more liberal Evangelical stance rather than a rigid Calvinist one. He saw harmony between faith and reason and expressed his concern for the socially repressed in espousing a social gospel. Through conciliation and compromise, in 1875 he helped unify disparate formations into the Presbyterian Church in Canada and became its moderator in 1889. Prominent in the Pan-Presbyterian Alliance, he travelled around the world in 1888 to study comparative religions, spoke at the Congress of Religions in Chicago in 1893, and published *The Religions of the World* in 1894.

Stirred by the idea of a Canadian federation, he expressed his own surge in national feeling by twice crossing the country from east to west with his close friend Sir Sandford Fleming. The first adventure resulted, in 1872, in Grant's book, *Ocean to Ocean*, which described the newly acquired lands on which the Canadian west would be built. Although both trips were undertaken to seek the most appropriate route for a transcontinental railway, Grant's fascination with the land and its culture resulted, between 1882 and 1884, in the vastly popular publication called *Picturesque Canada*. Grant's vision of Canada was very much a part of his wider concept of imperial federation in which the new country would become an equal partner in the British Empire. He was a founding member of the Canadian Branch of the Imperial Federation League in 1884. (His son William Lawson Grant married the daughter of another imperial promoter, Sir George Parkin, and their grandson, George Parkin Grant, became one of Canada's most prominent philosophers and nationalists.)

When Principal Grant of Queen's assumed his position in 1877, the Presbyterian college had a student population of only 90. When he died in 1902, he was the head of a non-denominational university of international reputation with an enrollment of 850. Grant instilled, in its faculty and students, an ethic of public service, promoted understanding between the sacred and the secular, and pioneered both scientific education and extension programs. Queen's pioneered advanced education for women when it admitted women to regular classes in 1879; furthermore, the institution opened a Woman's Medical College in 1883.

While political parties and business groups were putting a stamp on the new nation in late Victorian times, George Monro Grant – educator, minister, and author – had a broad cultural vision of the emerging country. Ultimately, Canada would become much greater than its disparate parts owing to the direction given by nation builders such as George Grant who saw the land and the culture and defined a purpose well before most Canadians had the opportunity of going from sea to sea themselves.

Larry Turner

A nation builder, George Munro Grant inherited a small and financially unstable denominational college in 1877 and for the next 25 years, until his death, turned Queen's University into one of Canada's most respected institutions of higher learning. Editor and co-author of the tremendously popular Picturesque Canada (1882), "Mr. Principal" was a charter member of the Royal Society of Canada and its president in 1901. [Photo, courtesy National Archives of Canada/C-37819]

ROBERT MUNSCH

Wizard of Kid Stories

FOR ROBERT MUNSCH of Guelph, Ontario, adult comment is fine, but the people he really listens to are children because they help him write his books. Since 1979, North America's most prolific modern-day children's author has written more than 20 books. With sales exceeding 21 million copies, he is the most popular writer of children's books in the English-speaking world. In 1994 his *Love You Forever* topped the *New York Times* bestseller list – more than eight million copies have been sold. Some of his books have been produced as CD-ROMs and some for the home video market.

Munsch's success lies in his deep and sensitive understanding of children and in his patience in creating oral versions of his stories and retelling them to groups of children – sometimes for two or three years – to test their response and participation before he ever writes his books. In fact, most of his oral creations are never printed because his young listeners have not given him the reaction he is looking for. "I figured out once that the stories the children kept requesting came to two per cent of my total output," laughs Munsch.

His storytelling began in 1972 when, as a student teacher at a nursery school near Boston, Massachusetts, one night he created a song story about Mortimer, a boy who did not want to go to bed, to entertain his young charges next day. It went over so well the children kept asking for it, and when he told it to his sister's children – Munsch, born in Pittsburgh, Pennsylvania, in 1945, was the fourth of nine children – they taught it to other children in the neighbourhood.

He was encouraged to write the story but didn't. He did, however, continue to make up tales, thinking of them not so much as stories but as "little machines that kept kids happy and occupied." In 1974, when he joined the University of Guelph's laboratory nursery school, he was again urged to put his stories into writing.

"At first I made the mistake of attempting to change my stories into what I considered good writing. They were terrible. Finally I tried keeping the text as close as possible to the oral version and that worked," he explained in a 1986 article.

Above: When an author's individual work sells more than 5,000 copies in Canada, he/she has a bestseller. Imagine selling over eight million copies of one work! That is exactly what has happened to Robert Munsch, author of Love You Forever, *first published in 1986 by Firefly Books. [Cover, courtesy Firefly Books]*

By then he had written and published a dozen stories with Toronto's Annick Press whose owners, Anne Millyard and Rick Wilks, decided to take a chance because "his approach was so crazy, but it was also fresh." That was in 1979. Since then one or two titles have appeared annually, many of them dealing humorously with the everyday situations preschool children experience: the dark, loneliness, putting on a snowsuit, mud puddles, going to the bathroom, and learning that families come in all shapes and sizes, including interracial adoption.

The last one is close to home, for Munsch's own life includes the adoption of three children after his wife's two unsuccessful pregnancies.

Before his marriage in 1972, Munsch had spent several years in a Jesuit seminary and taken an M.A. degree in pre-school education, but he says he isn't a "preachy" writer. Nevertheless, he believes conflict and confrontation – especially with adults – is an unavoidable component of children's lives. Munsch also designs his stories so that they mean different things to different people. As he succinctly wrote in 1986, "I spend time getting them to do that, so that the correct answer to 'What does a Munsch story mean?' is 'To whom?' "

That same year he published his most successful but controversial story, *Love You Forever*. This parable is about the relationship between a mother and son as both grow old. Annick felt it was for adults and turned it down, but Firefly Books of the U.S. cautiously printed a mere 50,000. By 1994, some eight million had been sold!

Munsch believes that *Love You Forever* has appeal on two levels. For kids it's a humorous look at family life; for adults it tends to be more a personal reflection on love that endures and on aging. Whatever the reason, "... this book," as Munsch says, "has a nice effect on people and families and I really like that."

Mel James

Robert Munsch has found his niche in writing books for children. To date, his works have sold in excess of 21 million volumes making him one of Canada's best-known authors – and most prolific. [Photo, courtesy Annick Press Ltd.]

Children's books written by Robert Munsch are known and loved around the world. Most are now available on CD-ROMS. Pigs (1989) *and* The Paperback Princess (1980) *represent two of his world-famous works.* [Covers, courtesy Annick Press Ltd./ Robert Munsch, author/ Michael Martchenko, illustrator]

An artist of rare ability and penetrating vision travelled the highways of the voyageurs in the middle of the last century sketching as she went. It is time that her sketches, paintings, and engravings should be brought to the attention of all who understand our North American wilderness, their fluid highways, and the voyageurs whose birch bark canoes sped over them in days gone by. For she, perhaps best of all early artists, has preserved the voyageur and his habitat most beautifully and at the same time most accurately.

[Nute, Grace Lee, "Voyageurs' Artist." *The Beaver* 248 (June 1947): 32-37]

THE FUR TRADE IN CANADA – an aggressive, expansionist, hierarchical regime – dominated the north and west until the transfer of Rupert's Land to the Dominion of Canada in 1870. It has been depicted as a man's world of native trappers, canoemen, clerks, and post managers, with only recent recognition of the role of both Native and European women in the trade. Frances Anne Hopkins, artist, wife, and mother, captured the essence of the canoe brigades in the decade before 1870 and dramatically documented her European perception of the wilderness waterways between Montreal and Manitoba.

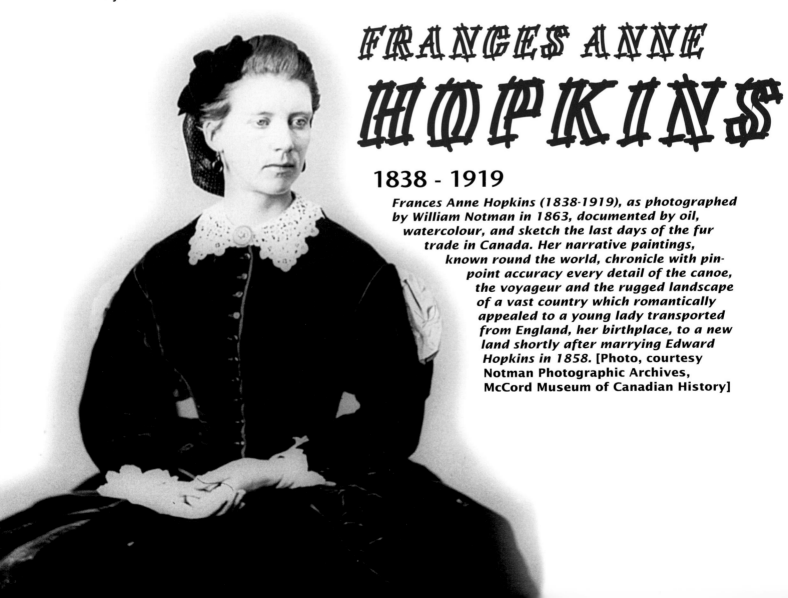

FRANCES ANNE HOPKINS
1838 - 1919

Frances Anne Hopkins (1838-1919), as photographed by William Notman in 1863, documented by oil, watercolour, and sketch the last days of the fur trade in Canada. Her narrative paintings, known round the world, chronicle with pinpoint accuracy every detail of the canoe, the voyageur and the rugged landscape of a vast country which romantically appealed to a young lady transported from England, her birthplace, to a new land shortly after marrying Edward Hopkins in 1858. [Photo, courtesy Notman Photographic Archives, McCord Museum of Canadian History]

Born Frances Anne Beechy in 1838, she married Edward Hopkins in London, England, in 1858. A widower residing in Lachine, Quebec, with three children, Edward, an employee of the Hudson's Bay Company, returned with his bride to Canada, settling in the Montreal area. When Frances witnessed the Grand Canoe Reception at Lachine given by Sir George Simpson for the Prince of Wales in 1860, little did she know that the canoe would play a significant part in her personal discovery of Canada. This was particularly true after she accompanied her husband on inspection trips after he was appointed Chief Factor in charge of the Montreal Department for the HBC in 1861.

Her canoe voyages became a window to several facets of Canadian life: the commercial lumber and fur trades, native life, and, most importantly, the role of the canoe. In 1869 she joined her husband on a leisurely canoe voyage from Thunder Bay to Montreal. Her documentary approach has been celebrated among historians, but only recently have her artistic skills been recognized and critically acclaimed. She painted in a British topographical landscape tradition and was influenced by John Ruskin who upheld the virtue of painting with a freshness of colour, boldness of conception, truth to nature, and originality of theme.

Art historian Robert Stacey has observed that Hopkins' vision and popularity foreshadowed a nationalist school of Canadian art. By painting Canadian subjects with the life and vitality of experience, Frances Anne Hopkins became "… a painter who captured something fundamental to a place, a people, and a way of life that nobody had looked at so closely or so lovingly before."

Hopkins rejected the Romantic Movement's preoccupation with the lone hero. Rather, her canvasses capture the notion of cooperation, not competition, on the canoe voyage, where group effort was necessary and vital. She also populated the wilderness with people, a human element lacking in the depiction of pristine nature by other contemporary artists. She also inserted her own authentic experiences into a scene and its action, unlike other contemporary women painters in England such as Lady Elizabeth Butler, who won fame for depicting wars she did not see. In the male world of the fur brigades, she was unique for her participation and her rendering of images of the past that few cared to record. She shares with William Armstrong and Paul Kane an important role as being among the first Canadian artists to paint the upper lakes region and the West. Stacey argues, "Her works need to be rescued from the dusty vaults of historical illustration, archival documentation, and sociological inquest and restored to their proper place: the repository of the living imagination."

The canvasses of Frances Anne Hopkins record for posterity a realistic portrait of the world-famous canoe brigades and lumber raft scenes of Canada's legendary waterways before such canoe travel, as a primary commercial system of transportation, succumbed to railways and before photographers replaced artists in documenting life in the wilderness theatre. Her images are far better known around the world than she as an artist in her own and adopted countries.

The north, the wilderness, the canoe and the fur trade help define a great deal of

Painted in 1879, "Shooting the Rapids," a dramatic oil on canvas, captures the essence of a thirty-six-foot long freight canoe being steered through treacherous white water by 16 voyageurs. The four passengers in the middle, side by side, include Edward and Frances Anne Hopkins. [Photo, courtesy National Archives of Canada/C-2774]

Canada's early history and are topics venerated by readers around the world, most of whom are familiar with the authentic and stirring images painted by Frances Anne Hopkins. An adventurous, stimulating, and creative artist, she, with such other women artists as Emily Carr, Paraskeva Clark, Peggy Nicol McLeod, Lilias Torrance Newton, Prudence Heward, was an imaginative interpreter of the Canadian experience.

Larry Turner

"Canoe Manned by Voyageurs Passing a Waterfall," *oil on canvas rendered in 1869, portrays a time of relaxation for exhausted voyageurs while Frances Anne Hopkins sketches the moment. It was not unusual for the artist to record her own likeness in her canvasses.* **[Photo, courtesy National Archives of Canada/C-2771]**

KAREN KAIN was eight when she wrote, "When I grow up I am going to be a ballerina. I will be in *Giselle*. It will be so much fun being a ballerina." After dancing *Giselle, Swan Lake, The Nutcracker, Romeo and Juliet, La Sylphide,* and hundreds of other classical and contemporary ballets, Karen expressed the same enthusiasm 35 years later in her auto-biography, *Movement Never Lies* (1994). While admitting that a dancer's life means pain, exhaustion, injuries, depression, dieting, and the hardships of touring, she called such drawbacks "negligible compared to the joys of creating a new role or learning an established classic and then getting out on the stage and performing, and the older I get, the more I relish it all."

A Canadian treasure, the divine Karen Kain was one of the world's most talented ballerinas during a 25-year career as a principal dancer with the National Ballet of Canada. [Photo, courtesy *The Toronto Star*/Reg Innell]

Audiences, too, have relished Karen who, in a *Maclean's* 1988 cover story to mark her 20th anniversary with the National Ballet of Canada, was described as "one of the most respected ballerinas in the world and – a living icon in Canada."

Karen's promise to be ballerina was prompted after seeing Celia Franca, the founding director of the National Ballet of Canada, perform in *Giselle* at Hamilton's Palace Theatre in 1959. Like many children she went to ballet classes at age six to gain poise and discipline, but her love, skill, and dedication to dancing prompted her parents to continue her lessons until she auditioned for the National Ballet School in Toronto. She enrolled in 1962 and spent the next seven years, often homesick but determined to do well, winning, at 18, an audition to join the corps of the National Ballet.

At the National she blossomed quickly from being a member of the corps to a dance soloist in *Mirror Walkers* in 1970. This led to a recommendation that she study the dual roles of the Queen and Black Swan in *Swan Lake* and in January 1971, she danced the two parts for the first time while on tour at Tempe, Arizona.

A year later, Rudolf Nureyev, the famous Russian-born dancer who defected to the West,

Canada's Prima Ballerina

came to the National to choreograph and dance in a lavish production of *Sleeping Beauty* in which Kain played the Principal Fairy, and would be Nureyev's partner in a new production of *Swan Lake* also performed that season.

"Rudolf helped me discover myself," Karen wrote in her autobiography. He taught me the joy and the necessity of a bold, clear, fully committed kind of dancing," adding, "Certainly I would never have reached my own potential as a dancer without Rudolf." Before the tour was over she also danced the lead role of Aurora in *Sleeping Beauty*. Nureyev returned the compliment in a *Time Magazine* interview: "The way she does Aurora," he said, "there is no one like that anywhere."

While Kain also attributes her international stardom to Nureyev, her first major step in that direction occurred when she and Frank Augustyn, also from Hamilton and a graduate of the National Ballet School, both went to the Moscow International Ballet Festival in May 1973. There she shared a silver medal for her solo performance. Together, the pair beat an elite field of dancers to take top honours in duet ensemble work for their performance of the Bluebird Pas de Deux from *Sleeping Beauty.* Tass called them a "a real discovery" who had won the sympathies of the Moscow audiences.

After that, the 1970s were a whirlwind of performances especially for Karen. Dubbed the "goldust twins" after their winning performances in Russia, audiences at home wanted to see them together, forcing the National to change its policy of not announcing who would dance in a performance to advertising their forthcoming appearances.

At the same time she was under pressure to dance in Europe and elsewhere. In Moscow she met Roland Petit, the renowned French dancer and choreographer who persuaded her to be a guest artist with his company, Le Ballet National de Marseille. Nureyev also pressed her into being his partner for appearances in Vienna, London, Washington, San Francisco, and a tour of Australia. She danced *Giselle* with the Bolshoi Ballet on a tour in Russia in 1977, and was also invited to perform in CBC television shows, the first of which, made on a cement floor, caused her considerable pain.

That, however, was minor compared to the turmoil and burnout she suffered as a person by the late 1970s. Always a perfectionist, she, and the critics, realized her performances were slipping, Anna Kisselgoff of the *New York Times* writing in 1979, "Miss Kain, once so radiant as Aurora now offered a sedate princess." Following a poor performance at Covent Garden in London, England, later that year, Karen quit dancing, sought help and through psychotherapy, learned "to shift from depending on having other people believe in me to learning to believe in myself."

By 1980, she resumed dancing with the National and for the next 15 years concentrated on performing with that company in Canada and on tour, with only occasional appearances in other countries including both China and Italy. By her 20th anniversary with the National in 1989, she had given up dancing some ballets, such as *Coppelia,* but continued dancing some favourites as *Swan Lake* and *Sleeping Beauty*, performing the later until the spring of 1994, her 25th anniversary year with the National, and giving a final performance of *Swan Lake* that fall.

Other ballets to reflect Kain's maturity both as a dancer and actress were created for her in the early 1990s and to celebrate her 25th anniversary, the National obtained permission to be the first outside of Britain's Royal Ballet to perform Sir Frederick Ashton's *A Day in the Country* that was first performed in London in 1976 by another Canadian born dancer, Lynn Seymour. The Royal had carefully retained its possession of the ballet until Karen indicated her interest in dancing the role of Natalia Petrovna which she considered one of the greatest ever created for a mature ballerina. On May 3, 1995, she performed it before yet another admiring audience and critical acclaim at Toronto's O'Keefe Centre.

After marking her second decade with the National in 1989, Karen was often asked how

long she would continue dancing. She ended the speculation in February 1996, when she announced her retirement. She will, however, continue being active in ballet circles. One of her special interests will be the Dance Transition Centre, founded in Toronto in 1985, to help dancers adjust when "they withdraw from the stage." Karen was elected its first president and shortly before her autobiography was published in 1994, wrote, "I recently accepted the title of 'president for life' and I consider my commitment to the Centre permanent."

Mel James

Karen Kain in The Actress, *choreographed by James Kudelka to celebrate her 25th anniversary season with the National Ballet in 1994.* [Photo, courtesy The National Ballet of Canada]

Wilfred Grenfell

Missionary Doctor of Labrador

1865 - 1940

Grenfell chose the rugged shoreland of Newfoundland and Labrador to serve humanity. Here, the medical missionary established schools, cooperatives, hospitals, nursing stations, and an orphanage to accommodate the immense needs of isolated communities located in bleak surroundings and harsh climate. [From Forty Years from Labrador, 1932]

S IR WILFRED THOMASON GRENFELL is one of Canada's most romantic heroes of the north. He was of an era when Victorian missionaries flung themselves into the far corners of the globe to bring civilization to the real or imagined uncivilized. Grenfell, motivated by both his religious and medical influences, brought to the coastal communities of Newfoundland, Labrador, and Quebec, a new degree of health care.

Born February 28, 1865 at Parkgate, Cheshire, England, Wilfred Grenfell received his medical education at Oxford University and London Hospital School. Converted to active Christianity in 1885 by Dwight L. Moody, an American evangelist, Grenfell practised his social gospel when he was fisherman's doctor in the North Sea in 1886. The National Mission to Deep Sea Fishermen made Grenfell a superintendent in 1889, and after an urgent call to visit Newfoundland in 1892, he returned to England where he pleaded passionately for funds to aid thousands of seasonal cod fishermen, over 3,000 permanent settlers, and the native people living on the coast who had been serviced only by one government doctor on an annual visit from the Newfoundland colony.

The first mission flag was planted at Battle Harbour on the eastern tip of Labrador at the entrance to the Strait of Belle Isle in 1893. Hospitals, orphanages, schools, nursing stations, industrial centres, agricultural stations, and cooperative stores soon followed at other locations in Quebec, Labrador, and at his eventual headquarters at St. Anthony,

First hospital established and built by Wilfred Grenfell was located at Battle Harbour, at the southern tip of Labrador, in 1893. Fire destroyed the mission in 1931. Stereograph depicts Dr. Grenfell leading a prayer meeting at Battle Harbour, circa 1895. [Photo, courtesy Charles J. Humber Collection]

Newfoundland. Facilities included a marine slip at St. Anthony to repair mission boats and fishing vessels, and a hospital ship used for annual cruises on the coast. There was also support of local handicraft business. The cooperatives helped break an economic dependence on unscrupulous merchants; the social clubs he promoted contributed to a sense of community and self-help.

As a widely read author and skilled lecturer, Grenfell brought attention and money to his mission. In 1909 he married the Chicago heiress, Ann MacClanahan, and a great deal of his support came from the United States. The International Grenfell Association was incorporated in 1912 as an umbrella of organizations in St. John's, Newfoundland; London, England; New York and Boston in the United States and the Grenfell Labrador Medical Mission of Canada. Also in 1912 Grenfell opened the King George V Institute in St. John's. Through hard work, courage, devotion, and a sense of mission for which the late Victorians were justly famous, Grenfell brought international attention to the plight of the cod fisherman.

Medical missionary, master mariner, and author, Wilfred Grenfell retired from active work in Labrador in 1927 and was living in Vermont still actively promoting his mission when he died on October 9, 1940. When Newfoundland joined the Canadian confederation in 1949, various segments of Grenfell's institutions were absorbed by government bodies, especially with the introduction of the Canada Health Act.

Peeling away the social mission behind the Grenfell effort, one finds a concerned medical man seeking practical means for providing a minimum level of health care on a rugged, isolated coastline. He was part of the advance force of authoritarian regenerators as represented by missions, police detachments, medical stations, and government agencies focusing on recognizing and assuming responsibility for the remote corners of Canada's North. Grenfell will be remembered as a pioneer in medical outreach, and for his delivery of vital services to remote regions of the far North. His personal papers are located at Yale University.

Larry Turner

In the late 19th century, St. Anthony, Newfoundland, became the mission headquarters for the International Grenfell Association. [Photo, courtesy Charles J. Humber Collection]

DOUGLAS SHEARER

*Originating
Sound for Film*

1899 - 1971

DOUGLAS SHEARER, a pioneer of motion picture sound, was born in Montreal in 1899. He left high school early, worked as a machinist, travelled for an industrial power plant, and learned signalling, photography, and flying.

At age 26 he journeyed to Hollywood not long after his actress-sister Norma joined Metro-Goldwyn-Mayer studio. He and Norma improved a system linking actors' voices, broadcast over radio, with a theatre screen, and his "movieola" used punch holes to indicate spoken words on strips of paper.

Jack Warner invited him to Warner Brothers studio where he worked in props but in 1927 he returned to MGM as an assistant cameraman. When Norma married studio boss Irving Thalberg, Douglas championed talking pictures, even to Louis B. Mayer. As its competitors moved to sound, MGM enlisted Shearer's assistance. "No longer were disks going to be used," he recalled in 1970. "Instead it was going to be done with a couple of ribbons that oscillated and a beam regulating the amount of light that reached the film, which, in turn, produced the sound change. So off I went to Bell Labs and learned about sound."

Shearer and a crew that he "stole from every which where" gave the famous MGM lion an audible roar and added sound (a thief cracking a safe) and dialogue to *Alias Jimmy Valentine*. They put music to film "in a church auditorium of the Victor Phonograph Company in Camden, New Jersey" and a music track on the documentary, *White Shadows in the South Seas*. Their work culminated in MGM's first musical, *The Broadway Melody*, which was named best picture of 1928-29 by the new Academy of Motion Picture Arts and Sciences.

At MGM's studio in Culver City, just outside Hollywood – where John Arnold ran the photography department, art director Cedric Gibbons reshaped the MGM backlots, and Thalberg "always wanted to know what was going on with the sound, costumes and photography" – Shearer set up and ran the sound department and recorded films. He accepted the first Academy Award given for sound for *The Big House* (1930) and worked on films that earned Oscars for Norma Shearer in *The Divorcee* (1930) and for Canadian-born actress Marie Dressler in *Min and Bill* (1931). He created the famous yell for *Tarzan the Ape Man* and took equipment up in his own plane to get realistic sound for *Night Flight*. And he recorded the films that brought Thalberg best-picture Oscars – *Grand Hotel* (1931-32) and *Mutiny on the Bounty* (1935).

His proudest accomplishment did away with the sound distortion troubling the MGM-controlled Loew's theatres. The two-element "Shearer horn" – tried out first at Loew's theatres in Montreal and New York in 1936, and used at the opening of *Romeo and Juliet* (Thalberg's last completed production involving both Shearers) – helped earn Douglas Shearer and the MGM sound department a scientific/technical award from the Academy's Board of Governors.

For improving the production and projection of motion picture sound and photography, Shearer and colleagues received six other scientific/technical awards. The first was for 1935 and the last for 1963, including one for 1959 for developing a method for producing and exhibiting 65-mm film which was used in MGM's film, *Ben Hur*, which swept the Oscars that year. For his work on individual films (some 1,400 in all, he estimated) Shearer received 20 Oscar nominations and accepted 7 Academy Awards (the last one for 1951) by the time he retired in 1968.

Shearer died in 1971 in Culver City. He had worked with many of the most able people in motion picture arts and sciences and earned enormous respect for his work that helped shape movie sound and photography worldwide.

John Parry

Douglas Shearer won the first Academy Award for sound recording for The Big House, 1930. **Born in Montreal, the older brother of Norma Shearer also devised Tarzan's famous electronic yell and solved the problem of Jeanette MacDonald's tendency to go flat on her high notes by adjusting the soundtrack frame by frame and "retouching" her voice. By the time he retired in 1968, he had won a total of seven Academy Awards. He also won an additional seven Academy citations for scientific and technological advances within the movie industry. In all, Douglas Shearer was nominated for 20 Oscars and his screen credits total some 1,400. This photo shows Douglas Shearer, on the right, at the 1935 Academy Awards dinner, March 1936, holding the award for sound recording for** Naughty Marietta **from presenter Hunt Stromberg. [Photo, courtesy Academy of Motion Picture Arts and Sciences via National Film Information Services]**

Abolitionist and First Black Woman Publisher in North America

IN THE 1850s MARY SHADD began and ran the little *Provincial Freeman* in Upper Canada (later Ontario), thereby becoming the first Black woman to found and edit a weekly newspaper in North America. Her own background lay in a United States still gripped by slaveholding throughout its southern half, until the American Civil war brought the abolition of Black slavery in the 1860s. And across the hectic mid-century years, this talented, enterprising woman boldly faced harsh racial prejudices and gender bias – forces that have scarcely vanished yet.

She was born in 1823 at Wilmington in the slave state of Delaware, the eldest of 13 children of Abraham and Harriet Shadd, "free Negroes." Her father had been a shoemaker but also an agent of the abolitionist press set up by white sympathizers in the Northern free states. He was also a "conductor" on the secret Underground Railroad that sheltered and forwarded escaped slaves on their northward flights to freedom.

In 1833 Abraham Shadd moved his family to West Chester in the Commonwealth of Pennsylvania, a free state where his children could be educated outside the world of slavery. Here, an alert, intelligent Mary did well in a Quaker school that crossed racial boundaries. In fact, she went on to teach school herself, variously in Pennsylvania, Delaware, New Jersey, and New York City. And in 1849, now an independent, travelled 26-year-old, she produced an influential pamphlet, *Hints to the Colored People of the United States*, which urged self-reliance and self-respect upon Black inhabitants. But very soon the American Fugitive Slave Law of 1850 violently shocked Black hopes and sent Mary wayfaring further northward on her own into the free lands of Canada.

This law of 1850 required federal authorities in Northern states to enforce the seizure of Black "runaways" for return to trial in Southern slave states. Still more, the law invited virtual kidnapping, since bounty-seeking slave hunters might grab Black suspects in the North for transfer to the mercies of Southern courts, thus destroying the Northern free haven of security. And so Black migrations rapidly swelled northward into British Canada where slavery had been illegal since Britain's own Imperial act of 1833 and where Upper Canada, which dipped down into the American mid-west, by law, had prohibited any future importation of slaves in 1793. Consequently, Blacks streamed into Windsor across from Detroit or over the Niagara frontier from upstate New York. Mary Shadd trekked north herself to examine this "Canada Venture."

She arrived in Toronto, the Upper Canadian capital, in September 1851,

Declared a National Monument in 1976, 1421 W Street N.W. in Washington, D.C., was the last residence of Mary Ann Shadd. [Photo, courtesy Dr. Daniel G. Hill]

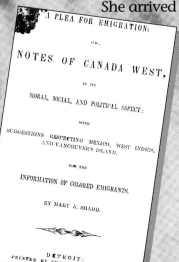

A PLEA FOR EMIGRATION:

OR,

NOTES OF CANADA WEST,

IN ITS

MORAL, SOCIAL, AND POLITICAL ASPECT:

WITH

SUGGESTIONS RESPECTING MEXICO, WEST INDIES, AND VANCOUVER'S ISLAND,

FOR THE

INFORMATION OF COLORED EMIGRANTS.

BY MARY A. SHADD.

DETROIT:
PRINTED BY GEORGE

Mary Ann Shadd produced a 44-page booklet, left, in 1852 for Blacks fleeing American slavery. The booklet evaluated Black settlements in Canada West. [Photo, courtesy Baldwin Room, Metropolitan Toronto Reference Library]
The **Provincial Freeman** *was first published in 1853 by Mary Ann Shadd, the first Black woman to publish a newspaper in North America. [Photos, courtesy Dr. Daniel G. Hill]*

Provincial Freeman.
DEVOTED TO ANTI-SLAVERY, TEMPERANCE, AND GENERAL LITERATURE.

TORONTO, CANADA WEST, SATURDAY, NOVEMBER 18, 1854.

VOLUME I.

and served as Secretary to a Black convention there. Capable and assured, eloquent and handsome, she was a striking figure with her light-brown skin and dark, commanding eyes. She liked Canada – "[I] do not feel prejudice," she wrote from Toronto to her brother – and afterwards she went on to Windsor where Black immigrants were settling to launch a much needed school for their children. Mary soon found, however, that Blacks disagreed among themselves over policies of setting up their own racial schools and areas or of pursuing integration into the general community – a key principle she backed aggressively. In any case, in 1852 she produced for new immigrants a 44-page booklet, *Notes of Canada West*, which evaluated the various Black settlements of Upper Canada. Yet her stand against segregation annoyed Black elements that favoured it and they attacked her views in their established newspaper, *The Voice of the Fugitive*. Thus Mary launched her own paper in response, the *Provincial Freeman*. It began in the spring of 1853 under the nominal editorship of a Black, male Presbyterian minister (who could accept a woman editor?) and it endured, even if its frequent shortage of cash impelled Mary to make lecture tours back into the United States to speak against slavery while her sister-in-law Amelia ran the paper in her absence.

Mary Ann Shadd

1823 - 1893

Mary Ann Shadd taught school in Windsor from 1851-53. She was founding publisher of a weekly newspaper in Chatham. A double-barrelled abolitionist, she recruited for the Union Army during the Civil War. She was a school principal in the United States before becoming a lawyer in Washington, D.C., where she died in 1893 at age 70. [Photo, courtesy Dr. Daniel G. Hill]

In 1854 Mary moved her influential paper to Toronto with its relatively sizable yet rooted Black community. The next year, she shifted it again, this time to Chatham which held some two thousand Blacks in its area, and which was near Buxton where her parents and others of her family had settled. Then in 1856 she married Thomas Cary, an industrious Black barber by whom she had a daughter and a son. In 1857 the spread of hard times across both the United States and Canada forced her to suspend her paper. Her husband died, all too prematurely, in 1860. Still, Mary Shadd went on, teaching, lecturing, writing until the coming of the American Civil War led finally to the end of slavery. Mary, indeed, was commissioned as a recruiting officer by the state of Indiana to help enlist Blacks for service in Union forces. And after the war, she decided to return to the United States and aid in the enormous task of educating and adjusting masses of ex-slaves for their new world of freedom. She went back permanently in 1868 to teach, write, and lecture tirelessly, settling in Washington – and also to become a lawyer by age 60. Her career as a committed activist (which further included support for woman suffrage) went on almost to her death in 1893, at 70. Over a courageous life, Mary Shadd had set her mark on two countries. And in Canada, she left descendants, close relatives, and friends in a maturing Black community, whose self-awareness and pride she herself had worked tirelessly to build.

J.M.S. Careless

Ralph Connor

Novelist with Muscular Spirit

1860 - 1937

CHARLES WILLIAM GORDON, pen name "Ralph Connor," clergyman and author, was perhaps the most successful Canadian novelist of the early twentieth century. Western missionary, Moderator of the Presbyterian Church, statesman of Church Union, army chaplain, diplomat, labour conciliator, and popular writer – at the height of his career he was arguably the best-known living Canadian and his name was a household word throughout the English-speaking world. As the prolific author of 24 novels, three separately issued extracts, three shorter tales, five religious pamphlets, one biography of his mentor and missionary superintendent, the Rev. James Robertson, and his unfinished autobiography, *Postscript to Adventure*, Connor ranks with Stephen Leacock, Mazo de la Roche, Lucy Maud Montgomery, Marshall Saunders, and Robert Service as the best-selling authors of Canada's first century.

Arguably the best-known living Canadian at the height of his career, Ralph Connor wrote many of his works in a cottage tower on Gordon Island in the Lake of the Woods. **[Photo, courtesy Charles J. Humber Collection]**

Charles W. Gordon was born in the Presbyterian manse at St. Elmo, Glengarry County, Canada West on September 13, 1860, the son of the fiery Rev. Daniel Gordon, Free Kirk minister in the Indian Lands, and the equally saintly Mary Robertson, a graduate of Mount Holyoke Female Seminary. Charles was named after one of his father's most faithful supporters, Charles McDonald, for 68 years an elder of the Indian Lands Church, a man of clear intellect and staunch integrity.

When Charles was not yet four, the Gordon Free Church was built in St. Elmo and officially opened by his father on July 20, 1864. Closely associated with the dedication of the new place of worship was the "Great Revival," a remarkable religious awakening in the Indian Lands of Glengarry that continued every evening with unabated fervour for well over a year. These spiritual stirrings made a lasting impression on the young Charles, as chronicled in *The Man from Glengarry* and *Torches through the Bush*, but it was the kinder, gentler faith of his mother that influenced him more profoundly than his father's strident sectarianism.

Charles Gordon left Glengarry at the age of ten when his father took on a new pastorate in Zorra, Oxford County, Ontario, in 1871. (By a strange coincidence, in that same year across the road in St. Elmo in the Congregationalist manse was born [Sir] Edward Peacock, later to become a prominent British financier and a Director of the Bank of England.) Gordon was educated at the University of Toronto, Knox College, and the University of Edinburgh. Ordained in the Presbyterian ministry in 1890, he undertook mission work for four years in Banff, Alberta, with his mission field extending to mining and lumbering camps and to Prairie pioneers. In 1894, he was called to the new parish of St. Stephen's in what was then the outskirts of Winnipeg. Serving on the Social Service Council of Canada, he became an early theorist and staunch advocate of the Social Gospel Movement. During World War I, he served with distinction in the front-line trenches as Chaplain of the 43rd Cameron Highlanders and was later appointed senior Protestant Chaplain to the Canadian Forces. In 1917 he was sent to the United States to enlist the American people to the Allied cause: at one point he aggressively lectured Woodrow Wilson on the moral inadequacies of American neutrality. In 1918 he returned to St. Stephen's and remained its pastor until his death on October 31, 1937, also serving as Chairman of the Manitoba Council of Industry set up following the Winnipeg General Strike and became one of the nation's most successful mediators of industrial disputes. As an ardent advocate of Church Union, he was instrumental in helping to create the United Church of Canada in 1925. Himself one of a family of six sons and one daughter, Gordon and his wife, Helen King, had a family of six daughters and one son, J. King Gordon, who followed in the footsteps of his father in his concern for social justice and progressive reforms.

Although Gordon always considered himself first and foremost a clergyman, it was as a tremendously popular author that he will be remembered. He believed that the novel was an instrument with which to teach and improve others: a secular sermon or parable. He could not have been less interested in the novel as an art form: for him it was a means of drumming up financial and spiritual support for missions in the West. If his novels were laced

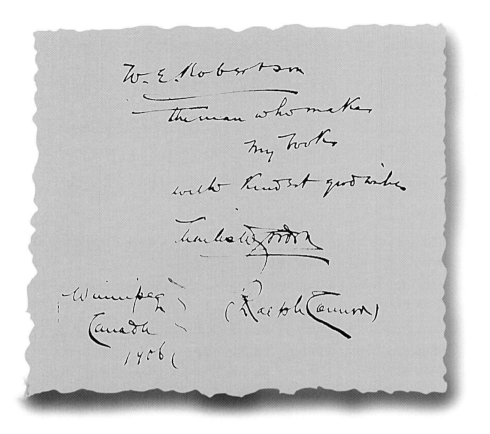

Rev. Charles W. Gordon, whose pen name was Ralph Connor, regularly autographed his novels with both signatures. [Photo, courtesy Masters & Fellows, Massey College, University of Toronto]

with melodrama, sentiment, and pathos, by his own admission he had not the slightest ambition to be a writer and paid little attention to literary style. His first novel, *Black Rock: A Tale of the Selkirks* (1898) originated in response to a request for a literary contribution from the Rev. James Macdonald, who had been with him at Knox College, and was then editor of the *Westminister* magazine (and later editor of the Toronto *Globe*). "Christmas Eve in a Lumber Camp" was expanded to nine chapters and renamed *Black Rock*. Macdonald asked his friend for a *nom de plume*: Gordon, who was then Secretary of the British Canadian Northwest Mission, glanced at the heading on his stationery, "Brit.Can. Nor.West Mission," and chose "Cannor." The telegraph operator mistakenly changed the message to "Sign article Connor" and Macdonald added "Ralph" because it sounded "euphonious." Thus was born "Ralph Connor." The first edition ran to 5,000 copies, an unheard-of figure for a first effort by an unknown Canadian novelist. In no time, a dozen American editions appeared, some of them pirated, that achieved a combined sale of more than half a million copies. *The Sky Pilot* the following year surpassed a million copies, and, with the appearance of *The Man from Glengarry* in 1901, the three novels achieved combined worldwide sales of over five million copies.

Connor himself attributed the great success of his novels in which "things just came to him and he put them down" to two factors: his novels presented a quality of religious life that "red-blooded" men could read and enjoy. And they gave an authentic picture of life in "the great and wonderful new country in Western Canada, rich in colour and alive with movement..., the land of the trapper, the Mounted Police, and that virile race of men and women, the first pioneers who turned the wild wilderness into civilization." This formula, applied to later novels, of the missionary-hero as larger than life muscular Christian who confronted spiritual issues with clear and strong action proved to be a phenomenally popular theme that Connor varied time and again. Connor's books were thus based on a religion which he felt represented "all that is virile, straight, honourable and withal, tender and gentle in true men and women." It was hard for an Edwardian to argue with such sentiments.

But Connor's best works from a literary perspective were those that centred upon the scenes of his youth in Glengarry. In this, he was profoundly influenced by an 1866 novel, *Shenac's Work at Home*, by Margaret Murray Robertson. It was set in the Maxville-St. Elmo area and described the customs of Glengarrians. And the author just happened to be his mother's sister. Connor's finest work, *The Man from Glengarry*, communicated the "Glengarry mystique" to an immense audience worldwide. Through a faithful rendering of dialect and the use of detailed local colour, Connor presented accurate, minute, and vivid recreations of the pioneer era in his native Glengarry for future generations. This penetrating realism was comprehensive, save for his glaring omission of local superstitions. The copious and authentic detail was

The most successful novel written by Ralph Connor was **The Man From Glengarry (1901) which, along with The Sky Pilot (1899) and Glengarry School Days (1902), had combined sales of 5 million copies, an unheard of tally at that time and a number that would make today's Canadian publishers drool. [Photo, courtesy Charles J. Humber Collection]**

repeated in *Glengarry School Days* the following year, 1902. However, the only Connor novel to make it to the silver screen was *Corporal Cameron* (1912), released in 1921 as *Cameron of the Royal Mounted*.

Ralph Connor will be long remembered for his two dozen phenomenally popular novels that spanned almost 40 years and addressed a wide range of contemporary social and economic issues in a compassionate and commonsense style. Vividly told with enthusiastic characterizations and unabashed sentiment, they celebrate the active commitment to faith of dedicated men and women. Ralph Connor may well have been the most popular novelist Canada has ever produced.

Murray Barkley

The Royal Canadian

ALTHOUGH he completed only grade school in his native London, Ontario, on May 25, 1971, Guy Lombardo received an honorary doctorate from the University of Western Ontario. The citation read in part: "Our distinguished graduate achieved early in life what many artists spend their lives searching for, a unique, distinctive and recognizable style."

Born in 1902, Lombardo considered this award his greatest lifetime honour. He had many others to choose from, for Guy Lombardo and his Royal Canadians – the band that played "The Sweetest Music This Side of Heaven" – had played at the inauguration balls of several United States presidents, had performed for Royalty, and had sold some 300 million records around the world.

By their early teens both Guy and younger brother Carmen were performing at church and other socials around London. Another London native, Freddie Kreitzer, joined them as pianist. Later, their brother, Lebert, born in 1905, and sister, Elaine, took part in local concerts, experimenting with different instruments to create the beginning of the band.

Carmen, a child prodigy with the flute, took up the saxophone, while Lebert moved from drums to trumpet. Other Londoners joined the group including drummer George Gowans, who, like Kreitzer, stayed a lifetime with the band.

The band got their first break in 1922 when they were booked into London's Winter Garden and at Port Stanley the next summer. Success, however, would be achieved only by their going to the United States and being heard on radio, a goal Guy pursued for months. Finally an agent booked them as one of eight acts at a club in Cleveland. While the band's sound was not a total success, word quickly spread around London that Lombardo's band was U.S.-bound. To avoid embarrassment, Guy pushed the agent into getting them another U.S. date – a one-week stint at Akron, Ohio. On the basis of that booking, the band boarded a train in London one Sunday at 1.00 a.m. with approximately a hundred people to see them off. Guy recalled years later, "I remember thinking I never would let them down."

He and the band didn't. The agent got them into the El Club of Cleveland and suggested a name change to "Guy Lombardo and His Royal Canadians." A local radio station gave them

That's where I

Guy Lombardo

1902 - 1977

air time and soon they were booked into a theatre in the afternoons and the club at night. They were taking on other jobs around Cleveland as well until Julius Stern of the Music Corporation of America signed them to a contract.

In 1927 Stern moved them to Chicago where arrangements were made to hook them up with Chicago's newest radio station, WBBM. The broadcast the first evening was supposed to last 15 minutes but went on until 1 a.m. as people jammed the station's lines every time Guy tried to sign off and crowds arrived at the club to see the band they were hearing. For the next two years they

Probably the best known band leader of his era, or any era, was Guy Lombardo. A native of London, Ontario, Guy Lombardo and his Royal Canadians made champagne bubbles dance each New Year's Eve to "Auld Lang Syne" in a career spanning nearly six decades. [Photo, courtesy The Toronto Star]

remained in Chicago. One reviewer described the band, after a performance at the city's Palace Theatre, as "the softest and sweetest jazzmen on any stage this side of heaven." The slogan lasted a lifetime.

In 1929 the Royal Canadians moved to New York's Roosevelt Grill and became so popular on radio that they ushered out 1929 for CBS and the New Year in for NBC. They also became the first band nationally sponsored on radio; to enhance their sponsor's product – cigars – Guy hired George Burns and Gracie Allen for comedy skits while his music played in the background. Two more Lombardos also worked with the band from time to time. Elaine, who became their female vocalist, eventually married their lead singer, Kenny Gardner, and a younger brother, Victor, joined them several times between stints with other bands or when not leading a band of his own.

When, because of the Depression, the Roosevelt Grill cut back on its contract, the Royal Canadians moved to the Coconut Grove in Los Angeles where numerous movie stars came to dance and became friends. In 1934, this led to their first of three movies, one in which Carmen had one of his many hit songs.

One-night stands while on tour for as much as nine months of the year was another reason for their popularity. One of the stops was London where the Lombardos always visited old haunts and invited the band's newest members to go along. In 1937 they made a special trip to London to play benefits for victims of the flood that devastated the city that year, a routine they were to continue, particularly during World War II.

Despite the demanding schedule of one-night stands or contract stays at such famous spots as the Coconut Grove, the Waldorf Astoria, and the Pavillion at Long Beach, New York, the band made numerous recordings. The first was cut in 1924, and for another 50 years Guy Lombardo records were produced and sold around the world –11 million of them in 1946 alone!

That year, Guy, an avid speedboat racer, won the Gold Cup at Detroit. Two years later he suffered a broken arm when he had to crash his boat during a race but he continued racing until 1954, when he was asked to produce musical extravaganzas at the Jones Beach Marine Theatre on Long Island, a job he and his brothers took on for the next 24 years. He produced such classics as *Show Boat*, *South Pacific*, *Oklahoma* and *The King and I* as well as other shows written by his brother Carmen with his song-writing partner, John Jacob Loeb.

The first major blow to the band was Carmen's death in 1971. For months Guy could not face the orchestra and led while facing the audience. But he continued because he couldn't think of what he would do in retirement. "Retire to what?" he asked in his autobiography published when he was 73. "I have been blessed with an occupation that enables me to make other people happy ... on the bandstand I am having a party every night I am working."

As a result he continued leading the Royal Canadians until his own death in November 1977, a death which "came as a shock to North Americans," one biographer wrote, because "the man was an institution and institutions don't die." Further honours were awarded to keep his memory alive. The city of London named a bridge after him and officials of

Guy Lombardo's "sweetest music this side of heaven" sold more than 300 million records throughout the roaring twenties, the dirty thirties, wartime forties, the jukebox fifties, the twisting sixties, and the Nixon seventies. [Photo, courtesy Charles J. Humber Collection]

Freeport, Long Island, his home city for many years, changed South Grove Street to Guy Lombardo Avenue and renamed the local marina to perpetuate his name.

The band kept on under the leadership of Lebert's son, Bill, but, as Guy had written in his 1973 autobiography, Rock 'n' Roll had replaced the big bands on radio. While he felt the Beatles were superb and imaginative musicians, he admitted that he "neither understood nor appreciated the new cacophony called music" being played by many groups. "I have never resisted change in our industry," Guy wrote, but "the deafening noise and lyrics that were suggestive and worse ... I didn't want to understand."

Mel James

CANADA owes much to its Irish-born physicians, and one of pre-eminence was Joseph Workman. Joseph, born near Lisburn, County Antrim, one of a family of ten, immigrated to Montreal with his parents in 1829. He entered McGill the following year and graduated from its medical school in 1835. His thesis explored cholera, a disease new to the world, that had seriously ravaged Canada in both 1832 and 1834. His thesis also demonstrated an independent mind, for the young Workman, in believing that cholera was contagious, differed from most of his profession.

He married a Montreal woman and practised there for a year, but his destiny awaited in Toronto. By 1836 he had become a full-time partner in his in-laws' hardware business and was a highly successful Toronto merchant. Other energies were channelled into local politics – for example, as alderman for St. David's Ward – and into the writing of biting, inflammatory prose in support of Upper Canada's Reform politics. He also became the first chairman of the Toronto School Board and strongly espoused the then controversial causes of free (i.e. tax-supported) and universal public school education.

In 1846, after John Rolph succeeded in inducing the middle-aged Workman to join the faculty of the medical school Rolph had founded in Toronto in 1832, Workman returned to medical practice. It says something for the casual nature of medical education that a man whose medical education had consisted of a year or so of practice in another city and whose chief concern for many years had been sales of hardware should have been sought out by Rolph as a teacher, first of midwifery and later of *materia medica*.

In the mid-nineteenth century, in efforts to house and treat the insane, politics were pre-eminently and directly involved. When Dr. John Scott, the fourth superintendent of the Toronto Asylum at 999 Queen Street, resigned, the Premier of Ontario had a candidate in mind for the post, a man with no psychiatric knowledge. Dr. John Rolph, a politician in 1853, also had a candidate with no psychiatric expertise. Whether Rolph somehow knew that his candidate would be successful or whether he was simply fighting another political battle at the pork barrel is unknown, but Workman got the job.

Fundamental to grasping and understanding Workman's position in Canada's history is seeing how the insane previously had been treated. In the absence of asylums, public or private, those who had any kind of mental difficulties serious enough to be publicly visible were often badly treated. Families tried to hide their shame by tying up the patient or by locking him or her in a closet or shed. When the "lunatic" became too loud or too violent, then appeal might be made to the local jail to take in the unfortunate.

By the 1830s, a definite change was necessary. The number of "lunatics" was increasing. Legislation was needed as well as a different approach to the problem. Dr. Charles

Joseph Workman

The Nestor of Canadian Alienists   1805 - 1894

Joseph Workman, viewed here circa 1849, was the compassionate superintendent of Toronto's Provincial Lunatic Asylum between 1853 and 1875. [Photo, courtesy Metropolitan Toronto Reference Library (T 10261)]

Duncombe issued a report in 1836 pointing to the high cure rates of some European institutions. The rates he cited were never achieved in Ontario or perhaps anywhere else, but the public was impressed by his vision and the government committed funds to build a provincial asylum in Toronto. It was perhaps just as well for Duncombe that he fled the country in the wake of the 1837 Rebellion in which he was a principal figure and thus never had to justify his optimistic predictions.

The Provincial Lunatic Asylum, as it was called, was not completed until 1850 and even then the work was inadequate. When Workman took over the Toronto Institution in 1853, among other messes he inherited was a basement full of sewage. Three years earlier, no arrangements had been made for the outflow.

But the real problems existed not so much in the basement as in the wards. Neither the physical nor the mental health of the patients had been attended to adequately. Daily meals were improved. Medications were decreased in amount, a salutary move since many of these were probably harmful. Instead of pills and potions, Workman prescribed alcohol. In one year the expenditure on wine, beer, and spirits was ten times that for medicines. The patients improved physically.

Workman was, of course, especially concerned about the mental condition of his charges. Over the previous half century, dating back at least to Philippe Pinel's memorable casting off of the chains confining the patients at his Paris hospital, an approach to madness had been worked out called "moral treatment." Kindness was the revolutionary ingredient along with

Superintendent of Ontario's Provincial Lunatic Asylum from 1853-1875, Joseph Workman (1805-1894), in his annual report to the provincial legislature of 1859, decried the underfunctioning of the province's mental health care system, claiming that "denying to the insane the benefits of early treatment is very erroneous public economy." Vigorously promoting public awareness of the plight of "lunatics," the legacy of Workman is that his mandate became a universal norm. [Photo, courtesy Museum of Mental Health Services (Toronto) Inc.]

encouragement of exercise and work rather than mandatory idleness within locked cells and wards. By the mid-nineteenth century, a few asylums doors were being unlocked.

The anticipated dramatic cures did not occur. Unquestionably, many patients did much better under the new regime, but Workman and his colleagues had optimistically expected a massive clearing out of the hospitals. Nothing of this sort occurred. Yet the basic premise was sound: mentally disturbed patients do better when they are treated with kindness than when they are ill-used. That the revolutionary Workman and his fellow asylum superintendents could go no further is no criticism of them. Even late in the twentieth century, cure of many mental disorders remains elusive.

Workman, as always with those in his position, continually requested more funds from government. The government of his time, like others, responded, not with more money, but with more control. It established a centralized system intended to cut costs, not increase them. And while the government did, over the next two decades, build additional asylums, increasingly the bureaucracy exerted tighter controls.

One of Workman's most important characteristics, given that he worked much of his adult life in the political arena, was his ability to fight the system and deflect, if not defeat, the politicians. Fearlessly he pointed out the stupidities that seemed inherent in a medical system controlled by politicians. Ultimately the system won and, in 1875, Workman resigned his position. He was then 70 years old with a distinguished and respected international reputation.

He had written much while becoming a pioneer in the field now known as psychiatry. His titles included *Asylum Management*, *Crime and Insanity*, and *Demonomania and Witchcraft* as well as the mandatory stream of official annual reports. He was a skilled linguist and translator: Canadian journals often carried his translations of Italian or Spanish medical papers.

Workman achieved widespread recognition among his peers, as evidenced by his presidencies of the Toronto Medical Society (later the Academy of Medicine of Toronto), the Ontario Medical Association, and the Canadian Medical Association, yet he remained a man of modesty with a low level of personal vanity. Late in his life, a group of colleagues commissioned a bust of the man at their expense. Workman put up with the necessity of spending several hours as the artist's model but afterwards concluded: "I would not sit again for all the busters in Canada."

Today as well as then, Workman's fundamental importance is his establishment of the role of asylum superintendent as an honourable one, with the consequence that the plight of the inmates began to be taken more seriously. Although the results of his moral therapy disappointed him, the approach was a fundamentally sound one. Though this policy did not originate with Workman, he promoted it vigorously, and it became a universal norm. He did much to humanize not only the treatment of "lunatics" but also their perception by the general public. These were real attainments deserving recognition.

Charles Roland

THE MEDIEVAL CATHEDRALS, churches, colleges, and choirs of Europe gave birth to a musical tradition that continues to resonate around the world. Masses, choral works, and organ compositions remained cloistered largely within the sanctuaries of the Christian church, but operas, orchestral works, madrigals, and folk songs flourished in the secular world. Healey Willan, one of the great composers of the twentieth century, transformed, interpreted, adapted, and composed works that sustained a tradition and took it to new dimensions. Composing more than 800 works including operas, symphonies, chamber music, a concerto, and pieces for band, orchestra, and piano, Willan was a consummate artist, a musician, composer, teacher, and conductor.

Healey Willan
1880 - 1968

Born in 1880, in Balham, Surrey, now a part of London, England, Healey grew up in a musical family, learned to play piano and organ, and attended St. Saviour's Choir School. As an organist and choirmaster within the Anglican church who supported the Oxford Movement which promoted Anglo-Catholic doctrine and ritual, he revived plainsong (or the Gregorian chant). He also edited and arranged Latin songs for English rendition, conducted choral and operatic societies outside the church, and was an esteemed member of the Gregorian Association from 1910.

Willan emigrated to Canada in 1913, accepting an offer to teach at the Toronto Conservatory where he served as vice principal (1920-1936) and became, in 1914, a lecturer, and, later, until 1950, a professor at the University of Toronto. In spite of Willan's ecclesiastical beginnings, he considered a career as a concert pianist. As music director of Hart House Theatre at the university between 1919 and 1925, he wrote and conducted incidental music for 14 plays.

In 1913 Willan accepted the position of organist-choirmaster at the prestigious St. Paul's Anglican Church on Bloor Street, Toronto, but jumped at the opportunity of serving a high

Viewed here playing the great Casavant organ in Convocation Hall, Healey Willan was organist for the University of Toronto, 1932-1964, giving recitals, presiding over ecumenical events and all graduations. [Photo, courtesy The Church of St. Mary Magdalene, Toronto]

Anglican church, the church of St. Mary Magdalene in the same city. Although he received less remuneration, he had far greater freedom in choosing the music, the form of worship, and even alterations to the building. As he commented in 1963, "You have a sense of home, absolute completion ... doing the work you want to do and the work you feel you can do." Willan remained as choirmaster for 46 years and it was there that Willan became a legend, creating two choirs (chancel and gallery) for special effects and playing a Casavant organ adapted for his tastes within a church structure designed for his purposes.

Writer and broadcaster Kenneth Winters described arriving at a Willan concert as a reviewer 15 minutes early and being unable to get in. "The hall was packed to bursting. All I could do was return to the office and write a brief disconsolate account of listeners standing in the aisles and hanging from the rafters, and no room for me. The lesson, which may still but should not surprise us, is that Willan's music has an audience, and that his music for the church can engage and touch a listener who may never set foot in a church."

In 1922 a correspondent for the *Montreal Standard* wrote of St. Mary Magdalene as the "most advanced" Anglican Church in Canada where the music was "an inspiration, an uplift, and a delight." The church vestry informed Bishop Sweeney in 1930 that the parish church had acquired a worldwide reputation for musical perfection and "All visiting artists, whether English, American, or continental European, come to St. Mary Magdalene's to hear the choirs." *Saturday Night* magazine in 1940 quoted an American stage star playing at the Royal Alexandra Theatre: "There are only two places in Toronto really worth visiting. One of them is the Chinese Collection at the Royal Ontario Museum and the other is the Church of St. Mary Magdalene."

The crowning achievements for Healey Willan were his being commissioned to write the homage anthem, "O Lord, Our Governour," for the Coronation of Elizabeth II in 1953; his receiving in 1956 the highest award an Anglican musician can attain, the Lambeth Doctorate from the Archbishop of Canterbury; and his being, in 1967, among the first Canadians to be honoured as a Companion of the Order of Canada. Many of his students became great musicians, including Louis Applebaum, Robert Farnham, and Godfrey Ridout. In 1980 Willan and Emma Albani shared the distinction of being the first musicians to be commemorated on a Canadian postage stamp.

Healey Willan was sometimes marginalized by contemporary Canadian composers and musical experts as a "church composer" who was more interested in transferring traditional medieval themes from Europe than in stirring a Canadian imagination. To the fine ear of a classicist, however, Willan with a mystical touch and a polyphonic approach within the ecclesiastical boundaries of musical tradition is one of this century's most significant composers. Like many Canadians, he was touched by several influences. He once commented, "I am English by birth, Irish by extraction, Canadian by adoption, and Scotch by absorption."

Larry Turner

This Healey Willan caricature was sketched by A.Y. Jackson on the back cover of a catalogue while both were attending the opening of the Maurice Cullen Exhibition at the Hamilton Art Gallery in 1956. [Photo, courtesy Mary Willan Mason]

Beatrice Lillie

"The Funniest Woman in the World"

1894 - 1987

Beatrice Lillie played to the troops during World War II. Recognized for her patriotic efforts, she was decorated by France's Gen. Charles de Gaulle. Her zany stage humour made her an international sensation. She published an amusing autobiography in 1972 called Every Other Inch a Lady. [Photo, courtesy Metropolitan Toronto Library Photo Collection]

IN APRIL 1964, Noel Coward made a diary notation: "Bea Lillie ... is mad about playing Acati. She will bring to it star quality, moments of genius and little or no acting talent, but I'll settle." The entry was typical of the relationship between Toronto-born Lillie and Coward who wrote numerous revues and shows for the woman who was to become globally known as "the funniest woman in the world."

Bea was approaching 70 when she played Acati in *High Spirits*, the musical version of Coward's play, *Blythe Spirit*. She had first appeared on the London stage fifty years earlier singing a boy's role in the André Charlot revue *Not Likely*. Before that, she had appeared in Toronto and numerous other Ontario towns as part of a family trio made up of her older sister Muriel, who was something of a child prodigy at the piano, and her musically ambitious mother, Lucy, who pushed Bea into taking singing lessons.

Bea went to Harry Rich, who had been a comedian before an accident confined him to a wheelchair. He taught Bea how to sing comic songs as well as gesture and grimace – her later repertoire trademarks. He also became booking agent for Lucy and her two daughters and got them engagements throughout the province. By her mid-teens Bea was attracting positive reviews. The Toronto *Globe* commented that she was a "remarkable clever artist with a sweet, powerful voice." The *Galt Reformer* reported that she "proved a great favourite and won much applause for all her numbers." Her mother's main interest, however, was in Muriel as a pianist. In 1913, she took Muriel to study in Germany but the threat of war caused them to settle in London. When Bea finished St. Agnes College in Belleville in 1914, she too wanted to try out for stage work; her father, John Lillie, saw her off to England but remained steadfastly in Toronto.

She got a part in an André Charlot revue and the following year, when she played a boy, one critic called her "one of the most dapper and accomplished of contemporary male impersonators." Other Charlot revues followed and, in 1917 when she appeared in *Cheep*, Noel Coward affirmed that "Beatrice Lillie appeared in her true colours as a comic genius of the first order."

Early in 1920 she married Robert Peel, the extravagant heir of Lord Peel, and by year's end their only son, Robert Jr., was born. Bea continued on stage, partly to keep her husband financially sound. Leaving her son much of the time with her mother over the next four years, she appeared in revues and vaudeville, including the 1922 hit, *The Nine O'clock Revue*, that featured music written by Muriel. The show lasted a full year.

Her New York debut in another Charlot revue won her instant recognition from the *New York Times* in January 1924. "There was no one in New York quite comparable to Beatrice Lillie." The show, originally booked for six weeks, lasted for nine months and went on tour for another six. She was in Chicago when, on the death of her father-in-law, she and Robert became Lord and Lady Peel.

Work as Beatrice Lillie continued unabated. In 1926 she was back in New York in another revue, made her first film with Mary Pickford's brother Jack, began performing in cabarets and in December appeared in *Oh Please*, a performance that caused critic Brooks Atkinson to write, "She is a comedienne with a divine spark, a mimic of the highest skill and everything she does is shot through with a piercing sense of humour." Walter Winchell also applauded her while panning the supporting cast, musical conductor, and stage crews. For the next decade Bea flitted between London and New York performing in numerous productions. She appeared in Coward's *This Year of Grace* and *After Dinner Music*, in some of Charlot's revues, and in Bernard Shaw's *Too True To be Good* opposite Claude Rains. Of this the *Herald Tribune* reported, "the Shavians speak of it with proper respect but unregenerate outsiders call it Beatrice Lillie's show."

In 1934 when her husband died of peritonitis, he left behind large debts. Beatrice had no choice but to continue her stage career. In 1935 she was at London's Palladium and that September at the Winter Garden in New York with Reginald Gardiner and Ethel Waters in

At Home Abroad. Cole Porter wrote a song for her and Bert Lahr was her co-star in *The Show is On* which lasted almost a year. In 1936 she tried the movies again appearing with Bing Crosby in *Dr. Rhythm*.

Movies, however, were not her forte. Critics felt she needed a live audience, and she got that in abundance by volunteering for troop shows one month after World War II was declared. She performed in England, the Mediterranean and the Middle East until illness forced her to quit in 1944. By then she had also learned that her son, reported missing in action in 1942, had been killed while serving in the Royal Navy.

In December 1944 she was back in New York and won the Donaldson Award for *Seven Lively Arts*. Then it

The revues of Beatrice Lillie (1894-1987) incorporated sketches, songs, and monologues parody and witty satire. Her uncanny ability to become intimate with audiences made her a stage success for over 50 years. This photograph was taken in New York city in the 1930s. By this time she was known as Lady Peel. [Photo, courtesy Charles J. Humber Collection]

was London again for *Better Late*, and New York in 1948 for *Inside USA* with Jack Haley, a revue in which Bea instituted her pearl-twisting bit. It was also during that revue that she met 26-year-old John Philip Huck, both a singer and actor, who became her manager and, despite their age difference, her companion for the rest of her life.

In the summer of 1952, she launched *An Evening with Beatrice Lillie* and for the next four years won rave reviews in the USA, Canada, and Great Britain. It was as a result of this show that the fabled Brooks Atkinson called her "the funniest woman in the world," and British critic Ronald Barker wrote, "Other generations may have their Mistinguette and their Marie Lloyd. We have our Beatrice Lillie and seldom have we seen such a display of perfect talent."

When that show had run its course, she appeared in the Golden Jubilee edition of the *Ziegfeld Follies* with Billy de Wolfe in 1957, then took over Rosalind Russell's role in *Auntie Mame* in 1958. As predicted by Coward and confirmed by Atkinson, she soon made "Mame her own."

By the early 1960s, however, the revue was becoming passé and so was Lillie. Following Coward's musical, *High Spirits*, in 1964, Bea made cameo appearances in two movies: *Around the World in 80 Days* and *Thoroughly Modern Millie* but it was obvious she was losing her memory. In 1967 when she shared double billing at Toronto's O'Keefe Centre, audiences found her material dated. Failing to make a comeback, she became more eccentric – she once attempted a striptease when one was neither intended or expected – and drifted into private life. In 1974 and 1975 she suffered strokes and was moved to a retirement apartment in New York where Huck, who had a fiery temper and was never popular with her friends, attempted to plead poverty on her behalf. Later they moved to a home she had purchased at Henley-on-Thames outside London. There, now blind, she lived as almost a total invalid, until her death in her 93rd year on January 20, 1987. Next day, Huck, her companion for almost 40 years, suffered a fatal heart attack and they were buried side by side near her mother and sister in a small cemetery near Peel Fold.   *Mel James*

Beatrice Lillie and Billy de Wolfe combined in 1957 to produce a smash hit golden anniversary revue of the Ziegfeld Follies at New York's Winter Garden. [Photo, courtesy Charles J. Humber Collection]

"BEATRICE LILLIE HAS NEVER BEEN FUNNIER!" —Chapman N. Y. Daily News

BEATRICE LILLIE ZIEGFELD FOLLIES BILLY DE WOLFE

The Glorified ZIEGFELD GIRLS in America's Most Famous Revue

Joseph Elzéar Bernier

Ulysses of the Arctic   **1852 - 1934**

Canada's vast arctic wilderness has always been perceived as just beyond the last line of civilization and cultivation, a permanent frontier. The immensity of the land inhibited thoughts of occupation or proprietorship, and it took men such as Joseph Elzéar Bernier to determine its extent and its boundaries and, most importantly, to establish its sovereignty. Whereas eighteenth and nineteenth century wayfarers had struggled to find passages west, master mariner Bernier explored and mapped the Arctic as an end in itself. In 1909 he unveiled a plaque on Melville Island that proclaimed, to the world, the Arctic Islands of Canada.

Born into a family of mariners at L'Islet, Quebec, on New Year's Day 1852, Bernier was bound for the sea as a cabin boy at 14 and was master of his own vessel at 17. His career involved commanding over 100 ships on many seas and crossing the Atlantic Ocean 269 times. Several years as a dockmaster for the Lauzon shipyard, managing the Dominion Ice Company, and serving as governor of the Quebec prison in the 1880s and 1890s allowed Bernier to plan and promote a strategy for polar navigation. He believed in a sector theory of Arctic sovereignty whereby a country facing the North Pole rightly should possess the islands within a triangle from the northern shore of its mainland to the apex at the pole.

Bernier campaigned for an expedition to the North Pole in 1902. As early as 1872, he acknowledged that Arctic region navigation had captured his imagination: "My knowledge of ice conditions in the St. Lawrence and in the North Atlantic, coupled with an experimental trend of thought, led me to read up the history of polar explorations in my spare time, and to study assiduously the problems of Arctic navigation. From 1872, my cabin library on shipboard consisted mainly of books on Arctic travel, and the latest Arctic maps were always in my chartroom."

Born at L'Islet, Quebec, on January 1, 1852, Bernier, at the age of three, embarked for the Mediterranean where he remembered the sacking of Sevastopol during the Crimean War (1854-56). Master of the 216-ton brigantine St. Joseph at age 17 – "the youngest skipper in the world" – he would command 105 ships and cross the Atlantic 269 times before he died.

Both the North Pole and the Northwest Passage frustrated Bernier, but he made a considerable contribution toward the understanding of Arctic travel and the management of such external threats as whalers penetrating the Arctic Ocean from the east. Bernier navigated Hudson Bay in 1904-05 and, from 1906 to 1911, made official voyages on behalf of the Dominion government to assert Arctic sovereignty. As Captain of the three-masted steamer *Arctic,* by 1910 Bernier had left documentation declaring sovereignty on most of the Canadian islands up to the 80th parallel.

Enticed by the rumour of gold on Baffin Island, Bernier left government service and made private expeditions into the Arctic archipelago from 1912 to 1917. He patrolled the eastern Arctic for the government from 1922-25, charting new territories until he retired at the age of 73. Two years later he was called back to the Arctic to plot a polar route for grain ships using the port of Churchill on Hudson Bay. Bernier, one of the world's most talented explorers, died at Levis in 1934 at age 82.

Other famous Arctic explorers received recognition for daring Arctic exploits, but much of their information was derivative and based on the navigation experience of J. E. Bernier. His reputation was built upon twelve Arctic expeditions in one of the most severe climates on earth. Bernier gave up his quest for the ever-elusive North Pole for the establishment of Arctic sovereignty. He claimed, "I regarded this work of greater importance than any attempts to reach the pole so far as Canada was concerned."

Although Bernier made mere inroads in the vast Arctic landscape, his stark flags were like the wands of a mystical sovereignty. It would later take the occupation of Hudson's Bay Company fur traders and the Royal Canadian Mounted Police to convince the international community and skeptical native people that Canada actually extended to the North Pole. As a symbolic gesture, Bernier proclaimed the Arctic Islands as Canadian; this was somewhat surprising to Inuit peoples who had known several of the islands as home for generations. The definition of sovereignty, self-government, and land management is still undergoing negotiations with original peoples, but Bernier ensured that it would be Canada that would do the negotiations in the Arctic Islands.

Larry Turner

The Arctic, a barquentine with a length of 165 feet, made 12 expeditions into the polar seas between 1904 and 1925. Captain Joseph Elzéar Bernier's chief purpose for these expeditions was to establish Canadian sovereignty over all the islands he could reach north of the mainland between the 60th and 141st meridans of west longitude.

CANADIAN GOLD RUSHES

El Dorado Fever

WHEN THE PADDLE WHEELER *COMMODORE* arrived at Fort Victoria from San Francisco on April 25, 1858, the 450 passengers on board more than doubled the size of the town that had no hotels or other public buildings to accommodate them. This did not really matter, however, as those arriving were eager to seek their fortune up British Columbia's Fraser River in the biggest gold strike since the California Gold Rush of 1849.

In the next three months an estimated 27,000 gold seekers sailed from San Francisco to Victoria. Another 8,000 travelled overland through the Oregon Territory to seek their fortune. Their first main stop was at the confluence of the Thompson and Fraser rivers. Then, in the 1860s, it was on to the Cariboo district until the dramatic discovery of gold in the Klondike brought worldwide fame to the Yukon in 1898....

Although reports vary, consensus is that the Fraser discovery was actually made in 1856. Donald McLean, the chief trader of the Hudson Bay Company in Kamloops, reported to James Douglas, the chief factor and acting governor of Vancouver Island, that Indians had brought him gold from the Fraser area. On receiving the letter in February 1857, Douglas asked McLean to "collect a large party of Indians," and proceed to the gold district, and "make them search and wash for the precious metal...."

Another letter from Douglas that November suggested that McLean send the gold to Fort Langley, near the mouth of the Fraser River, by February 1858, so that it could be sent the next month to England. A California newspaper on April 11, 1858, confirmed this when it reported that "*The Princess Royal*, a vessel belonging to the Hudson's Bay Company, sailed on the 29th ult. for England with 1,000 ounces of gold dust from the Thompson River Mines."

Nine days after that story appeared, the *Commodore* sailed from San Francisco for Victoria, where the prospectors, on realizing they still needed to reach the mainland, did not wait for

Background: *Some 35,000 goldseekers rushed to British Columbia's interior between 1858-1865. They came from around the world to seek their fortune, literally carving the 400-mile Cariboo Road out of rock, cliff, and canyon. [Photo, courtesy British Columbia Archives and Record Services]*

Left: *Barkerville grew up around the 50-foot shaft sunk by William Barker whose gold discovery along Williams Creek in 1862 yielded some $600,000 by 1866. The northern terminus of the Cariboo Road, Barkerville was inhabited by 10,000 stampeders by 1863. So much gold was being discovered in the region that some miners hired agents with guns, as this 1865 Barkerville photo demonstrates, to assure safe delivery of gold nuggets to Victoria.* [Photo, courtesy National Archives of Canada/C-088917]

"CARIBOO" CAMERON 1820-1888

Born in this township, John Angus "Cariboo" Cameron married Margaret Sophia Groves in 1860. Accompanied by his wife and daughter, he went to British Columbia in 1862 to prospect in the Cariboo gold fields. That year at Williams Creek he struck a rich gold deposit. While there his wife died of typhoid fever and, in order to fulfil her dying wish to be buried at home, he transported her body in an alcohol-filled coffin some 8,600 miles by sea via the Isthmus of Panama to Cornwall. She is buried in the nearby Salem Church cemetery. Cameron built this house, "Fairfield", in 1865, and in 1886 returned to the B.C. gold fields. He is buried near Barkerville, B.C.

Archaeological and Historic Sites Board of Ontario.

Above: *Born in Glengarry County, Upper Canada, John Angus Cameron travelled some 12,000 miles to stake claims in the Cariboo. Shortly before striking gold at Williams Creek in 1862, he lost his family to typhoid. To fulfil the dying wishes of his wife, it took "Cariboo" Cameron over one year to transport the remains of both wife and daughter from Barkerville, British Columbia, to Cornwall, Ontario.* [Photo, courtesy Charles J. Humber]

Above: *Although British Columbia's Cariboo district was mined into the 20th century, the spectacular discoveries were made in the early 1860s. Claims even then were feverishly reworked, redug, and rediscovered. This Grouse Creek sluicer from near Barkerville was still pocketing gold when Frank McLennan photographed him in 1867.* [Photo, courtesy National Archives of Canada/C-021575]

Right: *Getting supplies to the Cariboo district was a problem. Oxen-drawn wagons and mules were the main source of transportation. Of all the contrived methods for transporting freight, the most bizarre was by camel. The odour, personality, and soft hooves of the dromedaries proved, however, to be their shortcomings. By 1864 the Dromedary Brigade of 23 was disbanded.* [Photo, courtesy British Columbia Archives and Record Services/A-347]

steamers but built their own small boats, sailed across the Strait of Georgia and up the Fraser River during the low water season to Fort Yale. Even before reaching this isolated outpost, some began panning up to five ounces of gold a day while others moved up river hoping to find the mother lode.

Among the more experienced miners was Peter Dunlevy of Pittsburgh who, in May 1858, befriended Tomaah, the son of an Indian chief. Tomaah told Dunlevy and his four companions he could show them a river "where gold lay like beans in a pan." By the end of the month, these five were panning gold in Little Horsefly Creek, just 12 hours before a second party arrived. The two groups joined forces and started the Cariboo Gold Rush that drew thousands of prospectors over the next decade to numerous creek beds containing gold.

Keithley Creek, discovered in 1860 by veteran prospector Ben McDonald, was named for William Keithley, one of the original party of four. Before the year was out they made a second strike on Antler Creek. After staking their claims, William Keithley and a partner returned to get supplies at a camp that had sprung up at their initial strike. Their attempt to avoid alerting others came to nought when they discovered, on leaving after dark, that "hordes of men were packed and snow-shoed up, ready to follow the pair wherever they had come from." So wrote Donald Waite in *The Cariboo Gold Rush Story* (1988).

Other discoveries in 1861 at Williams, Lightning, and Lowhee creeks (250 pounds of gold nuggets were picked up in five weeks at the latter) prompted gold seekers, road contractors, traders, pack train operators, con artists, card sharks and prostitutes the world over, to go to British Columbia's interior. In 1862, Governor Douglas, who had earlier persuaded the miners themselves to build a four-foot-wide mule trail to the Fraser strike, commissioned an 18-foot-wide wagon road from Yale to the Cariboo, some 400 miles long. By awarding contracts to a number of road builders that included The British Army Royal Engineers, Douglas reinforced that the territory was British.

Not all, however, reached the Cariboo that way. A party of roughly 200 left Toronto by train in May 1862, bound for St. Paul, Minnesota, then by ox cart or ship to Winnipeg, and by ox cart to the Rockies. Despite assurances that a good trail to the gold fields existed, there were no good trails from the foothills of the Rockies and beyond. This caused incredible hardships and death before groups straggled into Fort George and Fort Kamloops in mid-September. Another party of 26 from the coal mines of Wales who sailed around Cape Horn to sink shafts at Lightning Creek in the summer of 1863 suffered from scurvy instead of reaping gold.

An enterprising American bought 23 camels from the U.S. Army (they could carry twice

the load of a mule) and shipped them to the Cariboo. Their soft hooves were not suitable for sharp rocks, however, and many went lame. They were outfitted with rawhide boots which worked, but the peculiar camel smell stampeded other horse and mule trains. As a result of law suits, the camels were turned loose, and so ended the "Dromedary Express."

Even though many of both groups squandered their fortunes one way or another, some who went to the Cariboo made fortunes as gold strikers, or as traders. Isaiah Diller, who struck gold on Williams Creek, vowed he would not leave until he had mined his 240-pound weight. Stories claim he left with more than his weight, returned to his mother's New York farm the day it was being auctioned, bought everything put up for sale, and returned it to his mother.

Another successful miner, German-born Edward Stout, was wounded by hostile Indians before discovering Stout Gulch on Williams Creek. He married and settled in Washington State where he died just shy of being 100 in 1924. Henry Beatty of Toronto returned home and invested his find in a shipbuilding venture that made him a millionaire. Bob Stevenson, who arrived with his father as a lad from Glengarry County, Ontario, and who stayed after his dad went home, became a shrewd trader and eventually a mine owner. One of the people he helped was another Glengarry native, John A. Cameron, who made and lost a fortune but is chiefly remembered as the man whose wife died and who, to keep a promise, had her body dug up twice before reinterment in Glengarry. Her remains were dug up a third time when a U.S. newspaper raised the suspicion that Cameron had hidden gold in her coffin. The newspaper was wrong.

Billy Barker, who left England and wife and daughter for the California Gold Rush, struck it rich in the Cariboo and married another English girl at Victoria in 1863. They returned to Barkerville, the town named after him, which became the largest community west of Winnipeg – a title that would be relinquished to Dawson City during the Klondike strike some 35 years later. As in Dawson, hurdy-gurdy girls were transported from California to dance with the miners at one dollar a fling.

An Anglican minister in Lillooet arranged to have English girls brought out to marry the miners, but some wed in Victoria and some who reached the Cariboo turned to prostitution. They were a tough lot according to the Victoria *Colonist*. "They dress in male attire and swagger through the saloons and mining camps with cigars and huge quids of tobacco in their mouths, cursing and swearing, and looking anything but the angels in petticoats heaven intended they should be."

The Cariboo was mined well into the twentieth century, long after the last and greatest gold rush of the period – the Klondike – was but a memory. As early as 1873 some prospectors were searching for gold in the Yukon. It took another 23 years, however, before there was a bonanza discovery. Two men are given credit for the strike: Robert Henderson, a native of Lunenburg, Nova Scotia, and George Carmack, the son of a Fortyniner.

Carmack, in the Yukon more as a trader than prospector, was married to an Indian and had two close friends, both native: "Skookum" Jim and "Tagish" Charlie. Henderson met and urged Carmack in 1896 to test the Rabbit Creek gravel bed near present-day Dawson City, cautioning the

Once the ice melted on the northeast side of the passes, flotillas, such a this one on Lake Marsh, captured on camera by E.A. Hegg on June 6, 1898, were set loose and the mad rush to see who first got to the Klondike was on. [Photo, courtesy National Archives of Canada/C-28615]

In the land of the midnight sun, one could "rock for gold" all day long and easily lose track of time. There was so much gold at Bonanza Creek, a tributary of the Klondike River, that it was difficult for a "rocker" to stop looking for gold for fear someone else might discover what he neglected to find. [Photo, courtesy National Archives of Canada/PA-16223]

California-born Carmack never to disclose his findings to anyone, especially his Indian friends. He didn't want Indians registering any gold claims! On August 16, 1896, Carmack discovered one of the world's richest gold beds at what later would be called Bonanza Creek. He not only disregarded Henderson's caution but happily shared his findings with anyone he met on his way to register his claims.

Within weeks prospectors from all over the territory converged near present-day Dawson City. News of the strike did not reach the outside world until 11 months later when two steamers arrived at Seattle and San Francisco in mid-July 1897 with tons of gold and a number of celebrating prospectors. This signalled a stampede "heard round the world."

Lured by both the thought of becoming rich and the adventure of finding gold in the depressed economy of the period, thousands from around the world stormed north to the Klondike. Some became rich, but thousands suffered incredible hardship and death in their quest for the elusive mineral that could be found in abundance in one spot and nowhere in the muck of shafts dug only a few feet away.

A dozen routes to the discovery were possible. The easiest but costliest was by sea from San Francisco, Seattle, or Victoria to St. Michael, Alaska, on the Bering Sea, where steamboats could travel 1,700 miles up the Yukon River to Dawson City. The winter freeze-up, however, stranded all but 43 of the 1,800 people who travelled that route in the summer of 1897, and it was July 1898 before those who persevered reached Dawson.

Another 3,500 took the all-American route from Valdez, Alaska, to avoid Canadian customs, but many could not cross the 20-mile-wide glacier they encountered beyond that port city. Only a few reached the Klondike taking this route. Two other all-American routes proved equal failures. Two Canadian routes, one through British Columbia and another from Edmonton, were equally devastating. Frostbite that caused gangrene, snowblindness, scurvy, starvation, even suicide were the result. There was no easy access to the gold fields!

Most of those who eventually made it did so through two passes, the White and Chilkoot. The White, a 45-mile narrow, winding route of gumbo, boulders, crevices, rivers, and hills, became the burial ground for more than 3,000 overworked, ill-treated, and ill-fed pack horses driven by some 5,000 people attempting the route. "The horses died like mosquitoes in the first frost and from Skagway to Bennett, they rotted in heaps," American reporter Jack London wrote.

Many who reached Skagway, at the head of Alaska's Lynn Canal, became victims of another kind – victims of the Soapy Smith gang that cheated, robbed, and even murdered at will, since Smith controlled the town, which NWMP Superintendent Samuel B. Steele described in his memoirs as "little better than a hell on earth."

On the Chilkoot Pass, people themselves became the beasts of burden as animals couldn't make the final four-mile climb from Sheep Camp to the summit. Everything had to be carried, and everything meant at least a year's supply of goods, a rule rigidly enforced by Steele and his North West Mounted Police stationed at the summits of both the White and Chilkoot passes. For those who couldn't afford to pay Indian packers to carry their supplies, it meant making 30 to 40 trips to the summit and beyond to Lake Bennett. Those who made it then worked feverishly building boats of every description to take them the remaining 500 miles to the gold fields.

Spring breakup occurred in late May and "the whole freakish flotilla of 7,124 boats loaded with thirty million pounds of solid food was in motion," wrote Pierre Berton in his 1957 best-seller, *Klondike*. On reaching Miles Canyon, however, 150 boats were destroyed and five people drowned in the first few days when they attempted the five-mile run of the Squaw and White Horse Rapids.

A handful of Mounties with Steele in command arrived. As he did in connection with the supplies required, Steele dictated rules. A corporal with riverboat experience was put in command to assess the suitability of each boat, provide experienced men to sail them when necessary, and ordered women and children to walk beyond the rapids five miles distant. A penalty of $100 was also imposed for anyone breaking these orders, and while some resented his dictum, few boats or lives were lost among the estimated 30,000 people who traversed the route that same summer.

As a result of this influx, Dawson became a city overnight. Unlike Skagway, there was little crime, even though the city was wide open six days a week, 24 hours a day. Only at Saturday midnight did the saloons and dance halls close until 2 a.m. Monday, another regulation imposed by Steele who turned a blind eye to prostitution and drinking but banned guns and imposed stiff penalties on card sharks and con men of any kind. Sentences for breaking the rules imposed by the NWMP were steep, the most severe being a sentence to the woodpile – which could mean months of hard labour sawing wood to heat the government buildings in Dawson.

Dawson remained the biggest city west of Winnipeg until the discovery of gold in Nome, Alaska, in mid-summer 1899. Within a week, 8,000 miners left and the Klondike rush was over. Gold continued to be mined by a few major companies with sophisticated equipment for another half century but Dawson's main interest and industry became tourism when Parks Canada rebuilt a number of the old buildings. Thousands visit the historic site each summer, lured in part by its history as one of the most romanticized gold strikes of all time, partly because of the imagination of a bank teller. His name was Robert Service, who in 1907 – a decade after the stampede began – created such legendary but fictional poems as "The Shooting of Dan McGrew" and "The Cremation of Sam McGee" in his first published book, *Songs of a Sourdough*.

Mel James

From 1896-1900, Dawson City grew from a murky swamp to become the biggest city west of Winnipeg. In 1898, 50,000 stampeders landed on the banks of the future city to seek their fortune. This view of Dawson was taken at midnight, June 2, 1899. [Photo, courtesy Charles J. Humber Collection]

1883 - 1955

Father of Ultrasonic Research

ROBERT WILLIAM BOYLE, a native of Carbonear, Newfoundland, is one of the truly unsung figures in Canadian scientific history.

Boyle was both an influential force in the development of modern physics methods within this country and one of the foremost researchers on radioactivity and ultrasonics in the first half of the twentieth century.

But even more significantly, he can be remembered as one of the fathers of "Sonar" (Sound Navigation and Ranging) discovered during World War I. Sonar became a crucial British antisubmarine tracking defence during World War II and is now a standard feature on virtually all commercial fishing boats (to locate schools of fish and underwater obstacles).

Boyle's academic career would foreshadow his greatness as a researcher. While in under-graduate studies at McGill University in Montreal, he qualified for several awards (including the British Association Medal) and it was there that he first came under the wing of Ernest Rutherford, the world's most prominent experimental physicist at the time, whose research on radioactivity won him the Nobel Prize for Chemistry in 1908. Boyle's important work on the properties of radium can be found in Rutherford's "Radioactivity," and for these efforts he was granted McGill's first Ph.D. in 1909.

That same year he followed Rutherford to Manchester University to undertake further research on radioactivity alongside several other notable young graduates including H.C. Mosley and Niles Bohr, the latter winning the Nobel Prize for Physics in 1923. In 1912 Boyle returned to Canada accepting, a position as the first head of the department of physics at the University of Alberta where he began his ground-breaking research on ultrasonics.

However with the outbreak of World War I, Boyle joined the staff of Britain's Board of Invention and Research, working for the Royal Navy at Parkeston Quay. In 1916 he was placed in charge of top secret research on "asdics" (the code name for Sonar) – submarine detection by the "echo method" using high frequency sound waves. By the end of 1918, Boyle's research team was obtaining ranges of 1400 yards with good bearing and the Royal Navy was ready to try out this new technology – which would later prove invaluable against German U-Boats.

This breakthrough was achieved without the benefit of modern electronics.

After the war, Boyle returned to the University of Alberta where he continued his research on ultrasonics (with his contributions cited in both the *Dictionary of Applied Physics* and

Encyclopedia Britannica). He was appointed Dean of the Faculty of Science in 1921 and became a member of the Alberta Council of Scientific and Industrial Research, positions that were instrumental in establishing western Canada as a presence for original scientific investigation.

In 1929 Boyle accepted another challenge, becoming Director of the National Research Council Laboratories' new Division of Physics and Electrical Engineering in Ottawa – a post he held until his retirement in 1948. Over the course of those 19 years, his division contributed major innovations in radar and related devices to the Allied war effort, helped to build up Canadian industry, and took root as a world-class scientific laboratory.

A garrulous bachelor known to friends as "Billy," Boyle was an avid fisherman and world traveller. He died suddenly in London, England, at the age of 71 with a long list of achievements to his name.

He was elected to The Royal Society of Canada in 1921 (serving as president of Section III in 1924-25), was awarded an LL.D. by the University of Alberta in 1933, was a member of the Engineering Institute of Canada and Chairman of the Imperial Oil Fellowship Selection Committee (1946-49), and sat on the advisory board of the Royal Military College (1927-38). Well-known and esteemed in international circles, he was a much respected Fellow of the American Physical Society and the Acoustical Society of America.

And while his name is conspicuously absent from the nation's annals, in 1940 Boyle joined the company of such celebrated Canadian scientists as Sir Frederick Banting, Dr. Wilder Penfield, and Michael Smith, Ph.D. as a recipient of the esteemed Flavelle Medal from the Royal Society of Canada (RSC). In handing down its annual award for Science, the RSC acknowledged Boyle's research on submarine detection during the latter part of World War I (specifically the development of asdics) "which led to results of great value during World War II and is cited as an important scientific contribution to the techniques of anti-submarine warfare and national defence."

Michael Beggs

Robert Boyle's mentor was Lord Rutherford, considered the greatest experimental physicist of the 20th century. Both Rutherford and Boyle were at McGill together, teacher and student respectively. Rutherford left for the University of Manchester in 1907. Following completion of his Ph.D. at McGill in 1909, the same year Rutherford won the Nobel Prize for Chemistry, Boyle rejoined his mentor at Manchester. Upon completion of his post-graduate studies there, Boyle accepted a position as the first head of the Department of Physics at the University of Alberta. There he began a lifelong career in ultrasonic research.
[Photo, NAC/C-37776]

FRANK STRONACH

FAIR ENTERPRISE Founder

HE CAME TO CANADA at age 22 with nothing more than a suitcase, a few hundred dollars and a penchant for hard work, and within several decades he parlayed his business hustle and toolmaking know-how into what would become one of the largest automotive parts manufacturing companies in the world.

His name: Frank Stronach. His company: Magna International Inc., the world's most diversified automobile parts supplier, with $6 billion in annual sales and 24,000 employees at more than 100 manufacturing and product development facilities. His vision: the creation of a revolutionary new economic culture known as Fair Enterprise, the cornerstone of which is a Corporate Constitution that guarantees the rights of employees, management and investors to share in the profits they all help produce. It was a brilliant business innovation that made Magna a world leader and Frank Stronach one of Canada's great pathfinders....

Frank Stronach was born in the small town of Weiz in the foothills of the Austrian Alps. He grew up in a working-class neighbourhood ravaged by war and depression, and left school at 14 to apprentice as a tool and die maker. Driven by a desire to travel the world, he arrived in Montreal in 1954 and travelled by bus to Kitchener, Ontario, where he landed a job as a dishwasher in a local hospital. After saving enough money, he moved to Toronto to look for work in his toolmaking trade.

By 1957, Frank had opened his own business, Multimatic Investments Ltd. Using personal savings and a $1,000 overdraft, he purchased some second-hand lathes and milling machines and set up shop in a rented gatehouse in Toronto's old manufacturing district. It was here, working long hours, spending the night on a cot next to his lathe, that Frank began building his small operation into Canada's largest automotive parts manufacturer. By the end of 1957, his company had ten employees. Soon after, the firm landed its first automotive parts contract – an order to produce metal-stamped sun visor brackets for General Motors in Oshawa. The company never looked back.

As the company grew, Frank held on to his best managers by giving them a share of the profits and ownership. In so doing, he was able to harness their entrepreneurial energy and enthusiasm and place the company on a path of phenomenal growth. Initially, only managers participated in the profit and equity sharing arrangement. But in order to generate even greater growth and to avoid the adversarial labour/management conflicts he saw taking shape around him, Frank wanted to give every employee a share of the company's profits and ownership, as well, making each of them a part-owner with a tangible stake in the company's success.

In the late 1960s, his company merged with Magna Electronics, a publicly-traded firm. As Chairman of the new firm, Frank expanded the profit and equity participation plan to include every employee, and the concept of "Fair Enterprise" was born.

Frank Stronach's Fair Enterprise business philosophy provided the foundation of Magna's unique corporate culture. At the heart of this culture is an operating philosophy based on profit-sharing between the three driving forces of the business: investors, employees and management. Each of these key stakeholder groups receives a pre-determined percentage of the company's annual pre-tax profits. This profit and equity sharing principle –sometimes referred to as Magna's "success formula" – is enshrined in a governing Corporate Constitution that clearly defines the rights of all employees and investors. Employees receive part of the profits in cash, while the remaining portion is used to buy Magna stock on their behalf, making them shareholders.

As a testament to the unique entrepreneurial culture established by Frank Stronach, Magna began booming in the 1970s. Over the next decade, company sales skyrocketed from $10 million to $180 million annually, and the number of factories grew to more than 40. A decade later, Magna had more than 100 factories throughout the world, and annual sales approaching two billion dollars. The company was opening a new plant every six to eight weeks and producing more than 5,000 different automotive components.

However, the company's meteoric expansion would eventually lead to problems. The company had borrowed heavily to finance its rapid growth. By 1989, in the throes of one of the worst industry downturns in decades, Magna became seriously overextended.

Frank worked with a special management team to restore Magna's financial health. In 1991 the company succeeded in raising a $100 million convertible bond issue. It marked the beginning of Magna's remarkable recovery and re-emergence as one of the preeminent auto parts suppliers in the world. Share prices, sales and profits all climbed to new record levels.

Today, Magna's Fair Enterprise culture stands as a role model of business success. Magna is not only expanding once again throughout North America, but also in Europe, where the company has made a number of strategic acquisitions, and where Frank Stronach, founder of Fair Enterprise, continues to play a key role in charting Magna's course as a global leader in the automotive industry.

Mel James

IT IS GENERALLY WELL KNOWN that the ingenious CANADARM manipulating device carried on all NASA Shuttle vehicles to launch and repair satellites and other spacecraft was designed and built in Canada by Spar Aerospace. The virtually faultless operation of the arm has been a major influence in the successful launch of a large number of important projects over fifteen years of Shuttle operations. However, less well known is Canada's tremendous contribution to the United States space programs in the pioneering days of the late '50s and throughout the '60s and early '70s when the single-man *Mercury,* the two-man *Gemini,* and the moon-landing *Apollo* projects were being developed.

The cancellation of the Avro *Arrow* supersonic fighter project on February 20, 1959, initiated the breakup of the extraordinarily talented team of engineers at Avro Canada, a team that had put Canada at the forefront of world aviation technology with the design and development of such projects as the *C 102 Jetliner*, the first jet passenger plane to fly in North America, the *CF 100* all-weather fighter, and the legendary *CF 105 Arrow.*

In the meantime, the newly formed Space Task Group at the National Aeronautics and Space Administration (NASA) facility at Langley, Virginia, led by Robert Gilruth, former Assistant Director of the National Advisory Committee for Aeronautics, was overloaded with urgent work on the *Mercury* space capsule design. At the time Gilruth was desperate to find experienced engineering personnel to develop the project. Gilruth had been involved in the wind tunnel and free-flight model testing of the *Arrow* models at Langley and the firing range on Wallops Island and was well aware of the unique capabilities of the Avro engineering team. He was quick to take advantage of their availability and made an arrangement with Avro to borrow a team of approximately 25 engineers to go to Langley and work on the development of *Mercury.*

The idea was to keep the ex-Avro engineers together as a team, with the intention of returning them when Avro sorted out the future of the company in the light of the *Arrow* cancellation. On the later demise of Avro Canada, the loan became permanent and the Canadian engineers were integrated into the Space Task Group, later contributing to both the *Gemini* and *Apollo* projects.

At the time of the *Arrow* cancellation, the Canadian team was led by the Chief of Design at

CANADA'S GIFT TO NASA

The Maple Leaf in Orbit

Avro, **Jim Chamberlin**. His career provides an example of the type of Canadian expertise made available to NASA at that time. Chamberlin was born in Kamloops, British Columbia, in 1915. He and his mother came to Toronto after his father was killed in World War I. He attended the University of Toronto Schools at Bloor and Spadina and is remembered by his colleagues and family for being, in his younger days, obsessed with model airplanes which he designed and flew in rapid succession.

He later graduated from the University of Toronto and also obtained a diploma from Imperial College in England. In the early 1940s he went as an aerodynamicist to work for Robert Noorduyn in Montreal. When A.V. Roe Canada (the parent company of Avro Canada) was established in 1945, he joined the engineering team as an aerodynamicist, later becoming head of the small initial project office and one of the senior designers at Avro. His work on the *C 102 Jetliner*, the first jet transport to fly in North America, the *CF 100 fighter*, and the supersonic *Arrow* was largely responsible for the remarkable flying characteristics of those aircraft.

On his appointment as team leader of the Canadians at the Space Task Group at Langley, Virginia, Chamberlin became Gilruth's close advisor and played a major role in the final design of the *Mercury* capsule that put John Glenn into orbit on February 20th, 1962 – ironically just three years to the day after the abortive cancellation of Canada's *Arrow* project. He became head of engineering and administration on the *Mercury* project and later head of the U.S. Space Task Group's engineering division, directing the multi-million dollar two-man *Gemini* project and becoming deeply

Canadian Jim Chamberlin played a major role in the final design of Mercury. This sketch of the Mercury spacecraft is the exact rendition of the one in which John Glenn orbited the earth on February 20, 1962 – just three years to the day after the Avro Arrow cancellation.
[Photo, courtesy NASA via William Mellberg]

involved in the project *Apollo* moon lander. Chamberlin received the NASA Gold Medal for his work on Gemini and was described by one of the NASA administrators as "one of the most brilliant men ever to work with NASA." At the time of his death in 1981 he was Technical Director for McDonnell at the Johnson Space Centre in Houston.

While Chamberlin's monumental impact on the United States space programs has to some extent been recognized in writings about that period, little has been written about the contributions made by the other members of the Canadian contingent who went with him to Langley. All of them contributed to the success of the American space programs, many becoming leaders of the NASA working groups involved in the design, development, launching, and tracking of the *Mercury, Gemini,* and *Apollo* vehicles. **John Hodge** became flight director on the *Mercury, Gemini* and *Apollo* spacecraft. **Fred Matthews** was a back-up flight director to the legendary Chris Kraft and was in charge of flight monitoring and the flight controllers at the tracking stations around the world. **Tec Roberts** was in charge of the trajectory group in mission control and in 1962 was largely responsible for the design of the Mission Control Center at NASA's Lyndon B. Johnson Space Centre in Houston, Texas. **Owen Maynard**, who became chief of the Systems Engineering Division on the *Apollo* spacecraft, was recognized as the focal point on that program and played a major role in the development of the Lunar Module *Eagle,* which placed Neil Armstrong and Buzz Aldrin on the moon in July 1969 – and the list goes on and on! Perhaps the most succinct categorization of their contributions is contained in *Apollo, the Race to the Moon* (1969) by authors Charles Murray and Catherine Bly-Cox:

> *As the Space Task Group's burden was threatening to overwhelm it, the Canadian government unintentionally gave the American space program its luckiest break since Wernher von Braun had surrendered to the Americans.... The Canadians ... never gained much public recognition for their contribution to the manned space program, but to the people within the program, their contribution was incalculable.*

One of the original American members of the Space Task Group recalled:

> *They had it all over us in some areas ... just brilliant guys ... they were more mature and were bright as hell and talented and professional to a man.*

Left: *Mission control for* **Mercury** *flights at Cape Canaveral, Florida. Ex-Avro engineer John Hodge was flight director on* **Mercury.** *The flight director of any space mission was described by astronaut Mike Collins as "the high priest."* [Photo, courtesy NASA via Fred Matthews]

Canadian Owen Maynard played a major role in the development of the Lunar module **Eagle.** *On July 20, 1969, Apollo 11 astronauts Neil Armstrong and Edwin ("Buzz") Aldrin touched down on the moon in the Lunar Module* **Eagle.** *The first lunar landing is recreated, right, with a spare LM at the Smithsonian's National Air & Space Museum in Washington, D.C.* [Photo, courtesy William Mellberg]

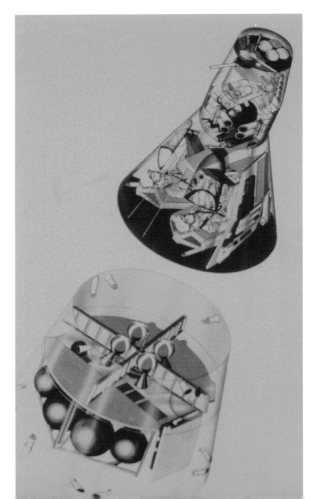

As head of the U.S. Space Task Group's engineering division, Jim Chamberlin, born in Kamloops, British Columbia, directed the multimillion dollar two-man **Gemini** *project. Viewed left, the* **Gemini** *spacecraft was much more than an enlarged* **Mercury.** *Though the two-man crew was still crowded inside a small cabin, much of their equipment was located in a two-part Adapter Module attached to the rear of the Re-Entry Module. Four solid rocket motors were housed in the Retrograde Section, while oxygen, propellants (for the thrusters) and fuel cells (for electricity) were housed in the Equipment Section. The astronauts sat side-by-side, each man having his own hatch and a forward-looking window.* [Caption and photo, courtesy NASA via William Mellberg]

Some of the exploits of the "famous twenty-five" have also been captured in other documents, but little has ever been revealed about the contributions to the American space programs made by other ex-Avro Canada engineers. **Robert Lindley**, chief engineer at Avro at the time of the *Arrow* cancellation, went to McDonnell Aviation in St. Louis and was in charge of their work on the *Gemini* spacecraft for NASA. He later joined NASA on the Shuttle program, becoming director of engineering and operations for manned space flight. In 1972 he was appointed director of project management at the Goddard Space Flight Centre. **Mario Pesando**, chief of project research at Avro, went to RCA headquarters in Massachusetts to work on the *Saturn V* project to launch the astronauts to the moon. **Carl Lindow**, formerly project manager on the *Arrow* project, went to Boeing and became project engineer on their *Saturn S-1* and *Saturn S-IB* rocket proposals. The list of contributions to the American space activity made by the great team of Canadian engineers from Avro could fill a book. It is to be hoped that some time in the future the entire story of this remarkable episode in the development of space technology will become better known.

On a wintry day in February 1962, as four million Americans watched with pride as a cavalcade of limousines slowly made their way along the streets of New York to wild cheers and mountains of ticker tape, America's first astronaut to orbit the earth, John Glenn, waved in appreciation to the crowds from the first car. In the second car was a quiet Canadian from Kamloops – James A. Chamberlin – Oh Canada!!

After the successful *Gemini* program in the late 1960s, a grateful American nation presented Jim Chamberlin with a certificate which was not only unprecedented, but which said it all:

> *National Aeronautics and Space Administration (NASA) Manned Spacecraft Centre presents this certificate of commendation to James A. Chamberlin for his outstanding contribution to this nation's space flight programs, for the technical direction and leadership of the Project* Mercury, *for his creation and promotion of the* Gemini *concept and for his guidance in the design of all manned spacecraft used in the United States' exploration of space to date.*
>
> Signed – Robert R. Gilruth, Director,
> Manned Spacecraft Centre, Houston, Texas.

Launch of the first manned Apollo *spacecraft on October 11, 1968. Chamberlin, Maynard, and other Canadian engineers were deeply involved in the* Apollo *spacecraft programs.* **[Photo, courtesy NASA via William Mellberg]**

Jim Floyd

Introduction

Diane Francis

HEIRLOOM PUBLISHING'S track record of celebrating Canada by launching quality productions without government funding is very impressive. Founded in 1985, this publishing house based in Mississauga, Ontario, has remarkably never been underwritten by taxpayers' money to publish its much-respected *CANADA Heirloom Series.*

The fact that corporations financially support opera, ballet, symphony, theatre, sporting and other cultural events convinced *Heirloom* some time ago that publications generating heritage awareness afford today's business establishments innovative opportunities....

Most Canadian corporations support a variety of cultural venues. *Heirloom* believes that business establishments, "from sea unto sea," should have similar opportunities to support nationally acclaimed specialty books. By accepting *Heirloom's* invitation to sponsor their all-Canadian productions, corporations are afforded an exceptional opportunity to identify with a visionary venture offering long-lasting, positive consequences....

What follows is a series of corporate profiles in one- or two-page vignettes showcasing some of Canada's most respected corporations. Each has accepted *Heirloom's* invitation to sponsor *WAYFARERS.* By spotlighting their own stories of corporate achievement in a "cultural ambassador" saluting Canada, they all are expressing support for the maple leaf at a critical time in their country's history.

Three out of the last five years the United Nations has saluted Canada as the best country in the world to live. It is therefore a distinct pleasure for me to introduce on the following pages the sponsors of *WAYFARERS: Canadian Achievers.* Each has contributed in a special way to make this innovative publishing venture possible. Without their support, *Heirloom's* mandate to spotlight Canada on the world stage would have been impossible.

Since 1991, Diane Francis has been editor of The Financial Post, *Canada's oldest and foremost business journal; She contributes a monthly column to Canada's only national news-magazine,* Maclean's; *She is a regular television commentator and is heard three times weekly on Toronto's CFRB and once a week on Vancouver's CKNW; She is a member of the Advisory Boards for the* Financial Post, *the Canadian Foundation for AIDS Research, and the York University East/West Enterprise Exchange Programme; She is also a Director of the Canada-Ukraine Chamber of Commerce and sits on the Advisory Committee of The Clarke Institute of Psychiatry. As a well-known author, she has written* Controlling Interest – Who Owns Canada *(1986),* Contrepreneurs *(1988),* The Diane Francis Inside Guide to Canada's 50 Best Stocks *(1990),* A Matter of Survival *(1993), and* Underground Nation *(1995). She was voted* Chatelaine *magazine's Woman of the Year in 1992.*

CORPORATE ACHIEVERS... *Generating Heritage Awareness*

Industry Canada

The Legacy of C.D. Howe

IN ONE WAY OR ANOTHER, business development has been the core theme of federal government policy since Confederation. It was formalized in the Department of Trade and Commerce Act of 1892. Then, as now, debates in the House of Commons stressed the importance of Canadian opportunities in the world economy.

Few, if any, articulated these goals more passionately than C.D. Howe. The American immigrant, who became an engineering professor at Dalhousie University, is, perhaps, best remembered as the architect of Canadian arms production during World War II.

On the strength of his inspired vision and fabled communications skills, Howe worked to mobilize Canadian industry to fight the Second World War; through his leadership on industrial development, C.D. Howe oversaw the emergence of a twentieth century power, from what was primarily an agricultural nation.

New challenges, new opportunities

A half century later, Canada faces new challenges – not from foreign enemies but from foreign competitors. It is fitting that many of the strategies for victory are, today, being developed in a building that honours Canada's great architect of industrial competitiveness – the C.D. Howe Building in Ottawa, centre for Industry Canada activity.

Industry Canada is the federal government department responsible for helping Canadian business grow, compete and create jobs: the department's sectoral, marketplace and industrial policies affect more than 70 per cent of Canada's GDP.

Within a single organization, Industry Canada encompasses the responsibilities for:

- international competitiveness, economic development and excellence in science and technology;
- telecommunications policy and programs;
- marketplace, business framework and consumer policy activities; and
- investment research, policy and review.

Growth through technology

Industry Canada, along with the agencies in the Industry portfolio, is the main focus and source of federal support for science and technology. The department's policies and programs, and those of the Industry portfolio agencies, are designed to encourage Canadian firms to develop and apply new technologies and innovative approaches.

The Communications Research Centre (CRC) is the federal government's principal research and development laboratory for advanced telecommunications and information technologies. The CRC fulfills scientific and technical responsibilities in telecommunications, for example, with regards to standards. It also helps companies by providing links between industry and government research and development activities, by fostering the transfer of knowledge and technology to the private sector, and by enabling the Canadian communications industry to compete in markets worldwide for its goods and services.

Fourteen Networks of Centres of Excellence, managed by the National Sciences and Engineering Research Council, coordinate basic and applied research in areas of strategic importance to foster the transfer of resulting technology to industry.

The Canadian Technology Network (CTN), coordinated by the National Research Council, is a national networks with international linkages for expert advice to assist small and medium-sized business to acquire technology and related business services, in order to expand their firms or increase profitability.

Trans-Forum, an Internet-based communication and information service, links higher education institutions across Canada in order to improve the transfer of their technology and expertise to Canadian firms, particularly small and medium-sized enterprises.

A pragmatic approach to industry sectoral development...

Support for science and technology also represents one of the four key pillars for Industry Canada's new approach to industry sectoral development – the other pillars being trade, investment, and human resources.

Canadian industry faces a challenge: advanced technology adoption rates are low; high technology is concentrated in a few sectors and large firms; and technology adoption by small and medium-sized enterprises remains a problem. Industry Canada has the sectoral knowledge and the analytical strengths to work with industry on pragmatic solutions to competitive challenges.

Electro Ceramics - ceramic cutting and polishing, Electrofuel Mfg. Co. Ltd. [Photo, courtesy Pierre St-Jacques/Industry Canada/NAC 6-Z-3-114]

The focus is on developing a shared view in both the private and public sectors on technology needs for the future and what the role of each sector should be in addressing these needs to encourage and influence technological innovation within Canadian industry.

Specifically, the department plays a lead role as a knowledge disseminator and network builder, delivering world-class information products related to technological issues and development; it advocates the needs and interests of Canadian industry in the development of innovative policies and programs which promote jobs and growth; and it provides a range of services to business, designed to enhance innovation, technology diffusion and adoption.

A new contract with industry

Industry Canada's expertise, information products and services are aimed at providing Canadian firms with a competitive edge in all aspects of business activity and at every stage of the business cycle. Information products include the largest single source of business information in Canada, benchmark studies and databases; analyses of markets, trade and investment, technology and innovation; and industrial research. Services are tailored to specific needs in 14 major industrial sectors ranging from pulp and paper to automobiles, aerospace to chemicals, and the health industry to telecommunications, as well as in enabling technologies such as advanced materials and advanced manufacturing technologies.

From support to small business to the promotion of science and technology, from establishment of a fair and efficient marketplace for businesses and consumers to leadership in the development of Canada's own Information Highway, Industry Canada's programs and services are creating a climate in which business can create jobs and all Canadians can prosper.

In all areas for which it is responsible, the department's policies reflect the needs of its clients. Whether they are designed to encourage economic development in Canadian regions, to increase beneficial flows of foreign investment, or to ensure the orderly introduction of new communications technologies – the department's policies are the result of close, working partnerships with the people it serves.

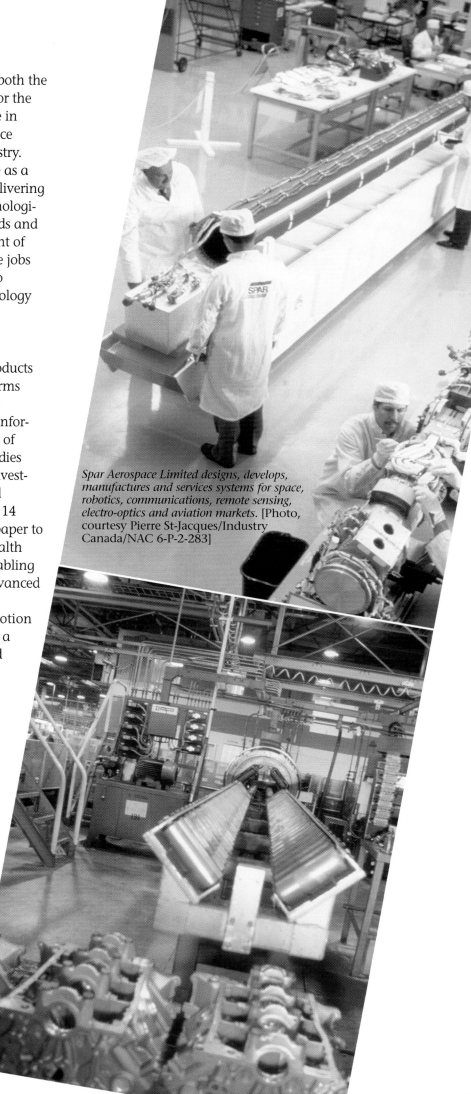

Spar Aerospace Limited designs, develops, manufactures and services systems for space, robotics, communications, remote sensing, electro-optics and aviation markets. [Photo, courtesy Pierre St-Jacques/Industry Canada/NAC 6-P-2-283]

Engine parts on an assembly line, Ford Plant, Ford of Canada Limited. [Photo, courtesy Brian Thompson/Industry Canada/NAC 6-R-1-45]

DOFASCO

A Canadian Success Story In Steel

DOFASCO BEGAN LIFE IN 1912 as a small foundry employing 150 people in Hamilton, Ontario. In 1996, in the same city, the company employs just over 7,000 people at a 700-acre site, producing about 30 per cent of Canada's flat rolled sheet steel shipments.

In the intervening eight decades, Dofasco developed a strong corporate culture and sense of family, based on the golden rule of treat others as you would like to be treated. Employees were respected for their individuality. In 1938 a 'Profit Sharing Fund' was instituted so that they might truly share in the company's success. The '30s also saw the first Christmas party for Dofasco employees and their families. The event grew to become known as Canada's largest Christmas party, with close to 30,000 adults and children (and Santa, of course) attending.

In 1943 Dofasco organized a Recreation Club. The company newsletter of the time said, "While still an experiment, we are confident that the club will grow and thrive and become a power in building healthy bodies and healthy minds and, just as important, contribute to the building of good-will among Dofasco folk." And "grow and thrive" it did, today occupying a 100-acre site as The Frank H. Sherman Recreation & Learning Centre, including baseball diamonds, soccer pitch, tennis courts, running track, golfing facilities, and twin hockey rinks, all for use by employees and their families, plus rooms allocated for employee meetings and skills training purposes.

Development of human resources is a priority at Dofasco. The company spends 15 to 20 million dollars a year on the training and development of employees, including team building, experiential learning, and providing the hard and soft skills that contribute to top level performance.

The values of caring and support which have evolved over the years at Dofasco are reflected in the roles that the company and its employees play in the community. Corporately and through the employees, support in the millions of dollars goes every year to the arts, education, health charities, and community causes, plus Dofasco employees give many hours of their time in support of local organizations and activities.

On the business side, the company has a history of innovation and leadership. In 1921 Dofasco introduced the first Universal Plate mill to Canada, and in 1935 pioneered the production of tinplate in this country. During World War II, the war effort required armour plate, a highly specialized product never previously made in Canada. Dofasco met the challenge and from late 1941 on, made all the armour plate, armour castings, and forged gun barrels for Canada until the end of the war. In 1954 Dofasco introduced the Basic Oxygen Furnace to North America, and in '55 started up Canada's first continuous galvanizing line.

Dofasco enjoyed an operating profit every year from the early '40s to 1991. Then as the company crossed the threshold into the '90s, it faced perhaps the most challenging period in its history. An economic recession combined with the phenomenon known as globalization to create unprecedented pressures on the

Our Product is Steel.
Our Strength is People.

Dofasco takes a holistic approach to the development of its human resource, and that involves providing facilities for playing hard, too – as well as encouraging employees to support the community through financial and volunteer contributions.

steel industry, resulting in virtually all North American mills operating at a loss. That the company has emerged from that difficult period vital and rejuvenated, and is now a leading performer among North American mills, building a strong foundation for future growth and enhanced shareholder value, is testament to the dedication and efforts of Dofasco people. As always, the company's strength.

Today, Dofasco is still a steel industry leader and innovator. In a decade-and-a-half, Dofasco invested over $3-billion in state-of-the-art technology. The company also entered into an international joint venture coating facility, DNN Galvanizing Corporation, which came on-stream in Windsor, Ontario in 1993. In 1995, a joint venture minimill, Gallatin Steel Corporation, began production in the United States in Kentucky. That same year, Dofasco announced a $200-million project to build an electric arc furnace/slab caster to become operational at the Hamilton plant in late 1996, with an operating expenditure of approximately $300-million finding its way into the local economy. The company's mix of facilities, with their respective world class production capabilities, positions Dofasco uniquely among North American steel mills and allows the company to compete effectively serving markets such as automotive, appliance, construction, and packaging in both Canada and the United States.

Dofasco is a participant in ULSAB (UltraLight Steel Autobody) – a global steel industry project aimed at energy conservation through significant vehicle weight reduction, made possible by innovative steels and processes.

As the third millennium looms large on the horizon, Dofasco is poised – a leaner, more responsive, flexible and profitable organization – to enter it successfully. Pursuing a strategy of operational excellence and growth, in order to improve the value chain of which it is a part, the company is building on a strong Hamilton operation and the values which reside there. Making steel is Dofasco's core business. Being successful allows the company to explore more options while meeting the challenge to grow revenue.

Steel production is an increasingly high-tech industry involving sophisticated systems pertaining to process control and the flow of information. Dofasco for instance spent a total of more than $50-million on information systems alone in 1994 and '95. The success of these improvement measures is evidenced by the achievement of such prestigious awards as Ford Q1 preferred supplier status, and Toyota's Pinnacle Award, their highest, for excellence in quality, delivery, service, and cost control. The restructured North American steel industry is proving to be a vibrant and dynamic entity, moving ahead with the times. And Dofasco is a leader of that industry in North America.

From the simple foundry of yesterday, to the unique technology, research, and customer service capabilities of today, Dofasco is a distinctly Canadian company, proud of its roots in Ontario and especially Hamilton, and of the values and relationships shared with its employees. A company whose strength is people, is going from strength to strength.

"Our product is steel" … Dofasco's state-of-the-art technology and commitment to continuous improvement has created one of the most successful steelmaking operations in North America.

"Our strength is people." Ongoing education and skills training, plus a problem-solving team approach, is focused on creating special value for our customers as seen through their eyes.

THE ECONOMICAL INSURANCE GROUP

125 Years a Canadian Success

AS Canada has grown and prospered, so has The Economical Insurance Group. In 1871, The Economical Mutual Insurance Company of Berlin issued its first policy when it insured a barn and a brick cottage in Berlin, Ontario (now Kitchener). In 1996, The Economical Insurance Group celebrates its 125 anniversary as one of the largest property and casualty insurers in Canada.

Economical grew in exciting times for Canada. During the company's first 25 years, the world's first long distance telephone call from Brantford to Paris was made and the Canadian Pacific Railway was completed. In 1879, the Canadian National Exhibition began and the first organized hockey game was played. In 1896, gold was discovered in the Klondike and the rush was on.

The Great War from 1914 to 1918 created tension surrounding the name "Berlin" in Canada. The city changed its name to Kitchener and Economical followed suit by dropping "of Berlin" from the company name.

The war years created the impetus for Canada to become a thriving industrial country. Over the ensuing 25 years, the rising population and the demand for building development created significant growth opportunities for Economical. During that time, the optimism of the '20s ended with the 1929 stock market crash. However, Economical, along with other companies, struggled on during the recovery years in the '30s and survived.

In 1935, Economical was federally incorporated and licenced for a broader range of insurance products. In 1937, Economical assumed the business of the Merchant's Casualty Co. of Waterloo, thereby adding automobile and accident and sickness products to the company product line. The purchase also provided access to business in Quebec and the four western provinces.

Economical introduced supplemental coverages for damage from perils such as wind and hail to fire policyholders in 1940. In the same year, Economical added burglary, robbery, liability and other casualty products. By 1946, premium volume had risen to $1,024,000.

Throughout the post-war years, economic expansion created a period of substantial growth for Economical. The company assumed the business written in Nova Scotia, New Brunswick, Quebec, and Ontario by the Northwestern Mutual Fire Association of Hamilton, Ontario, in 1947. This added branches in Hamilton, Ottawa, Moncton, and Halifax to existing branches in Toronto and Montreal.

The Missisquoi and Rouville Insurance Co. of Frelighsburg, Quebec, was purchased in 1956, marking the start of The Economical Group. The Missisquoi continues to operate independently.

Further strengthening occurred in 1968 when the Perth Mutual Insurance Company of Stratford was converted to a stock company and purchased by Economical. From 1971 to 1995, the company's sound financial base, solid management principles and strong independent sales force combined to develop premium volume to over $660 million.

The Waterloo Mutual Insurance Company of Waterloo was converted to a stock company and purchased in 1980. In 1995, Waterloo Insurance was reactivated to begin a new venture for The Economical Insurance Group by underwriting auto and personal property insurance on a group marketing basis.

The business focus and ethics of the founding leaders continues today. Through time and changes, prudent business practices and a clear sense of responsibility to customers have created a solid foundation for continued growth.

In 1908, the company boasted 250 agents selling fire insurance in all the principal centres of Ontario – the only province in which it conducted business. Today, The Economical Insurance Group markets personal and commercial property and casualty insurance and provides top-rated service through a force of 1,200 independent brokers, supported by an Economical staff of 1,200 located in 22 offices across Canada.

This Canadian-owned insurer has proven itself to be a strong, reliable company customers can count on.

1871
125
YEARS
A CANADIAN
SUCCESS
1996

**The Economical
Insurance Group**

**Economical Insurance
Waterloo Insurance
Missisquoi Insurance**

ALLIEDSIGNAL AEROSPACE CANADA

The company's 100K space clean room enhances its global reputation for leading edge manufacturing and state-of-the-art space products.

AlliedSignal Aerospace Canada Montreal's Coordinate Measuring Machine checks a fuel controller.

ALLIEDSIGNAL AEROSPACE CANADA is a premier market supplier of aviation, defence and aerospace products. The company is a pioneer in Canadian aviation and a recognized leader in technological innovation and engineering design. The company supports a corporate-wide mandate to constantly seek out and develop new solutions to enhance performance and reduce the acquisition and operating costs of commercial and military aircraft.

AlliedSignal Aerospace Canada is a unit of AlliedSignal Canada Inc., an advanced technology company with worldwide businesses in aerospace, automotive products, chemicals, fibres, plastic, and advanced engineered materials. Originally established to support AlliedSignal's corporate products in Canada, AlliedSignal Aerospace has developed its resources and capabilities, and also internationally markets its own products, systems, and services. It has developed into an acknowledged leader in the specialized fields of electronic environmental control systems, window heat control systems, de-icing/anti-icing systems, communication systems, electro-optics, aircraft engine controls and accessories, power management and generation systems, space products, and support services.

AlliedSignal Canada began as two separate Canadian companies, Garrett Canada and Bendix Avelex. In 1952, the Garrett Corporation, based in the United States, established a sales office in Montreal, offering the products and services of AiResearch Manufacturing Company of California. Three years later, it opened a repair and overhaul facility in Toronto to deal with the increasing level of business and Garrett's commitment to provide responsive and meaningful support of its products marketed in Canada.

The limited manufacture of avionics was initiated in 1956, and in 1960, Garrett Canada, as it was then known, obtained the contract to build the central air data computer for the CF-104 aircraft. After creating the technology base and capability to manufacture and test highly sophisticated electronic systems, the company acquired the World Product Mandate for the complete electronic temperature control systems product line. Since this transfer, these and many other products have been designed, developed, and manufactured exclusively in Canada and sold worldwide as major aircraft subsystems.

In 1989, Garrett Canada combined with Bendix Avelex to establish AlliedSignal Aerospace Canada. Bendix Aviation was first begun in Montreal in 1931 as Aviation Electric Limited. Growing into a world-class supplier of high-technology defence electronics, aerospace products and services, in 1985 it became Bendix Avelex Inc.

With customers around the world, AlliedSignal Aerospace Canada has become a major participant in the complex international arena of today's aerospace industry. Through international collaboration in North America, Europe, the Middle East, and the Far East, AlliedSignal Aerospace Canada is an experienced partner in multinational programs. The company's international activities span a wide range of intricate products and technologies in both commercial aerospace and defence programs.

Employing more than 1,600 Canadians, AlliedSignal Aerospace Canada has full-service operations in Toronto and Montreal; a regional airliner service centre at Summerside, Prince Edward Island; and an Aeromarine facility based in Richmond, British Columbia. Furthermore, the company has developed extensive repair and overhaul facilities at three locations across Canada.

AlliedSignal Aerospace Canada became an industry leader through its ongoing mission to exceed beyond the technical, quality, and reliability requirements of its customers. The company's dedication to customer satisfaction and a focus on quality, people, commitments have generated growth through innovative new product developments which will propel it into the future.

MANULIFE FINANCIAL

International Giant

Manulife Financial Corporate Head Office, North Tower Building, Toronto, Ontario.

Manulife Financial

MANULIFE FINANCIAL is one of Canada's largest, strongest and most successful financial services organizations. In 1995, Manulife's net income of $481 million represented record earnings for the second successive year, and an increase of $200 million over 1994. Manulife had the highest net earnings among all life insurers in Canada.

The company's roots are proudly Canadian: founded in 1887 in Toronto, its first president the first Prime Minister of Canada – Sir John A. Macdonald. The company lost no time in proving that it would become a force to be reckoned within the life insurance marketplace. By its first annual meeting in 1888, Manulife had sold over 900 policies worth $2.5 million – prompting the press to call the company, "The young Canadian Giant."

That "Young Canadian Giant" would soon also be a giant on the international scene. Very early in its history, the company set out boldly in search of global markets. In 1893, Manulife sold its first life insurance policy outside Canada. Four years later, its tenth anniversary, the Board of Directors endorsed Manulife's expansion into "China and other Eastern countries." In 1903, the company began selling insurance in the United States.

For over 100 years Manulife has followed a strategy of international diversification and, today, over half its revenue is generated outside Canada. While the United States accounts for most of the company's premium income outside Canada, Manulife's fastest growing market is Asia Pacific which comprises two regions. The Pacific Rim Division includes a branch in the Philippines, operations in Indonesia, South Korea, and Singapore conducted through subsidiaries in joint

Sir John A. Macdonald,
Manulife Financial's first President, 1887.

ownership with local enterprises, and a representative office in Vietnam. The Greater China Division includes Hong Kong, Taiwan, and five representative offices in the People's Republic of China. Manulife is also progressing rapidly toward obtaining a licence to do business in China, expected in 1996. This would make Manulife the first Canadian insurer to sell its products in the world's largest market.

Worldwide, Manulife operates more than 200 offices in 12 countries with more than 14,000 employees and agents.

Further diversification is achieved through subsidiaries. Altamira Management Ltd., in which Manulife holds a significant interest, and Elliott & Page Limited are among Canada's leading investment counsellors and mutual fund managers. Seamark Asset Management Ltd. provides investment management services to investors in Atlantic Canada. NAL Resources Management Limited manages investments in proven oil and gas properties for institutional investors.

Manulife Financial is known far and wide as an innovator. In 1913 the company became one of the first insurers in Canada to offer life insurance to women on the same basis as men. In 1940, Manulife became the first insurance company in North America to offer

insurance to controlled diabetics, and, in 1981, the first Canadian company to offer lower premium rates for non-smokers. In 1993, Manulife created The Manulife Bank of Canada, the first federally regulated bank opened by a life insurer.

Manulife's vision is to become the most professional life insurance company in the world, providing the very best financial protection and investment management services to customers in every market in which it operates. To help realize that vision, the company has launched several key initiatives. In 1994 Manulife acquired the Canadian group life and health insurance business of Confederation Life and the next year entered into a merger with North American Life – the first merger of two mutual life insurance companies in Canada. The result of this historic merger made Manulife Financial the largest life insurance company in Canada and one of the largest in North America with $46 billion in assets, revenues exceeding $10 billion and premiums of nearly $7 billion. The company now serves over three million customers throughout the world.

Manulife Financial's strategic focus on core businesses is critical to its ambition of becoming the leading, most professional insurer in every market where it does business. Today, Manulife is the largest group life and health carrier in Canada, with 13 per cent share of the market. It has one of the largest affinity group franchise's in Canada with, for example, 70 per cent share of the Canadian alumni insurance market and a 48-year history of serving Canadian professional engineers. In North America, it is the largest life retrocessionaire (retrocessionaires assume the reinsurance business of direct reinsurers) with 39 per cent share of the market. It is the largest individual annuity carrier in Canada with 22 per cent share of the market, the second largest provider of individual insurance in Canada with 10 percent of the market, and through subsidiary, North American Security Life, is one of the top ten variable life and variable annuity providers in the United States.

The company has a long tradition of supporting charitable organizations. Manulife directs funds to areas that will improve the quality of life for all people with emphasis on education and preventative health measures. In 1995 Manulife donated over $1.5 million dollars to over 280 non-profit organizations around the world and was designated "A Caring Company" by the Imagine program for its policy of donating and encouraging employee giving.

THE ROYAL CANADIAN LEGION

A Tradition of Service

possible by the work being done by the Great War Veterans Association which was one of the organizations amalgamated into the Legion.

By 1930 the Canadian Government had passed the War Veterans Allowance Act to provide assistance to those "aged" by the war but ineligible for disability allowances. The same year saw the Legion start to develop into what it is today.

The start of the depression propelled the Legion into activities at local, regional, and national levels to relieve the suffering of veterans made worse by the harsh economic conditions. These charitable activities, many of them for the benefit of all community members, continue today and have an effect on all of the communities in which Legion branches exist.

The Second World War brought the advent of the Canadian Legion War Services program and the Canadian Legion Educational Service provided correspondence services to the troops to prepare them for their return to civilian life. The Legion's work in securing pensions and benefits also intensified and increased again after the Korean War.

In 1958 the Legion dropped the BESL designation from its title and became The Canadian Legion. The adoption of the word "Royal" was approved by the Queen in 1960.

Today the Legion still maintains a nation-wide network of professional service officers who assist veterans, serving and ex-service members and their families in obtaining entitlements. These services are provided free of charge.

The 1,720 Legion branches in existence today concern themselves with many programs that improve the quality of life for all Canadians. Their total financial commitment and investment in those communities exceeds 200 million dollars annually for: *Veterans*

THE ROYAL CANADIAN LEGION was formed in 1926 from numerous groups that provided support to veterans and their families. Today it is the largest service club in Canada with more than half a million members and an 80,000 – member Ladies' Auxiliary in Canada, the United States, and Germany. Its major goals are still the provision of support to veterans and the perpetuation of remembrance, but it has many other programs that support the basis of community life as Canadians know it.

Following the First World War, and prior to 1925, veterans in Canada were represented by no less than 15 disparate groups whose efforts on behalf of veterans in regards to pensions, benefits, and their general well-being were not well coordinated. This changed in 1925 when the Dominion Veterans Alliance was formed and an amalgamation of a majority of the groups became the Canadian Legion of the British Empire Service League (BESL). By 1926 it was self sufficient and focussing efforts on service to veterans. This was made

Services – the continuous operation of programs supporting veterans, ex-service members and their families; *Remembrance* – perpetuating remembrance as a Canadian tradition with its annual poppy campaign, school programs, pilgrimages, and the conducting of Remembrance Day ceremonies at national, regional and local levels; *Senior Citizens* – providing care, housing, special support activities and facilities, specialized medical services, and the provision of geriatric training for those in the medical profession; *Community Service* – contributing money and volunteer hours to myriad charities and community projects; *Youth Activities* – operating a national track and field program, supporting cadet corps, Scouting, Girl Guides, youth sports organizations, and the provision of scholarships and bursaries to deserving students; *National Defence* – monitoring and supporting programs where necessary; *Canadian Unity* – Monitoring and supporting programs where and when necessary; Advocacy – participating in the debate and resolution of issues of importance to Legion members; and *Support to the British Commonwealth Ex-Services League (BCEL)* – supporting similar veterans service organizations in the Caribbean as part of a world-wide network that cares for Commonwealth veterans.

Probably the most recognizable symbol of the Legion in Canada is the bright red poppy it distributes to Canadians two weeks in advance of Remembrance Day on November 11 each year. Donations received for this symbol of remembrance are placed in trust accounts and are used only for specific activities including: Providing assistance to needy veterans, serving and ex-service members and their families; Purchasing medical appliances; Funding medical research and training; Providing bursaries and scholarships to the children and grandchildren of veterans and ex-service members; Funding accommodation and care facilities for veterans, seniors, and the disabled; and Operating the Legion's Service Bureau at its headquarters in Ottawa which acts on behalf of veterans, serving and ex-service members and their families in regards to pension submissions and appeals.

The Royal Canadian Legion is more than a social club for veterans. Working largely in the background, the Legion is able to make a significant contribution to the well-being of citizens and communities in which it exists. Without these efforts many of Canada's smaller communities would not enjoy the benefits they receive as a result of the hard work and dedication of legionnaires.

The Legion has become, and remains, an integral part of the Canadian way of life. It will remain this way into the next century and beyond. Its mission has always been, and will continue to be "to serve."

Hughy M. Greene, Dominion President, The Royal Canadian Legion, 1994-1996

RECKITT & COLMAN

Passion to be the Best

Today, Reckitt & Colman markets over 30 different brands in Canada.

TODAY, RECKITT & COLMAN is a world leader in the manufacture and marketing of household, toiletry, food and pharmaceutical products. Starting with only 25 employees the company now employs worldwide over 25,000 people. Reckitt & Colman's brands have become internationally renowned and are sold in over 40 countries. Its Canadian brands are not only familiar household names but many are also leaders in their categories. Examples include: Easy-Off Oven Cleaner, Zero Fine Fabric Wash, French's Mustard, Airwick and Wizard Air Fresheners, Sani-Flush Toilet Bowl Cleaners, and Lysol Disinfectants. Of course, this wasn't always so....

It was over 150 years ago, back in 1840, in the city of Hull, in what is now the county of North Humberside, in England, that Isaac Reckitt founded what was to become Reckitt & Colman.

Isaac Reckitt himself, was born in 1792 and had in fact established two previous businesses prior to this, both of which had failed! He was, however, a very determined man and the fact that he had now lost all his capital did not deter him. He borrowed money from his relatives and with it purchased a starch factory. His first business card simply read "Isaac Reckitt – Starch Manufacturer – late Middleton" for he had purchased the business from Charles Middleton. The factory was situated in Dansom Lane, which today remains the location for the company's U.K. pharmaceuticals factory as well as its main U.K. office. Its headquarters and Board of Directors are located in Chiswick, London.

Whilst Isaac started the business, there was no development until his four sons became old enough to help. Indeed, it was Isaac's son Frederick who became the company's first chemist and his other son, George, its first salesman. From this point on the business was known as Reckitt & Sons.

For the first nine years in the company's history, the only product sold was starch. But by 1854 Reckitt & Sons sold 22 products which competed in four product categories: starch, laundry blue, metal polish and washing paste. The company entered the pharmaceutical business in 1929 when they began the development of a liquid antiseptic that would not harm human skin. The leading brand on the market at that time was Lysol which was an excellent household disinfectant but was not designed to be used on skin. In 1932, Dettol antiseptic and disinfectant was launched and it became the company's biggest selling line. Little did they know that in just over 60 years the company would also come to own the Lysol brand!

Keen's Mustard was one of the original brands marketed in Canada.

During this time, the company began to expand its sales throughout England and to further diversify its product line into related areas. But despite this it took seven years for the company to make a profit! And it was a further eleven years before Isaac was able to pay off all his original loans. Unfortunately in 1862, only four years later, Isaac died at the age of 70.

Reckitt & Sons also grew through the development of new markets. Its first export to a Dominion took place in 1864 when it sent laundry blue to Montreal, Canada. The Canadian market was developed through agents until finally a branch was opened in Vancouver

and in 1924 a factory was acquired in Montreal. Today, factories and offices are still located throughout Canada with the Canadian Head Office in Etobicoke, Ontario.

Competition in these new markets was fierce and it was because of it that Reckitt decided to join forces with a company based in Norwich, England, by the name of J&J Colman.

Jeremiah Colman, like Isaac, was also from a family of millers. Jeremiah began milling mustard and flour in 1814. His diversification into starch and laundry blue took him into direct competition with Reckitt both at home and abroad. However, in 1913, the two decided to join the forces of their South American businesses. The partnership worked well and by 1921 they were working together in all their export markets until eventually, in 1938, they formed Reckitt & Colman Ltd.

Colman's expertise in the food industry was further enhanced by its purchase in 1903 of Keen, Robinson & Co. manufacturers of food and soft drinks. The acquisition of the RT French company based in New York, U.S.A., which made food, mustard and spices was appropriate and it strengthened the company's presence in North America.

Today, Reckitt & Colman continues to build on these solid foundations by concentrating on what it does best – marketing a wide range of quality, strongly branded consumer products. Its vision is to be an outstanding global company with leading brands and exceptional people.

Reckitt & Colman has continued to grow both through internal development of new products and the continuous improvement of existing lines. In order to fulfil its vision it has also pursued a strategy of acquisition to both strengthen its portfolio and its presence around the world. More recent purchases include: The Airwick Company in 1986 and with it the famous "Magic Mushroom" and "Stick-Up" products, Boyle-Midway in 1990 bringing with it many leading household brands and most recently, Lehn & Fink in 1995 which added Lysol and Prosolve to the fold.

With these leading brands and Reckitt & Colman's passion to be the best, it is well prepared to tackle the challenges of the 21st century.

Leading by
Building
Value

Construction of 12,000-tonne Cement Silo, 1965.

ST. LAWRENCE CEMENT

A PROMINENT MEMBER of North America's cement industry, St. Lawrence Cement's vision statement clearly identifies its goal for the future and the path this firm must follow to maintain a solid foundation in today's competitive marketplace. Over the past four decades, SLC's Mississauga Plant has built a solid reputation by providing value – value for all customers through innovative products and a keen service; value for employees through training and development; and value for community through philanthropic and volunteer support.

Whether we drive the highways of Ontario, depart the runways of Pearson International Airport, ride an elevator in an office highrise or play with children at a local playground, St. Lawrence Cement's products have become an integral and necessary role in our everyday life.

St. Lawrence Cement's Mississauga plant, which began production in 1956, proudly celebrates its fortieth anniversary in 1996. Located on Lake Ontario, 30km west of Toronto, this facility represents one of the largest and most technologically advanced cement plants in the Americas. Over the past 40 years, St. Lawrence has maintained this proud distinction through continual upgrading and improvement of its operations.

In 1968, the plant increased dramatically in size with the installation of the first large preheater kiln ever constructed in North America. The 3,000 tonne per day dry process preheater kiln more than doubled the plant's production capability while using substantially less fuel than the wet process kilns. In 1971, a 3,500 hp mill was moved from St. Lawrence Cement's Beauport plant for installation at the Mississauga facility addressing the need for increased cement grinding capacity. By 1974, cement mill # 7 powered by 9,500 hp, one of the largest cement mills in North America, was installed. Today, total plant capacity is 1.9 million tonnes of cement per year.

Improvements to the Mississauga Plant extend well beyond the grinding process. In 1988, the addition of a precalciner increased the capacity of Kiln #3 to 4,300 tonnes per day. Other operating features include the large storage hall, housing the coal and clinker used in the cement manufacturing process. Clinker is stored in two 75,000-tonne capacity silos. In 1989, a larger bag warehouse was constructed at the Mississauga plant to accommodate the increasing variety of bagged products. The heart of the plant's operations, the central control room, was upgraded in 1990 with a Honeywell TDC 3,000 control system.

This state-of-the-art high level supervisory system analyses every stage of the burning process for environmental, process, and quality parameters. The belt conveyor system, a reversible conveyor capable of transporting raw materials into the plant and conversely, clinker and cement from the plant to the dock for loading onto ships, is the lifeline of the plant. The entire conveyor system is enclosed and stretches 1.6 km from the northern perimeter of the plant to the shores of Lake Ontario.

Environmentally, St. Lawrence Cement's fortieth year began with the start-up of the $16 million baghouses designed to assist in the reduction of the amount of particulate emitted from the plant's 169 metre main stack. Operating similar to a vacuum cleaner, one baghouse replaces the electrostatic precipitators on Kiln #3, while the other replaces the gravel bed filters on the cooler. Coupled with improved maintenance and housekeeping programs, St. Lawrence Cement is committed to operating in a sound environmental manner.

1996 also heralded the implementation of SAP, a multimillion-dollar integrated business system designed to enhance St. Lawrence Cement's current information systems and business practices. Linking St. Lawrence Cement's many divisions throughout North America, SAP assists in guiding the Company into the twenty-first century.

St. Lawrence Cement's Mississauga facility is home to the Ontario Marketing Department, comprised of sales and technical service staff dedicated to meeting the demands of the ever changing marketplace. New market initiatives, such as HSF – high strength cement – and a new line of masonry cements were developed to meet the growing needs of the customer. Technical service staff are available, both at the plant and in the field, to deal with customer inquires and concerns, to assist with innovative solutions and to ensure that all industry codes and standards are maintained.

Located on the border of Mississauga and Oakville, St. Lawrence Cement is proud of its philanthropic role within both communities. Through financial and volunteer support, St. Lawrence Cement has supported such organizations as Foodshare, the Oakville Arts Council, Operation Lookout, the Living Arts Centre and the Mississauga YMCA. Proudly, St. Lawrence Cement was awarded the 1995 Mayor's Award for Business and the Arts from the Town of Oakville for its continued support of the Oakville Centre for the Performing Arts.

St. Lawrence Cement's North American operating centres include 5 cement plants, 23 cement distribution terminals, 46 ready-mix concrete plants, 17 quarries and sandpits, and 2 construction companies. The three Canadian cement plants, located in Mississauga, Joliette and Beauport (Quebec) supply 23 percent of Canada's cement production capacity.

During its 40-year history, St. Lawrence Cement's Mississauga Plant has played an important role in the industrialization and economic growth of both the Oakville and Mississauga communities. The plant's internal community of 200 employees, through their loyalty and commitment, have helped to ensure that the future of St. Lawrence Cement's Mississauga plant is as strong as the cement they produce.

Aerial view of St. Lawrence Cement's Mississauga plant.

Hatch's head office in the Sheridan Science and Technology Park, Mississauga, Ontario.

HATCH ASSOCIATES

Commitment to Excellence

IN 1955, a group of four civil engineers banded together in a small office on Toronto's Price Street. Full of talent, enthusiasm and energy, and poised to capitalize on post-war economic growth, they began what has become a firm of global reach.

The history of Hatch Associates is a story of hard work, imagination and vision. In 1958, Dr. G.G. Hatch implemented his far-sighted ideas about an integrated service. From an initial focus on heavy civil engineering in rail and transit projects, the firm expanded into process engineering in the metals industries.

Today, Hatch has grown into a consulting firm providing professional engineering, management and technology services to both the public and private sectors. The company provides a comprehensive service that ranges from research and development, design and engineering to operation assistance. Employee-owned, and driven by the talent and commitment of its people, Hatch has developed technical innovations that put it at the forefront of the world's consulting firms.

Peer recognition has been evident with seven top engineering awards: 1982 Schreyer Award, ISCOTT Greenfield Steelmaking Complex; 1985 Award of Excellence – Civil, Buffalo Light Rail Rapid Transit System; 1988 Award of Excellence – Metallurgical,

QIT-Fer et Titane Steelmaking Complex Expansion; 1988 Australian National Engineering Excellence Award – Building & Civil Design, Melbourne Underground Railway Loop; 1994 South African Project Management Excellence Award, Richards Bay Minerals – One-Million-Ton Expansion; 1994 Falconbridge Innovation Award; 1995 Award of Merit – Civil, Detroit River Tunnel Enlargement.

Among the firm's other accomplishments is its ISO 9001 registration. ISO 9001 is the new international quality management standard for product and service providers. Hatch is the first major engineering firm in North America to receive accreditation to the 1994 standards.

Today's achievements would be no surprise to the small company on Price Street – now a large multi-discipline consulting firm with over 1500 employees in 16 international offices, and projects worked in over 80 countries.

Hatch's story is a testament to the enthusiasm, vision and commitment of its employees. In meeting and exeeding expectations, and sharing the dedication and enthusiasm of its clients, the Hatch team has become a true partner in success – with an impressive past the prelude to a promising future.

SPAR AEROSPACE LIMITED

Up in the Sky ... And Down to Earth

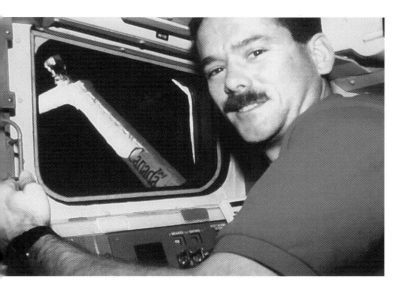

MONDAY, NOVEMBER 13, 1995, 11:45 p.m. Canadarm and Canadian astronaut Chris Hadfield are engaged in the first major task of mission STS-74. With his feet anchored in the flight compartment on the aft deck of the *Atlantis'* command station, Chris Hadfield grips the two joysticks that control the moves of the Canadarm. He lifts the 15-metre arm, emblazoned with the red and black CANADA wordmark, out of its cradle. Then, using the remote manipulator which, on Earth, cannot lift its own 410-kilo weight, the Canadian astronaut captures the five-ton Russian docking module and hoists it into position to await the coupling that will permanently attach the module to *Mir*.

During the 90-minute operation, Canadarm lifted the Russian module, tipped it 90 degrees, then positioned it less than seven centimetres from the docking ring of the *Atlantis* orbiter docking system (ODS). This was the most difficult part of the mission because both mechanisms had to be aligned with the greatest accuracy before locking. During the whole operation, Chris Hadfield kept an eye on the monitors of the new Canadian Space Vision System (CSVS). The monitors display images of small targets captured by cameras located in *Atlantis* cargo bay and on Canadarm.

Canadarm, used for the forty-third time on a Space Shuttle mission during STS-74, has never failed since it was first deployed on board *Columbia* on November 13,

1981. It has been used for such spectacular repair missions as that on the Hubble Space Telescope (1993) and communication satellites, *Intelsat* (1992), *Syncom* (1985) and *Solar Max* (1984).

The most prestigious offspring of Canadian space technology, Canadarm was born in 1974 when NASA entrusted Canada with the task of designing a remote manipulator arm for the new space shuttle program. Through the National Research Council of Canada, the federal government invested the $100 million required for its development. The challenge was tremendous: develop a tool that could reproduce in space the dexterity of the human arm and do so with bionic strength.

Spar Aerospace Limited of Toronto became the prime contractor for the project; CAE Electronic of Montreal built the training simulators as well as the arm's electronic systems; the joints were manufactured by DSMA Atcom in Toronto.

From the Canadarm's 15 years of operation, Spar has built a data base on space remote manipulators that is the only one of its kind in the world. Such expertise was put to good use in Spar's design and development of the next generation of Canadarm, the Mobile Servicing System (MSS), which will play a critical role in the assembly and maintenance of the International Space Station.

Thus, some time in 1998, astronauts on board the space station will be taking the controls of a 17-metre long remote manipulator arm able to detach itself by both its ends and crawl end-over-end, inchworm style, along the station's truss. This first element of the MSS, with its seven joints, will be able to lift objects weighing up to 100,000 kg—as heavy as the shuttle itself!

What about Earth? The technologies developed for the Canadarm and MSS programs have quite down-to-Earth spinoffs. For example, some remote manipulators, cousins of the space manipulators, have been developed for use in radioactive and hazardous environments. These remote handling systems will be used for tank waste characterization and retrieval, buried waste retrieval and stored waste handling.

These are perfect examples of the strategic wisdom shown by Canada in the development of its space policy: maximize the modest sums that our country invests in space by focussing on well-defined technological niches, with, ultimately, terrestrial applications of benefit to all of Canada.

FORD OF CANADA

Investing for the Future

The 1996 Ford Taurus

ALTHOUGH IT IS CANADA'S longest-established automobile company, Ford Motor Company of Canada, Limited, is looking more to the future than to its historic past.

In the five-year period ending in 1996, the company has invested nearly $5 billion in its Canadian plants in Oakville, Windsor, and St. Thomas. The investment exceeds spending

The 1996 Mercury Sable

The 1997 Ford Escort

by all other automobile companies combined in Canada during the same period.

Ford of Canada became the first Ford operation outside of the United States when it was established in 1904 by a group of young Canadian entrepreneurs who formed a partnership with Henry Ford. Today, it continues to play a leading role in Ford's worldwide automotive operations by producing vehicles and engines exported around the world.

Increased employment opportunities have accompanied Ford's massive investments. Compared with 1992 when the first investments were made, Ford's employment in Canada has increased by more than 2,000 to a total of 14,000 in 1996.

The investments are also paying off with world-mandate products that are built exclusively in Canada. The Oakville-built Ford Windstar minivan, for example, is exported to 40 countries around the world. Aluminum engine blocks produced at Windsor are shipped to Europe for use in Ford engines used in a number of countries.

The most recent investment announced by Ford of Canada involved the Ontario Truck Plant in Oakville, where a new paint facility and body shop were constructed, more than doubling the plant's size to 2.9 million square feet.

As a result of this project, the plant is producing the 1997-model F-Series pickup truck and thereby generating additional employment.

The 1997 Ford F-Series

Ford manufacturing plants in Windsor have an important role in the new F-Series, Canada's best-selling vehicle — car or truck — for several years. Essex Engine Plant produces the new truck's standard, split port, 4.2 litre V-6 engine, while the Windsor Engine Plant builds the optional, 4.6-litre V-8 engine. Two other Windsor plants — Essex Aluminum and Windsor Casting — produce cast iron and cast aluminum parts for the new engines.

Ford's successful 92 years in Canada can be attributed to the quality of its workforce and the quality of its products. Canadian plants have been honoured with the company's highest quality awards in competition with plants around the world.

New and exciting products that meet or exceed consumer expectations have always been "Job One" at Ford, according to Mark W. Hutchins, the company's 11th President and Chief Executive Officer.

Nearly half of the cars and trucks being offered by Ford today are new in technology, new in design and new in improved performance, Mr. Hutchins notes. Included in the new product offerings are the 1996 Ford Taurus and Mercury Sable, and the 1997 Ford Escort and F-Series pickup.

As Ford becomes a more globalized company, customers can expect even greater choice and quality in Ford cars and trucks.

Most recent investments by Ford of Canada include a new paint facility and body shop for Ontario Truck Plant, Oakville, part of nearly $5 billion invested in Canada since 1992.

W.C. WOOD COMPANY LIMITED

1996 Top Team at W.C. Wood Company

ON DECEMBER 6, 1896, when Wilbert Copeland (Bert) Wood was born, Ontario farmers like his grandfather John and his uncle Charles were still clearing land for farming. Bert was raised on that farm in Luther Township until 1909 when (again like many Ontarians) his family trekked to Saskatchewan where they took a homestead.

Bert Wood graduated in the early '20s from the University of Saskatchewan in Agricultural Engineering and joined Massey-Harris in Toronto where he worked as a research engineer on Massey's new farm machinery until the Great Depression forced Massey to lay him off in 1930.

Bert Wood saw the introduction of electric power across rural Ontario as an opportunity for a new business and founded W.C. Wood Company Limited in February 1930 to manufacture electrical farm equipment. His first product was an electrically powered grain grinder which would save farmers the necessity of having to transport grain from the farm to the feed mills for grinding and back to the farm for feed. He had

parts for his grinder cast and tooled at a local machine shop, assembled them on the back porch of his landlady's house and with the $150.00 he received from a Brampton-area farmer for his first grinder he established his new business.

Wood rented an empty candy shop on Howard Park Avenue in Toronto, bought a lathe, and machined the castings for his own electric grinders. From this one-man shop, his company developed over the next 66 years into Canada's leading freezer producer and the largest Canadian-owned appliance manufacturer.

By 1934 W.C. Wood Company had moved to a larger factory on Dundas Street north of Bloor in Toronto where it expanded its electrical farm equipment line to include an oat roller, a farm milking machine, and a farm milk cooler. In 1938 it was the refrigeration system designed for milk coolers that made it possible for W.C. Wood Company to develop its first electrically operated farm freezer. Little did the founder realize at that time that this product would be the stepping stone on the path from farm equipment to appliance manufacturer.

In 1941 W.C. Wood Company moved from Toronto to a 25,000 square foot factory at 123 Woolwich Street in Guelph, where for the next 15 years it grew, prospered and expanded to a facility of 40,000 square feet. By 1956 another move was necessary. The Company acquired the Taylor Forbes property and moved its manufacturing operation to an existing 90,000 square-foot plant at 5 Arthur Street South in Guelph where the company continues to grow to this day. By 1963, additional space was needed and the first of many additions was undertaken. As a result, the company operated two Guelph plants by 1985, totalling 600,000 square feet. By this time, the company's total manufacturing was devoted to appliance production: chest and upright freezers, compact refrigerators, compact kitchens, humidifiers, dehumidifiers, and rangehoods. More than 95 percent of the total production was for the domestic market with the remaining being shipped to the United States, South America, Europe, Asia, and the Caribbean.

By 1985 free trade was in the air and the company began focusing on a North American market strategy. As exports began to grow in the second half of the 1980s, it became apparent that the company would need a U.S. facility to take advantage of the lower operating costs in the U.S. and to broaden its product line. In April 1990, W.C. Wood opened a 137,000 square foot factory in Ohio to manufacture upright freezers for the North American market.

This new plant has provided numerous benefits to the corporation including significantly lower operating costs in serving the U.S. market, an expanded product line to meet North American needs, and significant additional capacity for its growing North American market. While most of the company's growth over the last decade has been outside Canada, and while the U.S. facility has expanded to over 370,000 square feet, the U.S. facility has given the company a broader product base which has resulted in a significant increase in exports of Canadian-made product as well.

Today, more than fifty percent of the company's Canadian production is exported. Employment at W.C. Wood Company has grown in both countries and in 1995, a third plant was added to the Canadian facilities located in Guelph.

Over the years, W.C. Wood Company has received many awards from various sources for its products including the National Industrial Design Award, presented by C.D. Howe in 1955, numerous customer recognition awards, the Province of Ontario "A" for Achievement Award, and the Canadian Award of Business Excellence.

In 1977 the company produced its one-millionth freezer and by 1991 the company celebrated the production of its five-millionth appliance. W.C. Wood Company looks forward to celebrating the production of its ten-millionth appliance before the end of this decade.

W.C. Wood Company is still a privately owned Canadian company with its owners continuing to work in the business. Its objective is to see that at the end of each year its suppliers, customers, employees, and shareholders are each a little better off as a result of it being in business. The company and its employees will continue to focus on productivity, quality, customer responsiveness, integrity, and organizational effectiveness as the cornerstone of its business.

Grandfather John Wood and Uncle Charlie in 1897 clearing family farm where W.C. Wood was born. *W.C. Wood, Founder of the Company*

Tetra Pak

The Multi-Product Company

Perhaps best known for the brick-shaped "juice box" it produces, Tetra Pak manufactures an array of packaging alternatives.

Tetra Pak packages safely and efficiently distribute a variety of liquid foods to consumers the world over.

ALTHOUGH PERHAPS still best known for the brick-shaped "juice box" carton it produces, today's Tetra Pak is a uniquely diversified company.

Uniquely diversified because this company can offer the Canadian food industry solutions to both their packaging and food processing needs. Founded in 1951 in Sweden, Tetra Pak grew to be one of the largest beverage carton manufacturers in the world. However, the company changed dramatically in 1993 when it acquired the internationally renowned food processing company Alfa Laval. From operating strictly in one industry, Tetra Pak now moved into two business worlds: food packaging and processing. Two different worlds, undoubtedly, yet very closely related.

Today, Tetra Pak can position itself as a single source supplier to its customers. State-of-the-art food processing solutions and an array of packaging alternatives are all a part of Tetra Pak's expertise.

The juice box, which today remains a popular food package of choice, is only one of many packaging options offered by Tetra Pak. The company is in no way limited to this type of packaging, instead it works to give its customers and consumers an ever-expanding spectrum of choices. For instance, Tetra Pak recently made its foray into the world of plastics. Plastic pouches and bottles are now a part of Tetra Pak's product mix.

Tetra Pak also supplies the food processing industry with processing and packaging solutions for viscous and solid foods, prepared food, fats & oils, and ice cream.

Tetra Pak is one of three divisions that makes up the Tetra Laval Group. The other divisions are:

Alfa Laval: Alfa Laval specializes in key products such as separators, flow equipment, heat exchangers, and computer-based control and monitoring systems. This company is the world's largest manufacturer of plate and spiral heat exchangers used in a variety of industrial applications including the heating and cooling of buildings.

Alfa Laval Agri: Alfa Laval Agri is the world's largest supplier of equipment, systems and accessories for dairy production and animal husbandry.

Each of the three divisions holds a strong position in its own field, and together the group of companies can service customers from the farmer's field to the consumer's table.

In Canada, the company's corporate headquarters is located in Aurora, Ontario. It is here that Tetra Brik Aseptic packages (or "juice boxes") are manufactured for dairies and juice manufacturers across Canada, and for export markets around the world. Tetra Pak has one other Canadian manufacturing facility in St-Leonard, Quebec. Here, gable top milk cartons are produced for customers across Canada and parts of the United States.

Additionally, sales and technical offices are located in Dorval, Quebec, and Vancouver, British Columbia. In Canada, Tetra Pak employs approximately 300 people in various positions including manufacturing, technical services, sales and marketing, and finance. Around the world, the company employs approximately 16,000 people in over 100 countries.

A S ANY CANADIAN CAN PLEDGE, our country is one of diversity and regionality. The sheer size of Canada contributes to this contrast. United Parcel Service Canada Ltd. (UPS), with over 20 years of service in this country, understands this diversity and helps link Canadians together by providing comprehensive package and document delivery services to every address in Canada. In fact, UPS presence in Canada currently resides with 5,600 employees and the 30,000 customers they serve each year.

UPS has followed a steady path of investment and development in Canada since commencing operations in 1975. Today, with 49 locations, 1,800 delivery vehicles and air hubs in Hamilton, Calgary, and Mirabel, UPS remains committed to Canadian business. In 1995, UPS reinforced its presence in Canada by opening a state-of-the-art call centre in Moncton and locating considerable presence in Fredericton, further enhancing its existing national distribution network.

But, as the largest package distribution company in the world, UPS' progress is not limited to its Canadian operations. UPS is no stranger to growth and adapting to changing environments. UPS is one of the few companies to provide Express package and document delivery service to more than 200 countries and territories worldwide. The company realizes that in order to compete in today's global market, it needs to respond quickly and efficiently to their customers and business partners wherever they may be.

For Canadians, that means next-day delivery of a package by 8:00 A.M. to the U.S. with UPS' Early A.M. service, and next-day service to any country in the world through its worldwide distribution network.

To ensure the company maintains its superior service commitment, UPS continues to invest in and rely heavily on technology. In 1994, UPS was the first courier in Canada to implement a fully integrated cellular network to allow faster exchange of information between dispatchers and drivers for increased speed of customer package pickup.

In early 1996, UPS introduced its Canadian-conceptualized on-line shipping software, UPS OnLine™... For The Office, which completely automates the customer side of preparing shipments, including calling for package pickup, preparing labels, and completing customs documents.

This year also marks UPS' worldwide sponsorship of the 1996 Centennial Olympic Games in Atlanta. In Canada, UPS is supporting many athletes on their road to Atlanta. The company is providing its services to demonstrate its commitment to globalism and cooperation around the world.

By continuing its local responsiveness and service approach with UPS' truly global network, UPS has become part of the landscape of Canadian business. This, combined with an ever-increasing reliance on technology, will allow UPS to continue supporting initiatives and progress of Canadians into the future.

UNITED PARCEL SERVICE CANADA LTD.

Continuing its commitment to Canada through a global approach

UPS serves every address in Canada and more than 200 countries and territories.

KRAFT CANADA INC.

JAMES LEWIS KRAFT was born in Stevensville, Ontario in 1875, and established his Canadian operations in Montreal during the 1920s. From a few horse-drawn wagons delivering innovative cheese products to grocery stores, the company's vision grew into a worldwide food business, drawing its strength from the trust of consumers, passed on from generation to generation.

To Canadian consumers, Kraft has always meant *good food and good food ideas*, and this purpose remains at the foundation of its success today. Kraft Canada employs over 4,000 Canadians and is the country's largest packaged food company with more than 30 leading brands and over 2,000 different products. Its vision is to see Kraft products on every Canadian table, at every meal.

Good Food. Good Food Ideas

To consumers, Kraft is synonymous with superior value in food – from its innovative products, recipes, and services to the way these products are marketed and distributed.

Consumers know Kraft products and the superior value they represent. Leading brand names, such as MIRACLE WHIP salad dressing, KRAFT DINNER macaroni & cheese, JELL-O gelatin, MAXWELL HOUSE coffee, POST cereals, and PHILADELPHIA cream cheese have earned consumer loyalty and become household words.

Consumers Want Value

Kraft is single mindedly focused on understanding and meeting the needs of Canadian consumers. Consumer tastes and expectations are changing constantly so Kraft continuously monitors lifestyles, trends, and changing food requirements.

Today's consumers have less time for shopping and preparing meals. They are more focused on health, more informed about nutrition and the importance of a balanced diet. Consumers want convenience, variety, and healthier options. They want superior value.

Kraft is a Leader in Innovation and Service

Process cheese as it is known today was first invented by J. L. Kraft more than 75 years ago. This dramatically changed the manufacture of cheese. J. L. Kraft's legacy has been nurtured over the years, making Kraft a leader in innovation.

In 1995 alone, Kraft introduced more than 25 new products and over 100 product improvements and line extensions – all with new relevance to today's consumer. Kraft is focused on anticipating and meeting the needs of its consumers faster and better than any of its competitors.

Kraft's consumer service goes beyond providing innovative products. On most Kraft products, consumers can find a toll-free telephone number which connects directly to the company's Consumer Response Centre. Through these toll-free numbers and its numerous consumer publications, Kraft encourages consumers to call or write for information and help regarding its various products and services. In 1995 alone, its Consumer Response Centre had more than 160,000 contacts with consumers.

Kraft knows and understands the needs of Canadian consumers.

Kraft's Consumer Response Centre has over 160,000 consumer contacts in a year.

More than 30 leading brands and over 2,000 different products.

The Kraft Kitchens bring good food and good food ideas to Canadian consumers.

Kraft's popular consumer magazine is full of tasty tips and quick and easy recipes.

Kraft Makes Healthy Eating and Grocery Shopping Easy

In 1924, J. L. Kraft hired a home economist and opened the celebrated Kraft Kitchens – one of the first of its kind in the food industry. Today's Kraft Kitchens are staffed with dietitians, home economists, food and consumer experts who form a vital link with consumers. They bring the "Voice of the Consumer" to the company, translating this voice into each food idea, program, or recipe they develop. With their consumer knowledge and food expertise, the Kraft Kitchens staff help consumers incorporate healthy, balanced eating into today's hectic lifestyles. In the course of a year, the Kraft Kitchens develop nearly 4,000 recipes as well as numerous helpful publications.

Information is Value

Kraft's *What's Cooking* publication is a unique consumer magazine full of exciting food ideas, quick and easy recipes, and tips to help consumers eat a healthy, balanced diet. It is distributed four times per year to four million Canadian households. An important aspect of this publication is consumer feedback. With each issue, consumers are encouraged to call or write-in ... and thousands do, many of them sharing how Kraft's *good food and good food ideas* are working for them. Kraft typically receives more than 4,000 valuable consumer contacts after each issue.

A Leader in the Grocery Store

Not only are consumer needs and expectations changing but so are their shopping patterns. Kraft understands how consumers shop today. It knows that consumers have less time to make purchasing decisions. With its recognized consumer expertise and its large share of the grocery store shelf, Kraft works in partnership with grocery retailers to position its products in line with consumer shopping needs. In this way, Kraft is leading the market in its consumer focused merchandising and in-store promotions.

A leader in consumer focused merchandising and in-store promotion.

MERCK FROSST CANADA INC. is Canada's largest fully-integrated pharmaceutical company. Its more than eleven hundred employees are engaged in the discovery, development, manufacture, marketing and sales of prescription and over-the-counter pharmaceutical products.

Most corporate activity takes place at the company's Kirkland, Quebec, headquarters, just outside Montreal. Regional offices are based in Vancouver, Calgary, Winnipeg, Edmonton, Toronto, Ottawa, Quebec City and Halifax.

Merck Frosst's roots in Canada stretch back nearly a century. The chemist Charles Frosst and four associates, including William S. Ayerst and Frank W. Horner, founded Charles E. Frosst & Co. in Montreal in 1899. The famous numbered analgesics such as 217® and 222® were the company's first products.

By the mid-twenties, the company was entirely family-owned. That same decade, Frosst became the first producer of synthetic vitamin D in Canada. The company's reputation as a leader in research was bolstered in the mid-1940s when Frosst pioneered the field of nuclear medicine with the development and commercialization of the first radioactive pharmaceutical products for sale in Canada and abroad.

Merck Frosst facility in Kirkland, Quebec

In 1965 Charles E. Frosst & Co. joined Merck & Co., Inc. of Whitehouse Station, New Jersey, whose history began with a German pharmacy acquired in 1668 by Friedrich Jacob Merck. The Merck family founded the American firm in 1891 and established a branch in Montreal in 1911. Towards the end of World War II, Merck & Co. Ltd. was producing penicillin in the first deep fermentation unit to be operated in the Commonwealth.

Merck continued to grow rapidly in the post-war period, merging with Sharp & Dohme in 1953 and then with Charles E. Frosst & Co. in 1965. In the late sixties, a Merck Frosst team in Montreal scored a pharmaceutical first with the discovery of timolol maleate, marked as BLOCADREN® (for the treatment of high blood pressure) and TIMOPTIC® (for glaucoma).

The Merck Frosst Centre for Therapeutic Research is the largest biomedical research facility in the country and employs more than 150 world class scientists. Since 1976 Merck Frosst researchers have been the lead team in the world in leukotriene research, naturally occurring substances implicated in respiratory diseases. Merck Frosst scientists are developing compounds that may one day represent breakthrough therapies for the treatment of asthma and other respiratory conditions.

Merck Frosst is also active in the communities it serves, particularly in the area of supporting and promoting science and science education. The company hosts dozens of field trips for students, has developed a program which sees Merck Frosst scientists visit local high schools to talk about the research they do, and is engaged in an ambitious nation-wide co-op student program. In addition to numerous other scholarships, research grants and university faculty sabbaticals, Merck Frosst also provides scholarships to pharmacy and medicine students across the country, research fellowships to medical and pharmacy schools and is a corporate sponsor of the Federal Government's Canada Scholars Program.

As the pre-eminent pharmaceutical company in Canada and as part of the world's leading pharmaceutical company, Merck & Co., Inc., the Merck Frosst name stands for superior research for superior products and for a highly desirable working environment.

ROYAL BANK OF CANADA

Fuelling Canada's Economy

IN 1864, when Royal Bank was founded (as the Merchants' Bank of Halifax), Canada's prosperity depended on trade.

> *"Every spring the arrival of the trade ships from Europe brought the harbour to life ... [with] the inflow of European goods.... In fall the pattern reversed as Halifax became the commercial centre through which passed Nova Scotia's exports of timber and fish and by-products of the port's West Indian trade in sugar, rum, and molasses."* *

If trade flows were predictable, financing was not. Merchants relied on an intricate system of bills of exchange and promissory notes which were subject to much uncertainty. Financing was dominated by London and New York.

The merchants who formed Royal Bank wanted to ensure that Canadian businesses would have access to a stable source of domestic financing. As Canada expanded westward, so did the bank, fuelling the new economy as it grew.

Some things haven't changed since 1864. Canada is still very much a trading nation. Exports generate almost a third of our Gross Domestic Product and one in four jobs. Canadian companies will always need reliable sources of financing to help them grow. And fuelling the economy is still a priority for the bank.

But who could have imagined back then that small business would become the driving force in the economy? At a time when new frontiers were defined geographically, who could have imagined that knowledge-based industries (KBIs) would redefine the frontier as an intellectual arena?

Today, close to a million small and medium-sized businesses fuel our economy. They range from tiny "mom and pop" shops to leading-edge visionaries in the global high-tech market. And they're critical to the well-being of the country.

Small businesses are job creators. They generate nearly 40 per cent of Canada's gross domestic product and employ about half its labour force. Typically, they are innovative, aggressive, and able to adapt quickly to change.

The port of Vancouver is an important gateway to the Pacific Rim. Royal Bank plays a leading role in financing Canada's exports and international trade around the world.

Royal Bank has been working aggressively to support entrepreneurs by creating policies and services that will improve lending practices, eliminate red tape, provide fast, professional assistance, and improve communication.

To continue to anticipate and meet the sector's rapidly evolving needs, banks must be just as entrepreneurial as the businesses. Among many other innovative programs, Royal Bank has: set up a national banking program for KBIs; established advisory councils with universities to better understand the needs of businesses specializing in agriculture biotechnology, and information technology; made it easier for small business to tap into government financial assistance programs by providing access to an electronic database; committed up to $300 million in a new loan program involving alliances with government agencies and targeted at export and growth-oriented small businesses; in 1994, added $125 million in new risk capital to provide equity financing to small and medium-sized enterprises.

Small business is important to our economy. And today, Royal Bank is making sure, just as it did more than 125 years ago, that the engine driving Canada's prosperity continues to be fuelled.

---

* (see, *Quick to the Frontier: Canada's Royal Bank,* 1993)

TEMBEC INC. is a leading Canadian integrated forest products company characterized by its motto, "A Company of People Building Their Own Future."

These words are more than a catchy slogan. They represent both an attitude and a commitment. They also illustrate how the company came into being and express fundamental values that still influence the company's activities today.

Tembec Inc. began in 1973 in Temiscaming, Quebec, when a group of people refused to give up their future without a fight. The town's economic lifeblood, a pulp mill owned by a large multinational, had been shut down. The mill's former employees and residents of Temiscaming gained national and international attention by effectively demonstrating how much the mill meant to them and to what lengths they were prepared to go to save it. A unique corporate entity was born when the employees joined with entrepreneurs to buy the mill and turn it into the fledgling company, Tembec Inc.

This unprecedented co-operation between unions and management wrote a new chapter in Canadian corporate history. It also brought opportunity to the employees and residents who bet their future on it and renewed economic vitality to Temiscaming and its region.

Today, Tembec Inc. has grown from the original pulp mill in Temiscaming, which is now a multi-process complex and the company's core operational centre, to a billion-dollar company with locations throughout Quebec, Ontario, and France. Tembec's original product line of sulphite pulp has expanded into a full range of forest products including specialty cellulose, high yield, chlorine free pulp, softwood kraft pulp, softwood and hardwood lumber, oriented strand board, coated paperboard, paper, newsprint, lignosulphonates, resins, and ethanol. Currently, Tembec's products are sold in 50 countries worldwide and the company and its Divisions and affiliates employ about 4,000 people.

Tembec's corporate philosophy and structure stress employee participation and intrapreneurship which generate innovation and growth and provide much of the company's vitality. Integrated operations make possible optimum control of such essentials as resource management, product quality, operational efficiency, cost and environmental impact. In addition to being a product innovation leader, Tembec is at the forefront of environmental responsibility and sustainable development. The company's environmental program was started in 1980 and targets "zero impact by the year 2005."

Tembec is a local enterprise that grew and is now making an impact worldwide. It is a concrete example of what a group of determined Canadians can do to build their own future.

TEMBEC INC.
A Company of People Building their Own Future

Tembec's Environmental program ensures that the company is a good corporate neighbour.

Innovation based on research and development is a key focus at Tembec.

SPRUCE FALLS INC.

Success Against the Odds

A group of Spruce Falls employee owners pose beside the No. 5 paper machine.

Spruce Falls newsprint contains environmentally friendly recycled and high yield pulps.

THE STORY OF SPRUCE FALLS INC. is the story of another company that fought to save its future.

In 1991, due to a realignment of corporate priorities, the newsprint mill in Kapuskasing, Ontario, was scheduled for a major downsizing by its long-time owners, the Kimberly-Clark Corporation and The New York Times Co. Located near vast forest resources and run by a skilled, experienced and dedicated work force who knew all about making newsprint, the mill was a viable operation in its own right and represented significant potential for success under a different management philosophy.

The employees, local residents and surrounding population, for whom the mill represented the core of their economic future, initiated the process of buying the mill. Tembec, a seasoned veteran of employee acquisition and co-operative management, and active in the same industry, became a partner in the venture.

The Spruce Falls acquisition was not easy, occurring during a cyclical downturn in the industry that reflected a worldwide economic recession. The Ontario government, intent on maintaining economic stability in the region, participated as facilitator during the acquisition negotiations. Rumours of subsidies, although there were none, made the rounds, and industry and financial analysts predicted the venture would fail.

The people of Spruce Falls carried on, raising millions of dollars on their own to make the acquisition possible. With unified determination and Tembec's 41 per cent participation and management expertise, Spruce Falls Inc. came to be.

It turned out to be the right combination because today Spruce Falls is a highly successful company that proved all the doomsayers wrong. Immediately after acquisition, Spruce Falls began a $360 million mill modernization program. Major projects completed over the next three years included a new, high-yield thermo-mechanical pulp plant which requires 50 per cent less trees than conventional chemical pulp, a recycling and deinking plant and a secondary treatment facility. These improved quality and environmental performance and contributed to Spruce Falls' increased competitiveness in today's markets. Integrated operations also contribute to competitiveness and have recently been enhanced with the completion of a stud lumber production facility at the Kapuskasing mill complex.

Major markets for Spruce Falls' products, which include recycled content newsprint and groundwood specialty paper for mass market paperback publishing, are concentrated in northeastern and northcentral United States and Canada. Due to growing demand for its products abroad, Spruce Falls has also recently made a strong entry into the world market.

Spruce Falls' long history of forest renewal (over 180 million trees planted as of 1995) and innovative program of ecological forest management position the company among leaders in sustainable forest management. The Spruce Falls approach emphasizes harmony with nature and ensures biological diversity and healthy, productive forests in perpetuity.

S&MG
Sales & Merchandising Group

Global Leader in Field Marketing Services

The S&MG Executive Team. From left: Lynn Dobson, Mike Feric, Shawna Weinman, Tony LaSorda, Jay Gordon, Joanne Krupa, Ken Pickthall, Nancy Gaeta.

THE entrepreneurial spirit that has propelled S&MG forward is apparent today in the way this Canadian business establishment services the individual needs of its diverse clients.

Founded in 1986, S&MG's vision is to provide sales organizations strategic and execution resources. Many of Canada's leading companies are S&MG clients. These are some of the prominent names that virtually reach into every facet of Canadian life and commerce. Because

control of their individual priorities. This customized service is extended to include automated field information systems, where valuable information is collected, analyzed and customized for each client.

Insight is derived from knowledge. The management team at S&MG, with experience and understanding of the retail environment, has provided many clients with invaluable insight and recommendations. Often this results from sharing best practices and experience

clients are innovative, entrepreneurial, and action-oriented, they expect the same from the professionals at S&MG.

The rules of success are always clear with hindsight. It is insight that creates new opportunities. As the retail environment experienced dramatic change in the '80s, companies initiated search for new ways to improve sales effectiveness at retail.

To succeed in a time of continuous change, limits must be stretched and old assumptions challenged.

S&MG provides a range of services including recruiting, training, and management of permanent part-time personnel. These teams sell, merchandise, and train retail personnel on a dedicated basis for each client. This means that each client has their own exclusive team of personnel where the client, at all times, is in complete

from clients in unrelated areas.

S&MG also offers Field Marketing Services targeted to clients who require shorter-term resources at critical times during the year (summer, Christmas). S&MG is one of Canada's largest recruiters at leading Universities and Colleges, hiring hundreds of students every year. Many of the S&MG alumni have utilized their seasonal work experience to help pursue permanent careers in sales and marketing management.

Just as clients have gone global, so too has S&MG. With international affiliates in 10 countries and, more recently, the full expansion into the U.S. market, S&MG is positioned for continued growth into the 21st century.

The firm's vision "To be recognized as the global leader in delivering leading edge Field Marketing Services" provides the guidance for all employees.

Mackenzie Financial Corporation.

*Building financial
independence
for Canadians
since 1967*

MACKENZIE FINANCIAL CORPORATION began its operations at a time of far greater financial simplicity.

Twenty-nine years ago, most Canadians didn't understand what a mutual fund was – much less own one. And even sophisticated investors largely restricted themselves to investing primarily in this country.

In the interim, there has been much progress. Canada's collective financial IQ has grown exponentially. More than 30 per cent of Canadians own at least one mutual fund. Many of these funds are invested in the United States and internationally as economic and financial borders have disappeared.

From a start with one client and one mutual fund, Mackenzie has grown today to manage 47 mutual funds – in four families: The Industrial Group of Funds, Ivy Funds, The Universal Funds, and The Mackenzie Group of Funds in the U.S. – with total assets of more than $17 billion. Serving nearly one million investors in Canada and the U.S., Mackenzie has evolved to become a significant player in North American capital markets, with 800 employees and listings on the Toronto, Montreal and Nasdaq Stock Exchanges.

But while change and expansion have been the watchword in many areas, much has remained unaltered at Mackenzie for more than two and a half decades.

For example, the company's basic investment philosophy – one of building growth and income for its investor clients without sacrificing safety of capital – is as much in force today as it was on day one.

Mackenzie's commitment to the independent financial professionals who ably represent it in the marketplace – and to the community-at-large in which

it operates – also remains undiminished.

It's internal investment management strengths notwithstanding, Mackenzie has always been quick to access specialized external assistance when this is of benefit to investors. In the management of international funds, the company has formed strong working relationships with independent international money management companies based in Europe and the Far East – as well as establishing an arms length investment management subsidiary, Mackenzie Investment Management Inc., in Boca Raton, Florida.

Whatever the location, each of the individual investment managers responsible for directing a Mackenzie mutual fund in any one of the four families of funds brings a distinctive management approach. The strategic breadth, in conjunction with a variety of asset classes and countries and industries in which to invest provides the broadest possible degree of diversification for client assets.

Continuing a tradition of innovation and development of investment vehicles, Mackenzie recently launched STAR, a strategic asset allocation program that packages Mackenzie's inherent diversity into 14 portfolios, from highly conservative to aggressive – each incorporating seven mutual funds.

Looking to the future, much more will change for Mackenzie Financial Corporation as part of the process of continuing innovation.

But as a matter of principle, much will again not change.

The combined result will continue to be greater financial gains – and independence – for North American investors.

RHÔNE-POULENC IN CANADA

Proud of Its Diverse Heritage

WITH ROOTS THAT TRACE to nineteenth-century France, the Rhône-Poulenc family of companies is proud of the role it has played in contributing to Canada's rich heritage of science and technology over the past 75 years.

Rhône-Poulenc's Canadian operations are represented by five companies spanning the chemical, pharmaceutical, human and animal vaccine, and poultry industries: Rhône-Poulenc Canada Inc., Rhône-Poulenc Rorer Canada Inc., Connaught Laboratories Limited, Rhône-Merieux, Inc., and Shaver Poultry Breeding Farms Limited. Together, the Rhône-Poulenc family of companies employ 1,600 people and had combined sales of $600 million in 1995. Research and development is a priority, with the Rhône-Poulenc group in Canada spending more than $40 million annually.

These companies are part of Paris-based Rhône-Poulenc S.A., the seventh-largest chemical and pharmaceutical manufacturer in the world. The company operates in 140 companies worldwide and employs 89,000.

Rhône-Poulenc's presence in Canada harkens back to 1920, with the establishment of Laboratoires Poulenc Frères du Canada Limitée – a small laboratory in Montreal with a staff of five. Today, Rhône-Poulenc Canada Inc. is one of the leading chemical companies in Canada and is a major exporter of products, with annual sales exceeding $300 million in 1995.

As a member of the Canadian Chemical Producers Association, Rhône-Poulenc Canada has made a public commitment to Responsible Care®, an initiative concerning health, safety and environmental management and product stewardship.

Like Rhône-Poulenc Canada, Rhône-Poulenc Rorer Canada can trace its beginnings to that same tiny lab in Montreal. Rhône-Poulenc Pharma, as it was originally known, soon established itself as a leader in pharmaceutical products. Merging with the Rorer Group in 1990, Rhône-Poulenc Rorer (as it is now known) ranks among the top ten pharmaceutical companies in the world.

Connaught Laboratories Limited is Canada's leading biotechnology research company and the country's largest producer of biological products for human health care.

Connaught's roots go back to 1914, when it was founded at the University of Toronto. Its achievements include being the world's first producer of insulin; working with Dr. Jonas Salk in developing and supplying the first polio vaccine; and assisting the World Health Organization to eradicate smallpox, a goal that was reached in 1977.

The newest edition to the Rhône-Poulenc group in Canada is Rhône-Merieux, Inc., a biotechnology company specializing in veterinary biologics and pharmaceuticals. With products available in Canada since 1985, Rhône-Merieux sells veterinary vaccines for dogs, cats, and horses.

Located in Cambridge, Ontario, Shaver Poultry Breeding Farms Limited is the only poultry breeding company in Canada and a significant supplier of layer strain and broiler breeding stocks to the international market. Founded in the early 1940s, the company has since developed into an industry leader in applying genetics to achieve production efficiency.

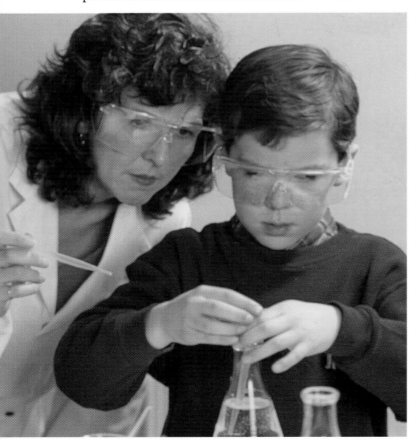

Oksana Mucyk, a chemist with Rhône-Poulenc Canada, has brought chemistry to life for hundreds of Canadian children.

CONNAUGHT LABORATORIES LIMITED

At the Frontier of Vaccine and Biotherapeutic Research

CONNAUGHT LABORATORIES' long-standing commitment to human health dates to 1914 when Dr. John FitzGerald set up a small laboratory at the University of Toronto to develop and produce serums and antitoxins. During World War I, the laboratory moved to its current location in North Toronto and adopted the name "Connaught" after the Duke of Connaught, then Governor General of Canada.

Connaught was the first company to mass produce insulin during the 1920s and a large scale producer of the first Salk polio vaccine in the 1950s. In 1978, Connaught acquired the research and production facilities of the Salk Institute in Swiftwater, Pennsylvania, and established its U.S. subsidiary, Connaught Laboratories Inc. In 1989, Connaught was acquired by Pasteur Mérieux serums & vaccins of France, a member of the Rhône–Poulenc global family of companies.

Today, Connaught's more than 1,700 employees work in 900,000 square feet of fully integrated research, development, manufacturing, and marketing facilities at these two locations. The company develops and produces effective adult and pediatric vaccines against influenza, diphtheria, tetanus, polio, pertussis, measles, and bacterial meningitis as well as vaccines for less common infections like rabies, tuberculosis, and cholera.

With annual sales of $408 million (Cdn.) in 1994, Connaught is a major supplier of vaccines and other biological products in Canada and the United States and exports its products to more than 130 countries.

Dedicated to research, Connaught currently spends about 15 per cent of sales revenue on research and development. Its Research & Development spending totalled more than $77 million in 1994.

Current research projects and recent product developments place Connaught at the frontiers of vaccine and biotherapeutic research. These include a) the development of a genetically engineered HIV pseudovirion for treating aids patients or as a vaccine against HIV infection; b) the first potential vaccine against Lyme disease, a crippling infection carried by ticks; c) the development of its multivalent "Penta"

Connaught Laboratories wants every child to have a better chance of realizing their potential in a world free from infection and disease.

vaccine that provides protection against five childhood diseases — Haemophilus influenzae type b, polio, diphtheria, pertussis,and tetanus — with one vaccination; d) a genetically-engineered vaccine against pertussis (whooping cough); e) improvements to its influenza vaccine to render it more effective in the elderly; f) a potential vaccine against otitis media (serious ear infections in children; g) new vaccine targeting systems that stimulate much more effective immune responses; and, h) an oral vaccine delivery system that could eliminate the need for injections.

Connaught has also extended its biological research into the emerging field of biotherapeutics, developing the first approved biological product for the treatment of superficial bladder cancer, now licensed in more than 20 countries.

Connaught also supports collaborative research through its Canadian University Research Fund which has dedicated $15 million to support projects with the University of Toronto and other Canadian universities over a 10-year period.

Wired for the 21st Century

WITH THE TWENTY-FIRST CENTURY looming, Canada rides the crest of the telecommunications wave, and, with it, Electro Source Inc., the manifestation of one man's vision and entrepreneurial spirit.

Each time a telephone is employed, numerous electronic components within each phoneset assures a completed call. These components, manufactured largely beyond Canada's borders, are among the many that are successfully used in the manufacturing of Canadian communications software. Electro Source Inc. buoyantly represents American and Japanese manufacturers to meet an aggressive North American demand for electronic components.

Electro Source facilitates the ever-changing needs of its Canadian customers by providing them access to state of the art electronic components manufactured worldwide. Its established and much-respected network assists Canadian companies such as Northern Telecom Canada Ltd., Newbridge Networks and Mitel Corporation to remain on the leading edge of design technology in the telecommunications field.

Founded in 1983 by its president, Sherman Cunningham, Electro Source has grown from one office in Toronto to five across Canada, with Western Canadian operations directed by Cunningham's son, Jeff. In addition, Electro Source has opened four offices in the United States, being the only Canadian representative to date to do so.

Sherman Cunningham, raised in Vancouver, gained electronics background as a radar ground technician serving in the Royal Canadian Air Force. Subsequent experience in the electronics industry led Cunningham to foresee the sturdy growth of new markets in the communications field. Electro Source is the culmination of his vision and entrepreneurial spirit.

Lauded by its American principals for outstanding sales and service, Electro Source is staffed by a team of highly motivated engineers and customer service representatives. Their motivation can be largely attributed to Sherman Cunningham's commitment to the well-being of his staff. Every employee is supplied with a cellular telephone to facilitate communications with business associates as well as family, and a lap-top computer which has brought the goal of being a "paperless office" well within reach. A state-of-the-art exercise facility complements the recent expansion of the Toronto head office.

Sherman Cunningham's dedication to Canadian sport and culture is evidenced by the proliferation of Canadian art and sporting memorabilia that accentuates the west-end of Toronto office headquarters. Electro Source sponsors numerous sports teams, and regularly contributes to the United Way, the Kinsmen and Lion's Club in addition to the Children's Wish Foundation. In 1993, a twelve-year-old boy's dying wish was to see in person a major league baseball game. Cunningham fulfilled that wish. He flew the young man and his family to Toronto to realize the boy's dream of seeing the Blue Jays and the Philadelphia Phillies play in the World Series.

Sherman Cunningham and Electro Source Inc. continue to be on the leading edge of the electronic components field as they look forward to the advent of video conferencing and other advancements in the rapidly changing world of telecommunications.

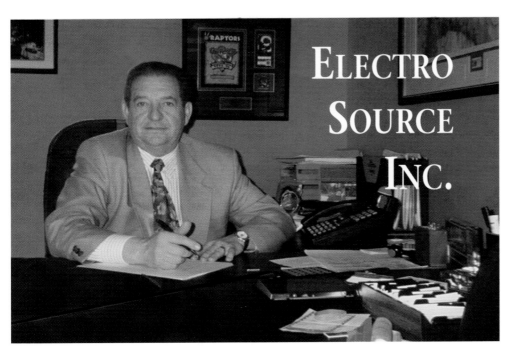

Sherman Cunningham, president, Electro Source Inc., represents many of North America's largest electronics components firms.

HOME HARDWARE STORES LIMITED

From Small-town Store to National Success

In Home Hardware, Walter Hachborn created a national retail force based upon old-fashioned principles of service, value, and quality. [Photo, courtesy E. Kohlmetz]

In 1979, Henry Sittler received a Gold Hammer Award for his 50 years of involvement in the hardware industry.

IN MANY WAYS, Home Hardware Stores Limited reflects the resourceful people who built a Canada-wide force of hardware retailers from a small, rural hardware store.

At the turn of the century a German immigrant, Henry Gilles, began selling hardware from his black-smith's shop in the village of St. Jacobs, Ontario. At that time, St. Jacobs was far removed from the larger industrial centres, but many of the area farmers and businessmen were industrially progressive. In 1932, the business was sold to a local businessman, Gordon Hollinger. Mr. Hollinger and his assistant, Henry Sittler, were very ambitious and aggressive hardware retailers. They used advertisements and loss-leaders to gain consumer confidence and increase sales. When Canadian manufacturers refused to sell their products to Hollinger Hardware because they were retailers, Mr. Sittler began importing products from the United States, Great Britain, and Germany. He also encouraged local industry to manufacture private product lines.

Walter Hachborn joined Hollinger Hardware in 1938 as an apprentice. Mr. Hachborn did everything from receiving stock, stocking shelves, serving customers, and shipping orders to sweeping floors. After serving as a Warehouse Foreman in World War II, Mr. Hachborn worked closely with Mr. Hollinger and Mr. Sittler. In 1948, Mr. Hollinger passed away and his family decided to sell the business. Mr. Sittler and Mr. Hachborn purchased the business with a third partner, Arthur Zilliax, and together they worked to compete with the increasing number of shopping centres, discount stores and franchised retailers.

To survive in this increasingly competitive retail environment, Mr. Hachborn began researching coop-eratives and dealer-owned companies in the United States. Mr. Hachborn met with hundreds of independent hardware retailers throughout Ontario and, in 1963, arrangements were made to purchase Hollinger Hardware and form a dealer-owned company with 122 independent retailers. On January 1, 1964, Home Hardware emerged as a new force in Canadian hardware retailing with Mr. Hachborn at its helm.

Home Hardware has grown immensely since its humble beginnings, but it has remained faithful to its basic principles of *quality, value and service*. Today there are almost 1,000 Home Hardware stores across Canada. Home Hardware also has distribution centres in Nova Scotia, Alberta, and an award-winning private label paint manufacturing plant in Burford, Ontario. Home Hardware's main office complex in St. Jacobs covers one million square feet. Home Hardware is a member of a North American buying alliance and a member of an international retail group which acts on a global level to share information and technology concerning the hardware industry.

Home Hardware has succeeded because of its resourceful staff, innovative technology and the vision of its founders. As Home Hardware continues to grow and increase its sales throughout Canada, there will be new goals, new technology, and renewed vision.

IMASCO

A Tapestry of Canadian Success Stories

IMASCO LIMITED, with headquarters in Montreal, is one of Canada's largest corporations. It was formed in 1970 to diversify Imperial Tobacco Company into other consumer markets.

Hallmarks of Imasco's growth have been investing in outstanding organizations and furthering the dreams of entrepreneurs. Each Imasco company is an important thread of success woven into the corporate tapestry. Each exemplifies Imasco's driving spirit: responding to consumer needs with the highest quality goods and services while helping to build strong communities. Imperial Tobacco, Shoppers Drug Mart, and Canada Trust are three Canadian success stories.

Imperial Tobacco Company: The Origins of Imasco

Imperial Tobacco Company was incorporated in 1912 when the Canadian tobacco industry was still in its infancy. It began as a consolidation of two Montreal companies and over its 80-year history has acquired many other tobacco businesses.

During World War II, Imperial embarked on a goodwill program of distributing its cigarettes to Canadian troops abroad, which also served to keep brand loyalty alive. The war stimulated Canadian economic growth and, during the post-war boom, Imperial constructed additional plants in Ontario and Quebec. Its engineers began experimenting with

In today's tobacco industry, being a cost-effective producer is a market imperative. Imperial Tobacco's new, high-speed cigarette makers are part of the company's $118-million investment in streamlining and modernizing manufacturing operations to increase productivity.

machinery for processing leaf tobacco, which was subsequently licensed to manufacturers around the world.

In the early '70s, TV and radio advertising of tobacco products were discontinued, and Imperial decided to channel some of its advertising and promotion budget into support for professional sports events and the arts. This support grew over the years and continues to this day.

By 1980, Imperial's *Player's* brand had become Canada's most popular cigarette and the company was the country's undisputed industry leader.

Today, Imperial Tobacco continues to flourish, led by the two largest selling domestic cigarette brand families, *du Maurier* and *Player's*. The company employs 2,700 people in all phases of the industry, from the purchase of raw tobacco leaf to the distribution of final products.

Shoppers Drug Mart: Joining forces with a Force

When scarcely 20 years old, Murray Koffler inherited two neighbourhood drug stores in Toronto. He went to pharmacy school, learned the heart of the business, then proceeded to redefine it. The end result was Shoppers Drug Mart.

For each new prescription, a Shoppers pharmacist reviews a personalized HealthWatch Reminder *with the patient. Private counselling is the fastest-growing area in pharmacy, and Shoppers healthcare advisory services are helping patients with chronic diseases better to manage their care.*

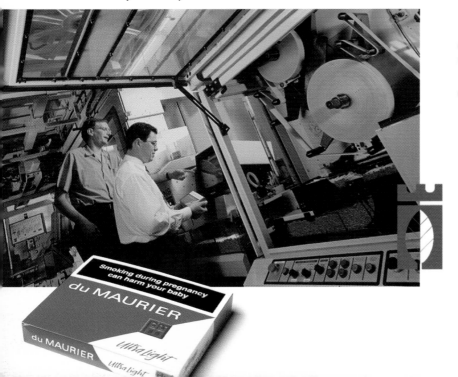

With typical bold strokes, Koffler revamped the concept of the twentieth century "drugstore" in Canada by ripping out the soda fountain and emphasizing the dispensary, requiring his pharmacists to wear starched white coats as a symbol of their professionalism. To that he added consumer-oriented approaches in merchandising and promotion. In the mid-'50s, he began acquiring other drug stores and organized them around a then-novel franchising concept: pharmacist "associates" would own and operate their own stores within the system and share in the profits. The concept turned out to be a cornerstone of the chain's success.

In 1962 Koffler's 17-store chain became known as Shoppers Drug Mart. It went public and major expansion occurred through acquisition and mergers in the '60s and in the '70s. Upon entering the chain, stores typically doubled their previous year's profits.

When it was time to sell his business, Murray Koffler chose Imasco largely because of its strong financial position but also because he liked Imasco's tradition of sponsoring worthy Canadian causes. A philanthropist in his own right, Koffler had seen to it that Shoppers had an established reputation as a leading educator on health issues as well as a supporter of hospital fundraising.

Shoppers Drug Mart continues to grow and develop under Imasco's ownership. In today's Shoppers, pharmacists serve as health advisors and are important liaisons between physician and patient. It's a far cry from soda fountain days!

Canada Trust: Helping to Build a Community

In 1986 Imasco acquired Canada Trust, one of the largest financial institutions in Canada. The company had its origins in the frontier days of Canada as the Huron & Erie Savings and Loan Society (H&E), a "building society" established in 1864 in London, Ontario, then the country's western edge. Formed by 25 London businessmen, the H&E was instrumental in shaping a stable and prosperous community.

Through building societies, people would pool their savings to finance the purchase of land by others. Innovative rules allowed borrowers to pay back their debts in monthly instalments of principal plus interest. The concept was ideally suited to the development of pre-confederation Canada. Capital was scarce in those days, for banks handled only commercial accounts and

people literally stashed their savings under mattresses.

Loans which enabled farmers to buy their land were H&E's dominant business for many years, and stories abound about the travelling valuators who had to conquer near impassable terrain on horseback to make their reports. In 1898, H&E acquired General Trust Corporation of Calgary which led to the formation in 1901 of an H&E subsidiary named Canada Trust.

The depression brought on difficult times, made more so in the prairies by drought and the subsequent abandonment of land and loans. The company supported its beleaguered customers, advancing money for seed, sometimes accepting harvested crops as payments on mortgages. Not surprisingly, profits dwindled and did not regain their 1930 level until 1950.

The outbreak of World War II began an economic recovery and by 1946, it was clear that if the company was going to grow, it would have to acquire other trust companies with good business volumes. This it did, and it also entered the field of corporate pension fund administration. By 1957, the company's two names began to meld into one corporate image, Canada Trust.

Over the course of the '60s and '70s, Canada Trust emphasized personal financial services and developed its well-earned reputation for friendliness and convenience. With the coming of the '90s, the company increasingly employed technology to serve customers better. And, through its active residential mortgage program, Canada Trust has remained true to its early mission of helping Canadians invest in their own communities.

Customers want to complete their financial transactions at times and places convenient to them, and Canada Trust is dedicated to "making banking easy." EasyLine *telephone banking (pictured) and ATM banking are well-used alternatives to the branch, and the company is now expanding to PC banking and secure Internet services.*

WHILE MOST ENTREPRENEURIAL stories begin with an entrepreneur chasing an idea, William J. Sutton & Co. Ltd. was founded by an idea chasing the appropriate person, a person that was transformed, somewhat reluctantly, into an entrepreneur.

Bill Sutton grew up in Brampton, Ontario, and during those long, winter hikes to the rink, hockey equipment swung over his back, he never imagined that his occupation would one day bring him face to face with the biggest names in the world of professional sports. His first order of business was education and Sutton achieved his accounting designation the old way, working in the field of accounting and auditing, while earning his Chartered Accountant requirements at night via correspondence. After various jobs in accounting and sales, Sutton eventually joined the firm of Ernst & Whinney in their management consulting practice, where he spent most of his pre-insurance career.

It was in 1974 that Sutton first entered the insurance business, intrigued by a company's involvement in sports accident insurance. This provided exposure to the industry's Special Risk classes, as well as the arena of professional athletics. Further, with the primary market for these coverages being Lloyd's of London and the company's significant operations in both Canada and United States, the firm had an appealing international focus.

When Sutton's relationship between the owner of that business changed in 1978, Sutton was sought out by the London contacts he had known, who, appreciating his contributions to the field and his integrity, encouraged him to establish his own business. He understood from the beginning that two fundamental qualities were required for success in this fast-paced segment of the insurance business: an unshakable commitment to superior client service; and, a continuing, unquestionable integrity in working with both clients and the supporting underwriters in London. Based on these two cornerstones, the business grew from two employees and $700,000 in sales in 1978, to over 40 employees, in three different companies, with combined revenues in excess of $50 million in 1995.

William J. Sutton & Co. Ltd. was established as a Managing General Underwriter, providing various specialty Accident & Health products on behalf of supporting underwriters, primarily at Lloyd's. The firm's emphasis was on delivering the flexibility and capacity of the large insurance market at Lloyd's, through a small but highly technical and service conscious owner-

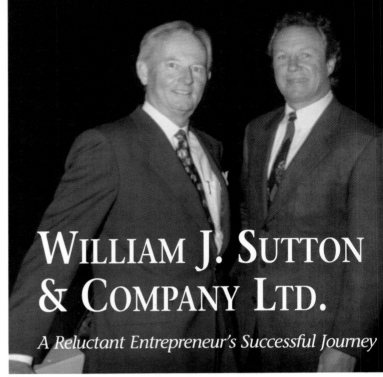

WILLIAM J. SUTTON & COMPANY LTD.

A Reluctant Entrepreneur's Successful Journey

President Bill Sutton, left, with Darryl Sittler, a popular former captain of the Toronto Maple Leafs hockey team. Sittler, an early client of Sutton & Co. while a player, is now a senior executive with the Maple Leafs, which, in 1978, became the very first client of the firm and continues to be to this day.

managed company, to insurance agents and brokers throughout North America. Recently, Sutton's supporting underwriters have expanded to include leading Canadian life insurers.

It was Sutton & Co.'s experience in markets outside Canada that led Bill Sutton to the observation that the Canadian Life Insurance industry is held in particularly high regard. This reputation for outstanding management and fairness, as reflected by Sutton & Co., resulted in the establishment of the Canadian Accident Reinsurance Facility, CARF, managed by a new company, Tri-Can Reinsurance Inc., founded by Sutton in 1986 as a joint venture with the principals of a similar company, Reinsurance Management Services in Wayne, New Jersey. As an extension of the Sutton & Co. capability in specialty accident products, Tri-Can provides reinsurance coverage to international insurers wishing to reduce their exposure to catastrophic loss. To take advantage of growing international opportunities outside North America, Tri-Can launched a second office in 1995, based in Hamilton, Bermuda.

The success of both Sutton & Co. and the two units of Tri-Can bear out Bill Sutton's belief that Canadians are very highly regarded worldwide, and specifically, well-thought-of in the insurance world. The Canadian reputation for integrity and fair dealings, combined with the strength and conservative nature of their Life Insurance companies, have been significant factors in the success of all three companies.

SAMUEL MANU-TECH INC.

Preparing for the 21st Century

SAMUEL MANU-TECH INC., a Canadian-owned and operated company, is a shining example of the successful outcome of time-honoured traditions combined with innovative forward thinking.

Opening its doors as a publicly owned company in 1985, Samuel Manu-Tech Inc. has enjoyed unqualified success and remarkable growth in its first decade. This success is not the least bit surprising as the foundations of Samuel Manu-Tech Inc. are built upon the same corporate philosophies, business ethics and standards of excellence as its parent company, Samuel, Son & Co., Limited.

With roots going back to Lewis Samuel, Samuel, Son & Co., Limited has been family owned and operated for over 140 years. Now captained by great-grandson Ernest, the company maintains its position at the forefront of the marketplace through innovation and expansion as required to address the ever-changing and increasing needs of the Canadian and international steel markets. One such landmark expansion was the formation of Samuel Manu-Tech Inc., incorporated to facilitate the company's pursuit of opportunities in metals manufacturing and technology.

Samuel Manu-Tech Inc. began its history with three core divisions, comprised of Canadian Metal Rolling Mills, Nelson Steel and Samuel Strapping Systems. These three original foundation divisions have grown to incorporate four additional divisions. The 23 plants, operating in both Canada and the U.S., manufacture and sell a wide variety of products ranging from metal pickling technology to stainless steel piping to custom roll-formed products and steel strapping. Record sales and earnings were reported in Samuel Manu-Tech Inc.'s tenth anniversary year, with net sales reaching 397.6 million dollars – quadruple those of 1986.

At the helm of Samuel Manu-Tech Inc. is Mark C. Samuel who carries with him

to future frontiers a five-generation tradition of excellence, dependability and durability. Samuel Manu-Tech is dedicated to supporting each decentralized division. That employees are the company's strength is reinforced by Samuel Manu-Tech's dedication to the well-being of its employees, shareholders, and environment. Continuous reinvestment in state-of-the-art equipment ensures the safety of Samuel Manu-Tech Inc.'s employees, and secures the company's position at the forefront of its industrial segments by providing customers with the highest quality products available. The company's Corporate Environmental Policy ensures that environmental compliance is continuously examined, with results reported to the Board of Directors.

With time-honoured traditions as its guide to the future, and an unwavering commitment to its employees and to quality, productivity, and environmental protection, Samuel Manu-Tech Inc. has positioned itself for the push toward the 21st century.

Mark Samuel, president, Samuel Manu-Tech Inc., is the fifth generation of Samuels involved in the family business.

Lewis Samuel (1827-1887), industrialist, merchant and philanthropist, began the family business in Toronto over 140 years ago.

SHAKLEE CANADA INC.

A Company with a Conscience

ITS PRODUCTS have been to the North Pole – several times. They've been consumed at Lillehammer, Albertville, and other Olympic venues. And they're used, daily, by tens of thousands of Canadians who benefit from them just as much as Arctic explorers and world-class athletes do.

Now celebrating its 20th anniversary, Shaklee Canada Inc.'s long-term commitment to quality and personal service has distinguished it as one of the country's leading suppliers of nutritional, personal care, household and other products that contribute to a healthy lifestyle.

Shaklee's growth and sophistication have been phenomenal, but every operating aspect of the company has evolved out of its founding philosophy of "products in harmony with nature and good health." It has earned the enviable reputation of being a company that cares: its nutritional supplements help thousands maintain a healthy diet; its household cleaners are kind to the environment; it does not request or require animal testing on any of its products; and its independent business opportunity provides a secure and significant livelihood to hundreds of people.

This philosophy – combined with strong executive leadership, consumer awareness, and a dynamic partnership with Shaklee U.S. – has propelled the Canadian subsidiary of the worldwide Shaklee organization to national prominence since it was founded in 1976.

Although well-established in the United States, the corporation moved northward in a modest way. Its first Canadian president, Stephen J. Locke, started the business from the kitchen table of his Burlington, Ontario, home, working to supply 12 initial distributors with Shaklee products. By the end of 1976, there were four employees and more than 1,000 distributors. The company soon outgrew its makeshift office, and operations were moved to a local industrial complex.

In June 1981, the rapidly growing enterprise underwent a major relocation to its own home office: an award-winning, 39,000-square-foot building, also in Burlington, designed specifically to reflect the Shaklee philosophy of co-operation with nature and concern for the environment.

Today, under the leadership of President Vic Prendergast, Shaklee Canada Inc. has a permanent staff of 45, over 600 "Sales Leaders," and more than 100,000 "Members" and distributors across Canada. Each month, more than 2,500 orders for Eastern Canada are packed and shipped from Burlington, while approximately 1,300 orders for Western Canada are dispatched from an office and warehouse facility in Calgary.

From the Atlantic to the Pacific, Shaklee representatives and customers alike are routinely educated and

The award-winning Home Office building in Burlington, Ontario.

informed by the company's two lifestyle consultants, Allan Somersall, Ph.D., M.D. of Oakville, Ontario, and Christopher R. Scott, M.D., of Saskatoon, Saskatchewan. These highly respected physicians tour the country, giving presentations in the interests of sound nutrition, health, physical fitness, and the environment.

Medical consultation for better health is consistent with the principles and practices installed by corporate founder Dr. Forrest C. Shaklee. A noted physician, author and lecturer who had dedicated his life to the study of nature and nutrition, the late Dr. Shaklee came out of retirement in 1956 to start a small family business that would soon become Shaklee Corporation.

Dr. Shaklee poured years of careful research and development into each of his products, and subjected them to endless quality tests before introducing them to the public. From the outset, he knew that he wanted his products to be distributed by people who used them and believed in them. Retail sales would not allow for this personal approach, so the Shaklee marketing plan was developed around the person-to-person concept of multi-level marketing. Throughout the world, this is how Shaklee products continue to be distributed today.

Dr. Shaklee's practice of combining nature's ways with state-of-the-art technology is perpetuated at the research centre that bears his name in Hayward, California. This outstanding facility is staffed by nutritionists, microbiologists, biochemists and other specialists who regularly collaborate with experts from leading universities to extend the borders of scientific knowledge. Over the years, Shaklee has spent more than $100 million on research and development activities.

But the ever-increasing variety of rigidly tested products that flows from the unique Shaklee system is only half the story. The comprehensive business opportunity offered by the two longest-standing subsidiaries – Shaklee U.S. and Shaklee Canada Inc. – is unparalleled in the industry. Part-time, entry level distributors enjoy excellent supplementary earnings, while the average income for full-time, top-ranking Sales Leaders is at a high executive level. Whether part-time or full-time, people who "share" Shaklee have the opportunity to receive brand new cars every three years and major-expense-paid convention travel at least once a year.

Shaklee Canada Inc. also contributes in a meaningful way to a host of amateur sports teams and individual athletes, as well as community services. It's the official nutritional supplier to the Canadian Olympic rowing, alpine, cross-country ski, freestyle ski, biathlon, ski jumping/nordic combined, and cycling teams, and has nutritionally sponsored record-breaking Arctic journeys involving Canadian explorer Richard Weber in 1988 and 1995. Shaklee also supports community programs in the Burlington-Hamilton area, including the annual United Way Campaign and Salvation Army Food Drive, and has made several contributions to its world-famous neighbour, the Royal Botanical Gardens.

As the turn of the century draws near, Shaklee's approach to health, philosophy of harmony with nature, unlimited financial opportunity, and concern for others continue to flourish across provincial boundaries, national borders – even oceans.

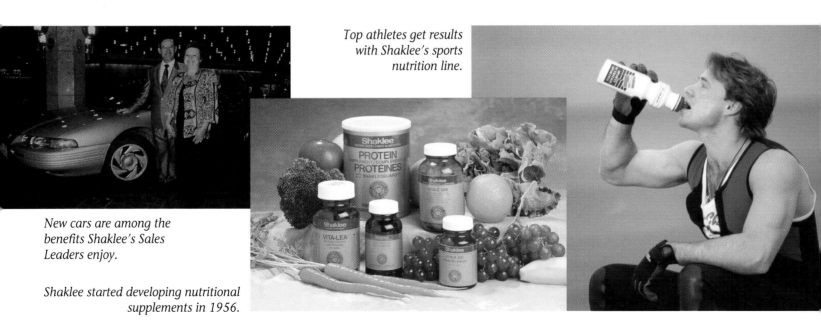

New cars are among the benefits Shaklee's Sales Leaders enjoy.

Shaklee started developing nutritional supplements in 1956.

Top athletes get results with Shaklee's sports nutrition line.

IN 1858, six years after moving to Montreal as oil commission merchants, William C. Macdonald and his older brother Augustine launched McDonald Brothers and Co. Tobacco Manufacturers. Initially the company imported tobacco from Kentucky and manufactured chewing and smoking tobacco plugs. The business prospered and in 1866 underwent a name change to W.C. McDonald Tobacco Merchants and Manufacturers. That same year the brothers initiated a heart-shaped logo and coined the phrase "tobacco with a heart" – a trademark that lasted more than a century.

Many changes took place in the business. Augustine eventually left the company giving William full control. By 1876 expansion was necessary and the company moved its manufacturing facilities to Ontario Street East in Montreal, where the original building is still used today. The present buildings house both research and manufacturing facilities under the name RJR-Macdonald Inc.

With the growing financial success of the business, William became an integral part of the financial establishment of Montreal and the nation. Named a director of the Bank of Montreal, he established himself as a leading philanthropist, ultimately pouring millions of dollars into health and educational causes, particularly McGill University. Besides funding both a student and science building, he quietly provided numerous scholarships and endowed a number of chairs, one of

them filled by Ernest Rutherford, famed pioneer of atomic research and future Nobel laureate.

For his generous support of various health and education causes he was knighted by Queen Victoria in 1898. At that time he changed the spelling of his thriving tobacco company name from McDonald to Macdonald. As Sir William, he continued to support rural education, providing funding for colleges in agriculture and household sciences in Prince Edward Island, Nova Scotia, New Brunswick, Quebec and Ontario. He also provided funding for the consolidation of Vancouver and Victoria colleges into the McGill University College of British Columbia, which later became the University of British Columbia.

Upon his death in 1917, Macdonald, a bachelor, left the company to the Stewart brothers who had started their careers with the company as clerks. Walter Stewart became president and under his management, the company extended production to cut pipe tobacco and the first "roll your own" finecuts. In 1922, cigarette production was added, cigarettes being sold in packages of 10s, 20s, and 50s. In 1928 *Export* cigarettes were introduced. First known as *British Consol Export*, the cigarette package became distinctive in 1935 with the addition of a Scottish lassie wearing a Macdonald of Sleat tartan kilt. Created by Canadian artist Rex Woods, the Lassie has remained a company symbol ever since.

During World War II, the company provided cigarettes to Canadian troops overseas. By 1945 fifty percent of the Canadian forces smoked *Export* cigarettes. This helped the company maintain a dominant share of the domestic market during the first postwar decade. Under Walter's son David M. Stewart, the company diversified into cigar making during the '60s.

RJR-MACDONALD INC.

Since Before Confederation…

RJR-Macdonald has carried on manufacturing in the Ontario Street, Montreal, building since 1876.

The process of manufacturing tobacco products has evolved to present-day high-tech, state-of-the-art equipment. RJR-Macdonald Inc. produces more than 15 billion units annually for domestic and worldwide distribution.

The Stewarts retained ownership of the Macdonald Tobacco company until 1974 when it was bought by R.J. Reynolds Industries of Winston-Salem, North Carolina. Four years later the name was changed to RJR-Macdonald Inc. to take advantage of the growing recognition of R.J. Reynolds as a major multinational corporation that was made even more so with the merger of R.J. Reynolds and the Nabisco Corporation of New York in 1985.

As a subsidiary of R.J. Reynolds International, RJR-Macdonald, now headquartered in Toronto, has the capability of drawing on the financial, technological and research resources of its international parent. It continues to produce a full range of Canadian cigarette brands, fine cut tobaccos, cigars, and cigarette papers. Most of its Canadian products are produced from Virginia flue-cured tobacco grown in southwestern Ontario. It also imports and distributes several well-known American brands which are manufactured by its sister company R.J. Reynolds Tobacco Co. in Winston-Salem, North Carolina.

The plant in Montreal has seen many changes, undergoing a major program of modernization and renovation during the '80s. With state-of-the-art equipment, the plant is capable of producing more than 15 billion units annually, and has a reputation for producing high quality products, some of which are produced for and distributed by RJR affiliates in other parts of the world, such as Japan, Eastern Europe, and the Middle East.

Operating in Canada for more than 138 years, RJR-Macdonald has been associated with many special causes and sporting events. For years it has provided financial assistance and marketing expertise to help promote sports such as downhill and freestyle skiing, curling, windsurfing, hockey, fishing, and recently hydroplane boating and golf. While sponsorship of such programs may be curtailed in the future by government legislation, the company remains committed to providing assistance to cultural, recreational, educational, and humanitarian institutions for as long as it can. It is also proud of its role as an equal opportunity employer, its long-standing record of good management-employee relations and its identity as a successful company with roots clearly and firmly established in Canada.

Hugo Sørensen, Managing Director of Olsten Staffing Services.
[Photo, courtesy Gregory Petkovich]

OLSTEN SERVICES LIMITED

Setting Strategies. Seeing Results.

employing over 600,000 people annually for more than 100,000 local, regional, national, and international clients.

In Canada, Olsten Staffing commenced operations in 1965 and has grown steadily to create an extensive coast to coast network that provides innovative staffing solutions to thousands of clients. Since 1995 Hugo T. Sørensen, Managing Director, has overseen rapid strategic expansion to 16 new locations in Canada through client centered startups and assertive new market acquisitions.

Ward Associates, formerly P.J. Ward Associates, a Toronto-based staffing company specializing in the Information Systems/Technology (I.S.T.) marketplace, is a significant point of differentiation for Olsten and represents considerable growth opportunities for Olsten as more and more corporations seek staffing solutions for systems support and development. Peter Ward, founder and president of Ward Associates, continues to lead this first-class organization into the future.

FOUNDED IN 1950, the Olsten Corporation today is one of the world's leading staffing and health care providers. Through two primary operating units – Olsten Staffing Services and Olsten Kimberly Quality Care – assignment employees are provided to business, industry and government, while caregivers service the home, health, institutional and hospital-based health agencies. Canadian headquarters are located in North York, Ontario.

By early 1996, the office network of Olsten Corporation has globally grown to over 700 offices throughout Canada, USA, Mexico, South America, Great Britain, and Europe,

Olsten's ISO 9002 registration assures clients of consistent processes, procedures, and quality all across Canada. Staffing solutions are designed to meet a full range of business needs including traditional temporary help, project staffing, professional level and accounting resources, strategic partnerships, permanent placement, testing, recruiting, applicant screening and more.

In a business environment demanding ever increasing quality and flexibility, Olsten's staffing solutions help companies of all sizes to increase productivity and stay competitive into the next century....

The Integral Group, Inc

"A Taste of Things to Come"

Try this one at home: take twenty-some programmers, five sales reps, forty-plus computers, and a couple of executives determined to make waves; mix and stir; then bake in today's computer marketplace for ten years. This recipe, mixed with care, is the culinary combination that produced today's Integral Group, Inc.

This recipe has other effects, characteristic traits which define the flavour of the company: reliability, quality, integrity and perseverance – it's amazing what those ten years will do! Soon you will discover the enticing aroma bringing legions of satisfied customers back again and again for Integral's rare blend of talent, knowing that their AS/400 and Electronic Commerce related dilemmas will be resolved immediately, or sooner....

"But what makes The Integral Group tick?" you ask.... There's a story behind that....

Established in 1986, Integral began early in both of its specialty fields. Zoltan Karacsony (programmer number three from the recipe) was involved in the development of the first Electronic Data Interchange (EDI) software for IBM midrange computers. With demand for EDI functionality growing at a phenomenal pace since then, The Integral Group has actively stayed ahead of the race. A glance through The Integral Group's brochures reveals an assortment of EDI software for a range of platforms, some of them third-party, some of them innovatively developed by The Integral Group. Foremost among these

products is SolutionPak, Integral's answer to their clients' Electronic Commerce needs including EDI and bar-coding. As the mass migration to the Internet and other electronic communications media induces companies to reassess their business practices, adopting Electronic Commerce in order to remain competitive, The Integral Group is there to provide necessary solutions.

The Integral Group, Inc. is equally agile in the AS/400 marketplace. Emma Perlaky and company co-founder Merrie Lee prudently secured the very first production B10 AS/400 for their own uses, assuring right from the beginning that they would have the technology needed to tackle the latest trends. Since then, The Integral Group has worked with an impressive variety of AS/400 products and situations. From CASE tools to data ware-

housing and from manufacturing to distribution to finance, The Integral Group has the experience to make AS/400 systems work. Always exploring new territory, in 1995 Integral announced the release of its premier AS/400 client/server tool, DCS/400, which provides accelerated performance for client/server applications between AS/400s and PCs.

Once familiar with The Integral Group, there is incentive to know it better. You will soon see that this well-stirred, upbeat firm is ambitious and responsive, possessed by a flair for quality solutions. You will absolutely ascertain that Integral's culture is ready to enhance your future just as surely as it has successfully dealt with the past.

MOORE CORPORATION LIMITED

Global Leader in Information Handling

Moore is expanding and enhancing its range of products and services through leadership and innovation in business forms and systems, business equipment, print management outsourcing, commercial and digital printing, labels, personalized direct mail, statement printing and related services.

MORE THAN ONE HUNDRED YEARS AGO, a salesman named Samuel Moore introduced what would be a revolution in the business world – the multi-part sales form. The modern day business forms industry was launched via this simple product and Moore Corporation was born. Today, this Toronto based, Canadian company is a global leader in the analysis of customer information flows and in the communication of business information through the design, development, manufacture, and implementation of forms, printing, labels, and direct mail, systems and services.

Moore Corporation had sales of over $2.6-billion in 1995. It operates in 50 countries with over 100 manufacturing facilities worldwide. Moore has approximately 19,000 employees in four major markets – North America, Latin America, Europe and Asia Pacific. Moore specializes in an integrated product and service offering that is focused in three main areas – Forms and Print Management; Labels and Label Systems; and Customer Communication Services.

From the beginning, Moore Corporation has focused on not only selling to customers, but on helping customers anticipate needs and stay in touch with the latest developments. It is the company's commitment not only to serve existing customers or attract new ones with existing products, but to lead customers, new or old, to fresh and unanticipated offerings, thereby creating new competitive space and opportunities for growth. Moore is the only business forms company to have its own research facility. In 1995, Moore spent more than $28 million on research and development. The technical skill sets within Moore can be categorized into: 35 percent software engineering, 25 percent materials development, 20 percent mechanical engineering and 20 percent electronic engineering. These provide Moore's key technology differentiators: electronic and mechanical system integration; applications and workflow software; variable print software; high speed print engine technology; paper handling engineering; and adhesive and label technologies. These differentiators provide Moore customers with the very best and latest in products and services to meet their needs.

Moore has been rewriting the parameters of the forms business throughout the company's history. Samuel Moore's original precept to "Let one writing serve many purposes" has been adapted to help present and future customers: "Let one entry serve many functions." Today, this means helping customers along the migration path from paper to electronics. Moore Corporation applies technology to build integrated solutions for the collection, formatting, management and distribution of information. Customers' needs are complex, so the solutions provided are complex. They can – and do – embrace both paper and electronics.

Moore's offering includes the design and manufacture of custom business forms and systems, commercial printing services, digital colour printing, print outsourcing services, electronic forms and services, forms handling, and document processing equipment. By focusing on vertical markets, Moore ensures a thorough knowledge of business processes and specialized technical skills and technology applications for customers. Primary vertical markets include banking, insurance, government, and the healthcare sector. Moore is also developing strategic alliances with marketing partners, such as Indigo and JetForm, to provide integrated solutions for customers.

Just-in-time – a buzzword of the '80s – a reality for the '90s. One of the major current technology development activities for Moore is in digital colour printing. The ability to furnish short run colour and commercial printing services enables Moore to serve the total print management requirements of customers. Print-on-demand capabilities put just-in-time theories into practice and allow subscribing businesses to focus on their core competencies by off-loading the responsibility of print management to Moore. Instead of "print and distribute," it is now "distribute and print."

One of the fastest growing industries in the world is labels and label systems. Moore Corporation is one of the world's leading labels and label systems providers with products and services that include pressure sensitive labels, linerless labels, variably imaged bar codes, form label combinations, integrated software, product and applicator solutions, and specialty materials and adhesives. Moore is dominant in the secondary labels market segment – these are label systems that transfer unique data for shipping, tracking and inventory control. Moore also leads the industry in new product development including the linerless label, the direct thermal and the thermal transfer label. Key vertical markets include transportation, manufacturing, retail and government. Moore's ability to leverage label systems capability with forms technology provides a unique offering for customers.

To create efficiency and enhance competitiveness for customers is the basis of Moore's value proposition. The Customer Communication Services division plays a key role in achieving these goals for many customers. As the world's largest provider of personalized direct mail and the dominant provider of real estate systems in North America, Moore provides complete project management – from program strategy through production with unique and personalized customer communications. Moore is the leading North American information processing service bureau specializing in statement printing and imaging, processing, distribution and year-end tax mailings. CCS products and services include the creation and production of personalized mail, direct marketing program development, database management and segmentation services, database publishing, on-line real estate systems, and mail production outsourcing services. These unique offerings blend in Moore's vertical market focus including the financial, retail, telecommunications, insurance, government, automotive and real estate fields. With extensive industry experience and a strategic business approach, Moore is able to offer its customers products and services that are second to none.

Moore has come a long way since the multi-part form in 1882, but the basic values that underlie the company and its people have not changed: to provide the best for customers, so they can provide the best to theirs, to help customers do business better, faster and smarter. Moore Corporation greets the new century with a history of innovation and a long and proud history in Canada and around the world.

INDEX

Bold – Feature article; *Italics* – Illustration or Caption reference